François Villon Revisited

Twayne's World Authors Series
French Literature

David O'Connell, Editor

Georgia State University

TWAS 864

AN ILLUSTRATION FROM THE 1485 EDITION OF GUYOT MARCHANT'S *LA DANSE MACABRE*

François Villon Revisited

David A. Fein

University of North Carolina at Greensboro

Twayne Publishers
An Imprint of Simon & Schuster Macmillan
New York

Prentice Hall International
London • Mexico City • New Delhi • Singapore • Sydney • Toronto

Twayne's World Authors Series No. 864

François Villon Revisited
David A. Fein

Twayne Publishers
An Imprint of Simon & Schuster Macmillan
1633 Broadway
New York, NY 10019

Library of Congress Cataloging-in-Publication Data

Fein, David A.
    François Villon revisited / David A. Fein.
        p.   cm. — (Twayne's world author series ; TWAS 864. French literature)
    Includes bibliographical references and index.
    ISBN 0–8057–4564–5
    1. Villon, François, b. 1431—Criticism and interpretation.
    I. Title   II. Series: Twayne's world authors series ; TWAS 864.
    III. Series: Twayne's world authors series. French literature.
    PQ1593.F45   1997   96–38633
    841'.2—dc20   CIP

10 9 8 7 6 5 4 3 2 1

Printed in the United States of America

For Rita

Contents

Preface

Having taught Villon for 20 years, and having written two books about the poet (not including the present study), I am keenly aware of the difficulties facing the uninitiated reader, difficulties that I will describe in chapter 1. It is certainly not my intention to catalog and identify every site and person appearing in Villon's work. Other scholars (including Pierre Champion in 1913) have already carried out this task. Moreover, the mere identification of a site, person, or event does not necessarily contribute significantly to our understanding of a given passage. I firmly believe, however, that in order to appreciate Villon's poetry and have a sense of its true character, the reader must be acquainted with the unique relationship between the text and the historical context. After exploring various approaches in my teaching and in my writing, I am convinced that an appreciation of this particular feature of Villon's poetry, whether we choose to identify it as "referentiality" or "historicity," is essential to any meaningful reading of the work. Those of us who regularly teach Villon are accustomed to familiar refrains such as "I don't understand this part," "What is he trying to say?" and "What does this mean?" And whenever possible, of course, we attempt to address these concerns by elucidating a particular reference, a particular passage, or at least *our own* sense of its meaning. But in all honesty, we must often confess that neither we nor anyone else is able to explain the precise meaning of a given verse or verses.

These days, as I teach Villon, I do so with the hope that my students will accept their ignorance, my ignorance, and the ignorance of all the scholars who have ever studied Villon when it comes to understanding certain obscure portions of his poetry. Indeed, my hope is that students will not equate the inability to understand with a failure to appreciate. Rather than allow themselves to become frustrated by the lack of knowledge that prevents them from unlocking the meaning of a specific reference or passage, I would like to see them attempt to grasp a larger understanding of the work, grounded in discernible patterns of language and images, changing voices, and familiar thematic strands. The kind of question that I would like my students to reflect on is not "Why does Villon choose this particular tavern? Where is it located? How does he exploit its name for humorous purposes?" (although these are all legitimate questions for a scholar to ask), but rather "Why are there so many references to taverns in Villon's poetry? What connotations are attached to these taverns? What element do these passages contribute to the work?" Thus, I confess that I am less concerned with the import of particular details than with the cumulative and composite effect of these details. Given, however, that so much of Villon's poetry is grounded in specificity, one can hope eventually to gain a sense of the larger picture only through examination of individual details.

It is in this spirit that I have undertaken the present study. Throughout the writing of this book, I have kept before me a map of fifteenth-century Paris. The diagram allows me to chart Villon's wandering through the city, but it also serves as a continual reminder that the poetry of François Villon, for all its imagination and fantasy, is firmly rooted in the buildings, walls, and streets of an actual city, and that this poetry is filled with one man's memories of all that he has experienced as a citizen of Paris.

Acknowledgments

I wish to thank my university, the University of North Carolina at Greensboro, for granting me a research leave in the spring semester of 1996 for the purpose of completing this study, and especially the head of my department, Professor Kathleen V. Kish, who endorsed my project. I am very grateful to Professor David O'Connell for allowing me to contribute another volume to the Twayne World Authors Series. I owe much of my knowledge on Villon to preparation for various courses on medieval French literature and to the insightful questions and comments of some of my students. It is my hope that this book, generated partly from their curiosity and enthusiasm for Villon, will help other students to gain a deeper understanding and appreciation for this remarkable poet. Finally, I wish to thank my wife, Rita, for her confidence, patience, and support, all of which have sustained me through the writing of this book.

Chronology

1431 Birth of François Villon. (Joan of Arc burned to death in Rouen by the English.)

1449 Villon receives his bachelor of arts degree from the University of Paris.

1452 Villon receives his master of arts degree.

1455 Involved in a violent dispute leading to the death of a priest, Philippe Sermoise, Villon flees from Paris.

1456 Two royal pardons are issued, exonerating Villon, who subsequently returns to Paris.

Navarre robbery. Composition of the *Lais*.

1457 As a result of the Navarre affair, Villon leaves Paris again.

1457–1461 Villon wanders in the provinces, spending an undetermined period of time at Blois as a guest of Charles d'Orléans.

1458 Arrest of Guy Tabarie, a participant in the Navarre robbery. Tabarie implicates Villon as an accomplice.

1461 By the summer, Villon is jailed in the dungeon of Thibaut d'Aussigny, bishop of Orléans, charged with an unknown crime.

In October, Villon and other prisoners are liberated in commemoration of the entrance of the new king, Louis XI.

1462 Toward the end of the year, Villon begins composition of the *Testament*.

In November, Villon is arrested for a minor theft, incarcerated at the Châtelet, and released after a few days. Some weeks later, as a result of a street brawl, he is jailed again and condemned to be hanged.

1463 In January, the death sentence is commuted to a 10-year exile from Paris. No trace of Villon exists beyond this point.

Chapter One

Introduction

Special Problems in Reading Villon

Numerous challenges confront those students who read Villon for the first time. First, there is the problem of language. Despite similarities between Middle French and modern French, many differences in spelling and syntax can easily confuse the reader accustomed to current French usage. Then there is the problem of vocabulary. Although readily recognizable to any contemporary of Villon, words such as *anten, courcez, havet,* and *guisarme,* having all but disappeared from the language, will not be found in most current French dictionaries. Villon's reader may be further perplexed by an abundance of references based on biblical and classical sources. The most serious obstacle to the modern reader, however, is the wealth of historical information contained in this body of verse. Villon's poetry abounds with references to sites—churches, monasteries and convents, cemeteries, markets, municipal buildings, prisons, taverns, and certain well-known private houses—that would be familiar to any fifteenth-century Parisian citizen residing in the area that we now call the Left Bank. More problematic are the names of Villon's contemporaries who appear so often in his poetry. Some are well-known figures of the period, men in high positions of civil or ecclesiastical authority, for example. Most, however, are lesser-known personages, including friends or acquaintances of the poet, as well as a variety of characters representing all walks of life. Here, lay readers (and frequently even scholars) find themselves at a loss. Writing primarily for a small circle of acquaintances, Villon enjoyed making private jokes that only his immediate audience would be able to understand and appreciate. Thus even many of Villon's contemporaries, unfamiliar with the poet and his immediate acquaintances and therefore incapable of deciphering the meaning of many verses, would find themselves precluded from understanding large portions of Villon's poetic corpus.[1] The following stanza from the *Testament* is one of many passages whose mean-

ing, although undoubtedly transparent to Villon's original audience, has
now become obscure:

> De moy, povre, je vueil parler:
> J'en fuz batu comme a ru telles,
> Tout nu, ja ne le quiers celler.
> Qui me fist macher ces groselles,
> Fors Katherine de Vauselles?
> Noël, le tiers, ot, qui fut la,
> Mitaines a ces nopces telles!
> Bien eureux est qui rien n'y a!   (657–64)

> [About poor me I want to speak,
> Beaten like laundry at a stream,
> Nude, I don't try to hide the fact.
> Who was it made me swallow this
> Except Katherine de Vausselles?
> Noël, the third party there,
> Got, as I did, some festive thumps.
> Happy the man who keeps away!]²

Given the passage's context, a long ballade recounting the misfortunes
of various literary personages caught in the snares of love, it is evident
that Villon is referring here to an amorous misadventure involving a certain Katherine de Vausselles and an acquaintance by the name of Noël.
We know nothing of Katherine, although a family named Vaucelles
resided in the general neighborhood where Villon grew up. Noël may
well be the Noël Jolis who reappears in lines 1636–43 of the *Testament*
as the recipient of 220 lashes. Other than that he was implicated in an
adultery case prosecuted in 1461, we know nothing of him or his relationship with Villon. The second and third verses may refer to a publicly
administered punishment resulting from the incident. The penultimate
verse apparently refers facetiously to the custom of exchanging punches
(somewhat softened by gloves) as part of traditional wedding festivities.
We can only speculate about the incident to which Villon refers in this
stanza. Were he and Noël coparticipants in the adventure? Did Noël fail
to warn François of an unexpected intrusion? Or did Noël, perhaps,

denounce his acquaintance after the incident while in the process of confessing his own role in the affair? Did the episode mark the bitter end to a long friendship, or were the verses written with a note of banter, in a playful spirit of male camaraderie? To Villon's acquaintances, aware of the circumstances surrounding the incident in question, the meaning of these verses would be immediately apparent. Deprived of essential information, we, on the other hand, cannot possibly decipher the meaning of this enigmatic reference.

This passage, one among dozens that could be chosen by way of example, illustrates the relative opacity that characterizes much of Villon's poetry. Five and one-half centuries after the first published commentary on Villon's poetry, we are still no closer to discovering the meaning of many problematic verses. Exhaustive archival searches have failed to yield the slightest hint of information that would allow us to penetrate a little deeper into this or many similar passages. Yet, despite the frustrating silence surrounding this particular secret, these verses nevertheless reveal a certain aspect of the poet and his work. He participated in a sexual escapade that went awry, resulting in a beating and public humiliation. Yet, despite the unflattering nature of this episode and the unpleasant memories it undoubtedly evokes, Villon chose to include the incident as one of several defining moments that cumulatively convey an image of the *povre Villon,* the sometimes tragic, sometimes comic victim of the *Testament.*

Trends in Villon Scholarship

Owing in part, perhaps, to its difficult nature, the poetry of François Villon has generated a tremendous amount of scholarly interest over the years, particularly in the twentieth century.[3] In the first half of the century, the dominant approach to Villon was grounded in a historical and biographical perspective. Eagerly searching for connections between the poetry and the life of Villon, critics did not always rigorously differentiate between evidence and conjecture. The basic weakness of this approach lies in the relative scarcity of biographical information, occasionally tempting well-meaning scholars to fill in the gaps with speculative reasoning. Nevertheless, the period produced a number of outstanding works of scholarship. Pierre Champion's two-volume study, *François Villon* (1913), despite its shortcomings, contains a wealth of historical information on fifteenth-century Paris.[4] Louis Thuasne's annotated edition of Villon's complete works (1923) offers many enlightening commentaries and provides numerous examples of fifteenth-century French usage, which are especially useful for philological analysis.[5] By the 1960s and 1970s, with the advent of new approaches in French literary criticism inspired by the work of pioneers such as Levi-Strauss, Derrida, and Lacan, Villon scholarship began to take on a different look. The field of medieval French literature was revitalized and, to a certain degree, revolutionized by Paul Zumthor's *Langues et techniques poétiques à l'époque romane*.[6] Critics began to look more carefully at the text itself, separating it from its historical and biographical context. David Kuhn's *La Poétique de François Villon* (1967) marks a turning point in Villon criticism.[7] The study's controversial readings of Villon (which, according to some critics, reveal more about the richness of Kuhn's imagination than about the richness of Villon's text) helped liberate Villon scholarship from the constraints of historicity and opened the door to a variety of fresh perspectives. Reacting against the excessive reliance on the biographical and historical approach that characterized so much of earlier Villon scholarship, critics now began to distinguish the poetic persona from the man, François Villon. Nancy Freeman Regalado, in her insightful article "*Effet de réel, Effet du réel:* Representation and Reference in Villon's *Testament*," reminds us that the poetic reality of the *Testament* does not necessarily correspond to the historical reality on which it appears to be based, and she cautions us against excessive reliance on historical sources:

> Efforts at historical reconstruction, however, have invariably resulted in fragmented readings of the *Testament*. As its verses have been traced piecemeal into archives, the complete poem of the *Testament* has been left pecked apart like the faces of the hanged men in Villon's *ballade*.[8]

Despite Regalado's reminder that the *Testament* is not a historical document, the connections between Villon's poetic masterpiece and the historical context in which it was written continue to preoccupy many of the most active and influential Villon scholars today. In the international colloquium organized in Paris in 1989 in commemoration of the 500th anniversary of the first published edition of Villon's poetry, papers were delivered on topics such as Villon's original audience, the relationship between François Villon and Charles d'Orléans, the legal documents exonerating Villon of certain crimes, medieval winter carnivals, and the *neiges d'antan*. However, informed and enlightened by recent developments in literary criticism, historical approaches to Villon are generally less naive than in the past. Villon scholarship now embraces a richer and more diverse array of critical approaches than ever before. Yet, as Jean Dufournet, the renowned Villon scholar and one of the organizers of the Villon colloquium, reminds us, Villon's poetry continually invites reflection: "L'œuvre, étant inépuisable, à jamais ouverte, il faut continuer à l'interpréter dans sa profondeur et dans son étendue . . ."[9]

Villon, Poet of Paris

Clément Marot, the sixteenth-century poet who first edited Villon's poetry, describes in the introduction to his 1533 edition the extent to which Villon's poetry is inextricably tied to the city of Paris:

> Quant à l'industrie des lays qu'il feit en ses testaments pour suffisament la cognoistre et entendre, il fauldroit avoir esté de son temps à Paris, et avoir cogneu les lieux, les choses et les hommes dont il parle: la mémoire desquelz tant plus se passera, tant moins se coignoistra icelle industrie de ses lays dictz.

> [As for the ingenuity of the legacies he makes in his testaments, in order to understand and appreciate it, one would have to have lived in the Paris of his day and would have to have known the places, things, and men of whom he speaks; the more the memory of these things disappears, the less will be recognized the ingenuity of these legacies.][10]

Like Baudelaire, Villon is very much a poet of the city, and in some ways, Villon's Paris is not terribly different from Baudelaire's Paris. The city already contained some of the landmarks for which it is known today—the cathedral of Notre Dame and the Sainte Chapelle, the Latin Quarter and the Sorbonne, and the bridges of the Seine. Paris was a lively, flourishing city—already one of the largest in Europe—full of taverns (the ancestor of the nineteenth-century café) and all the colorful life normally associated with these public houses. On the other hand, Villon's Paris had all the characteristics that distinguish medieval cities from their modern counterparts. Completely enclosed by walls (broken only by a few well-fortified gates), the inhabitants of the city were effectively isolated from the outside world. The landscape of the city was dominated above all by churches—cathedrals, chapels, and monasteries.

The part of Paris that appears most frequently in Villon's poetry is the area around the Sorbonne, the Latin Quarter, and the Left Bank. As for the characters who inhabit Villon's poetry, they represent practically every segment of the Parisian population—shopkeepers, members of the Parisian police, jailers, various municipal and ecclesiastical bureaucrats, students, professors, clerks, clerics, monks, priests, lawyers, tavern owners, criminals, and prostitutes. Villon's poetry, by and large, is the work of an urban poet, and the city of Paris and its inhabitants continually intrude into his verse. They give the poetry its shape, its individuality, and its vitality.

Chapter Structure

The little information available on Villon's life (until his disappearance in 1463) is presented in chapter 2, "Biographical Sketch." Chapter 3, "The *Lais*," examines the 320-verse poem composed by Villon at the age of 25 in 1456. Too long and complex to be adequately treated in a single chapter, Villon's poetic masterpiece, the 2,023-verse *Testament*, provides the focus for the next three chapters. Chapter 4, "The *Testament*: Sites," concentrates on locations cited in the poem, including public houses and churches and other religious buildings. The following chapter, "The *Testament*: Characters," examines Villon's presentation of various groups of characters, including men associated with the legal and penal system, men serving an ecclesiastical function, friends and acquaintances, and women. Chapter 6, "The *Testament*: The Ballades," is based on the premise that the ballades interspersed throughout the *Testament* illustrate certain "voices" with which Villon experiments in the *Testament*. Five of Villon's other ballades, not included within the *Testament*, are treated individually in chapter 7. The next chapter focuses on various biblical subtexts and on the manner in which these texts are integrated into Villon's poetry. Chapter 9, "The *Danse Macabre*," studies the origin of this literary and artistic motif and its appearance in Villon's poetry.

Chapter Two
Biographical Sketch

Student Days

Although certain aspects of Villon's life, particularly his role in various criminal activities, are well documented, there are long stretches of his life about which we know virtually nothing. These significant gaps preclude the reconstruction of a continuous biography. The little biographical information we possess comes partly from archival sources—university records, judicial proceedings, and royal pardons—and partly from internal evidence found in Villon's poetry. From the latter, for example, we know Villon's approximate date of birth and the dates he composed his two major poems. Born in 1431 (the year that Joan of Arc was burned at the stake), fatherless at an early age, François was placed by his mother in the care of Guillaume de Villon, the chaplain of Saint-Benoît-le-Bétourné (a church in the Latin Quarter) and a professor of canon law. Originally known variously as François de Montcorbier and François des Loges, Villon eventually took the name of his adopted father and, after 1456, was known only as François Villon.

In the *Testament,* François speaks of Guillaume with affection and perhaps a touch of remorse:

> Item, et a mon plus que pere,
> Maistre Guillaume de Villon,
> Qui esté m'a plus doulx que mere,
> Enffant eslevé de maillon
> (Degecté m'a de maint boullon,
> Et de cestuy pas ne s'esjoye;)   (849–54)

> [Item, and to my more-than-father
> Master Guillaume de Villon,
> Who's been to me more kind than a mother,

7

A child just out of swaddling bands
(He's got me out of many a scrape
And at this one he doesn't rejoice;)]

Guillaume de Villon, apparently, was frequently compelled to intervene in order to extricate his adopted son from various unpleasant situations, some of which undoubtedly involved possible legal complications. Yet, despite whatever challenges may have arisen from his young charge, Guillaume provided François with a solid education, enabling him to enroll in the Faculté des Arts at the University of Paris, where he successfully completed the course of study leading to the bachelor of arts degree in 1449.

The Faculté des Arts of the University of Paris was actually a conglomeration of 10 schools, and the area around the university was divided into "nations" in which students from various locations were housed—the *Nation de France,* the *Nation de Normandie,* the *Nation de Picardie,* and the *Nation d'Allemagne* (in which all the foreign students resided). The university (and the surrounding area) constituted a kind of city within a city, which had its own hierarchy, its own government, and its own rights and privileges. In 1444, for example, a dispute arose between the university and the city of Paris over the imposition of a new tax. The anonymous author of *Le Journal d'un bourgeois de Paris* chronicles the event:

> All sermons were stopped on September 4th until March 13th, the Sunday before Ramis Palmarum. . . . The reason was that a heavy tax had been proclaimed and they tried to make it apply to all members of the University of Paris. The Rector, therefore, to defend and protect the liberties and privileges of the university, went to see the tax officials, some of whom laid violent hands upon the Rector, so that all sermons stopped.[1]

The temporary termination of sermons, normally delivered by members of the university's theology faculty, presumably resulted as a mark of protest over the incident on the part of outraged faculty. If the rector of the university could let himself become involved in a fistfight over the collection of taxes, it is not surprising that student life was especially tumultuous and often violent. One contributing factor was the high rate of unemployment among university graduates.[2] Those unable to find legitimate employment were forced to rely on their own resourcefulness and a variety of illicit activities to secure income. Drifting along in hopes of a change in fortune, these young men spent their time drinking, gambling, singing lewd songs, and brawling in the streets. They were well acquainted with the darker side of Paris—its taverns, prisons, prostitutes, corrupt police, and a wide assortment of related criminal activity documented in court records from the period. One of the favorite activities of students and ex-students was to steal the painted signs that identified private homes (before the advent of street numbers). Nocturnal confrontations with the Parisian police were frequent.

In 1452, the year before the Hundred Years' War ended with the liberation of Bordeaux, Villon received his master of arts at the age of 21. Although he satisfactorily completed his course of study, a comment in the *Testament* raises questions concerning Villon's later appraisal of his formal education:

> Bien sçay, se j'eusse estudïé
> Ou temps de ma jeunesse folle
> Et a bonnes meurs dedïé
> J'eusse maison et couche molle—
> Mais quoy? Je fuyoie l'escolle
> Comme fait le mauvais enffant.
> En escripvant ceste parolle
> A peu que le cueur ne me fent. (201–8)

> [If I had studied (well I know)
> In the time of my imprudent youth,
> And if I had been well-behaved,
> I'd have a house and a soft couch now—
> What then? I stayed away from school,
> As a bad boy is wont to do.
> While I am writing down these words
> My heart is just about to break.]

The passage is the only direct reference to Villon's education to be found in his poetry, and like so many other passages in the *Testament*, these verses are marked by ambiguity. Given Villon's pronounced penchant for irony, we should listen cautiously, if not suspiciously, to his confession. Is there a note of self-mockery here, a hidden contempt for the bourgeois values embedded in the phrase "maison et couche molle"? Or could there be a note of genuine contrition in the phrase "a peu que le cueur ne me fent"? The tone of voice here, as so often in Villon's work, is subject to interpretation, and there are few if any contextual clues that would provide a definitive answer. Regardless of how one chooses to read these verses, the admitted rejection of *bonnes meurs* (together with similar references in his poetry and external evidence in the form of court records) would seem to strongly suggest that Villon, both as a student and as a recent graduate, actively participated in various "extracurricular" activities for which the university quarter was famous.

The Sermoise Incident

Perhaps the best-documented and most famous episode of Villon's life is the violent encounter with a priest, Philippe Sermoise (or Chermoye), which resulted in the death of the latter. Two *lettres de rémission,* royal pardons exonerating the defendant, provide detailed information that allows us to reconstruct the incident.[3] The episode allows a rare glimpse into Villon's life from the perspective of external rather than internal sources. Around nine o'clock on the evening of June 5, 1455, following the celebration of a religious holiday (the Fête-Dieu), François was seated with two acquaintances on a stone bench in front of Saint-Benoît-le-Bétourné, the church where his adopted father served as chaplain. With François were a priest named Gilles and a young woman named Isabeau. Their conversation was abruptly interrupted by the arrival of another priest, Philippe Sermoise, and his friend Jehan le Mardi. One of the *lettres de rémission* recounts the beginning of the altercation in this manner:

> [Sermoise speaking to Villon] "I deny God! I've found you!"; and immediately the defendant stood up to give him a place on the bench, saying to him, "Good brother, what are you angry about?" The forementioned Chermoye as the defendant arose to give him a place, shoved him forcefully back onto the bench. Seeing this, Mardi, Gilles, and Isabeau, supposing from the manner of his arrival and demeanor that Chermoye had come only with the intention of making trouble for the defendant, left the scene, leaving only the defendant and Chermoye. Chermoye immediately afterwards . . . drew a large dagger from underneath his cloak and struck the defendant in the face on both lips causing a great flow of blood. . . . Seeing this, the defendant, who was dressed in a coat because

of the coolness of the evening, and who carried a dagger on a belt under this garment, to avoid the furor and ill will of Chermoye ... drew the said dagger and struck him, as it seemed to him, in the groin or there-about, not believing he had actually struck him.

Following the initial encounter, Villon withdrew into the cloister, but Sermoise pursued him, shouting insults and threats. At this point (according to the version provided by one of the royal pardons), the man accompanying Sermoise on his arrival, Jehan le Mardi, attempted to intervene. Finding Villon with a rock in his right hand and a dagger in his left, le Mardi succeeded in disarming Villon by wresting the knife from his possession. Now unarmed and still pursued by Sermoise, Villon hurled the rock at the priest, striking him in the face and knocking him to the ground. Seeking assistance for his wound, Villon found a barber, a certain Fouquet. Required by law to report the incident, Fouquet asked for the names of the parties involved in the fight. Villon revealed the identity of his assailant but identified himself with a fictitious name, Michel Mouton. Philippe Sermoise was taken to the Hôtel-Dieu, where he died two days later. Fearing the consequences of the altercation, Villon immediately fled the city of Paris and remained in hiding (probably close by) until formal notice of his pardon was given, six or seven months later. The fact that two royal pardons were issued (at approximately the same time—January 1456) seems to suggest two separate efforts on the part of Villon's friends and other interested parties (perhaps including Guillaume de Villon). Although the two versions agree on the essential facts of the case, one version presents a more detailed account, including the attempted intervention of le Mardi and the assertion that Philippe Sermoise, while on his deathbed and under questioning by the authorities, forgave his assailant.

The willingness of Philippe Sermoise to pardon Villon undoubtedly played a major role in the decision to exonerate the latter. The royal pardons also speak of Villon's good character ("il a esté et est home de bonne vie"), and it is evident that François had not yet compiled any significant criminal record. The most influential factor in the pardon, however, may have been the behind-the-scenes negotiations carried on by friends and acquaintances of François and Guillaume Villon on behalf of the defendant. Also in Villon's favor, no witnesses were present to contest or corroborate his version of the initial encounter. Although the claim of self-defense may well be legitimate, certain details of Villon's version raise questions about the completeness, if not

the accuracy, of his account. We note, for example, that Villon answers
Philippe's ferocious verbal attack with cordiality, offering him a seat on
the bench in an act of courtesy that can only have further inflamed the
aggressor's passion. Nor is there any explanation for the cause of Sermoise's rage, although it is clear that Villon is somehow implicated in
the priest's anger. We also note that although Villon carried a dagger of
average size, Sermoise is said to have drawn a large dagger (*une grant
dague*). The wound on Villon's lip is said to have bled profusely, but no
mention of blood is made in connection with Sermoise's wound. Perhaps the most revealing detail is the assertion that after stabbing his
assailant in the groin, inflicting a potentially fatal wound, Villon
(according to his statement) did not believe he had actually made contact with his assailant.

Villon never refers directly to this episode in his poetry. One cannot
help but wonder whether the experience is present in the poet's mind
when he thanks his adopted father, Guillaume, for extricating him from
many difficult situations (*Testament*, 853). It is also difficult to imagine
how the memory of Sermoise's death, unintentional though it may have
been, can be separated from Villon's confession of sin in the *Testament:*

Je suis pecheur, je le sçay bien;
Pourtant ne veult pas Dieu ma mort,
Mais convertisse et vive en bien,
Et tout autre que pechié mort.   (105–8)

[I am a sinner, I know well,
And yet God does not wish my death
But that I may amend, and live,
And likewise all who're gnawed by sin.]

Granted, by the time François Villon wrote these verses in 1462, he
certainly had no shortage of sins to draw upon, and the death of
Philippe Sermoise was already deeply buried in his past. Whatever personal significance the experience may have carried for Villon, the events
that transpired on June 5, 1455, are the first recorded evidence of his
troubles with the law, the beginning of a long police record that would
later return to haunt him as he quickly lost his reputation as an *home de
bonne vie*.

The Navarre Affair

The next entry in Villon's criminal record relates to an event that took place around Christmas Eve of 1456, less than a year after the royal pardons had been issued. On this night, five young men, including François, broke into the College of Navarre and stole 500 crowns from the college treasury. Again, the episode is well documented, thanks to police records based largely on the confession of one of the participants.

Entering a popular tavern, la Mule, on a night shortly before Christmas Eve, Villon and his friend Guy Tabarie encountered two acquaintances, Colin de Cayeux and Petit-Jean, who were already preparing for the burglary. Enticed by their plan, Villon and Tabarie decided to participate. The four were eventually joined by a Picard monk named Dom Nicolas. Colin de Cayeux, the son of a locksmith, had already been jailed at least once for theft and appears to have been the ringleader. Petit-Jean also brought to the group valuable experience and expertise in lock picking. The other three were relative novices.

Around midnight, the five assembled outside one of the college walls, removed the long robes that distinguished them as clerics, and scaled the wall. Tabarie and Villon kept watch in different positions while Cayeux and Petit-Jean entered the chapel where the treasury was located. It is not known how the fifth member of the band, Dom Nicolas, was occupied during this time. Once the strongbox had been opened and a substantial number of coins removed, the group quickly dispersed.

Villon immediately left Paris for Angers, where according to the later deposition of Guy Tabarie, Villon planned to carry out another theft. His 320-verse poem, the *Lais,* was supposedly written, according to a questionable claim that will later be discussed, on the same evening of the Navarre affair. The burglary at Navarre was not discovered until March 1457. Several months later, Tabarie boasted of the incident to a new acquaintance, a country priest by the name of Pierre Marchant. Once he had collected enough information on the crime, Marchant reported it to the authorities, who promptly arrested Tabarie and held him for questioning. After repeated interrogations and torture, Tabarie confessed the details of the crime, and it is from his deposition that we are able to reconstruct the series of events.

Although Villon does not refer directly to the Navarre incident, the names of Guy Tabarie and Colin de Cayeux appear in the *Testament.* De Cayeux, who went on to compile a long criminal record and was eventually

hanged in 1460, is cited in a warning to those who might follow the same
destiny (*Testament*, 1675). Guy Tabarie is mentioned in connection with a
literary work, the *Roumant du Pet au Deable* (that may well be fictitious):

> Lequel maistre Guy Tabarye
> Grossa, qui est homs veritable.   (859–60)

> [Which text Master Guy Tabarie
> Copied, who is a truthful man.]

Whether Villon is implying that Tabarie exaggerated Villon's role in the
Navarre escapade or suggesting that his former friend betrayed his
accomplices by his confession, there is clearly nothing flattering or
respectful in Villon's characterization of Tabarie as an *homs veritable*.[4]

Meung-sur-Loire

Villon's whereabouts during the next five years are something of a mystery. Unable to return to Paris because of the Navarre robbery, François
wandered about the provinces. We know that he lived for a period of
time in Blois, the residence of Charles d'Orléans, the duke who had
spent 25 years as a hostage in England. Villon's sojourn at Blois
occurred sometime between 1457 and 1460, although the exact dura-
tion of his stay there cannot be determined. At Blois, he participated in
at least one of the *concours poétiques,* the poetic contests that Charles
d'Orléans was so fond of organizing. Three of Villon's poems may be
found in the duke's poetic album, including a long poem in honor of
Charles's daughter, Marie, probably written on the occasion of her
entrance into the city of Orléans on July 17, 1460. One somewhat enigmatic portion of this text suggests that Villon may have had personal
reasons to celebrate the event:

> Cy devant Dieu fais congoissance
> Que creature feusse morte
> Ne feust vostre doulce naissance
> En charité puissant et forte.
> Qui ressuscite et reconforte
> Ce que Mort avoit prins pour sien.   (73–78)

[Here before God I do declare
That I was just as good as dead
Had it not been for your sweet birth
In strong and potent charity,
Which comforts and resuscitates
What death has taken for its own.]

The most plausible explanation is that Villon was among the prisoners in the city of Orléans who were released in commemoration of the event. It is difficult to explain the especially strong language in which Villon frames his expression of gratitude, without supposing a personal context for these verses.[5]

Although we can only speculate about Villon's possible release from the prison of Orléans in 1460, we know for certain that by the summer of the following year, he was jailed in the dungeon of Thibaut d'Aussigny, bishop of Orléans, for an undetermined crime. As a cleric, and thus subject to ecclesiastical authority, Villon evidently was charged with some transgression of church law. Thibaut d'Aussigny had a reputation as a strict administrator who closely regulated the lives of the priests, monks, and clerics under his control and was not a man to tolerate any infraction of ecclesiastical law. In the absence of any official record relating the crime with which Villon was charged, and in the face of Villon's silence on the subject, we can only speculate about the nature of his offense. According to one tradition, dating back at least to the eighteenth century, Villon was charged with the theft of a sacred object from the sanctuary of a church under Thibaut's jurisdiction. According to another hypothesis, Villon had violated the ecclesiastical code of conduct for clerics by joining a company of itinerant actors and entertainers. Whatever the offense, Thibaut deemed it serious enough to warrant imprisonment under the harshest conditions. While in prison, Villon composed the ballade that has come to be known as the *Epitre a ses amis,* a poetic plea for assistance, addressed to his Parisian friends:

Aiez pictié, aiez pictié de moy,
A tout le moins, s'i vous plaist, mes amis.
En fosse giz, non pas soubz hous ne may,
En cest exil ouquel je suis transmis.   (1–4)

[Have pity, do have pity upon me,
You at least, if you please, who are my friends.
In a pit I lie, not under holly or may,
Within this prison where I am consigned.]

This period of confinement provided Villon, as far as we know, with his
first real taste of prison life. It was an especially bitter experience. His
world was suddenly reduced to the confines of a small, dark cell; his diet
was limited to bread and water; and he was repeatedly tortured and
abused by his sadistic jailers (according to various statements and implications found in the *Testament*). Imprisonment at Meung-sur-Loire
deeply marked François Villon, leaving him (again, according to his own
account) a physically and spiritually broken man. The experience also
left him with a profound hatred for his jailers, particularly the man
responsible for his imprisonment. The memory of Meung-sur-Loire, still
painfully fresh, intrudes almost immediately into the *Testament*:

Non obstant maintes peines eues,
Lesquelles j'ay toutes receues
Soubz la main Thibaut d'Aucigny . . .
S'esvesque il est, signant les rues,
Qu'il soit le mien je le regny.   (4–8)

[Notwithstanding many pains,
Every one of which I've had
Under Thibaut d'Aussigny—
If he's a bishop, blessing streets,
That he is mine, this I deny.]

Of the various enemies whom Villon singles out in the *Testament*, it is
Thibaut d'Aussigny for whom Villon reserves the longest and most
vehement attack. Although there is no firm evidence to substantiate the
hypothesis, it is possible that Thibaut deprived Villon of his status as a
cleric, a fact that would explain Villon's forceful rejection of Thibaut's
authority. (As a resident of Paris, Villon would have been subject to the
diocesan authorities of his city, who would be the only ones properly
empowered to carry out such an action.) The hypothesis would explain
why Villon's appeal of a later criminal indictment (in 1463) was

addressed to civil rather than ecclesiastical authorities. It would also justify, in part, Villon's deep-seated animosity toward the bishop.[6]

In commemoration of the ceremonial arrival of the newly crowned Louis XI, who had included the city of Meung on his procession route, a group of accused prisoners, including François Villon, was released from prison on October 2, 1461. The event is recorded in the *Testament:*

> Lors que le roy me delivra
> De la dure prison de Mehun
> Et que vie me recouvra   (82–84)

> [When the king delivered me
> From the hard prison of Meung
> And restored to me my life]

Returning to his native Paris, François Villon now began the composition of his poetic masterpiece, the *Testament.*

Return to Paris

Still wanted for his role in the Navarre affair, Villon presumably tried to keep a low profile while in Paris. Nevertheless, on November 2, 1462, he ended up in the Châtelet, the central prison of Paris, apparently charged with a minor theft. Alerted to his presence in Paris, the administrators of the College of Navarre intervened; when Villon was released from the Châtelet on November 7, it was on the condition that he repay his share of the stolen money, 120 *écus,* in installments over the next three years. For a man without any source of substantial revenue, this sum represented a crushing debt, the equivalent of 20 years' rent for a shopkeeper's house situated on the Pont Notre-Dame in the heart of Paris.[7] The Navarre authorities must have realized that even partial restitution was unlikely, but the arrangement virtually ensured that Villon would no longer be able to remain in Paris after the three-year deadline had passed.

Within a few weeks, however, Villon found himself back at the Châtelet, facing much grimmer prospects for release. One evening in December, Villon and three acquaintances, having just eaten supper together, were walking down the rue de la Parcheminerie when they passed the workshop of François Ferrebouc, a pontifical notary. Several

apprentices of the notary were working late that night, and a member of
Villon's party, Roger Pichard, who was known for his hot temper, began
trading insults with the apprentices inside the building. When Pichard
spit into the open window, the quarrel quickly escalated as the apprentices rushed into the street. In the ensuing brawl, another member of
Villon's group, Hutin de Moustier, was cornered by the clerks and
dragged screaming into the workshop. The other three members of Villon's band threw themselves against the door, attempting to rescue
Hutin. At this point, the notary, Ferrebouc, opened the door and
entered the fray, striking a certain Robin Dogis and knocking him to the
ground. Villon and Pichard, seeing that the incident was taking a turn
for the worse, immediately left the scene, probably heading for Villon's
room, located in a nearby quarter. Dogis, perhaps without knowing the
identity of his assailant, drew his dagger and struck the notary before
fleeing the scene.

Unfortunately for Villon and his three companions, they had crossed
a powerful and respected citizen, a wealthy man with important political connections. What could have been a simple street brawl, with only
minor and inconsequential results for the participants, took on the proportions of a major crime. All four young men were arrested and sentenced to be hanged. Although Villon played only a small role in the
disturbance, he simply had the misfortune of being in the wrong place
at the wrong time. The four appealed their sentences. Two, Villon and
Dogis, were successful. The other two were not and eventually paid for
their crime on the gallows.

Villon's sentence was commuted to a 10-year banishment from the
city of Paris. It is clear that interested parties must have interceded on
his behalf, because Villon no longer possessed the good reputation that
had led to a reprieve in the Sermoise case. Villon's record was now that
of a *récidiste*, a habitual offender, a hardened criminal.[8] In a terse statement commuting the death sentence, the court record cites "la mauvaise
vie du dit Villon" as grounds for the 10-year exile.[9]

In a ballade titled "La Question que fist Villon au clerc du Guichet,"
addressed to Etienne Garnier, doorkeeper of the Châtelet prison, Villon
speaks triumphantly of his successful appeal:

> Mais quant ceste peine arbitraire
> On me juga par tricherie,
> Estoit il lors temps de moy taire?   (14–16)

[But when that brutal penalty
In all unfairness was imposed,
Was that the time to hold my tongue?]

At the same time, Villon addressed a poem, "Louenge et requeste a la Court," to the judges who had commuted his sentence, thanking and praising them for their mercy but ending with a request that they grant him a brief extension:

Prince, troys jours ne vueillez m'escondire
Pour me pourveoir et aux miens adieu dire;
Sans eulx argent je n'ay, icy n'aux changes.   (31–33)

[Prince, please do not deny to me three days
To make provision, take leave of my friends;
Without them I've no cash, here or in banks.]

These are the last two existing poems written by Villon. The document commuting the death sentence is dated January 5, 1463. By January 8 of this year, then, François Villon had left Paris. There is no record of his life beyond this date.

Chapter Three

The *Lais*

Although it was long believed that Villon participated in the Navarre theft and wrote the *Lais* on the same night—Christmas Eve of 1456—most critics now doubt that these events occurred so close together. First, we must remember that Villon's dating of the poem is somewhat approximate:

> En ce temps, que j'ay dit devant,
> Sur le Noël, morte saison   (9–10)

> [At the time I said before,
> Toward Christmas, the dead time of the year]

The phrase "Sur le Noël" can be read as either "at Christmas" or (as Barbara Sargent-Baur translates it) "toward Christmas." The latter reading would appear to be justified by the next few lines of the stanza, in which Villon describes the general conditions of the season (hungry wolves and people confined to their houses) rather than making any specific reference to the celebration of a religious holiday. It must also be noted that the dating of the Navarre escapade as Christmas Eve of 1456 is based on a rather imprecise reference in Guy Tabarie's deposition: "*circa* festum Nativitatis Domini" (my emphasis). Both Tabarie's statement and the *Lais* concur on Villon's immediate destination of Angers. According to Tabarie, Villon intended to use Angers as the base for another theft. Villon, on the other hand, claims in the *Lais* that he is leaving Paris to escape an unhappy love affair. These conflicting explanations have led some critics to conclude that Villon composed the *Lais* shortly before or shortly after the Navarre theft and included the references to Christmas and Angers as an alibi.[1]

Using the popular literary device of a mock will, Villon frames the prologue to his poem within the conventional language of a legal will:[2]

Mil quatre cens cinquante et six—
Je François Villon, escollier
Considerant, de sens rassis   (1–3)

[Year fourteen hundred fifty-six—
I, a scholar, François Villon,
Considering, while of sound mind]

The series of fictitious bequests that follows may be divided into three basic categories—various personal acquaintances, police and officers of the law (many of whom the poet also knew personally), and an assortment of well-known Parisian citizens of the day. Many of the figures appearing in the *Lais* will resurface six years later in the *Testament*.

Personal Acquaintances

Heading the procession of legatees is Guillaume de Villon, to whom Villon bequeaths his *bruyt* (renown). Next comes the unidentified woman whose rejection, according to Villon, is the cause of his imminent departure for Angers. Although we know nothing of the woman's identity, the circumstances of her relationship with the poet, or the veracity of Villon's claim (which some readers interpret as a complete fabrication), there is reason to believe that references to the mysterious woman are at least partially grounded in reality. Given that Villon places his bequest to her immediately after the bequest to Guillaume, and that all of the other legatees in the poem have been identified as Villon's contemporaries, it is quite plausible that Villon expects his audience of close acquaintances to readily recognize both the woman in question and the younger, richer rival for whom she apparently rejected François:

Autre que moy est en quelongne
Qui plus billon et plus or songne,
Plus jeune et mieulx garny d'umeur.   (52–54)

[Another man is on the scene
Whose money makes a louder clink,
Younger than I, more cheerful, too.]

Although the possibility of fabrication cannot be flatly rejected, it would be difficult to reconcile this explanation with the fact that the poem is so firmly anchored in every other respect within a biographical context. It would also be difficult to explain the obvious importance of the unidentified woman (she occupies five stanzas and is clearly assigned to a preeminent role over the other legatees of the poem) and specific details concerning Villon's successful rival.[3]

An old acquaintance prominently featured early in the poem is Robert Valée, whom Villon met during his student days. Possessing all the advantages offered by a wealthy and well-connected family, Valée (who received his master's degree three years earlier than Villon) had quickly advanced through the various stages of a successful law career and, by 1455, secured a prestigious appointment as a public prosecutor in the Châtelet. To this man—whom Villon facetiously identifies as a *povre clergon* (poor little clerk)—possessing an ample income from his profession, family sources, and various properties, the poet leaves, among other gifts, his underwear:

> J'ordonne principalement
> Qu'on luy baille legierement
> Mes brayes, estans aux Trumillieres,
> Pour coyffrer plus honnestement
> S'amaye, Jehanne de Millieres.   (100–104)

> I will, as principal bequest,
> That he be given without delay
> My underpants, now at the Cuisses,
> To deck more suitably the head
> Of his girl, Jeanne de Millieres.]

The undergarment, allegedly left as security for an unpaid bill in a local tavern, typifies the legacies of the *Lais*. A variety of personal belongings (frequently an object with obscene overtones)—some real, some imaginary—are bequeathed for purposes that, although undoubtedly apparent to Villon's immediate audience, we can only guess. In the case of the preceding passage, for example, some scholars speculate that Jeanne de Millieres (about whom we know virtually nothing) deserves the gift because she is the one who "wears the pants" (an expression that already existed, in a variant form, in fifteenth-century French) in the couple's relationship.

A second reading of the passage also reveals something about Villon's self-characterization. Whereas the designation of the legatee as a *povre clergon*, the choice of the *brayes* as a bequest, and the suggestion that the undergarment should be given to Robert's mistress all clearly belong to the realm of fantasy, the statement that an article of Villon's clothing lies in a tavern in lieu of payment is arguably the aspect of the stanza that comes closest to the truth. The protest of poverty will echo repeatedly in Villon's poetry, especially in the *Testament*. As M. J. Freeman points out, Villon's self-portrayal in the *Testament* is primarily based on his financial condition: "Villon defines himself, then, in terms of his poverty. He is, after all, a 'povre petit escollier' (*Testament,* v. 1886) both penniless and humble."[4] Even six years before the *Testament*, we can see that Villon is already beginning to define himself in the same fashion, depicting himself (in a detail that his contemporaries may have found amusingly accurate) as a man who must occasionally resort to desperate measures to indulge his often costly habits. Underlying the attack on Robert Valée and his mistress, then, we find a discernible note of self-mockery, one that will ring consistently throughout Villon's later poetic production.

A legatee whose financial and social condition more closely resembles Villon's own station is Jacques Raguier, the son of a royal cook:

Et a maistre Jacques Raguier

Laisse l'Abruvouër Popin,

Perches, poussins au blanc menger,

Tousjours le choiz d'un bon loppin,

Le trou de la Pomme de Pin

Cloz et couvert, au feu la plante.   (153–58)

[Also to Master Jacques Raguier,

I leave the Popin water-place,

Perch and pullets with almond sauce,

A tasty something every day,

The tavern called the Pine Cone, too,

Cozy and snug, feet to the fire.]

From a reference in the *Testament* (1038–45), it is clear that François and Jacques were longtime drinking partners and that the Pomme de Pin, a tavern located on the rue de la Juiverie in the Ile de la Cité, was apparently one of the pair's favorite meeting places. The stanza partially quoted above is particularly rich in sexual innuendos, the subject of numerous commentaries, but the most important feature of the passage may be not its content but its tone.[5] The Abruvouër Popin, a watering place for horses on the Right Bank, clearly targets Raguier's apparently well-known thirst, for which the Popin would have provided a most unsatisfactory remedy. Unlike so many of Villon's legacies, however, there is nothing cruel or nefarious in the subsequent gifts the poet bestows upon Raguier—the culinary delicacies and the tavern with its warm fire—or the sexual innuendos implied by alternative readings of the stanza. The image of Jacques Raguier that emerges here is simply that of a man who enjoys the sensual pleasures of life, and Villon freely bequeaths Raguier these pleasures in abundance, without any perceptible trace of accusation or bitterness. The stanza is pervaded by a spirit of playful camaraderie, friendly banter, and the rough jokes of male companionship.

Police and Officers of the Law

The second category of legatees includes various representatives of municipal authority charged with enforcing the law—police, officers and examiners attached to the Châtelet, and others. To the captain of the night police and his men, Villon makes the following bequest:

> Item, au Chevalier du Guet,
> Le Hëaulme luy establis;
> Et aux pietons qui vont d'aguet
> Tastonnans par ces establis,
> Je leur laissë ung beau riblis:
> La Lanterne a la Pierre au Let.   (145–50)

> [Item, to the Knight of the Watch,
> To him I allocate the Helm;
> As for the foot patrol, with care

Groping among those merchants' stalls,
I leave some nice pickings to them:
The Lantern in Pierre-au-Lait Street.]

In order to understand the implications of Villon's bequest, a little background information on the Parisian night police is essential. The security of the city was ensured by two groups, the *guet des bourgeois* and the *guet royal*. The former was comprised of artisans and shopkeepers who formed a kind of citizens' militia. Established merchants, except those granted special exemptions, were required to serve once every three weeks. Each night, a group of 60 of these men was scattered throughout Paris, stationed at certain strategic locations. The permanent guard, the *guet royal* (known simply as the *guet*), consisted of 20 mounted officers and 40 on foot, led by the *Chevalier du Guet*. This group was charged with the dangerous job of policing the dark streets of Paris at night. Although Parisian citizens were theoretically required to be off the streets after the curfew and were forbidden to carry weapons, the *guet* kept busy breaking up street brawls, pursuing thieves, answering complaints about vandalism and student pranks, arresting prostitutes, and generally attempting to ensure the peace and security of the citizens of Paris under adverse conditions. The darkness of the narrow Parisian streets (in an era long before the advent of public lighting), the wide area the *guet* had to police, and the relatively modest size of their force (only one-third of which was mounted on horseback) all contributed to the difficulty of the task.

The man serving as *Chevalier du Guet* at the time Villon wrote the *Lais* was Jean de Harlay, appointed to the position a year earlier, in 1455. The holder of the position, however, had to possess a title of nobility, and Jean's social standing, and hence his right to the title, were presently a matter of public dispute. Philippe de la Tour, a military leader who had distinguished himself in the Hundred Years' War, had formerly held the position of *Chevalier du Guet* and insisted that the appointment rightfully belonged to him because he, unlike his rival, could claim to be a bona fide knight. The lawsuit dragged on for 13 years before it was finally resolved in favor of Philippe.

Thus, by offering Jean the *Hëaulme*, actually a street sign designating the Porte-Baudoyer tavern, Villon not only acknowledges the disputed nature of Jean's claim to nobility but also undercuts his authority by calling into question the legitimacy of his appointment. The attack on Jean de Harlay tells us something about the intended audience of the *Lais*. The Parisian police were no more in favor with the students of the fifteenth century than they are with Villon's counterparts today. Thus, any verbal assault on such a visible figure of authority as the *Chevalier du Guet* is likely to have been received with great amusement and appreciation. The stanza in question, which could be interpreted (leniently) as a cruel joke at Jean's expense or (harshly) as a flagrant act of provocation, could not fail to draw the ire of its victim if he ever became aware of its existence. Moreover, since Villon immediately identifies himself in the second verse of the *Lais,* the attack hardly could be kept anonymous. In fact, had the original manuscript of the poem fallen into the hands of the police captain (or any of several other powerful figures targeted with similar mockery), Villon would likely have sooner or later, directly or indirectly, felt the unpleasant consequences of his indiscreet and indiscriminate attacks. His audacious bouts of verbal aggression may be partly explained by the fact that he wrote the poem just before leaving Paris for the safety of the provinces, where he intended to remain for an undetermined period of time. It is also quite possible, however, given the sensitive and potentially dangerous nature of some of the bequests, that Villon confided the manuscript, and hence the safety of his own person, into the trusted hands of a few close personal acquaintances.

To the *piétons* (those who patrol on foot), Villon leaves another house sign, a lantern, representing a private house on the street Pierre-au-Lait. Although nothing is known of this particular house, we know that the street in question ran through one of the less reputable neighborhoods in fifteenth-century Paris. Thus the house, or at least the street, with which the lantern is associated could well represent exactly the kind of illicit activity that the *guet royal* was responsible for suppressing.[6]

In an age when houses were identified by decorative signs displaying a particular emblem in the form of an animal or object (a horse, a lion, a donkey, a basket, or a lantern), a favorite student prank was to steal these signs and display them in front of different houses or "marry" two signs (a horse and a mule, for example). The nocturnal patrols attempted to prevent this activity whenever possible, of course, but given the *guet*'s insufficient resources, the enormous area that it was forced to cover, and the relative ease with which a sign could be removed, the *guet* proved ineffective in protecting these property markers, which disappeared and reappeared with irritating frequency. Villon, who enjoys playing his own game with signs (more than 30 appear in the *Lais* and *Testament*), is taunting Jean de Harlay and his men with their inability to protect the property of the honest Parisian citizens who employ them.

The theft of signs, it may be argued, represents more than just the antics of mischievous students. Symbolizing the property, wealth, respectability, and authority of the bourgeois and aristocratic residents of Paris, the house signs represented a level of material comfort and social standing—the *couche molle* (*Testament*, 204)—unattainable by many of the students and unemployed clerics with whom Villon associated. By removing the signs, relocating them, and combining them with other signs, the young men were, in a symbolic sense, restructuring the society that the signs represented. There was even, it may be further argued, a poetic dimension to the criminal act. By situating a sign in a new context, often in conjunction with another sign, the authors of the act endowed the object with an original and unexpected meaning. In fact, Villon as a poet proves quite adept at displacing signs (both material and semantic), "stealing" a word from a "proper" linguistic register (perhaps a semantic field associated with the legal profession, financial transactions, or religious life) and inserting the word into a context where it takes on a comically obscene connotation. Thus the activity of sign stealing becomes an especially apt metaphor for much of Villon's mischievous poetic pranks.

Perrenet Marchant (an officer attached to the Châtelet and a member of the bodyguard assigned to protect the *prévôt*, Robert d'Estouteville) is another officer of the law honored by a bequest:

Item, a Perrenet Merchant,
Qu'on dit le Bastard de la Barre,
Pour ce qu'il est ung bon merchant
Luy laisse troys gluyons de feurre
Pour estendre dessus la terre
A faire l'amoureux mestier,
Ou il luy fauldra sa vie quere,
Car il ne scet autre mestier.   (177–84)

[Item, to Perrenet Merchant
Who's called the Bastard de la Barre,
Because he's a good businessman
I leave to him three bales of straw
To be spread out upon the ground
And carry on love's traffic with,

Wherein he'll seek his livelihood,
For it's the only trade he knows.]

The implication of this gift, according to Jean Dufournet, is that Perrenet supplements his modest income as an officer of the law with prostitution, as either a pimp or a gigolo.[7] Another possibility, one not mentioned by Dufournet but one that cannot be excluded entirely, is that
Villon is using the word *mestier* in a figurative sense to designate not so
much a source of revenue as a way of life.[8] Perrenet Marchant, a favorite target of Villon cited three times in the *Testament,* was apparently
a less-than-honorable character who had acquired a reputation as either
a womanizer or a pimp and (according to a later reference in the *Testament*) as a cheating gambler. One can easily imagine the advantages
to which such a man could exploit his power as an officer in the
Châtelet, connected with a variety of well-placed (and possibly corrupt) officials.

   As in many bequests, Villon makes no effort to identify the legatee
in terms of his actual profession (although he does add an alias under
which Perrenet may also have been known). The activity by which
Marchant is identified has nothing to do with his official function as an
officer of the Châtelet, but rather with a more intimate aspect of his
life. In a pattern repeated throughout the *Lais* and the *Testament,* Villon
defines many of his legatees in terms of their well-known weaknesses,
obsessions, shameful incidents, private failures and humiliations, and
illicit activities, all of which are masked by their honorable *mestier.*

   Immediately following his bequest to Marchant, Villon turns his
attention to two other individuals, one of whom, Casin Cholet, was also
employed as a member of the Châtelet police:

Item, au Loup et a Cholet
Je laisse a la foys ung canart
Prins sur les murs, comme on souloit,
Envers les fossés, sur le tart   (185–88)

[Item, to Loup and to Cholet,
To both at once, I leave a duck
Caught at the walls, as custom was,
Around the moats, when the hour is late.]

One of the favorite activities of this pair (who also resurface in the *Testament*) was stealing poultry from the outskirts of Paris, but their thefts apparently included firewood, coal, crops, and swine. Le Loup and Cholet preferred, of course, to operate under the cover of night, and the *Lais,* like the *Testament,* is in many respects a poem of darkness. The *Lais* is, after all, written during the season of the winter solstice, the darkest period of the year. There are references to various nocturnal activities (the lantern bequeathed to the foot patrol of the night watch, the sexual escapades of Perrenet Marchant, and the thefts committed by Le Loup and Cholet under cover of night) and to taverns, which were perpetually dark by day or night. Finally, Villon finishes (or at least claims to finish) the poem at night:

> J'ouys la cloche de Serbonne,
> Qui tousjours a neuf heures sonne
> Le salut que l'ange predit.   (275–77)

> [I heard the bell of the Sorbonne
> Which always sounds at nine o'clock
> The greeting that the angel spoke.]

The world of the *Lais,* with all its colorful inhabitants, truly comes alive during the night.

The Rich and Powerful

The majority of bequests go to men with whom Villon had very little— if any—contact, wealthy financiers and merchants, members of parliament, and high-ranking members of the clergy. Generally belonging to an older generation, these well-established men enjoyed power and privileges to which Villon and his acquaintances, humble and largely unemployed clerics, could never aspire. Before the rich and powerful are allowed to enter into the world of the *Lais,* however, they are forced to undergo radical transformation. Rich men become paupers, old men become children, the powerful become helpless, the corrupt become innocent, the arrogant become humble. Thus, three elderly usurers, Colin Laurens, Girard Gossuin, and Jehan Marceau, who have amassed considerable fortune at the expense of others, are transformed into ragged orphans:

Item, et je lesse, en pitié
A troys petis enffans tous nudz
Nonmés en ce present traictié—
Povres orphelins inpourveuz,
Tous deschaussez, tous despourveuz
Et desnuez comme le ver . . .
J'ordonne qu'ilz seront pourveuz,
Au moins pour passer cest yver—   (193–200)

[Item, I leave in charity
To three small youngsters, naked all,
Named in this present document—
Poor orphan boys without support,
All of them barefoot, all deprived
And mother-naked, every one . . .
I will they be provided for,
To live this winter through, at least—]

By the repeated use of antiphrasis, Villon teaches the reader to substitute the opposite meaning of certain relevant signifiers (when alerted by appropriate clues). Thus, the initiated reader, once having made the connection between the three elderly financiers and the *troys petis enffans tous nudz*, would be well equipped to appreciate the humorous portrayal of the *povres orphelins*. By insisting on the vulnerability of the "orphans"—*tous nudz, inpourveuz, deschaussez, despourveuz, desnuez*—Villon comments implicitly on the material comfort of the three men in question. By the end of the sixth verse, having emphatically and repeatedly drawn the reader's attention to the wealth and material possessions of his legatees, Villon now concludes the stanza with an unexpected twist. In a gracious act of charity, he wills that the orphans be provided for long enough to survive the coming winter. A note of truth pierces the carefully constructed fiction at this point, for with each passing year, Laurens, Gossuin, Marceau, despite all the comfort and protection afforded by their excessive wealth, are indeed, at their advanced age, at greater and greater risk of not surviving the winter. The danger, then, to which Villon alludes in the last verse is very real. In effect, the stanza redefines the traditional concepts of poverty and wealth. Villon seems to

suggest that a true sense of wealth derives not from affluence and material comfort, but rather from youth, health, and physical well-being.
Lacking these attributes, the three men targeted by Villon are truly
povres, that is, worthy of pity although they are not financially destitute.
The poet himself, on the other hand, although lacking the financial
advantages of his legatees, boasts one possession that all of them are
wanting, the vigor of a 25-year-old man.

The transformation of the elderly financiers into defenseless orphans,
like the displacement of the house signs, restructures the existing world
of Paris in 1456 according to the inner logic of the *Lais,* which is a
poetic world of its own, a world whose intelligibility resides in the minds
of the poet and his intimate acquaintances. The same process transforms
two elderly canons in the cathedral of Notre-Dame, Guillaume Cotin
and Thibaut de Vitry (both wealthy members of parliament), into the
following:

> Deux povres clercs, parlans latin,
> Humbles, bien chantans au lectry,
> Paisibles enfans, sans estry.   (219–21)

> [Two poor clerks, Latin-speaking both,
> Humble, good singers in the choir,
> Peaceable youngsters, free of strife.]

As canons of the cathedral of Notre-Dame, both men were involved in a
long and bitter lawsuit between their church and Saint-Benoît-le-
Bétourné, the church with which Guillaume de Villon was affiliated,
and which was subject to the control of Notre-Dame. Deciphering the
antiphrasis of Villon's description, we may conclude that he is drawing
attention to the advanced age of the canons, their poor knowledge of
Latin, their broken voices, their arrogance, and their contentious nature.
As a cleric himself, Villon is taking on two very powerful and potentially
dangerous adversaries, men capable of doing him even more harm than
a civil authority such as Jean de Harlay, the *Chevalier du Guet.* In the
world of the *Lais,* however, all power is concentrated in the pen of the
poet, who playfully reduces his enemies to ludicrous figures, deprived of
all authority and dignity. Elderly financiers are forced to masquerade as
naked orphans; pompous prelates are forced into the robes of choirboys.

Cruel Gifts

Not all of the recipients of Villon's "charity" are politically and financially empowered. As one would expect in an actual will, the testator
turns his attention to the poor and disenfranchised:

> Item, je lesse aux hospitaux
> Mes chassis tissus d'arignee;
> Et aux gisans soubz les estaulz
> Chacun sur l'eul une grongniee.   (233–36)

> [Item, to the poorhouses I leave
> My window frames of spider webs;
> To the sleepers under the merchants' stalls
> A good punch in the eye for each.]

The poor and helpless—including the blind, the lame, and the mentally
handicapped—are frequent targets of derision in medieval literature,
appearing as stock characters in the *fabliaux* of the thirteenth century
and later in the *farces* of the fifteenth century. Thus, although the sensibilities of the modern reader may be offended by the apparently sadistic
humor of which these characters are often the victims, it is important to
recognize that Villon is working within a well-established comic tradition. Yet even taking into account the literary precedent, we should note
that Villon's bequest to the *gisans soubz les estaulz* (those whom we would
call the homeless today, and who still populate the streets of Paris five
centuries later) does not end with a quick blow to the face. The second
half of the stanza, written in some of the most vehement language to be
found in the *Lais*, is nothing short of a violent curse, as the poet details
the suffering that he wishes on these unfortunate creatures:

> Trambler a chiere renfrongee,
> Megres, velus et morfondus,
> Chausses courtes, robe rongnee,
> Gelez, murdriz et enfondus.   (237–40)

> [To shiver with their faces drawn,
> All thin and hairy, with heavy colds,

Trousers too short and gowns all frayed,
Chilled through, in pain, and soaking wet.]

Here Villon goes far beyond the cursory slap in the face, the casually
offered blow he has delivered, in keeping with medieval tradition, in the
first half of the stanza. The passage illustrates an undercurrent of violence that runs throughout the *Lais* and will become even more prominent in the *Testament*. The motivation for these passionate outbreaks is
usually transparent, as in the case of the bequest reserved for an anonymous "benefactor":

Et pour celluy qui fist l'avangarde
Pour faire sur moy griefz exploiz,
De par moy, Saint Anthoine l'arde!   (261–63)

[And that man who began it all
To bring down trouble on my head,
Saint Anthony burn him, in my name!]

With convincing logic, Jean Dufournet identifies the legatee as Jean
le Mardi, the companion of Philippe Sermoise who disarmed Villon during his struggle with the priest and in a subsequent deposition presumably implicated Villon to some extent in the incident.[9] If Dufournet is
right, then the vehemence of the bequest, which brings down the curse
of Saint Anthony's fire (probably erysipelas, an acute infectious disease
causing particularly painful inflammation of the skin), can be readily
understood. On the other hand, the curse delivered to the *gisans*, who
could hardly have posed any threat to Villon, is more difficult to explain,
except as an expression of gratuitous cruelty. It is worth noting, however, that despite the sadism that apparently underlies the bequest, the
passage reveals a remarkable sensitivity to the plight of the homeless
victims. Villon describes their physical condition with an exceptional
attention to detail—the trembling of their limbs, their facial expression,
their thin bodies and unkempt appearance, symptoms of respiratory
infection caused by prolonged exposure to inclement weather, the worn
condition of their ill-fitting clothes, and the misery of their condition as
they lie huddled, thoroughly soaked, shivering with cold and pain under
the merchants' stalls. These men whose gaunt and trembling bodies are
depicted with graphic detail are not the familiar puppets that one sees

slapped about in the *fabliaux* and the *farces*. Whatever else the bequest
to the *gisans* may represent, it acknowledges at least the reality of their
suffering. Abandoning his favorite technique of antiphrasis, Villon
observes with painful and compelling realism the pitiful state to which
these *clochards* have been reduced. Unlike so many of the caricatures we
find throughout the *Lais*, the *gisans* are real men whose condition is
straightforwardly portrayed without even a hint of verbal deceit. There
are, then, rare and almost startling moments of authenticity in which
the Paris of 1456 and the world of the *Lais* are allowed to briefly coin-
cide. The stanza dedicated to the street people of Paris represents, at one
level, a testimonial to the poet's sensitivity and power of observation, as
well as his capacity for cruelty. These are qualities that will all be developed in the *Testament*.

Chapter Four

The *Testament:* Sites

Churches, Monasteries, and Convents

Villon's *Testament,* by far the longest, most important, and best known of Villon's works, is an exceedingly complex text. One of the elements that contributes to the *Testament*'s difficulty, as stated in chapter 1, is the wealth of references pointing to actual people and locations from Villon's Paris. Although the poem contains occasional references to sites outside the city, the topography of the *Testament* is based largely on the streets of fifteenth-century Paris. One way to enter this complicated work, one step in the long and difficult process of reading and deciphering the poem, is to begin by simply observing these locations. As Villon wanders through the city streets he knows so well, where precisely does the poet lead his reader?

Unlike the sprawling metropolitan area that Paris is today, fifteenth-century Paris was fairly compact, completely enclosed within the walls that fortified the city. Many of the sites now situated near the heart of Paris—St. Germain des Prés, for example—were actually located outside of the city walls. From a distance, the profile of late-medieval Paris was largely dominated by the silhouettes of its churches (ranging from modest chapels to the cathedral of Notre-Dame)—bell towers, monasteries, cloisters, convents, and related buildings. Every major religious order had its own enclave. Thus the mere mention of any order would inevitably suggest to Villon's contemporaries a series of associations, including the site that served as a locus for the order's activities. Two of the monastic orders in particular, the Célestins and the Chartreux (Carthusians), were known for their large and prosperous communities. Reflecting on the destiny of various acquaintances from his student days, Villon refers specifically to these two monasteries, which symbolize a way of life that was the envy of many of his less-fortunate comrades:

Les autres mendient tous nuz
Et pain ne voient qu'aux fenestres;

Les autres sont entrez es cloistres
De Celestins et de Chartreux.   (235–38)

[Still others, naked, have to beg
And see bread only in shop displays.
Others again have entered cloisters
Of Celestines and of Chartreux.]

The opposition between the two groups of former students, the haves
and the have-nots, is sharpened by the accompanying visual imagery.
One group is situated in an unspecified commercial district of Paris,
wandering aimlessly before the shop displays, hungrily eyeing the bread
in a baker's window, reduced to depending on the charity of strangers. If
the have-nots cannot afford even such an essential commodity as a loaf
of bread, one can only imagine the humble nature of their residence. Villon situates the second group in a far more comfortable environment,
the cloisters of a large and affluent monastic community. Whereas the
monastery of the Chartreux, located in the environs of Paris outside the
city walls, may have been less familiar to some of Villon's original readers, the house of the Célestins (an order founded in the thirteenth century by Pope Celestine V), situated on the Right Bank in the southern
section of the city near the Porte Saint Antoine, would have been well
known to any resident of Paris. With its high walls and imposing tower,
handsomely endowed by Charles V and other royal patrons, the
monastery of the Célestins housed the ornate tombs of many members
of the aristocracy (including the family of the poet Charles d'Orléans).
The image of the cloisters of the Célestins, then, clearly represents affluence, elegance, and material comfort. The interior walls of the church of
the Célestins, painted with scenes depicting the joys of heaven and the
torments of hell, provided a powerful warning on the perils of a sinful
life. It is this scene, presumably, to which Villon refers in the ballade
that he leaves to his mother, a prayer to the Virgin, which has come to
be known as the *Ballade pour prier Notre Dame:*

Au moustier voy, dont suis parroissiënne,
Paradiz paint, ou sont harpes et leuz,
Et ung enffer ou dampnez sont bouluz;
L'un me fait paour, l'autre joye et liësse.   (895–98)

[At the church where I'm a parishioner, I see
Paradise painted, where there are harps and lutes.
And also Hell, wherein the damned are boiled.
One gives me fear, the other joy and gladness.]

The dramatic representation of heaven and hell embodies one of the dominant preoccupations of medieval life (one frequently reflected in the *Testament*), the struggle between the forces of good and evil. By referring the reader to a familiar mural in a well-known church, Villon adds another dimension to the imagery, enriching it beyond the limits of verbal description. By limiting himself to one particular aspect of each scene (the harps and lutes of heaven, the boiling of the damned in hell), by selecting one out of many details that must have constituted a rich and colorful panoply, Villon creates a scene that is more emblematic than descriptive. Rather than attempt a visual representation of the entire mural, he chooses a single, salient feature that eloquently expresses the essence of the scene: the harps and lutes represent the celestial joy and peace of salvation, and the boiling of the damned represents the eternal torment of the unrepentant sinner. The full impact of the verses depends on the audience's ability to bring to the reading the rich and dramatic imagery from the interior of the church of the Célestins. (To approximate this imagery, we may consult certain manuscript illuminations from the late medieval period, or the famous depictions of hell by Hieronymous Bosch, who was roughly a contemporary of Villon.)[1]

As the site of his burial, Villon chooses a much more modest church, the chapel of Saincte Avoye:

Item, j'ordonne a Saincte Avoye,
Et non ailleurs, ma sepulture;

. . . .
De tombel? Riens; je n'en ay cure,
Car il greveroit le plancher.   (1868–69; 1874–75)

[Item, I wish my burial to be
At Saincte Avoye and nowhere else;

. . . .
As for a tomb? I care for none,
For it would overload the floor.]

A convent of Augustinian nuns, Saincte Avoye housed its chapel on the upper floor of one of its buildings, a fact that explains Villon's reference to a possible collapse of the chapel floor beneath the weight of a heavy stone sepulchre. There is also a play on *Avoye* and *avoier*, "to guide, to put on the right path." Wills dating from the fifteenth century typically include (near the opening of the document) a phrase stipulating where the testator wishes to be buried—for example, "il voult et ordonna sa sepulture de son corps en l'eglise Saincte Katheline du Val des Escoliers a Paris."[2] Both in life and in death, Villon repeatedly defines himself in relation to the city of Paris and its inhabitants.

Taverns

Like the *Lais*, the *Testament* includes frequent references to drinking and taverns. According to a 1457 census, the city of Paris included at least 200 taverns. Although spread throughout the city, these establishments were concentrated in certain quarters, notably the streets of St. Jacques, St. Denis, la Harpe, and the quarters of St. Martin, les Halles, and the place de Grève. To Etienne Genevoys, a lawyer affiliated with the Châtelet, who apparently had a reputation as a heavy drinker, Villon bequeaths the tavern called the Barillet (Wine Keg). Another tavern, the Mulle, located on the rue St. Jacques, appears both in the *Lais* and the *Testament*. It was at the Mulle, shortly before Christmas in 1456, that Villon and Guy Tabarie happened to meet Colin de Cayeux in a chance encounter that led to the Navarre burglary. To Jacques Raguier, the notorious drinker already cited in the *Lais*, Villon leaves the tavern called Grant Godet (Big Goblet). Situated on the place de Grève, an important commercial port on the Seine, the Godet was probably among the rougher taverns in the city. In the same stanza, Villon, in a somewhat enigmatic allusion, implies that he and Raguier frequent (or used to frequent) another tavern, the Pomme de Pin (mentioned in connection with Raguier in the *Lais*):

> Se sans moy boit, assiet ne lieve,
> Au trou de la Pomme de Pin.   (1044–45)

> [If, without me, he drinks, sits, stands
> Inside the tavern called the Pine Cone.]

The Pomme de Pin appears to have special personal significance for Villon, for it is the only tavern whose proprietor, Robin Turgis, is mentioned. Along with Jean Moreau, who sold roast meats, and Jean de Provins, a pastry chef (*Testament,* 774), Turgis is included in the list of Villon's principal creditors, to whom Villon claims to be so deeply indebted that they own even his bed. In a mocking challenge to Robin Turgis, Villon offers to pay off all his debts, provided that the proprietor of the Pomme de Pin can locate the poet's present place of residence (where he remained in hiding during the first months after his return to Paris):

> Item, viengne Robert Turgis
> A moy, je lui paieray son vin;
> Combien, s'il treuve mon logis,
> Plus fort fera que le devin.   (1054–57)

> [Item, let Robin Turgis come
> To me, I'll pay him for his wine;
> However, if he finds my place
> He'll do far better than the seer.]

By the time Villon composed the *Testament,* the Pomme de Pin, which had been owned by the Turgis family for several generations, had achieved a reputation as one of the best taverns in Paris, supplying wine for various official occasions. (The tavern's reputation was even known by Rabelais, who mentions it in his work.)[3] Approximately the same age as Villon, Robin Turgis may have been a friend (as Pierre Champion speculates), or he may simply have known Villon well enough to extend him credit.[4] At any rate, it is clear from internal evidence that at the moment Villon was writing the *Testament* in 1462, he had consumed far more of Robin's good wine than he had actually purchased, and that the proprietor of the Pomme de Pin now figured prominently on the poet's list of creditors.

The *Testament* is filled with references to wine and drinking, from the opening verses:

> En l'an de mon trentiësme aage
> Que toutes mes hontes j'euz beues   (1–2)

[In my thirtieth year of life
When I had drunk down all my shames]

to the conclusion of the poem:

Sachiez qu'il fist au departir:
Ung traict but de vin morillon,
Quant de ce monde voult partir.   (2021–23)

[Here's what he did on taking leave:
He drank a draft of dark-red wine
When just about to leave this world.]

The free flow of wine and the often crude and raucous outbursts of joy
that generally result contribute in part to the sense of unity in this
complexly structured work. The locus of drinking—at least within the
context of late medieval Paris—is the tavern. As Jean Favier points
out, "C'est donc sans le dire que Villon fait du monde des tavernes, qui
est aussi celui du théâtre, le monde de son *Lais* et de son *Testament*."[5]
Favier points out the connections between taverns and theater in Villon's time: taverns were popular settings for comic scenes in medieval
French theater, and on the other side of the coin, comic theater was
often performed in taverns. The tavern serves as the locus where many
motifs, memories, and characters of the *Testament* seem to intersect. In
the refrain of one of the final ballades of the *Testament*, Villon claims
that for himself and for many of his acquaintances, the ultimate destination of any financial gain is always prostitutes and taverns: "Tout
aux tavernes et aux filles" [All to the taverns and the girls] (1699).
Those to whom the poem is addressed—cardplayers, gamblers, robbers, counterfeiters, itinerant entertainers, and actors—are clearly
among the steady clientele of many of the taverns that Villon frequented. Although we know nothing of the conditions under which
the *Testament* was originally disseminated, it is plausible that taverns
played a role in the clandestine circulation of the manuscript. At the
very least, one can state with certainty that the poem, with its many
inside jokes, sexual innuendos, and sarcastic treatment of well-known
figures of the day, would have been appropriately directed to an intimate circle of the poet's drinking partners.

The Bobignon Property

Among the many bequests contained in the *Testament*, one of the most enigmatic concerns a piece of property that Villon leaves to Jean Cornu, a high-ranking government official:

> Pour ce, le jardin luy tranffaire
> Que maistre Pierre Bobignon
> M'arenta, en faisant reffaire
> L'uys et redrecier le pignon.   (994–97)

> [So I transfer the garden to him
> That Master Pierre Bobignon
> Rented me, provided he fix
> The door and raise the gable again.]

The house to which Villon refers, owned by a Châtelet lawyer, Pierre Bobignon, had obviously been allowed to fall into a state of disrepair, if not total abandonment. It is highly doubtful, given the condition of the property and the dubious purposes for which it seems to have been used (as will soon become apparent), that Bobignon and Villon ever entered into any contractual arrangement regarding the property, and the term *arenta* undoubtedly represents a comic veneer of respectability thinly concealing certain suspicious activities associated with the premises. The last two verses would seem to strongly suggest that the house was virtually unfit for human habitation and perhaps even had a missing door and a collapsed roof. Villon continues to describe the building in the following stanza:

> Pas faulte d'un huys, g'y perdiz
> Ung grez et ung manche de houe.
> Alors huit faucons, non pas dix,
> N'y eussent pas prins une aloue.
> L'ostel est seur, mais qu'on le cloue.
> Pour enseigne y mis ung havet;   (998–1003)

> [For lack of a door, there I lost
> A hoe handle and a paving stone.

Then eight falcons, even ten,
Wouldn't have caught a lark in there.
The place is safe, so long as it's locked.
For house sign I put up a hook.]

Hoe handles and paving stones were often used as weapons. Were these
objects simply stolen in the absence of their owner, or should we read
these verses as a veiled reference to a skirmish in which Villon was disarmed? The next two verses suggest that the house is so dark, or perhaps that the roof has so many holes in it, that a lark could easily elude
10 pursuing falcons. The subsequent assertion that the house is safe,
provided it remains locked, is obviously an ironic commentary on the
total lack of security afforded by the dwelling. The meaning of the last
verse is subject to interpretation. The *havet,* which Villon claims to have
hung as a house sign, was a hook for extracting meat from a hot pot, but
the *havet* also served as a favorite weapon of thieves and murderers. Ironically, this particular hook, like so many Parisian house signs, seems to
have mysteriously disappeared.

Villon's commentators agree on the relative obscurity of the passage,
recognizing that a lack of circumstantial information precludes any
definitive interpretation. Most scholars would agree with Louis
Thuasne's assessment: "Le sens du huitain ne laisse pas d'être obscur
comme cette masure abandonnée qui servait sans doute de réfuge, la
nuit venue, aux vagabonds en quête d'un mauvais coup à faire."[6]
Indeed, all the evidence solidly supports the supposition that the abandoned property became the site for less-than-honorable occupants
(whether they were squatters, vagabonds, or professional criminals) with
whom Villon may well have been associated. The references to the hoe
handle, the paving stone, and the hook would also strongly suggest the
potential for violence and perhaps criminal activity. Beyond these observations, we can only speculate on the purposes for which the Bobignon
property was used by its illegal occupants.

The passage is significant to the present study not only as an excellent illustration of the intimate connection between text and biographical context in Villon's poetry but also as one of many problematic verses
that raise fundamental questions concerning the reading of Villon. If we
are simply unequipped to decode the meaning of these seemingly
impenetrable passages, then how are we to read them? Or should we
even attempt a reading? Should we not focus our attention on more

transparent portions of the *Testament,* certain ballades, for example, that do not contain obscure, personal allusions, or on certain passages alluding to biographical data with which we are familiar? There is an understandable tendency among modern readers of Villon—students and critics alike—to devote more attention to those passages that, for all their inherent difficulties, are amenable to informed interpretation, if not total comprehension. Seen from this point of view, the *Testament* becomes a kind of patchwork of light and shadow, some portions revealing various degrees of illumination while others remain steeped in obscurity. The problem with this approach, in spite of its defensibility and legitimacy as a critical stance, is that it fails to recognize the nature of the poem, the fact that so many personal memories are inextricably woven into the very fabric of the *Testament.* It may be that we are simply asking the wrong question as we read these so-called impenetrable passages, a question that can only result in puzzlement and frustration. Instead of asking, "What does he mean? What is he *really* trying to say?" perhaps we should ask, "What is going on at this moment? What is Villon doing here" and thus shift attention away from the hidden message (which we are admittedly incapable of deciphering) to the process by which the message is delivered. We may also discover, if we momentarily renounce the search for the "true" meaning of a particular passage, that we can reasonably arrive at certain well-grounded assumptions related to the reference in question. Whereas many portions of the *Testament* will inevitably remain partially concealed by shadow, they need not remain totally obscure.

In the passage cited above (998–1003), for example, we can reasonably assume that the location in question, the abandoned house owned by Bobignon, does not appear in the *Testament* as a randomly chosen site devoid of any personal significance, but represents instead certain episodes of Villon's life (whether recent or distant) that he finds meaningful enough to include in the poem. We can also reasonably assume that Villon's decision to renounce the comforts of conventional housing for an abandoned building in a state of total disrepair, with all the attendant risks and discomforts, implies either a sense of impending danger or the need for secrecy. Perhaps more important than the mysterious purpose of the occupancy, at least in terms of the poetic patterns that characterize the *Testament,* is the manner in which Villon represents his period of residence. By transforming a simple case of wanton trespassing (and perhaps more serious crimes) into a legitimate contractual arrangement (Villon, a tenant of Pierre Bobignon, agrees to sublet the property to Jean Cornu, provided that the latter agrees to carry out certain essential repairs and thus maintain the residence), Villon disguises a questionable and probably criminal venture in the language of bourgeois respectability. Rather than contributing to the further detriment of the building by forcing it to serve a function for which it is no longer fit, Villon (like any good tenant who cares about the residence entrusted to his care) is actually enhancing the value of the property by tending to its needs. His first concern, the first concern of any honest resident of the city, is the security of his home: "L'ostel est seur, mais qu'on le cloue" (*Testament,* 1002). To properly identify the residence and establish its legitimacy, he hangs a sign: "Pour l'enseigne y mis ung havet." Now that he has placed his personal mark on the property, he becomes a home owner rather than a mere tenant. Having thus discharged his moral responsibilities as the legitimate owner of the residence, he can only react with outrage at the disappearance of his house sign, cursing the thief:

Qui que l'ait prins, point ne m'en loue: . . .
Senglante nuyt et bas chevet!   (1004–5)

[Whoever took it, I'm not pleased . . .
A bloody night and a low bed!]

Thus, the aspect of the passage on which we should ultimately focus the most attention is not the mystery of the Bobignon residence but the mask of the respectable and indignant bourgeois that Villon assumes at this point in the poem. Earlier in the poem, the *povre Villon* claims, among other regrets, that he could have had a proper house if only he had adhered to socially accepted norms of behavior:

Et a bonne meurs dedïé
J'eusse maison et couche molle.   (204–5)

[And if I had been well behaved,
I'd have a house and a soft couch by now.]

Ironically, the only time he shows himself residing in a house is as the dubious "proprietor" of Pierre Bobignon's run-down estate.

In the previous chapter, we witnessed Villon's penchant in the *Lais* for stealing and relocating various house signs. Now his own sign has been stolen, and both the sign and the theft deserve a little reflection. If the *havet* signifies thievery, then the irony of the theft and of the righteous indignation shown by the home owner are immediately obvious. As already mentioned, the appropriation of house signs serves as an apt metaphor for one of Villon's favorite techniques. In lines 994–1005, Villon appropriates certain words associated with property ownership and situates them in a context where they now appear incongruous and ironic. Thus, the *jardin* is probably in reality an uncultivated, overgrown piece of land. In all likelihood, the contractual arrangement suggested by *arenta* represents a pure fiction. The *ostel* is nothing of the sort, and it certainly is far from *seur*. The *enseigne* is nothing but a crude iron hook. By this misappropriation of bourgeois language, and by assuming the mask of the respectable home owner outraged at the theft of his property, Villon comically undercuts the values he claims to defend.

Cemeteries

Claiming that he has inherited his state of poverty from a long family tradition, Villon describes the unadorned character of his ancestral tombs:

> Povreté tous nous suit et trace.
> Sur les tumbeaux de mes ancestres,
> Les ames desquels Dieu embrasse!
> On n'y voit couronnes ne ceptres. (277–80)

> [Poverty tracks us, every one.
> Upon the tombs of my ancestors
> (The souls of whom may God embrace!)
> Sceptres and crowns aren't to be seen.]

Because we know virtually nothing about Villon's father and the poet's family origins, we cannot ascertain whether the allusion to family tombs refers to a visual image taken directly from the poet's memory, or whether the allusion derives instead from the realm of poetic imagination. A second reference, this time to his father's gravestone, may indicate a firsthand acquaintance with the family burial plot:

Mon pere est mort, Dieu en ait l'ame!
Quant est du corps, il gist soubz lame.   (300–301)

[My father's dead, God keep his soul!
His body lies beneath a slab.]

If Villon's father was buried in Paris, the poet's mother would likely
have occasionally taken the young François to visit the grave. The simple phrase *gist soubz lame*, however, can also be taken as a figurative
equivalent for "deceased," akin to our phrase "dead and buried," and
does not therefore necessarily imply that Villon has actually seen the
lame. In any case, the two references to family graves, containing specific
allusions to the tombstone (*tumbeaux*, *lame*), lead us into the domain of
the cemetery. A reference to a much less modest tomb separates these
two passages but also serves as a link in the thematic chain to which
they belong:

Se tu n'as tant qu'eust Jaques Cueur,
Mieulx vault vivre soubz gros bureau
Pouvre, qu'avoir esté seigneur
Et pourrir soubz riche tumbeau.   (285–88)

[If you've got less than Jacques Coeur had
Better to live, though coarsely clad,
Poor, than to have once been a lord
And now to rot in a rich tomb.]

Jacques Coeur, an extremely wealthy merchant and financier who died
in 1456, six years before the composition of the *Testament*, was famous
for his wealth, and his *riche tumbeau* contrasts sharply with the modest,
unadorned tombs of the poet's ancestors. The contemplation of these
tombs inspires Villon to initiate a theological discourse on mortality,
which he abruptly terminates:

Il n'appartient a moy, pecheur;
Aux theologïens le remectz,
Car c'est office de prescheur.   (294–96)

[It's no affair of sinful me.
To the theologians I defer,
For it's a Preaching Friar's job.]

The conjunction between the cemetery and the *prescheur* is a natural juxtaposition for the medieval mind, for cemeteries furnished a favorable
location for the wandering friars, whose vocation was to preach. Sermons on the dangers of sin and damnation were especially popular, and
what more effective backdrop could be chosen than a public cemetery?
The Cemetery of the Innocents (to which Villon refers later in the *Testament*), the largest in Paris and capable of accommodating especially large
crowds, was a favorite site for such sermons. The anonymous author of
the *Journal d'un bourgeois de Paris* describes the preaching activity of an
itinerant friar who chose this Parisian cemetery as the site for his sermons in April 1429:

> About a week later a grey friar called Brother Richard arrived in Paris.
> He was a man of great judgment, wise in prayer, a sower of sound doc-
> trine for his neighbour's edification. He worked tremendously at this
> task; one could scarcely believe it without having seen it—all the time he
> was in Paris he preached every single day except one . . . He would begin
> to preach at about five o'clock in the morning and go on till between ten
> and eleven o'clock and there were always five or six thousand people lis-
> tening to him. He preached from a high platform . . . with his back to
> the charnel-houses opposite the Charronnerie near the Danse Macabré.[7]

Early in the *Testament,* Villon leads his reader into the cemetery.
Although the Cemetery of the Innocents was not the only public cemetery in the city (the Cemetery of St.-Jean, for example, situated close to
the Hôtel de Ville, served as another important burial site), none could
rival the Innocents in size and grandeur. The rectangular enclosure—
divided into three sections belonging to the adjoining Church of the
Innocents, the Hôtel de Ville, and those churches without their own
cemetery—covered a wide, grass-covered expanse of land dominated by
several large stone crosses and a platform erected for the use of preachers
such as Brother Richard. On days when the weather was inviting, the
cemetery often served a variety of social and commercial functions. Visi-
tors strolled among the tombs or gathered to listen to the occasional sermon. Beggars chose strategic positions to solicit alms. On feast days,
processions often ended their itinerary at the Innocents. Merchants even

set up stalls in or around the cemetery, and the location served as a convenient site for a variety of illicit activities. In short, if the cemetery carried inevitable associations of death, it was often a place filled with life.

Among the beggars who were allowed to station themselves in the Cemetery of the Innocents, Villon chooses to include the residents of the Quinze Vingts, a hospice for the blind situated in the vicinity of the cemetery, as recipients of his generosity. To them he wills his spectacles:

> Sans les estuiz, mes grans lunectes,
> Pour mectre a part, aux Innocens,
> Les gens de bien de deshonnestes.   (1733–35)

> [Without the case, my spectacles,
> To sort out, at the Innocents,
> Good people from dishonest ones.]

Once back within the cemetery, however, the mocking voice that joked of leaving *grans lunectes* to the blind quickly recedes, yielding to a more somber voice that reflects on the futile pursuit of gratification by which so many lives are driven. This radical and abrupt transition, triggered by the seemingly casual reference to the Innocents, marks a shift of attention from the superficial aspect of the cemetery, the variety of social interaction localized within its confines, to its essence as a place of death. Wealth, unlimited consumption of food and wine, sexual gratification, and all manner of worldly pleasure all mean nothing in the face of death.

The confrontation of mortality in the Cemetery of the Innocents is not an abstract experience. Despite its size, the cemetery had well exceeded its capacity by the time the *Testament* was written, necessitating the removal of human remains in order to dig new graves. During the years of the plague, especially during the early part of the fifteenth century, the cemeteries of Paris proved inadequate for the massive burials that had to be carried out without proper preparation. The *Bourgeois of Paris* reports that in the fall of 1418, Parisian grave diggers were particularly overworked:

> All October and November people died as fast as ever. When it got so bad that no one could think where to bury them, huge pits were dug, five at Holy Innocents, four at the Trinity, and the others according to their capacity, and each pit held about six hundred people.[8]

Now, some 40 years after the event, these burials and others were routinely excavated for lack of space. The skeletal remains were unceremoniously piled on wood platforms erected above the cloisters that partially enclosed the cemetery. A great many of these skeletons came from the *fosse aux povres*, but this common grave yielded the remains of the rich as well as the poor, for many prominent figures stipulated burial in this grave as a sign of humility.[9]

Among the disinterred remains, the skulls—and all they represent—especially attract the poet's attention:

Quand je considere ces testes
Entassees en ces charniers,
Tous furent maistres des Requestes,
Au moins de la Chambre aux Deniers,
Ou tous furent portepaniers.   (1744–48)

[When I reflect upon those heads
Heaped in those charnel galleries,
They all were royal officers
Or of the king's household, at least,
Or else were peddlers, all of them.]

Villon continues with a poetic rendition of the *danse macabre*, which we will examine more closely in chapter 9. For the purposes of the present commentary, however, the essential feature of this passage is the link that binds the verses to the source of their inspiration, the *charniers* of the Cemetery of the Innocents. Jean Meschinot, roughly a contemporary of Villon, but a poet of far less talent, is inspired to similar reflection by the same scene:

Se tu vas a sainct Innocent
La ou sont d'ossemens grands tas,
Ja ne cognoistra entre cent
Les os des gens de grans estas.[10]

[If you go to Holy Innocent
There where lie great piles of bones,

You will never be able to distinguish among a hundred
The bones of people of high station.]

In contrast to Meschinot, Villon selects certain salient details that create a
graphic realism lacking in Meschinot's poem. Whereas Meschinot speaks
vaguely of a pile of bones (*d'ossemens grands tas*), Villon specifies the location
(*en ces charniers*) and the anatomical portion of the skeleton that inspires
the most interest (*ces testes*). He comments on the jumbled mass of human
remains, where even the skeletal integrity of individual bodies has been
destroyed, leaving a disordered and indistinguishable collection of bones:

> La les voys toutes assouvies,
> Ensemble en ung tas pesle mesle.   (1756–57)

> [I see them there, all at an end.
> Together in a heap, pell-mell.]

Whereas Meschinot portrays the subject in strictly static terms, Villon
represents the scene as a moment in the continuing process of decay.
The flesh has already disappeared:

> Or sont ilz mors, Dieu ait leurs ames!
> Quant est des corps, ils sont pourriz.   (1760–61)

> [Now they are dead, God keep their souls!
> As for the bodies, they have rotted.]

The degeneration of the body, however, is only partially complete, and
close observation reveals that the relentless process of decomposition
continues even at this moment:

> Et les os declinent en pouldre.   (1765)

> [And the bones are becoming dust.]

The *charniers*, of course, would have been a familiar scene to any Parisian
citizen of the day. Villon's original audience was therefore equipped to
read this portion of the poem against the actual scene that inspired the

verses' composition. It may be argued, in fact, that the full power of the passage derives from the contextual imagery, that is, the *charniers,* that frames the text. Deprived of this essential imagery and the attendant associations that would inevitably color the original reading of the poem, the modern reader, it may be further argued, perceives the text from a fundamentally different perspective.[11]

The Streets of Paris

To move from site to site in Villon's Paris, from churches to cemeteries to private houses or taverns, one was obliged to follow the Parisian streets, most of which, long before the advent of the boulevard, were narrow, winding, and often crowded with beggars, itinerant merchants, and livestock. Many streets bore the name of a saint (St. Antoine, St. Martin, St. Denis); others carried more picturesque names (rue de la Juiverie, rue des Ecrivains). Then there were the bridges connecting the Ile de la Cité to either bank of the Seine: the Pont Notre Dame, the Pont aux Marchands, the Petit Pont, the Pont St. Michel, the Pont au Change, and others. The streets of Paris provide the backdrop for much of Villon's poetic masterpiece, and if the *Testament* is a poem of the tavern, it is also in many senses a poem of the streets.

It is significant that the word *rue* occurs in the opening stanza of the poem. The memory of Thibaut d'Aussigny, in whose jail Villon had spent the bitter summer of 1461 immediately prior to the composition of the *Testament,* evokes an image of the bishop blessing the streets, either at the head of a religious procession or standing on a balcony or platform overlooking such a procession.[12] Villon may well have in mind a particular ceremony that he witnessed, such as the annual commemoration of the liberation of Orléans by Joan of Arc (May 8), over which the bishop always presided:

> S'esvesque il est, signant les rues,
> Qu'il soit le mien je le regny.　　　　　　　　　　(6–8)

> [If he's a bishop, blessing streets,
> That he's mine, this I deny.]

The image of a bishop blessing crowded streets with the sign of the cross occurs casually, inserted almost parenthetically into a prologue domi-

nated by anger and resentment. Nevertheless, it emerges as the most
sharply defined image of the stanza, and given its strategic placement at
the very outset of this lengthy poem, this image deserves more than
passing acknowledgment. If we separate the actual gesture from the
source of the gesture—the bishop Thibaut d'Aussigny, and all the
intensely negative memories and feelings that Villon obviously associates with this figure—two important aspects of the scene emerge. In
spite of the striking nature of the image and its privileged position in
the poem, these verses have inspired surprisingly little critical commentary. David Kuhn, while characterizing the passage as a *tableau saisissant*,
proposes an alternative reading to the verse in question, "on devait voir
Thibault signant les rues, du signe de la croix, mais aussi les *saignant* à
mort."[13] Although Kuhn's interpretation, as always, provides a provocative reading, it deflects attention from the essence of the image. Given
the prominent thread of spirituality that runs throughout the
Testament—references to sin and salvation, Christ images, biblical subtexts—it is no accident that the poem opens under the sign of the
cross.[14] The second important aspect of the verse, and the one most relevant to the present chapter, is the reference to the street. From the context, it is clear that these are not empty streets, but streets teeming with
humanity. It is not so much the street as a physical entity, then, that
receives the blessing, but the people who fill the streets. Thus the word
rue, which appears only once in the *Testament*, signifies here a human as
well as an inanimate presence—indeed, it is the human element that
implicitly dominates the scene.

Although this particular word does not reappear in the poem, many
scenes of the *Testament* are distinctly set against the backdrop of the
street. Although the poet does not usually reveal the precise location of
these scenes, the reader can clearly sense the presence of the street. In
the following passage (already cited in connection with a different aspect
of the poem), Villon notes that some of his former companions have
fallen on hard times:

Les autres mendient tous nuz
Et pain ne voient qu'aux fenestres.   (235–36)

[Still others, naked, have to beg
And see bread only in shop displays.]

Whereas *tous nuz* must be taken as a bit of hyperbole, the poet's acquaintances described here have obviously been reduced to a state of utter poverty, forcing them to beg for their living. The reference to shop displays, juxtaposed with the allusion to begging, situates the scene squarely within the realm of the street, possibly within one of the more prosperous quarters of the city, where beggars might expect to find more generous patrons.

Ironically, when Villon does refer specifically to the physical aspect of a street (without, however, using the word *rue*), the street turns out to be entirely imaginary. To a certain Guillaume Charüau (who may have been an acquaintance from Villon's student days), he bequeaths the equivalent of one *reau* (a gold coin that had practically disappeared from use by this time), which he claims to have found on the street:

> Il avra avec ce ung reau
> En change, affin que sa bourse enffle,
> Prins sur la chaussee et carreau
> De la grant closture du Temple. (1026–29)

> [Along with that he'll have a *reau*
> In small change, to fill out his purse,
> Picked up off the pavement and street
> Of the enclosed lands of the Temple.]

The *closture du Temple,* also known as the *marais* (swamp) *du Temple,* refers to cultivated fields belonging to the Order of the Knights Templar. Some of these fields were located inside the walls of Paris, and some were situated just beyond the city's fortifications. The *chaussee* and *carreau,* then, like the *reau* and the coins for which it has supposedly been exchanged, are completely fictitious. The most striking feature of this particular gift is that it represents not only a sleight of hand (Villon, as we have seen, enjoys giving away possessions that actually belong to others), but also a restructuring of the Parisian topography, the laying of a finished road over a swamp. Thus, Villon expands the world of familiar streets into corners of the city where streets have not yet spread.

Toward the end of the *Testament,* when the dying narrator prepares to make his peace before departing, he turns to the people of the street, taking his leave and asking their forgiveness:

A fillectes monstrans tetins
Pour avoir plus largement hostes,
A ribleurs, meuveurs de hutins,
A battelleurs, traynans mermoctes,
A folz, folles, a sotz, a soctes,
Qui s'en vont cyfflant six a six
A vecyes et marïoctes,—
Je crye a toutes gens mercys.   (1976–83)

[Of girls who wear their gowns cut low
In order to make business brisk,
Of robbers and makers of brawls,
Of showmen with monkeys in tow,
Of male and female Fools by trade,
Who go about in groups of six,
Whistling, equipped with jesters' toys—
I ask pardon of everyone.]

The common thread connecting all these figures—prostitutes, robbers,
thugs, itinerant entertainers, and actors—is precisely the street. All these
characters make their living off the street and, more specifically, off
passersby—the street people's clients or victims. Like Villon, the street
people are all marginalized residents of the city, excluded from respectability by their social station, lack of wealth, and dubious livelihood. However, these street people, constantly circulating through Paris (especially at
night), endow the city with a vigorous and sometimes dangerous life.

     In the final ballade of the *Testament,* an unidentified voice announces
the death of the *povre Villon* and invites us to attend his funeral service:

Icy se clost le testament
Et finist du povre Villon.
Venez a son enterrement,
Quant vous orez le carillon.   (1996–99)

[Here closes and comes to an end
The testament of poor Villon.

Come to attend his burial
When you hear the carillon.]

The carillon, a bell rung by the *semoneor de cors* who passed from door to door announcing funerals, invites Villon's mourners to leave their homes and file through the streets to his burial site. Thus the *Testament*, which opened (at least implicitly) with a religious procession (*signant les rues*) closes with another procession, inspired by the *carillon*. The poem has come full circle.

The *Testament*, as we have seen, is firmly attached to certain physical aspects of Villon's Paris. If we look briefly at the points where the text and the physical environment intersect, certain patterns become apparent. Each cluster of site references connects to a major thematic strand of the poem. Churches and monasteries, for example, reflect the spiritual dimensions of the work. Private houses (and the signs that represent these houses) connote wealth and the values implied by the pursuit and accumulation of wealth. Taverns evoke associations of joy, camaraderie, coarse humor, and physical excess. The streets connote vigor, violence, and human diversity. By tying these thematic strands to certain sites in the city that he and his immediate audience know so well, Villon endows his poem with a sense of specificity and physicality.

Chapter Five

The *Testament*: Characters

The *Testament* derives much of its character (and its difficulty) from references to Villon's contemporaries. These references basically fall within five categories: personal acquaintances, members of the clergy, representatives of civil authority (police, officers of the law, lawyers, and government officials), the wealthy and politically powerful, and women. As we have already seen, one path toward understanding the *Testament*, or least deepening one's appreciation for the poem in the absence of complete understanding, leads through the various sites included in the poem. Another path leads through the list of names cited in the Testament and, more important, the ways in which Villon defines himself in relation to the people identified by these names. A word of clarification is in order here: Strictly speaking, it is the *je* of the *Testament* that defines itself in relation to the various legatees cited in the poem. Some critics would argue that the poetic *je* cannot necessarily be equated with the historical François Villon. Indeed, there are moments when the poet puts on a mask that conceals his true identity (the mask of the courtly lover in the *Ballade de la Grosse Margot,* for example). Some of the self-portraits of the *Testament* are admittedly exaggerated caricatures, if not total fabrications, but one cannot deny that the vast majority of the names cited in the poem represent actual contemporaries with whom Villon was either directly or indirectly acquainted. As Stéphane Gombertz points out, Villon reaffirms his identity not in self-referential terms, but in terms of his relationships:

> . . . un moi obligé de revenir sur son passé pour se prouver qu'il existe en tant qu'homme et que poète, et qui ne peut s'exprimer que dans une référence constamment renouvelée à autrui. La relation à autrui, qui a fondé et exprimé la difficulté d'être soi, permet seul au poète d'exister vraiment.[1]

Thus the dozens of names that appear in the *Testament* represent more than gratuitous digressions. The names constitute a means (according to Gombertz, the *only* means) by which the poet can validate his identity. If Villon identified himself strictly within self-referential terms, the poem would lack any firm points of reference. If the self-characterization were limited to Villon's relationship with any one group of legatees—members of the clergy, for example—we would see only a single facet of Villon's personality (or his poetic personality, to be more accurate). It is precisely the diversity of the relationships in the *Testament* that allows the *moi* to acquire such a deep, rich, and authentically human identity in the course of the poem. Gombertz also draws attention to the instability of the *moi:* "un moi fragile, instable."[2] In spite of the fragility of the poetic identity, laced with contradictions and inconsistencies, a certain wholeness emerges from the poem. This is not to say that Villon reveals himself completely in the *Testament,* but the *moi* that does gradually reveal itself possesses all the complexities, mysteries, paradoxes, and range of emotion that we normally associate with genuine human experience. Self-characterization in the *Testament* becomes a kind of organic process. It involves a complicated constellation of relationships, each of which contributes in some way toward the global identity of the poetic voice. Far from mere ornaments, the portions of the poem devoted to these relationships constitute in many cases important and revealing attempts toward self-definition.

Thibaut d'Aussigny

The first name cited in the *Testament* is that of the bishop Thibaut d'Aussigny, in whose prison Villon had spent the summer of 1461. Both by its appearance in the opening stanza of the poem and by the strong and angry denial that immediately follows, the name immediately claims the reader's attention:

> En l'an de mon trentïesme aage
> Que toutes mes hontes j'euz beues,
> Ne du tout fol, ne du tout saige,
> Non obstant maintes peines eues,
> Soubz la main Thibault d'Aucigny . . .
> S'esvesque il est, signant les rues,
> Qu'il soit le mien je le regny.   (1–8)

> [In this my thirtieth year of life
> When I had drunk down all my shames,
> While *compos mentis* (more or less)

Notwithstanding many pains,
Every one of which I've had
Under Thibault d'Aussigny—
If he's a bishop, blessing streets,
That he is mine, this I deny.]

The will proper does not actually begin until verse 792, "Et vecy le com-
mancement" [And here begins the testament], initiating the long series
of bequests. The official testament is preceded by a lengthy prologue in
which Villon introduces the poem's major thematic strands, one of
which relates to injustice and the desire for revenge. Especially significant is the sudden force with which Thibaut d'Aussigny intrudes into
the poem. The *Testament* opens with an attempt to situate the work
within an autobiographical context. Whereas an actual will would typically begin with a chronological reference, helping to establish its
authenticity as a legal document, Villon situates his poem within a personal chronology—the 30th year of his life. The narrator defines his
state of mind in ambiguous terms, "ne du tout fol, ne du tout saige," in
other words, somewhere between wisdom and insanity. The reference to
shame, "toutes mes hontes," evokes memories of suffering, "maintes
peines," and these memories are quickly localized at their source: "Soubz
la main Thibault d'Aucigny." Once the bishop's name appears, the progression of the stanza, which has followed a certain logic to this point—
the dating of the will, the affirmation of the testator's state of mind—
breaks down completely. Even the syntax is radically disrupted as the
enterprise of the will is abruptly interrupted by a vehement rejection of
the bishop's authority.

The first stanza of the *Testament*, significantly, begins with an attempt
at self-definition (the narrator's age), an attempt that immediately fal-
ters (in the failure to characterize a clearly identifiable state of mind),
and ultimately fails completely, truncated by the sudden entrance of the
bishop. Ultimately, the salient feature emerging from this stanza is not
the poet's age but his relationship with Thibaut d'Aussigny. Even the
reader who is unaware of the biographical context can easily perceive the
intensity of the experience underlying the second half of the stanza.

Despite the syntactical disruption that immediately follows the mention of Thibaut, the following verse reveals a certain continuity of
thought. The punishment that Villon experienced as a prisoner in
Meung-sur-Loire was inflicted "Soubz la main Thibault D'Aucigny," the

very hand that we see blessing the streets in the next verse. Having suffered the violence of the hand that punishes, Villon vehemently rejects
the authority of the hand that blesses. His rejection of Thibaut, out-
wardly an attempt at control and an affirmation of independence, ironically reveals the bishop's continuing power over the poet, for Thibaut's
very name is strong enough to totally disrupt the framework that Villon
has barely begun to build for his poem. The bishop completely dominates the next five stanzas of the poem, in which Villon, under the thin
disguise of a mock prayer, curses Thibaut repeatedly for the experience
at Meung-sur-Loire. None of Villon's many enemies will receive this
amount of sustained attention during the remainder of the *Testament.*
Although his body has been liberated from the bishop's prison, it is evident that Villon's spirit still remains partially under Thibaut's control.
Nor does this outpouring of anger successfully exorcise Villon of his
demon. Twice more in the course of the poem, Thibaut and Meung will
return to haunt the poet.

Later in the prologue, Thibaut appears again, but without warning or
any evident link to the portion of the text immediately preceding his
entrance. Villon has just finished a digression in which he renounces
love, "Amans ne suiveray jamaiz" [I'll follow lovers nevermore] (718),
and claims that women find him unappealing, taking him for an old
man in spite of his relatively young age.

> Dieu mercy—et Tacque Thibault,
> Qui tant d'eaue froide m'a fait boire,
> En ung bas, non pas en ung hault,
> Menger d'angoisse mainte poire. (737–40)

> [Thanks be to God—and Tacque Thibault
> Who forced so much cold water on me
> (Downstairs it was, and not upstairs),
> And made me eat much bitter fruit.]

Tacque Thibault, whom Villon associates with Thibaut d'Aussigny, was
commonly rumored to have been the lover of Duke Jean de Berry (who
died in 1419, 12 years before Villon's birth). The reference to the
drinking of cold water may refer to the standard prison regimen of bread
and water, or the practice of water torture, in which large quantities of

water were forced down the throat of the victim. The *poire d'angoisse* can either serve as a figurative designation of suffering or as a specific reference to an instrument of torture (a pear-shaped funnel used to force water down the throat), thus picking up the allusion to cold water in the second verse of the stanza. Juxtaposed with the phrase *Dieu mercy*, Villon's enemy is ironically endowed with a kind of divine empowerment, condemning Villon to the hell of the dungeon ("en ung bas, non pas ung hault") where he will pay the price of his sins. At this point, as we saw in the opening stanza of the *Testament*, the intrusive memory of the summer in Meung-sur-Loire disrupts the syntactical flow of the text:

> Enferré . . . Quant j'en ay memoire,
> Je prie pour luy *et relicqua*
> Que Dieu luy doint, et voire, voire!
> Ce que je pense, *et cetera.*   (741–44)

> [Chained up . . . When I remember it,
> I pray for him, *et relicqua*
> That God may give him (yes, oh yes!)
> Just what I think, *et cetera.*]

The mock prayer of forgiveness, thinly disguising the real prayer for divine punishment, parallels the lengthy discourse of which Thibaut is the object early in the *Testament*. In fact, the second passage on Thibaut, quoted above, functions as an intratextual reference, bringing us back to variants on the same theme:

> Sy prieray pour luy de bon cueur   (33)

> [Yet I'll pray for him willingly]

> Je veul que le Dieu eternel
> Luy soit dont semblable a ce compte.   (27–28)

> [I wish that the eternal God
> Be so to him, in equal scale.]

The long diatribe directed at Thibaut at the outset of the poem, which appears at first to have purged all bitter memories associated with his name, now resumes for two stanzas. The memories have merely been momentarily suppressed. Thibaut again exerts his tyranny over Villon, or at least over his poetic creation. In the following stanza, Villon vents his bitterness toward the bishop's three subordinates, Pierre Bourgoing, Etienne Plaisance, and a certain Maistre Robert (all participated to some degree in the poet's condemnation and subsequent imprisonment), all of whom Villon claims to have forgiven:

> Je les ayme, tout d'un tenant,
> Ainsi que fait Dieu le Lombart. (751–52)

> [I love them, no distinction made,
> Just as the Lombard loves his God.]

Jean Frappier has convincingly demonstrated that Villon is probably referring here to the Trinitarian doctrine of Pierre Lombard, a twelfth-century theologian whose *Liber Sententiarum* was studied in universities throughout the Middle Ages.[3] Lombard insisted on the unity and the inseparability of the three persons of the Trinity. Villon, then, claims equal love for the three persons of his unholy Trinity—Pierre, Etienne, and Robert. It is no accident that Villon chooses to frame the attack on Thibaut and his cohorts in religious language: three mentions of God, the reference to prayer, and the allusion to the Trinity. These are, after all, men connected with the church, charged with enforcing the authority of the church. It is fittingly ironic that Villon should appropriate religious language in assaulting his enemies, attacking them with their own weapon, as it were.

Thibaut and his subordinates refuse to disappear, even after this second attack. Toward the end of the poem, in the ballade with the refrain, "Je crye a toutes gens mercys," the men responsible for his suffering at Meung-sur-Loire return. Although they are unnamed this time, their identity is unmistakable:

> Synon aux traitres chiens matins
> Qui m'ont fait ronger dures crostes,
> Macher mains soirs et mains matins,
> Que ores je ne crains pas troys croctes. (1984–87)

[Except for those vile, treacherous dogs
Who caused me to gnaw on hard crusts
And chew them many a night and day,
Whom now I fear less than three turds.]

The mock prayers and the pretense of forgiveness have now completely disappeared, and the language is strikingly, even uncharacteristically, direct. The ballade ends with a curse on the poet's enemies:

C'on leur froisse les quinze costes
De groz mailletz, fors et massiz,
De plombees et telz peloctes! . . .
Je crye a toutes gens mercys.   (1992–95)

[Let someone crush their fifteen ribs
With heavy strong mallets, massive and strong,
Lead balls, and playthings of that kind! . . .
I ask pardon of everyone.]

This ballade marks the end of the will proper, or at least the silencing of the narrator's voice, for the final ballade of the poem (referring to Villon in the third person) supposedly belongs to another voice. Thus Thibaut and the memory of Meung-sur-Loire both open and close the poem. The rage so thinly concealed in the opening of the work, rage that resurfaces again tenuously contained by a mask of sarcasm and irony, now finally explodes to the surface in some of the most violent imagery anywhere in the *Testament*. The last occurrence of the refrain "Je crye a toutes gens mercys" may be read in at least two ways. Given its ironic juxtaposition with the violent images immediately preceding it, the plea for forgiveness may be taken as another comic posture, that of the dying penitent. On the other hand, now that the poet has fully vented his rage and cursed his enemies with a physical suffering that will repay his own, some measure of equilibrium is restored. Having finally exorcised one of the demons that has haunted him throughout the poem, Villon is perhaps finally ready to include Thibaut and his henchmen in the long list of those to whom the poet turns for pardon at the moment of his fictive death.

Other Members of the Clergy

Although Thibaut d'Aussigny is singled out for special treatment, members of the clergy, especially those belonging to the monastic orders, provide Villon with a favorite target. His attacks are inscribed within a long medieval tradition of anticlericalism. Monastic orders inspire particularly sharp criticism throughout medieval literature, and in fifteenth-century French monasticism, especially in those chapters located in Villon's Paris, corruption and violations of monastic rule were not unusual. Although instances of flagrant corruption were well known, Villon and many of his contemporaries were also troubled by the hypocrisy that allowed an unconscionable degree of material comfort to exist in monastic orders founded on principles of austerity, discipline, and even deprivation. Thus, among Villon's clerical legatees, we find mention of the *freres mendians* (the Mendicant friars, including the Franciscans, Dominicans, and Carmelites) and the Devotes and the Beguines, religious communities of women not formally bound by vows (1158–61). To all these religious orders, Villon offers the following bequest:

> De graces souppes jacoppines
> Et flans leur faiz oblacïon;
> Et puis aprés, soubz ces courtines,
> Parler de contemplacïon. (1162–65)

> [Of rich roast birds and cheese on toast
> And of flans I make them oblation.
> Thereafter, with bed curtains drawn,
> Let them discourse on contemplation.]

This passage actually parallels and extends a previous bequest made to the same group in the *Lais:*

> Savoureux morceaulx et fryans:
> Chappons, flaöns, grasses gelines (252–53)

> [Some good and tempting things to eat:
> Capons, pâtés, and meaty hens.]

In some ways, the passage from the *Testament* appears to represent a mere reworking of the earlier text. The religious communities are cited in an identical order, and in both cases, the bequest includes roast fowl and pastry. One important difference, however, separates the two texts. Whereas Villon makes the first bequest in straightforward terms ("Je laisse aux Mendïans," v. 249), he couches the second in religious terminology: "Et flans leur fais oblacïon." The term *oblacïon* belongs strictly within the semantic field associated with sacred rites, specifically, the celebration of the Mass—*quam oblacionem*—designating the eucharistic bread.[4] Thus connected to the most sacred and dramatic moment of the Mass, the word is charged with spiritual significance, evoking the divine presence associated with the Eucharist. By stealing the term from its liturgical context and relocating it within a profane context, Villon (playing the familiar game of stealing signs that we have already witnessed in the *Lais*) effects a radical dislocation of semantic meaning. The same is true of *contemplacïon,* which, although perhaps less charged with sacred meaning than *oblacïon*, clearly belongs within a spiritual context.[5] The bequest in the *Testament* strikes a more powerful blow than the earlier version presented in the *Lais*. Whereas the first text simply leaves rich food to poor friars who should be subsisting on a much more austere diet, the second text, through the misappropriation of religious terminology, draws attention to the flagrant hypocrisy of the group in question.

As the religious communities of women (the Devotes and the Beguines) quickly disappear from sight, the Mendicant friars eventually receive the brunt of Villon's attack. The sexual allusion appearing in the last two verses of the passage develops into scathing sarcasm in the following stanza. Villon claims that is not he who bequeaths the monks the sexual pleasure to which he has just alluded. Rather, it is the mothers of Paris, and God himself, who thus reward the good friars for the bitter pains they have endured:

> Il faut qu'ilz vivent, les beaulx peres,
> Et mesmement ceulx de Paris.
> S'ilz font plaisir a noz commeres,
> Ils ayment ainsi leurs marys.   (1170–73)

> [These Fathers must live, after all,
> Especially the Paris ones.

If they give our married women pleasure,
That's how they show, to husbands, love.]

The force of Villon's attack resides in a skillful manipulation of double
entendre. The friars, having presumably fathered their share of illegitimate children, doubly deserve the appellation of *beaulx peres*. The phrase
font plaisir can be taken figuratively (as it is normally used in modern
French) or in a cruder, physical sense, more fitting to the spirit of the
text. The last verse can be read (in accordance with Sargent-Baur's
translation) as "This is the manner in which they demonstrate love for
their husbands" (that is, as good Christians), or "This is how they show
the degree of love they have for their husbands" (that is, none at all).

Another intertextual reference, bringing the reader back to the *Lais*,
concerns Thibaut de Vitry and Guillaume Cotin, two elderly canons
affiliated with Notre-Dame (who appear in a passage previously analyzed in chapter 3). As in the earlier bequest, Villon focuses particular
attention on the advanced age of his legatees:

Quoy que jeunes et esbatans
Soient, en riens ne me desplaist.   (1314–15)

[Although they're young and frisky boys,
That doesn't bother me a bit.]

By transforming the elderly clergy into frolicking boys, the poet applies
the familiar technique of antiphrasis that we have seen him favor so
often in the *Lais* (in which Vitry and Cotin are characterized as *povres clercs*,
humbles, and *paisible enfants*). Now, however, Villon adds an ironic twist
by the use of another double entendre:

Dedans trente ans ou quarante ans
Bien autres seront, se Dieu plaist.   (1316–17)

[Within some thirty, forty years
They'll be much changed, if it please God.]

Within the fiction of the *Testament*, the youths will be men in their prime
within 30 or 40 years, but the phrase *bien autre seront* obviously carries a

macabre meaning when applied to Vitry and Cotin, already well into their eighth decade of life. Likewise, the normally innocuous phrase *se Dieu plaist* takes on darker connotations in the present context.

The elderly canons are identified in the previous stanza only as *mes povres clergons* (1306). In order to understand and appreciate the significance of this passage, it is essential that the reader connect these poor little clerks with Thibault de Vitry and Cotin, and this identification necessitates a familiarity with the *Lais*. Furthermore, Villon provides a clue to guide the informed reader:

> Item, a mes povres clergons,
> Auxquelz mes tiltres resigné   (1306–7)

> [Item, and my poor little clerks,
> Whom I ceded my titles to]

This connects neatly to the 28th stanza of the *Lais*, in which Villon clearly identifies the *povres clercs*. The *Testament*, as this passage illustrates, occasionally invites (indeed requires for proper understanding) a degree of intertextual intervention. Villon often revisits the legatees of the *Lais*, but usually with a sharper tongue and wit the second time.

Villon concludes his unflattering presentation of the *povres clergons* on an ironically cautionary note:

> Il fait mal qui ne leur complest,
> Ilz sont tres beaulx enffans et gens.   (1318–19)

> [He's wrong who doesn't treat them well,
> They're handsome youngsters and so nice]

It is, of course, the poetic attack just unleashed that the first verse immediately brings to mind. The second verse, especially in the antiphrastic use of *gens*, strongly suggests that Vitry and Cotin are dangerous and powerful men, not to be crossed. As already mentioned in chapter 3, Villon's treatment of these two prominent figures (among others) inevitably entails a degree of risk. As long as the text remains within the hands of trusted acquaintances, Villon is safe, but his security is fragile at best and could be seriously compromised by public release of the poem. The risk of offending a powerful and well-connected citizen of Paris is not to be lightly dismissed, as the disastrous consequences of the Ferrebouc affair (resulting in Villon's banishment from Paris and the hanging of two acquaintances) forcefully demonstrate.

One of Villon's most vicious attacks is reserved for an elderly Carmelite friar, Baude de la Mare, to whom Villon leaves various weapons with which the friar might defend himself against the loss of a certain prized possession:

> Une sallade et deux guisarmes,
> Que Detusca et ses gens d'armes
> Ne lui riblent sa caige vert. (1193–95)

> [A sallet, two halberds as well,
> So that Detusca and his guards
> Will not steal from him his "green cage."]

A number of factual explanations are in order here. A sallet is a light helmet that has a vision slit or a movable visor. A halberd, a cross between an ax and a spear, is a shafted weapon that has an ax blade on one side, a spike on the other, and a point on the end of the shaft. Detusca, it is generally believed, refers to Jean Turquant, a high-ranking member of the Parisian police and a friend of Guillaume de Villon, a fact that would explain Villon's deformation of Turquant's name in an effort to avoid offending the poet's adoptive father. The precise meaning of the "green cage" remains a subject of conjecture. It could refer to a sign showing a cage and identifying a house of ill repute situated across from the Carmelite monastery. The cage also appears in literature of the period symbolizing women or, specifically, female genitals. Evidence suggests that the green cage may be connected to prostitution.[6] Extrapolating from the available evidence, we can reasonably conclude that Villon is referring here to an affair that Brother Baude is alleged to have had (with a mistress or possibly a prostitute), which was eventually terminated (or perhaps was soon to be terminated) thanks to the intervention of Jean Turquant.

Villon transforms Baude de la Mare into a young soldier, "Portant chierre hardie et baude" [Wearing a visage bold and brave] (1192), well equipped, and manfully prepared to defend his rights to the woman in question. The ludicrous picture of an elderly friar armed as a warrior dressed for battle, although somewhat lost on the modern reader, would be readily apparent to a member of Villon's original audience, who, acquainted both with the physical appearance of Brother Baude and with the image of a soldier appropriately armed and accoutred for battle, could easily visualize the incongruous juxtaposition of these two images.

Villon singles out a canon of Notre-Dame by the name of Pierre Lomer for an especially trenchant assault. Lomer, according to a church document dated to 1456, received the unenviable assignment of eliminating prostitution from certain infamous houses on the Ile de la Cité:

Item, donne a maistre Lomer
Comme extraict que je suis de fee,
Qu'il soit bien amé (mais d'amer
Fille en chief ou femme coeffee,
Ja n'en ayt la teste eschauffee)   (1796–1800)

[Item, I give to Master Lomer,
As one who am of fairy line,
This: to be loved (if he loves
Bare-headed girl, or woman coiffed,
Let him not worry his head for that!)]

The second verse implies that nothing short of magic could make any woman love Lomer. Some commentators believe these verses suggest that Pierre Lomer was more attracted to men than to women, hence necessitating a magical spell.[7] Such an interpretation would lend additional irony to the last two verses. Although the sexual orientation of the legatee cannot be definitively determined on the basis of textual evidence, the sharpness of the personal attack becomes quite apparent by the end of the stanza:

Et qu'il ne luy couste une noix
Faire ung soir cent foiz la faffee,
En despite d'Augier le Danois.   (1801–3)

[And this: that he may, at no cost,
Perform a hundred times a night
And show up Ogier le Danois.]

Ogier le Danois, an epic hero noted for his sexual prowess, obviously has nothing to fear from Pierre Lomer.

The Wealthy

Another group of legatees includes men who hold positions of power based on their social standing, political connections, and especially wealth. These are the men who indirectly or directly controlled Paris. Villon and his fellow unemployed clerics, forming a kind of underclass, resented such power and privileged position, and considered their wealthy adversaries fair game for verbal attack and occasional vandalism. Villon's bequests to these prosperous and influential members of the bourgeoisie generally relate to power—the exercise, distribution, abuse, and deprivation of power. In actuality, Villon and his fellow clerics, disenfranchised and marginalized, somewhere beyond the fringe of social respectability, found themselves virtually powerless against their wealthy adversaries. However, in the poetic world of the *Testament*, governed by its own laws and hierarchy of power, the wealthy find themselves dispossessed and under the total control of the poet. One of the major preoccupations of the *Testament*, one of the strongest unifying forces of the poem, is the restoration of justice. The poem is pervaded by a sense of protest against the injustice and victimization that have been inflicted on the poet (or that he claims have been inflicted on him) from various quarters—members of the clergy, judges, prosecutors, sadistic jailers, former friends turned traitors, unfaithful mistresses, and wealthy men in positions of power. The *Testament* is, among other things, simply a payback, a forceful and often bitter act of retaliation, an attempt to right past wrongs and thus reestablish a sense of justice. Thus the *Testament* represents at one level the empowerment of a man who knows the experience of total helplessness, and this restitution of power is carried out through the medium of poetry.

One would expect the most common bequest of any will, of course, to take the form of financial gifts, and Villon does in fact leave various sums of money to some of his legatees, although he generally favors more unusual and imaginative gifts. Michel Culdou and Charlot Tarrenne, two extremely wealthy financiers, are favored with a bequest of a hundred sols, a paltry sum by any standard:

Item, donne a Michault Culdou
Et a sire Charlot Tarrenne

Cent solz. (S'ilz demandent: 'Prins ou?'
Ne leur chaille; ilz vendront de manne.)   (1338–41)

[Item, I give to Michault Cul d'Ou
And also Sir Charlot Tarrenne
A hundred *sols* . . . (If they ask, 'Where from?'
Never mind; they'll drop like manna.)]

The skeptical response that Villon anticipates from the ungrateful beneficiaries of his charity *(Prins ou?)* points to the avarice of the recipients as
well as to the total poverty of the donor. The suggestion that the coins
will fall like manna from the sky reinforces the impecuniosity of the testator and heightens the ludicrousness of the bequest. Villon has
reserved, however, a more malicious gift, which he now bestows on his
wealthy beneficiaries:

Et unes houlses de basenne,
Autant empeigne que semelle,
Pourveu qu'ilz me salueront Jehanne,
Et autant une autre comme elle.   (1342–45)

[Also a boot made of old skin,
Both the upper and the sole,
Provided they greet Jeanne for me
And one more of her sort as well.]

The *houlses de basenne* carries obscene connotations, which color the final
two verses of the stanza.[8] *Jehanne* designates a woman "d'une vertu peu
farouche" as one commentator delicately puts it.[9] As he does with certain members of the clergy, Villon is casting doubt on the virility of his
legatees. The juxtaposition of the bequests (100 sols and an old boot,
two appropriate gifts from a man who owns practically nothing) provides a skillful transition from one domain of power (financial) to
another (sexual). If the two financiers have unquestionably demonstrated their potency in the former realm, the status of their virility is
less established, particularly in light of their age.

     Given that Villon establishes and maintains his authority over the fic-
tional world of the *Testament* through the medium of poetry, it is appro-

priate that several of the bequests consist of poems (which Villon himself actually characterizes as songs), short lyric insertions inscribed within the testamentary framework of the larger poem. Unlike the fictional gifts that dominate the *Testament*—gifts of money, property, potency, and so forth—these poems represent a genuine source of wealth (one might say the only true source of wealth to which Villon can lay claim), that of poetic talent. To Ythier Marchant, possibly an acquaintance from Villon's student days, who by the time the *Testament* was written had attained a high position in financial administration, Villon leaves a short piece that he calls a lay, although the poem properly belongs to the genre of the rondeau:

Donne (mais qu'il le mecte en chant)
Ce lay contenant des vers dix,
(Et au luz) ung *De profundiz*
Pour ses ancïennes amours   (972–75)

[I give (provided he makes a song
Of it, and for the lute) this lay,
A *De profundis* ten lines long,
To celebrate his former love]

Villon makes a point of concealing the identity of the woman in question (and, paradoxically, announces the concealment), and there is some speculation that Marchant and Villon may have been rivals at one time for her affection. The lay that follows, based on the refrain

Mort, j'appelle de ta rigueur,
Qui m'as ma maistresse ravie   (978–79)

[Death, I appeal your harsh decree,
You who have snatched my love away]

is written in the courtly register to which the genre typically belongs. This lay is in some ways quite conventional and (like other lyric insertions) may well have been composed prior to the genesis of the *Testament*. Although Ythier Marchant undoubtedly lacks the talent to write the musical accompaniment stipulated as a condition for the bequest, it is

significant that Villon leaves him a song. Whatever advantages
Marchant may boast in the realm of finances or amorous relations, he
clearly lacks the poetic gift of Villon, a lack highlighted in the mention
of the lute, which symbolizes poetic creation.[10] By lending his song to
Marchant, Villon also lends his poetic voice, thus subordinating Ythier
to the poet's control.

To Jacques Cardon, a prosperous cloth merchant whose shop was situated on the Place Maubert, Villon leaves another rondeau, which he
terms a *bergeronnecte,* a genre designating popular songs often containing
obscene allusions. Villon even suggests two possible musical arrange-
ments based on the melodies of popular songs of the day. It is generally
thought that the rondeau, like the poem bequeathed to Ythier
Marchant, antedates the composition of the *Testament.* The somber tone
of the rondeau, as the refrain indicates, is hardly a tone that one would
expect from a *bergeronnecte:*

> Au retour de dure prison,
> Ou j'ay laissié presque la vie,
> Se Fortune a sur moy envie,
> Jugiez s'elle fait mesprison!   (1784–87)

> [Returning from imprisonment
> In which I nearly left my life,
> If Fortune bears ill will to me,
> Judge whether she is wrong or right.]

Although some critics have attempted to explain the connection
between the rondeau and its immediate context, such conjectures
remain basically unconvincing in spite of their ingenuity.[11] As Barbara
Sargent-Baur states, "It is hard to know what to make of this rondeau,
whose spirituality and elevated tone seem to belie the offhand, if not
obscene, manner in which it is introduced."[12] Indeed there is no reason
to assume a priori that there is necessarily a meaningful connection
between the rondeau and its context. After all, Villon begins by saying
that he actually has nothing suitable to leave Cardon:

> Item, riens a Jacquet Cardon,
> Car je n'ay riens pour luy d'onneste   (1776–77)

[Item, to Jacquet Cardon, nil;
For him I've nothing suitable]

Why should Villon choose to leave a poem that in all probability represents a deeply personal meditation on an experience (the prison at
Meung-sur-Loire comes immediately to mind) that has profoundly
marked his life? Rather than attempt to force an explanation, the
reader should perhaps simply accept this as one of many paradoxes,
many mysteries, that make the *Testament* such a fascinating and problematic text.

By comparison, the bequest for two prominent merchants—Jean de
la Garde, a grocer, and Guillaume Volant, a salt merchant—is unequivocal. Villon appoints them to ring the bells that will announce his
death and stipulates how the merchants are to be compensated for their
service:

Les sonneurs avront quatre miches
Et, se c'est peu, demye douzaine;
Autant n'en donnent les plus riches—
Mais ilz seront de saint Estienne.   (1912–15)

[The bell-ringers will get four loaves
And if that's too few, a half a dozen;
The richest don't give as much as that—
But they'll be of Saint Stephen's kind.]

The last verse, evoking the stoning of Saint Stephen, abruptly transforms the life-sustaining gift of bread into lethal stones. The passage
reveals another major thematic strand of the *Testament,* violence, which
runs through and unifies so much of the poem (and will be prominently
displayed in the next group of beneficiaries: police, officers of the law,
and bureaucrats). Under the guise of a dying sinner who has forgiven his
enemies and made peace with the world and can now look with compassion and munificence on those whom he leaves behind, the narrator of
the *Testament* dispenses an astounding variety of cruel and violent "gifts."

The "three orphans" whom Villon cites in the *Lais*—Colin Laurens,
Girard Gossuïn, and Jehan Marceau, all extremely rich usurers—will
receive a less severe punishment:

Sy vueil qu'ilz soient informez
En meurs, quoy que couste basture;   (1298–99)

[Still, I desire that they be taught
Their manners, and the rod not spared.]

Following a familiar pattern, Villon reverses the power structure of his
world. Wealthy and influential men are transformed into defenseless
orphans. Rather than enforcing *meurs* with the police, courts, prisons,
and laws (all of which protect the orphans' property and security, validating their privileges and authority), these unruly youths need to be
beaten into submission for their own good and for the good of society.
Villon's true feelings toward his legatees are clearly less than generous,
and yet these radical transformations could also represent, at one level, a
restitution of innocence.[13]

Police and Officers of the Law

One of the most important group of legatees in the *Testament* consists of
men charged in various capacities with enforcing the law. The long tradition of antagonism between Parisian students and police, which even
today resurfaces more than occasionally, dates back to the medieval
period, and Villon, for reasons already cited, had special reasons for personal animosity toward anyone representing the legal or penal system.
Accordingly, it is not surprising that this group should be prominently
featured in the poem. If political power is concentrated in the hands of a
few wealthy and influential individuals, it is the judges, prosecutors, jailers, and especially the municipal police who bear the responsibility of
maintaining the authority and protecting the property and privileges of
these individuals.

The actual gifts—all comic bequests relating mainly to money, wine,
violence, and sexuality—that Villon leaves to this group of beneficiaries
are less important than Villon's inclusion of so many of these men
among his legatees. Their names, and especially the physical appearance, demeanor, and personality traits that Villon's immediate audience
would inevitably associate with these names, contribute greatly to the
color and character of the poem. The *Testament*, among other things, is a
poem of the underworld, inhabited by the underclass—marginalized
individuals familiar with the darker side of Paris, its taverns, street

brawls, prostitutes, corrupt police, jails, and a wide assortment of criminal activity. A brief overview may help the reader appreciate the prominence of police in the *Testament*, the degree to which they occupy Villon's attention and thus shape large portions of the poem.

Perrenet Marchant, an officer attached to the Châtelet, one of the 12 personal police of the *prévôt*, Robert d'Estouteville, appears once in the *Lais* and three times in the *Testament*. The coat of arms that Villon designs for Perrenet reveals one of his favorite activities:

Trois dez plombez, de bonne quarre,
Et ung beau joly jeu de cartes.   (1098–99)

[But three dice, loaded but well-shaped,
And a most handsome deck of cards.]

According to an earlier bequest (*Lais,* 177–84), Marchant was also known for his unspecified involvement in prostitution. Two other members of d'Estouteville's personal security detail, Jean Raguier (1070) and Jean Chapelain (1836), also appear. The nature of Villon's relationship with these three men is impossible to determine from internal evidence. The bequests can be taken as disparaging remarks directed against enemies or as a bit of rough teasing reserved for close acquaintances, or as something between these two extremes. Without characterizing the nature of the relationship, we can be reasonably sure that the poet was familiar with the milieu frequented by the three.

One of the officers of the Châtelet prison responsible for administering interrogation and torture, Jean Mahé, cited by his nickname, Orfevre de Boys, "the Goldsmith of Wood" (1118), receives a mysterious and highly obscene bequest that has never been satisfactorily explained, but possibly refers to his involvement in prostitution or to his own sexual practices. Casin Cholet, another officer attached to the Châtelet, appears several times in the *Lais* and the *Testament* in the company of Jean Le Loup, a jack-of-all-trades who had some loose connections with the police. Cholet and Le Loup were apparently fond of stealing fowl from the farms around the Seine, an area the pair was supposed to police, and Villon leaves to Le Loup a hunting dog for this purpose:

Ung beau petit chiennet couchant
Qui ne laira poullaille en voye.   (1114–15)

[A handsome little pointer dog
That'll miss no chicken in its way.]

The *Chevalier du Guet*, Jean de Harlay, chief of the night police, who received a helmet in the *Lais*, makes a return appearance in the *Testament* (1828). Villon singles out Denis Richier and Jean Valet, two members of the *unze vings sergens*, the main body of the Parisian police, as exemplary members of their corps:

Et sont bonnes et doulces gens   (1088)

[And they are good and gentle folk].

This is a clear sign that Richier and Valet are among the most dishonest and ruthless of the lot. Jean Riou, captain of a company of 120 archers, a kind of citizen militia recruited to assist the regular police, receives six wolf heads cooked in cheap wine to share with his men, as a token of Villon's obviously high esteem and affection.

Unlike the bequests made to the clergy and the wealthy bourgeois, there is a certain intimacy to many of these gifts. Whereas the beneficiaries holding positions of power in society and the church often appear radically deformed by extreme caricature, Villon's presentation of the men charged with enforcing the law, many of whom represent social stations equivalent to or lower than the poet's own, demonstrates an intimate knowledge of their passions and weaknesses, occasionally almost suggesting a hint of sympathy.

Close Personal Acquaintances

One of the features that gives Villon's poetry, particularly the *Testament,* its distinctive character and texture is the degree to which the poetry reflects concrete aspects of the poet's life. Although any lyric poetry, by definition, may be termed "personal," Villon's work redefines the term, at least by medieval standards. Earlier medieval poets such as Colin Muset and Rutebeuf, who wrote in the thirteenth century, occasionally include autobiographical information in their poetry, but they generally present the information in such a way that allows the audience, even if unacquainted with the poet, to appreciate the significance of a given reference within a broad biographical context. In one poem, for example, Colin Muset describes the unfavorable reception he receives from an angry wife when he returns with an empty saddle pack from an unsuccessful tour as an itinerant poet and singer. Rutebeuf frequently refers to his poverty, illustrating in graphic terms the material conditions of an impoverished life—worn clothing, the scarcity of food, and so forth. In general, however, lyric genres, from the early songs of the troubadours in the twelfth century to the ballades of Charles d'Orléans in the fifteenth century, tend more toward abstraction than specificity. Indeed, the work of Charles d'Orléans provides an enlightening backdrop for Villon's poetry. Charles's ballades are deeply personal, but they are also highly self-referential. As a hostage of war, held under house arrest and confided to the custody of various aristocratic families in England, Charles writes to his wife Bonne, lamenting their separation:

Pour ce que veoir ne vous puis,
Mon cuers se complaint jours et nuis,
Belle, nompareille de France,
Et m'a chargié de vous escrire
Qu'il n'a pas tout ce qu'il desire
En la prison de Desplaisance.

[Because I cannot see you,
My heart complains day and night,
Lovely lady, peerless one of France,
And has charged me to write you
That he does not have all he desires
In the prison of Discontent.][14]

Charles, in typical fashion, transforms the experience of confinement from external to internal terms. The circumstances of his actual sequestration are subordinated to the internal conflict, which the poet represents in metaphorical language, specifically with the image of the heart confined in the *prison de Desplaisance.*

Villon, of course, experienced a very different kind of confinement at Meung-sur-Loire, which he represents in much more graphic terms. The essential point of the comparison, however, is not related to the physical conditions surrounding each confinement. More important, François Villon and Charles d'Orléans choose to represent in fundamentally different fashions a profoundly influential experience. Charles presents the event in psychological, symbolic, introspective, and self-referential terms. Villon, on the other hand, presents his experience by securely attaching it to the external circumstances that frame the event—the location of the prison, the date of the imprisonment, the harsh conditions of his confinement, and the identity of the men who were responsible for his suffering. To be sure, moments of abstract lyricism are to be found in Villon's poetry, especially in some of the ballades inserted into the *Testament* (the subject of the following chapter), but many of the most emotionally charged moments involve episodes and personal relationships that remain largely mysterious to the modern reader. If we eventually begin to comprehend the complex persona of the *Testament*, with all its inconsistencies and contradictions (or at least, in the absence of complete comprehension, begin to attain a sense of its complexity), it is thanks to the many relationships in which the *je* of the poem presents itself, each of which reveals a different facet of the poetic personality. There is, for example, Guillaume de Villon:

> Item, et a mon plus que pere,
> Maistre Guillaume de Villon,
> Qui esté m'a plus doulx que mere   (849–51)

> [Item, and to my more-than-father
> Master Guillaume de Villon,
> Who's been to me more kind than a mother]

Nothing in the tone of the passage, the context of the bequest, or the identity of the individual would suggest any ironic or devious meaning to the poet's affectionate description of his adoptive father.[15] Indeed, the transparent benevolence of the passage distinguishes it from the vast majority of references to male figures in the *Testament,* particularly those of an older generation, whose relationship with Villon is generally characterized by conflict, jealousy, anger, or a combination of all three. More than a father, kinder than a mother, Guillaume represents, if we are to take Villon's depiction of his adoptive father at face value, the purest example, perhaps the only example, of disinterested love to be found anywhere in the *Testament*. The following verses attest to the fidelity of Guillaume's support, a fidelity severely tested by his recalcitrant charge:

> Degecté m'a de maint boullon,
> Et de cestuy pas ne s'esjoye (853–54)

> [He's got me out of many a scrape,
> And at this one he doesn't rejoice.]

Although we cannot know to which particular crisis Villon is referring in the last verse (the prison at Meung-sur-Loire? the Ferrebouc incident? an unidentified crime whose consequences Villon is trying to escape?), we can be reasonably sure that the verse alludes to another of Villon's many misfortunes, which, insofar as we can judge from contextual evidence, will probably necessitate another intervention on the part of the ever-patient and generous Maistre Guillaume.

Where Villon makes ambiguous bequests that clearly reveal a mocking intent, we cannot always ascertain the nature of his relationship with the recipient. When the heir represents the church, the law, or the upper class, we can usually assume that the bequest reveals a malicious intent. If, on the other hand, the recipient bears no affiliation to any of these groups and is not known to have wronged the poet in any way, then it is quite conceivable that Villon makes the bequest in the spirit of good-natured teasing. Here is another aspect of the poem's complexity. To read *all* the bequests as evidence of malicious intent would inevitably give rise to misinterpretations and would inevitably result in an impoverished (and predictably mechanical) reading of this unpredictable poem. Thus, the relationship between Villon and Jacques Raguier, cited a total of three times in the *Lais* and the *Testament*, is somewhat problematic. Jacques receives the tavern called the Grant Godet, along with a stipulation:

> Pourveu qu'il paiera quatre placques,
> (Deust il vendre, quoy qu'il luy griesve,
> Ce dont on coeuvre mol et greve,
> Aler nues jambes, en chappin),
> Se sans moy boit, assiet ne lieve,
> Au trou de la Pomme de Pin. (1040–45)

[Provided that he'll pay four *plaques*
(Even if he were forced to sell
What's used to cover calf and shin
And go bare-legged, slipper-shod)
If, without me, he drinks, sits, stands
Inside the tavern called the Pine Cone.]

The joke, at Jacques's expense, involves a double reading of *placques*, coins of little value and also scabs, apparently a reference to an unsightly skin condition affecting Raguier's legs. That the earlier bequest to Jacques Raguier (*Lais*, 1038–45) also entails a reference to the Pomme de Pin (as well as an allusion to Raguier's penchant and capacity for drink), in conjunction with the lack of any apparent motive for malice, would seem to strongly suggest that Jacques Raguier, the son of a royal cook, is known to Villon chiefly through their mutual patronage of the Pomme de Pin, the tavern whose owner, Robin Turgis, appears among the list of Villon's principal creditors. It is hard to know how else to interpret the last two verses of the stanza, which, whatever their implied meaning, appear based on the assumption that Jacques Raguier and François Villon at one time drank together at the Pomme de Pin.

A personal acquaintance who does not receive the benign treatment accorded to Jacques Raguier is Noël Jolis, who apparently played a role in a sexual escapade that led to disastrous results. On the basis of textual evidence, it appears that Noël and François were both beaten in punishment for the incident, and Villon makes it clear that he did not get off lightly:

J'en fuz batu comme a ru telles,
Tout nu, ja ne le quiers celler.   (659–60)

[Beaten like laundry at a stream,
Nude, I don't try to hide the fact.]

Later in the poem, Villon leaves Noël a punishment, which the poet does not even attempt to conceal under the pretense of a gift:

Chastoy est une belle aulmosne,
Ame n'en doit estre marry:

Unze vings coups lui en ordonne
Livrez par les mains de Henry. (1640–43)

[Chastisement is good charity,
At which no soul should take offence:
I order for him twenty times
Eleven blows, at Henry's hands.]

Exactly why is Henry Cousin, the city executor of justice (authorized to carry out floggings and to implement death sentences) commanded to administer such a harsh punishment? We can only assume that Villon blames his accomplice for failing to protect him, or even (given the severity of the punishment) for committing an act of betrayal. The woman involved in the incident, Katherine de Vausselles, appears blameless. However, like other women in the *Testament*, she is implicated in an act of violence and degradation. This leads us to a consideration of the final group of heirs.

Women

With the exception of references to Villon's mother and the Virgin and one ballade (which will be discussed in chapter 6), the modern reader will find little to mitigate the poet's harsh treatment of women. It should be pointed out, by way of explanation rather than justification, that Villon's misogynist digressions were undoubtedly appreciated (and expected) by his male audience. Love between men and women, with the notable exception of the ballade written for Robert d'Estouteville, quickly degenerates to pure sexual attraction, which in turn degenerates to exploitation, cruelty, violence, and even death. This jaundiced view of love reveals itself particularly in the poem that has come to be known as the *Double Ballade,* in which Villon chronicles a long series of famous anecdotes (from biblical and mythological sources) demonstrating the catastrophic results of uncontrolled lust. If women are indicted in the poem, it is only by indirect implication, for they are practically invisible. Violence is limited exclusively to men, and men and women alike fall victim to male lust. Samson loses his eyes, but Delilah is never mentioned (631). David sends Uriah to his death in battle in order to have his wife, Bathsheba, who is reduced in the poem to a pair of shapely thighs, "cuisses bien fetes" (647). Amnon clearly bears the

responsibility for the incestuous attack on his sister Thamar (651), and
thus deserves his subsequent death at the hands of Absalom. Herod
orders the decapitation of John the Baptist, but the role of Herodias
and Salome (neither cited by name) is reduced to "dances, saulx et
chansonnectes" [dances, skips, and little songs] (655). In the passage
cited in connection with Noël Jolis, Villon takes his place among the
martyred lovers, but Katherine de Vausselles, like her biblical counterparts, appears to play an almost marginal role in the episode. Women,
it may be argued, serve as the temptation that ultimately instigates
male violence, but (with the exception of Delilah) cannot be held
morally responsible for the disastrous triumph of male lust over reason.

The women who figure most prominently in the *Testament* are prostitutes. In a lengthy digression, Villon considers the causal chain that
leads an honest woman into prostitution:

> Assavoir mon se ces fillectes
> Qu'en parolles toute jour tien,
> Ne furent ilz femmes honnestes?   (590–92)

> [But this is what I'd like to know:
> Those girls I chat with all day long,
> Were they not honest women once?]

The narrator makes no effort to distance himself from these disreputable
fillectes. In fact, as we will soon see, he not only portrays himself associat-
ing with prostitutes, but even identifies with them to a certain extent.
The process that leads women to compromise their honor, he maintains,
begins with a lust that is satisfied by a single lover:

> L'une ung clerc, ung lay, l'autre ung moyne,
> Pour estaindre d'amours les flasmes
> Plus chaudes que feu saint Antoine.   (598–600)

> [A clerk, a layman, or a monk,
> In order to put out love's flames,
> Hotter than Saint Anthony's fire.]

To this point, the digression appears almost a defense of women who
have compromised their virtue. After all, they begin as *femmes honnestes*,

initially limit themselves to one lover, and maintain a certain discretion concerning the relationship. Eventually, however, promiscuity sets in, drawing the following censure from the poet:

> Qui les meut a ce? G'ymagine,
> Sans l'onneur des dames blasmer,
> Que c'est nature femeninne
> Qui tout unyement veult amer.   (609–12)

> [What drives them to it? I suspect
> (Without impugning ladies' fame)
> That it is femininity
> That wants to love men generally.]

In attributing promiscuity to the insatiable nature of female lust, Villon echoes the sentiments of Jean de Meung and other medieval writers who are less than charitable in their attitude toward women. The pretense of respect for women, "Sans l'onneur des dames blasmer," is immediately undercut by the sarcastic use of *dames* to designate prostitutes, and by the obvious implications of the proverb selected to end the stanza:

> Que six ouvriers font plus que trois.   (616)

> [Six workmen can do more than three.]

Greed and lust merge in Villon's portrayal of the woman identified only as *ma chiere rose,* to whom he will not leave his heart (or his liver) because

> Elle aymeroit mieulx aultre chose,
> Combien qu'elle ait assés monnoye.
> Quoy? une grant bourse de soye,
> Plaine d'escuz, parfonde et large.   (912–15)

> [There's something else that she'd prefer
> Although she isn't short of cash . . .
> What's that? A big purse made of silk,
> All full of coins, and deep and wide.]

Given that the anatomical references seem to follow a descending order, beginning with the heart, and also given the obscene nature of the subsequent stanza, the erotic overtones of the passage are fairly obvious. Although Villon never discloses the identity of the woman in question, the name Marthe appears as an acrostic in the first stanza of the following ballade, a poem that, according to Villon's instructions, is to be delivered by Perrenet Marchant (one of Robert d'Estouteville's bodyguards, whom Villon connects to prostitution in other passages) with the following salutation:

Orde paillarde, dont viens tu?   (941)

[You dirty whore, where have you been?]

Whether the woman in question (Marthe?) deserves such a harsh greeting, and the extent of Villon's relationship with the *fillectes*, whom he claims to know so well, can only remain a matter of conjecture. It is certain, however, that at least one of the women named in the *Testament* is a known prostitute:

Item a Marïon l'Idolle
Et la grant Jehanne de Bretaigne
Donne tenir publicque escolle—
Ou l'escolier le maistre enseigne.   (1628–31)

[Item, to Marion the Idol
And to tall Jeanne of Brittany
I give the right to keep a school—
Where the pupils educate the staff.]

From court records of 1461, we know that Marion l'Idole (alias Marion la Dentue) shared a house with other women of her trade (one of whom may well have been Jeanne de Bretagne).[16] Both Marion and Jeanne, we may assume, were known to Villon's original audience by reputation if not by personal acquaintance. Indeed, there is reason to believe that some of Villon's contemporaries may have had more than a passing acquaintance with Marion, who is cited again a little further in the poem. In a play on the *enfants trouvés,* orphans housed in a church institution located on the Ile de la Cité, Villon refers to the *enfants perdus,* probably unemployed clerics like himself:

> Mais les Perdus fault que consolle.
> (Sy doivent estre retrouvez,
> Par droit, sur Marïon l'Idolle.)   (1661–63)

> [But the Lost Ones I must console.
> (They ought to be found once again,
> Of course, at Marion the Idol's.)]

Prostitutes and prostitution, it may be argued, represent more than a mere ornament in the *Testament.* In the ballade entitled by Marot *Ballade de bonne doctrine a ceux de mauvaise vie,* Villon reminds his dissolute comrades that everything they possess will ultimately end up in one of two places:

> Tout aux tavernes et aux filles.   (1699)

> [All to the taverns and the girls.]

The flow of money (including all forms of legal and illicit financial transactions—bequeathing, donating, lending, borrowing, stealing, begging, buying, selling, and bargaining) provides one of the principal unifying strands of the *Testament.* And what is the final destination of this flow of wealth, where does it all end up? The ultimate beneficiaries are the taverns and the prostitutes. One is tempted to speculate that Villon is speaking here, at least partly, from personal experience. What happened, for example, to his share of the Navarre theft, a substantial sum of money that by his return to Paris in 1461 had completely disappeared? Villon's connection to prostitutes, however, can also be viewed in a different light. Because the *Testament* presents, at least on one level, a reflection or a projection of the poet's interior world, is it not possible that the fallen women who wander through the poem represent something in him—a corruption of innocence, a moral failure, or a betrayal of integrity? In the *Ballade de la Grosse Margot,* the poet, in a most unflattering self-portrait, presents himself as the procurer of a fat prostitute, well past her prime. Although the authenticity of the relationship

is debatable (it is possible, for example, that Margot represents a caricature of all Parisian prostitutes), the essential feature of the poem is not
the historical authenticity of the particular woman described in the
poem, but rather the self-characterization of Villon, where again we see
the narrator defined by his relationships:

> Vente, gresle, gesle, j'ay mon pain cuyt.
>
> Je suis paillart, la paillarde me suyt.
>
> Lequel vault mieulx? Chascun bien s'entressuyt.
>
> L'un vault l'autre; c'est a mau rat mau chat.
>
> Ordure aimons, ordure nous assuyt;
>
> Nous deffuyons honneur, il nous deffuyt,
>
> En ce bordeau ou tenons nostre estat.   (1621–27)

> [Come wind or hail or frost, I've got it made.
>
> I am debauched; so's she who shares my life.
>
> Which of us is the better? We're well matched,
>
> Each worth the other: for bad rat, bad cat.
>
> It's filth we love, and filth runs after us.
>
> We fly from honour, honour flies from us
>
> Inside this brothel where we hold our court.]

The separate identities of the poet and the woman whom he comically
calls *la belle* in the opening verse of the ballade gradually merge in the
course of the *envoi* (final stanza). The gender may differ, but not the
essence (*paillart, la paillarde*). Each resembles the other (*Chascun bien
s'entressuyt*). One is the equivalent of the other (*L'un vault l'autre*). By the
closing of the stanza, the individual identities are subsumed within the
inclusive first-person plural: *aimons . . . nous assuyt . . . nous deffuyons. . .
nous deffuyt . . . tenons nostre estat*. The acrostic signature further solidifies
the conflation. Is it by accident that in the one instance where Villon
chooses to fuse his identity completely with that of another individual,
that person turns out to be a prostitute?

Chapter Six
The *Testament*: The Ballades

Villon has interspersed a series of fixed-form poems, 16 ballades and three rondeaux, throughout the *Testament*. Scholars generally believe that the composition of these poems antedates the composition of the *Testament*, and during the writing of the *Testament*, Villon decided to incorporate the collection of earlier poems into the longer poem at appropriate junctures. Sometimes the lyric insertion is skillfully integrated into the body of the *Testament*; at other times, the transition is more abrupt. Any thoughtful consideration of the *Testament* must include attention to not only the will proper but also the lyric insertions that the poet has integrated into this matrix. The ballades enrich the work with "a remarkable variety of voices," to borrow the perceptive observation of Sylvia Huot.[1] Whereas Huot and other critics study the thematic connections between the ballades and the *Testament*, the present chapter will focus more on the nature of the voices themselves, the associations they bring to the poem, and the manner in which they blend with or play against other voices.

The Courtly Voice

One of the poetic traditions in which Villon inscribes portions of the *Testament*, in fact one of the oldest and most important of all medieval poetic traditions, is that of courtly ideology. Villon and his fellow fifteenth-century poets had at their disposal an abundant stock of conventional language, images, and poetic conceits dating back to the *trouvères*, the earliest French poets to compose verse (actually songs) on themes of love. In the ballade entitled by Marot *Ballade à s'amie*, addressed to a woman whose identity (although the subject of much speculation) has never been conclusively established, Villon draws much of his language from the courtly register:

Cherme felon, la mort d'un povre cueur,
Orgueil mussé, qui gens met au mourir,

Yeulx sans pitié, ne veult Droit de Rigueur,
Sans empirer, ung povre secourir?   (946–49)

[Charm bringing woe, the death of a poor heart.
Occult conceit, that sends folk to their death,
Inhuman eyes—Does Justice not enjoin
Sparing a poor man, not destroying him?]

Here Villon is simply reworking familiar courtly motifs—the power of
feminine charm and pride, the spell of the woman's eyes, the appeal to
reason and compassion, and the subordination of the poet to the
woman's will. Especially conventional is the invocation of death, associated with the suffering of the lover (highlighted twice within two verses,
la mort . . . met au mourir). The following stanza develops the motif of
death, introducing a new personification:

Et qu'est cecy? Mouray sans coup ferir?
Ou Pictié veult, selon ceste teneur,
Sans empirer, ung povre secourir?   (955–57)

[Enough! Now shall I die without a fight?
Or does Pity decree, from what's been said,
Sparing a poor man, not destroying him?]

However, despite certain conventional elements, the ballade does not
strictly conform to the poetic norms of the courtly lyric. In this poem,
abstract lyricism is methodically punctuated and punctured by more
earthy forms of expression. Love, the very essence of so many abstractions associated with the courtly lyric, receives a decidedly uncourtly
characterization:

Amour dure plus que fer a macher   (944)

[A love more hard than iron to chew].

The description of the poet's plight culminates in a cry for help that
sharply contrasts with the elevated tone of the preceding verses:

Haro, haro, le grant et le mineur! (954)

[Help! help! I send my cry to all and some.]

A glimpse of the future brings to mind a famous sonnet by Ronsard, who will attack the same theme in similar language a century later:

Ung temps viendra qui fera dessechier,
Jaunyr, flectrir, vostre espanye fleur. (958–59)

[A time will come that will quite desiccate,
Yellow, and wither that full-blown flower of yours.]

A contemplation of the destructive effects of time should, according to the conventional norms of the love lyric, lead to an eloquent and impassioned plea to profit fully from the present moment. Instead, the thought of the woman's withered body inspires a very different reaction:

Je m'en reisse, se tant peusse macher
Lors; mais nennil. Ce seroit donc folleur. (960–61)

[I'd laugh, if I could move my jaws that much
Then; but no. So it would be foolishness.]

The eventual carpe diem sounds more like an impatient command than an invitation to savor the sweetness of the present:

Or buvez fort, tant que ru peult courir! (963)

[Now drink up well, as long as the stream flows!]

The *envoi*, addressed to a figure identified as *Prince amoureux* (generally thought to be either Charles d'Orléans or René d'Anjou, established poets whose patronage Villon sought during his wanderings following the Navarre incident), squarely resituates the refrain within a non-courtly context:

Vostre mal gré ne vouldroye encourir,
Mais tout franc cuer doit, par Nostre Seigneur,
Sans empirer, ung povre secourir.   (967–69)

[I shouldn't like incurring your ill will,
But, Lord! Each noble heart's duty is this:
Sparing a poor man, not destroying him.]

Here the word *povre* (the signature of the *povre Villon*) reverts from its figurative meaning (*la mort d'un povre cueur*) to the familiar financial sense in
which Villon typically uses the word.

Without knowing the precise circumstances surrounding the composition of the ballade, we can nevertheless observe that Villon is playfully
assuming the guise of the martyred lover, a mask he has already
assumed in the *Lais.* He will continue to play with this mask during the
remainder of the *Testament.* Courtly terminology and references to
beauty, love, honor, charm, death, the heart, pity, and justice fail to conceal a genuine personality that repeatedly breaks through the courtly
veneer. The plea for love eventually becomes a plea for money.

A ballade more closely aligned to the courtly tradition, the *Ballade
pour Robert d'Estouteville*, remains something of a mystery. The circumstances leading to this ballade's composition (and, presumably, its eventual delivery) are totally unknown; there is no internal or external evidence illuminating the relationship (if any) between Villon and Robert
d'Estouteville, the *prévôt* of Paris. The poem celebrates the conjugal love
of Robert and Ambroise de Loré. Was the ballade commissioned by
Robert as a gift for his wife? Does the poem represent a token of gratitude on the part of Villon, in return for a favor? Despite the enigmatic
nature of the ballade's composition, it seems clear that Villon wrote the
poem specifically for Robert d'Estouteville, whose marriage is presented in appropriately elevated language. The ballade opens with
images of birds—a soaring sparrow hawk and fluttering blackbirds
preparing to mate. The speaker of the poem, Robert, thus leads
Ambroise from the natural and innocent mating of birds to the expression of his own desire, decorously couched, however, in suitably
abstract language:

Offrir vous vueil, ad ce desir m'alume,
Joyeusement ce qu'aux amans bon semble.   (1382–83)

[Out of desire I wish to offer you
Joyously that which to lovers seems good.]

The union of husband and wife is blessed with a triple sanction. First, like the birds whose activity is held forth as a model, the lovers are responding to a natural and basic desire. Second, bound by the law of Love, they are obligated to carry out the will of their sovereign:

Sachiez qu'Amour l'escript en sa volume.   (1384)

[Such is the law Love inscribes in his book.]

Last, and most important, the sexual act is divinely sanctioned when fulfilling (according to church teachings) its intended function, that of procreation:

Sy ne pers pas la graine que je sume
En vostre champ, quant le fruyt me ressemble.
Dieu m'ordonne que le fouÿsse et fume;
Et c'est la fin pour quoy sommes ensemble.   (1398–1401)

[And thus I do not lose the seed I sow
In your field, when the fruit resembles me.
God orders me to delve and fertilize;
Engendering's the reason we're together.]

The poem contains an unusual blend of earthy, nature-based imagery (birds in flight or mating, smoke dispersing in the wind, the sowing of a fertile field) and the highly refined and abstract language typically associated with the courtly lyric:

Dame serez de mon cueur sans debat,
Entierement, jusques mort me consume.   (1386–87)

[Doubtless you'll be the lady of my heart,
Entirely, till I am consumed by Death.]

It is also significant that the physical union celebrated in various forms
throughout the ballade has evolved into a purely spiritual union by the
envoi:

> Que le mien cueur du vostre dessassemble
> Ja ne sera; tant de vous en presume;   (1403–4)

> [That my heart should detach itself from yours
> Will never be; I expect of you the same;]

The most striking feature of this poem is that it treats human sexuality
with extraordinary tenderness and respect, an attitude diametrically
opposed to the crude, cynical, and often cruel treatment of sexuality
typically manifested in the *Testament*. The intimacy of the relationship
described in the poem gives credence to the theory that Villon wrote the
piece at the behest of Robert d'Estouteville, who may even have given
specific instructions concerning the nature of the poem. At any rate, the
poem detaches itself like a ray of sunlight from the obscurity of the *Testament*. Indeed, the opening verse,

> Au poinct du jour, que l'esprevier s'esbat   (1378)

> [At daybreak, when the sparrowhawk beats his wings],

provides the only image of daylight in the 2,000 verses of this otherwise
dark poem.

The Homiletic Voice

The formal discourse with which Villon and his contemporaries were
perhaps most familiar was the homily. The historian Jean Favier explains
that a variety of ecclesiastical appointments involved the right—or even
the duty—to preach, creating occasional conflicts and rivalries within
the church:

> Il y a la doctrine du prédicateur, de celui qui, du haut de la chaire ou
> dans le secret de la confession, met le dogme à la portée des intelligences
> et harmonise les devoirs du chrétien avec les possibilités du bourgeois
> ... Le curé prêche, le moine prêche, le frère mendiant prêche. Le frère

prêcheur voit même en la Parole sa raison d'être dans l'Eglise et se pose
en rival du curé.[2]

As we have already seen in the passage from the *Journal d'un bourgeois de
Paris* (quoted in chapter 4), mendicant friars, whose vocation involved
preaching, drew large crowds in Paris, especially in the Cemetery of the
Innocents, which provided such a dramatic and effective backdrop for
the friars' stern warnings. Villon's poetry picks up the many sounds of
the streets—songs, curses, jokes, and obscenities—and among these
sounds we should not be surprised to find the preacher's voice. One of
the salient features of the *Testament* is its orality, the extent to which the
poem replicates, distorts, and playfully mixes various aspects of oral discourse taken from the poem's immediate environment, the streets of
fifteenth-century Paris. The voice of the preacher represents an important aspect of this orality. The trilogy of ballades beginning with the
famous *Ballade des dames du temps jadis* bears all the hallmarks of a popular sermon—repeated rhetorical questions, a dramatic insistence on
human mortality, and an abundance of illustrative examples. Highlight-
ing the pedagogical function of the popular sermon, Favier points to the
importance of citing historical examples for rhetorical purposes:

> Il faut être compris, et la pédagogie n'est pas moins simple: paraboles,
> exemples tirés de l'histoire sainte ou de la vie des saints. Tout est exemple.
> Toute anecdote porte son triple sens, historique, allégorique et moral.[3]

The trilogy of ballades, and in particular the *Ballade des dames du temps
jadis*, drawing on historical, mythological, literary, and religious sources,
sets forth a series of names, each evoking a story (often of a tragic
nature) that enriches and dramatizes the *ubi sunt* theme. As Pierre Le
Gentil points out, the compelling effect of the *Ballade des dames du temps
jadis* derives not only from poetic technique but also from the very resonance of the names cited in the *ballade:*

> Plus encore qu'une Christine de Pisan ou un Charles d'Orléans, Villon
> s'est intéressé à la sonorité de la parole . . . de même il a su découvrir dans
> la *Ballade des dames* des noms propres qui à eux seuls—sans qu'ils évo-
> quent aucun être précis—suggèrent par le timbre de leurs syllabes la
> fragile beauté dont le poème déplore la rapide et définitive destruction.[4]

A skilled rhetorician, Villon immediately engages his audience in the
opening verse of the *Ballade des dames du temps jadis:*

Dictes moy ou, n'en quel paÿs
Est Flora la belle Romaine   (329–30)

[Tell me where, and in what land,
Flora the lovely Roman is]

The remainder of the ballade is framed by a series of questions all related
to the *ubi sunt* motif. This rhetorical device appears even more prominently in the following ballade, the *Ballade des seigneurs du temps jadis*.
The self-conscious manner in which the question is posed (and consequently the speaker's awareness of his relationship with the audience)
and the use of a succession of short, pointed questions for dramatic purposes all strongly suggest a homiletic tone:

Encor faiz une question:
Lancellot le roy de Behaygne,
Ou est il? Ou est son tayon?
Mais ou est le preux Charlemaigne?   (377–80)

[Yet I shall ask one question more:
Lancelot, the Bohemian king,
Where is he? Where's his grandsire gone?
But where's the worthy Charlemagne?]

The wealth of allusions that fills these first two ballades of the *Testament* has inspired extensive commentary focusing on the content of the
poems—examination of Villon's sources, explanations of the juxtaposition of certain names, thematic progressions, and so forth. Scholars
have devoted considerably less attention to the tone of the poems.
Although the poems are obviously inscribed within the well-
established *ubi sunt* genre, there are moments of homiletic discourse
that distinguish these pieces from the often stiff and formal language
of their literary antecedents. The second ballade, for example, concludes with a simple list of names, rattled off in quick succession,
where the poetry (as Le Gentil has explained) lies in the resonance of
the names, and presumably in the delivery of the speaker, rather than
in poetic technique:

Ou est Clacquin le bon Breton?
Ou le compte Daulphin d'Auvergne
Et le bon feu duc d'Alençon?
Mais ou est le preux Charlemaigne?   (381–84)

[Where is the brave Breton, Claquin?
Or the count, dauphin of Auvergne?
And the brave late duke of Alençon?
But where's the worthy Charlemagne?]

The homiletic voice reappears in the final ballade of the *Testament*. Here, an unidentified speaker presents a eulogy for the *povre Villon*, who has now joined the ranks of the departed souls cited in the poem's first two ballades, having, like certain of his predecessors, achieved a legendary status by the heroic nature of his death:

Car en amours mourut martir   (2001)

[A martyr did he die, in love].

Rather than disappearing into self-effacement, however, the voice continues to remind us of its presence, as the speaker repeatedly intervenes in an apparent effort to corroborate the authenticity of his account of the "martyr's" life and death:

Ce jura il sur son coullon
. . . .
Et je croy bien que pas n'en ment
. . . .
Il est ainsi et tellement
. . . .
C'est de quoy nous esmerveillon   (2002–18)

[He swore it on his testicle
. . . .
And I think he's telling no lie

. . . .
The way of it's exactly this

. . . .
That's what we find astonishing]

The preacher's voice, not limited to lyric insertions, surfaces occasionally at other junctures in the *Testament*, especially at moments where the
poem reveals a didactic thrust. Thus, the poet's companions are repeatedly warned to abandon the sinful paths that threaten their physical and
spiritual well-being:

> Ce n'est pas un jeu de troy mailles,
> Ou va corps, et peult estre l'ame.
> Qui pert, riens n'y font repentailles
> C'on n'en meurre a honte et diffame.   (1676–79)

> [It's not any threepenny game
> Where body—perhaps soul—is risked.
> The loser's not helped by remorse
> Or kept from a disgraceful death.]

The moralistic tenor of these passages is unmistakable. The warning
cuts directly to its target:

> A vous parle, compaings de galle
> (Mal des ames et bien du corps)   (1720–21)

> [I'm talking to you, comrades in pleasure
> (Illness of soul, and body's gain)]

The question of separating irony from sincerity in the *Testament* is often
highly problematic. In the moments where the poem warns the *com-
paigns de galle* of the grim destiny that awaits the unrepentant sinner,
however, it is difficult to find any evidence of humorous intent, especially in view of the shadow of the hanged Colin de Cayeux (one of Villon's accomplices in the Navarre theft, later sentenced to death for
another crime) that swings over the passage (1673–75).[5] The call for

penance, in preparation for a death that may strike at any moment, echoes through virtually every medieval sermon:

> Et pour Dieu, soiez tous recors
> Une foyz viendra que mourrez. (1726–27)

> [And for the love of God recall:
> the time will come when you will die.]

Verses such as these, no doubt, lead Pierre-Yves Badel to find one of the salient features of the *Testament* to be its didactic purpose: "Son intention [Villon] n'est pas de se chanter ou de se plaindre, mais d'abord comme celle de Bodel, Rutebeuf, et Jean de Meun, d'enseigner."[6] The didactic dimension of the *Testament* will become even more apparent in the passages representing the *danse macabre* (the subject of chapter 9) where the homiletic voice merges with graphic images of death as the preacher returns to the cemetery.

The Sacred Voice

Not from the Cemetery of the Innocents but from the chapel of the Celestines emanates another voice, not one with moralistic and didactic overtones, but with the fervent tone of true prayer. The *Ballade pour prier Nostre Dame*, the one genuine and prolonged prayer of the *Testament*, stands in marked contrast to the mock prayers for Villon's enemies, especially Thibaut d'Aussigny. This ballade is an extension of the *Ave Maria* ("Holy Mary, Mother of God, pray for us sinners, now and at the hour of our death"). In the poem, which Villon presents as a gift to his mother, who will in turn recite the poem to the Virgin, we witness a conflation between the poet's voice and that of his mother, although the latter ostensibly delivers the prayer. The prologue, beginning and ending with Villon's mother, actually places the poet himself figuratively and literally at the center of the stanza:

> Item, donne a ma povre mere
> Pour saluer nostre Maistresse
> (Qui pour moy ot douleur amere,
> Dieu le scet, et mainte tristesse)—

Autre chastel n'ay ne forteresse
Ou me retraye corps ne ame,
Quant sur moy court malle destresse,
Ne ma mere, la povre femme!—   (865–73)

[Item, to my poor mother I give
(For her to hail our Mistress with)—
Who for me has had bitter grief,
God knows, and many sorrows too,—
No other castle have I, or fort
Where I may shelter body and soul
When harsh distress comes down on me,
And neither has my mother, poor thing!]

What begins as a minor digression in the presentation of the bequest—
"Qui pour moy"—which the editor aptly encloses in parentheses, ultimately subordinates the mother's relationship with the Virgin to the
son's: "pour *moy*," "Autre chastel *n'ay*," "Ou *me* retraye," "Quant sur *moy*."
The adjective *povre*, Villon's signature that repeatedly appears in first-
person and third-person references designating the poet in the *Testament*
(e.g., 178, 273, 274, 949, 1811, 1997), appears twice in the prologue
applied to Villon's mother, "ma povre mere" (865), "la povre femme"
(872), and once in the ballade, "Femme je suis povrecte" (893), further
reinforcing the conflation of the two identities. In the second stanza, the
speaker entreats the intercession of the Virgin, citing the example of two
infamous sinners who, thanks to a change of heart and prayers for divine
deliverance, eventually moved from a state of sin to a state of grace:

Pardonne moy comme a l'Egipcïenne,
Ou comme il fist au clerc Theophiluz   (885–86)

[Let him (Jesus) forgive me as He did the Egyptian,
Or as he did the clerk Theophilus].

The Egyptian is Mary, a prostitute of Alexandria who converted to Christianity and dedicated the rest of her life to serving the Virgin. Mary's story
is told by the thirteenth-century poet Rutebeuf. Theophilus was a priest

who, according to legend, entered a pact with the Devil, from which Theophilus was ultimately freed by the intervention of the Virgin. His story is the subject of Rutebeuf's *Le Miracle de Théophile*. Why Villon would choose to compare two of the most notorious sinners with the figure who characterizes herself in the poem as a humble Christian, a poor and aged woman, remains something of a mystery until we juxtapose this passage with the other passage in the *Testament* dealing with sin and conversion:

> Je suis pecheur, je le sçay bien;
> Pourtant ne veult pas Dieu ma mort,
> Mais convertisse et vive en bien,
> Et tout autre que pechié mort.   (105–8)

> [I am a sinner, I know well,
> And yet God does not wish my death
> But that I may amend, and live,
> And likewise all who're gnawed by sin.]

The signature words *povre* and *pecheur* lead us back, through a series of intratextual references, to Villon himself. It is thus significant that the feminine form *pecheresse* (879) evolves—through *pechiez* (884)—to the masculine form *pecheurs* (900). Also significant is the expansion of the first person singular in the opening stanza into the plural by the end of the poem: *nostre* (905), *nous* (906), and *nostre* (908). The acrostic signature, VILLON, in the *envoi* completes the conflation of mother and son.[7]

Despite their obvious differences, the *Ballade pour Robert d'Estouteville* and the *Ballade pour prier Nostre Dame* bear certain similarities. Both represent moments of spiritual elevation in the *Testament,* one a celebration of the beauty of conjugal love; the other, a hymn to divine love. Both concern an intimate relationship, one in the physical domain, the other in the spiritual domain. Last, both ballades are written to be recited by another person. Thus, paradoxically, the two poems that represent the most intense lyricism of the *Testament* are meant to be delivered by a voice other than the poet's.

The Dionysian Voice

In contrast to the elevated style of the *Ballade pour prier Nostre Dame*, Villon offers a very different kind of prayer (*orroison*, v. 1237) for the soul of

Jean Cotart. Cotart, a diocesan prosecutor, whom Villon claims represented him in a defamation case (1230–35), had died on January 9,
1461, shortly before the composition of the *Testament*. Given that most of
the ballades were probably written prior to the *Testament*, it is very possible that Villon composed the *orroison* upon learning of Cotart's death.
The nature of Villon's relationship with Cotart has never been definitively
established. Some critics maintain that Villon's treatment of the lawyer
(who, like Villon, was charged with several crimes, and was once even
jailed in the Châtelet) suggests a sympathetic point of view. Others,
believing that Cotart was among the officials responsible for prosecuting
Villon for various crimes, find in the prayer for Jean Cotart a cruel and
heavy-handed attack. Deprived of essential information about the case to
which Villon refers (and for which he claims to be figuratively and literally in Cotart's debt), we cannot conclusively characterize the tone of the
ballade as either sympathetic or vicious. We can, nevertheless, ascertain
the humorous intent of the poem. Jean Cotart, regardless of his professional successes or failures, had apparently acquired quite a reputation as
a drinker, and Villon celebrates this aspect of Cotart's life in the *orroison*:

> Luy qui buvoit du meilleur et plus cher,
> Et ne deust il avoir vaillant ung pigne;
> Certes, sur tous, c'estoit un bon archer:
> On ne luy sceust pot des mains arracher;
> De bien boire ne fut oncques fetart.   (1247–51)

> [He who'd drink of the costliest and best
> Even if he didn't have a comb's price left.
> Truly, as a tippler he outran the rest.
> You couldn't have snatched a pot out of his hands;
> He never was slack where drinking was concerned.]

The last verse could easily be a pejorative reference to Cotart's professional shortcomings, implying that he is *fetard* (lazy) as a lawyer but not
as a drinker. However, the reference could represent a good-natured
observation as well as a critical remark, and therefore does not provide a
clue to Villon's attitude toward the subject of his poem. Those who find
in the poem a note of sympathy probably see in the figure of the impe-
cunious drinker a reminder of various passages in the *Lais* and the *Testa-*

ment in which Villon refers to his own tavern debts.[8] Not only was Cotart no slacker when it came to drinking, but he actually excelled in this domain, rising above all competitors: "Certes, sur tous, c'estoit un bon archer" (1249). Cotart's excesses are corroborated by the personal testimony of the narrator:

> Comme homme viel qui chancelle et trespigne
> L'ay veu souvent, quant il s'alloit coucher,
> Et une foiz il se fist une bigne,
> Bien m'en souvient, pour la pie juchier.   (1254–57)

> [Like an old man who totters and stamps his feet
> I've seen him often, as he'd go off to bed.
> And once he raised a good bump on his skull,
> I well recall, when he'd been on a binge.]

Using the first-person narrative intervention, Villon personalizes the account of Cotart's exploits, authenticating the lawyer's reputation with claims that the poet witnessed firsthand the damaging results of Cotart's drunken binges: "L'ay veu souvent . . . Bien m'en souvient." Whether these assertions are based on firsthand accounts, as they purport, or whether they actually represent fictitious embellishments designed to convey the illusion of authenticity, they implicate Villon to some extent as a witness, if not an accomplice, in Cotart's drunken escapades. Where was he (or where does he claim to have been) when he so often observed Cotart staggering home at night? How is it that he recalls so well Cotart's self-inflicted injury?

At the same time that the poem includes specific information about this particular notorious drinker—his name, his profession, the fact that Villon owes him money, his taste for more expensive wine than he could afford, and the sometimes disastrous results of his inebriation—the poem also inscribes itself within a well-established tradition of songs commemorating drinkers and the act of drinking. Numerous medieval songs in Latin, related to the goliard tradition, celebrate the joys of drinking:

> Meum est propositum in taberna mori . . .
> Tunc cantabunt laetius angelorum chori:
> "Deus sit propitius huic potatori."

[It is my intention to die in a tavern . . .
Then the choirs of angels will joyfully sing:
"May God be kind to this drunkard."][9]

These songs enjoyed special popularity with university students (and
former students) all over Europe.[10] Like the excerpt of the Latin song
quoted above, the *Ballade pour Jehan Cotart* glorifies the fate of the
drunkard, adding a pseudo-sacred dimension with an obviously parodic
intent. Roger Dragonetti comments on this aspect of the ballade:

> Que dans l'ivrognerie dionysiaque de *Cotart*, Villon ait rendu inséparables
> l'ivresse et le supplice du désir en donnant à la soif du héros une dimen-
> sion sacrée, c'est ce qui nous paraît certain du seul fait que dans la Bal-
> lade, le poète interpelle en faveur de l'ivrogne les ancêtres bibliques de la
> vigne, Noé et Loth, tous deux victimes du vin.[11]

The pattern of biblical subtext in this ballade and other portions of the
Testament will be treated in chapter 8. The essential point for the present
is that Villon attempts to heroize a most unheroic character, an aging
drunkard who habitually drinks himself into a stupor before stumbling
and staggering his way into the night. Cotart, paradoxically, achieves
greatness in his weakness, attaining the epic proportions of what Dragonetti calls "un exemplaire pré-pantagruélique."[12] In effect, Villon and
Rabelais both encourage their audience to drink, the former by the
example of *le bon feu maistre Jehan Cotart*, the latter by a more explicit
invitation: "Beuvez donc un bon coup sans eaue."[13] Ultimately it is not
the person of Jean Cotart whom Villon celebrates in the ballade, but the
act of drinking itself.

   The theme of drinking resurfaces later in the *Testament* in the *Ballade de bonne doctrine,* based on the refrain "Tout aux tavernes et aux
filles" (1699). As we have already seen in chapter 5, the poem
addresses the socially marginal characters associated with the locus of
the tavern—sellers of indulgences, robbers, counterfeiters, wandering
actors and entertainers, and gamblers. The Dionysian voice of the
poem derives, however, not only from the setting of the tavern and the
act of drinking that implicitly unites this disparate group of characters, but also from the stream of words that flow with intoxicating
energy:

Ryme, raille, cymballe, fluctes,
Comme folz fainctilz, eshontez;
Farce, broulle, joue de fluctes;
Faiz, es villes et es cytez,
Farces, jeux et moralitez;
Gaigne au berlanc, au glic, aux quilles   (1700–1704)

[Try rhymes and jokes, sound cymbals and flutes
As do those lying, shameless Fools;
Hoax, do sleight of hand, deceive;
In villages and towns put on
Farces, plays, moralities;
Win at the dice, or skittles, or cards]

The series of enumerations, verbal chains that lead from music to magic
to theater to gambling, build momentum before terminating in a rapid,
almost frenzied list of dispossessed articles of clothing:

Chausses, pourpoins esguilletez,
Robes, et toutes voz drappilles,
Ains que vous fassiez piz, portez
Tout aux tavernes et aux filles.   (1716–19)

[Your hose, your doublets with their laces,
Your gowns and all the clothes you own,
Before you do a worse thing, take
All to the taverns and the girls.]

Villon, of course, refers on several occasions to various garments he has
left behind in lieu of payment in certain taverns. What we witness here,
however, is more of a general disrobing, a stripping away of all clothing,
along with all the social and personal inhibitions clothes represent, as a
gradual process of dispossession and liberation accelerates with comic
speed and abandonment. The driving force behind this violent divesti-
ture, the force that unifies the marginal characters of the poem, and
indeed the poem itself, is simply the lust for women and wine.

The Obscene Voice

In the *Testament,* Villon mixes moments of intense lyricism with repeated obscenities. These range from subtle innuendo to transparent double entendre to coarse and undisguised vulgarity. Indeed, the strand of obscenity (along with the strand of violence with which obscenity is often intertwined) emerges as one of the strongest unifying features of the *Testament.* Villon stipulates that his epitaph be written with coal, a fitting medium for graffiti:

> Qui n'avroit point d'escriptouoire,
> De charbon ou de pierre noire   (1879–80)

> [If writing tools weren't to be had,
> Carbon would do, and so would coal.]

In fact, one may argue that the *Testament* (or at least a significant portion of the poem) functions as a kind of graffiti, leaving obscene testimony to the life of the *povre Villon.* Thus, the epitaph, in the form of a rondeau, which Villon instructs his executors to write on his tomb (in *charbon* or *pierre noire,* if necessary), contains an appropriate obscenity:

> RIGUEUR LE TRANSMIST EN EXIL
> ET LUI FRAPPA AU CUL LA PELLE   (1900–1901)

> [A HARSH DECREE SENT HIM TO JAIL
> AND STRUCK HIS BACKSIDE WITH A SPADE]

On the other hand, much of the "scribbling" of the *Testament* represents (in another of the many paradoxes that characterize Villon's poetry) exceptionally refined, extraordinarily artistic graffiti. Yet there are moments when Villon drops all pretense and simply allows himself to indulge in the crudest forms of obscenity. To Jean Mahé, one of the guards at the Châtelet charged with inflicting torture, Villon leaves a hundred cloves of Arab ginger, a supposed aphrodisiac:

> Mais pour joindre cuz et coiectes
> Et couldre jambons et andoulles   (1122–23)

[But to join male and female parts
And attach hams and sausages]

The translation "male and female parts" provides a more delicate rendering of the cruder *cuz et coiectes;* the literal rendering of *jambons and
andoulles,* of course, speaks for itself. To the clerks of the *Chambre des
Comptes,* Villon leaves a highly undignified gift:

Et ceulx qui ont les culz rongneux,
Chascun une chaize percee   (1208–9)

[And those whose bottoms bother them
Will have a privy seat apiece.]

Again, the translation "whose bottoms bother them" represents a dis-
creet rendering of a flatly obscene phrase *culz rongneux.* Toward the end
of the *Ballade de la Grosse Margot,* which begins in a mock courtly style,
Villon presents himself in a most uncourtly posture, flattened beneath a
lustful prostitute:

Monte sur moy, que ne gaste son fruyt.
Soubz elle geins, plus q'un aiz me fait plat.   (1617–18)

[She climbs on me so as not to waste her fruit.
I groan beneath, more flattened than a plank.]

In one of the last self-portraits of the *Testament,* contained in the eulogy
of the final ballade, Villon leaves two conflicting images:

Car en amours mourut martir:
Ce jura il sur son coullon   (2001–2)

[A martyr did he die, in love;
He swore on his testicle]

The second verse clearly undercuts the courtly language of the preceding verse, effectively removing the last remnants of dignity from the
"martyr of love."[14]

Although obscene references are widely distributed throughout the work, prevalent in some of the fixed-form pieces as well as in the body of the *Testament*, the most concentrated and extended example of obscene language appears in the *Ballade des langues ennuieuses*. The circumstances surrounding this ballade remain highly obscure. It appears to be directed at François Perdrier, a wealthy Parisian merchant and money changer who probably (directly or indirectly) caused Villon a great deal of hardship:

> Langues cuisans, flambans et rouges,
> My commandement my priere
> Me recommanda fort a Bourges.   (1411–13)

> [Half by order, half by prayer,
> Much recommended to me at Bourges,
> Some tongues, well-spiced and flaming red.]

The passage in question has inspired a great deal of interest and speculation. An older generation of Villon scholars once offered a charmingly naive but improbable interpretation based on the assumption that Villon wished to repay François Perdrier for a plate of excessively spiced tongue that the latter had recommended he taste at Bourges.[15] One of the most intriguing and persuasive interpretations, although by no means definitive, is that of Jean Dufournet, who explains the exceptional vehemence of the ballade as an act of retribution for a grievous injustice:

> il y a dans ce huitain une allusion à un supplice qui devait terroriser le povre [sic] François, et qui était loin d'avoir disparu. . . . Le bûcher. Perdrier aurait, par envie, porté contre Villon les dénonciations qui tendaient à le faire condmaner à cette mort atroce, où ces langues auraient bien été cuisantes, flambantes et rouges.[16]

Whatever the offense, the extraordinary and sustained violence of the ensuing ballade forcefully conveys feelings of anger and deep resentment. At the same time, certain connections loosely bind this piece with the ballade almost immediately preceding it, the *Ballade pour Robert d'Estouteville*.[17] The poem, presented as a recipe, consists of a lengthy list of unsavory ingredients in which the *langues ennuyeuses* are to be fried.

First comes a group of inorganic ingredients—arsenic, saltpeter, quick-lime, boiling lead, soot, and pitch. These are followed by lye made from an organic base:

Faicte d'estront et de pissat de juifve,
En lavailles de jambes a meseaux   (1426–27)

[Made from a Jewess's feces and urine;
In water used to wash the legs of lepers]

Intermingled with these humanly generated elements we find various materials of animal origin—asp blood; the gall of wolves, foxes, and badgers; a cat's brain; and dog drool. In the ingredients of human origin, however, the poem attains the highest degree of repulsiveness:

En sang c'on voit es poillectes sechier
Sur ces barbiers, quant plaine lune arrive,
Dont l'un est noir, l'autre plus vert que cyve   (1444–46)

[In the blood that we see drying in bowls
At barber's shops, when the full moon arrives,
Of which one's black, the other greener than chives]

In Villon's time, one of the frequent duties of barbers, who also served as surgeons, was to bleed their patients as a remedy for a variety of ailments. Barbers collected the blood in brass basins called *pallettes* or *poil-lectes*. Although they were supposed to dispose of the blood within a few hours, and were even subject to fines for noncompliance, some barbers, perhaps through reasons of neglect or superstition, would leave bowls containing blood on their windowsills, often for an extended period of time, thus explaining the unpleasant sight recounted in the final verse of the preceding excerpt. The obscene imagery continues:

En chancre et fix, et en ces ors cuveaux
Ou nourrisses essangent leurs drappeaux   (1447–48)

[In ulcers and sores, and in those filthy tubs
In which the nursemaids rinse their diapers out]

The term *chancre* was most frequently applied to an ulcer of the tongue or nasal passage, while *fix* generally designates a sore located in the genital or rectal area. Thus, by association, the poem leads from unspecified illness (the *poillectes*) to various sores to the scatological imagery of the last verse. At the same time, another line of imagery leads from the contents of the barber's basin to the tub water where diapers have been rinsed to the water from a prostitute's bath:

> En petiz baings de filles amoureuses
> (Qui ne m'entant n'a suivy les bordeaux)   (1449–50)

> [In little baths of girls who live by love
> (Don't understand? You haven't haunted brothels)]

The *envoi* picks up the poem's scatological strand, which develops into the closing images. All the ingredients listed in the course of the recipe are to be filtered thus:

> Parmy le fons d'unes brayes breneuses
> Mais, par avant, en estrons de pourceaux
> Soient frictes ces langues ennuyeuses!   (1454–56)

> [Right through the seat of a pair of dirty pants;
> But before that in the feces of pigs
> —In all this may those spiteful tongues be fried!]

It should be pointed out that Barbara Sargent-Baur, despite the admirably high standards of accuracy that she maintains throughout most of her translation of the *Testament,* has somewhat softened the highly obscene tone of the *envoi,* rendering *breneuses* as "dirty," and *estroncs* as "feces." Rychner and Henry provide a less delicate translation of *brayes breneuses,* "une paire de caleçons merdeux."[18]

In spite of the distasteful imagery of the poem, there is an undeniable element of artistry here. The list of ingredients, although seeming at first glance to be arbitrarily chosen and arranged, represents a process of careful selection. Furthermore, a careful reading will uncover chains of imagery skillfully connected by well-defined internal logic. Oddly enough, the recipe's enumeration of repulsive ingredients, each more repugnant than the last, actually generates a curiously captivating cadence, an incantatory rhythm that builds in intensity as the poem progresses. The result is a strangely powerful lyricism that, in its own way, matches the poetic force of some of the more frequently studied ballades such as *Nostre Dame* and *Robert d'Estouteville*. The *Ballade des langues ennuieuses* is in its own right a masterpiece of obscenity.

Conclusion

The 16 ballades of the *Testament* represent a striking range of human experience and poetic voice. Yet, despite the seeming disparity of these poems, they are unified by their source, as Sylvia Huot aptly reminds us:

> The one constant is the identity of the author, creator of all poetic voices and personae. From the multiplicity of poetic stances emerges the voice of the poet, who, though frequently associated with members of the poetic world (most closely and more frequently with the protagonist of the huitains), is not ultimately contained by that world.[19]

Although some scholars have demonstrated remarkable imagination and ingenuity in making connections between the ballades of the *Testament,* it is difficult to demonstrate a tightly logical progression in the sequence of these lyric insertions within the overall structure of the *Testament*. Indeed, given the virtual certainty that the majority of these poems were composed prior to the body of the *Testament*, any attempt to uncover a cohesive design in the arrangement of the ballades may ultimately be misguided. Rather than search for an overarching and unifying structure in the ballade sequence, we should perhaps reflect on the remarkable diversity of poetic voices that alternately blend with and oppose one another, creating a sense of harmony that is progressively deepened as the reader moves through the world of the *Testament*.

Chapter Seven

Other Poems

In addition to the *Lais* and the *Testament,* Villon's poetic corpus includes 15 ballades, a *quatrain* (a four-verse poem), and at least six ballades written in the jargon of the Coquillards, a criminal society with which Villon appears to have had some connection. Some of these poems bear obvious connections to circumstances and events in Villon's life—the ballade written in praise of Marie, the young daughter of Charles d'Orléans; a request for money addressed to a royal patron; a plea from the prison at Meung-sur-Loire to the poet's friends; a poem to Etienne Garnier (doorkeeper of the Châtelet prison) boasting of the poet's successful appeal of his death sentence; and a versified appeal to parliament requesting a three-day extension of his banishment. Other ballades, more philosophical in nature, cannot be connected with any degree of certainty to a specific biographical context.[1]

Requete au prince

The stated purpose of this poem is to request the financial support of an unidentified royal patron, generally believed to be either Jean II, Duke of Bourbon, or Charles d'Orléans. Rychner and Henry offer compelling evidence supporting the hypothesis that Villon addressed the request to Charles d'Orléans during one of the poet's visits to Blois.[2] It is also possible that the poem was addressed to Jean II, at a time when both he and Villon were enjoying the hospitality of Charles d'Orléans at Blois. Whether addressed to Jean II or Charles d'Orléans, the ballade clearly appeals to the charity and goodwill of Villon's patron, speaks of past sufferings, alludes specifically to a previous gift from the same source, and manipulates humor and self-deprecation to achieve the stated objective.

The ballade opens with an appropriately deferential form of address, stressing the high aristocratic standing of the patron:

Le mien seigneur et prince redoubté,
Fleuron de lis, roialle geniture   (1–2)

[My natural lord and my redoubted prince,
Fleur-de-lys, scion of royal line]

The four forms of address highlight the royal lineage of the addressee: *seigneur*, *prince*, *fleuron de lis*, and *roialle geniture*. In striking contrast to the suitably elevated language reflecting the elite social status of the *seigneur*, Villon again proceeds to characterize himself in comically graphic terms as the victim of Fortune:

François Villon, que Travail a dompté
A coups orbes, a force de batture   (3−4)

[François Villon, whom travail's broken down
With bruises left behind by many a blow].

The abstract description of past sufferings, "que Travail a dompté," immediately leads to a more concrete restatement, personalizing the relationship between Travail and François Villon, the latter presenting himself as the battered victim of a physical assault. The poem now sets forth its raison d'être, the request for financial assistance, framed in quasi-legal terms:

Vous supplie par ceste humble escripture
Que luy faciez quelque gracïeux prest.   (5−6)

[Entreats you through this humble document
To make to him some sort of gracious loan.]

Qualifying his poem as an *escripture* and referring to the requested donation as a *prest*, Villon now continues his request along the lines of a mock promissory note. It is not his intent, he implies, to ask for an outright gift of money. Any financial assistance will be duly repaid. The poem now shifts into the register of legalistic language, which Villon manipulates so skillfully in the *Testament* (perhaps from personal experience). The *escripture* (referring appropriately to Villon in the third person) vouches for the applicant's willingness to repay his debt:

De s'obliger en toutes cours est prest
Se doubte avés que bien ne vous contante   (7−8)

[He'll swear to repay, in any court you like,
If you have doubts of being satisfied.]

The term *s'obliger* (to make a formal and legally binding promise) carries
definite legal connotations, leading into the assertion that the party
requesting the loan is prepared to formally recognize his debt in any
court of law. The image of the *povre Villon* solemnly and publicly swearing to honor his debt, allegedly put forth to assure the creditor and
relieve him of any possible doubts concerning the debtor's willingness or
ability to offer restitution, comically undermines the credibility of the
whole enterprise. The stanza ends with an extension of the contractual
language that characterizes the proposed transaction:

Sans y avoir dommage n'interest,
Vous n'y perdrés seulement que l'attente.   (9–10)

[Without incurring harm or prejudice,
All you will lose will be the waiting time.]

While *interest* is properly translated as "prejudice" (thus reinforcing *dommage*), in the context of a request for a *gracïeux prest,* the term also
implies an interest-free loan. The refrain "Vous n'y perdrés seulement
que l'attente" is actually a phrase taken from legal protocol indemnify-
ing a creditor against possible loss.[3]

    The second stanza opens with an allusion to a previous gift of six *écus*
(a significant sum for a man of Villon's modest means) from the same
source, money that Villon claims to have spent long ago on food. This
previous debt will be combined with the new one, all to repaid
promptly:

Tout ce paiera ensemble, c'est droicture
Mais ce sera legierement et prest   (15–16)

[All this he'll pay together, as is right,
But soon, and without any argument.]

And how does a man who portrays himself as the constant victim of bad
luck and claims that he has been forced to borrow money in order to

subsist intend to repay the sizable debt that he is accumulating? Villon attempts to relieve any doubts concerning his solvency by pointing to a rather curious source of income:

> Car se de glan rancontre la forest
> D'entour Pactay, et chastaignes ont vente,
> Paié vous tient sans delay ny arrest   (17–19)

> [For if he comes upon the acorn woods
> Around Patay, and chestnuts can be sold,
> He holds you paid, without let or delay.]

Exactly how the acorn forest of Patay will generate the revenue required to pay the poet's debt is unclear. First, Villon stipulates two conditions: "*se* de glan rencontre . . . et chastaignes ont vente." In other words, the absence of these two conditions (if he does *not* come upon the acorn forest of Patay, and if chestnuts *cannot* be sold) would effectively invalidate the rest of the contract. Furthermore, what is the relationship between an acorn forest and the selling of chestnuts? Last, Clément Marot, Villon's first editor, who lived close enough to the period when the poem was composed to speak authoritatively on the subject, maintains that there is no acorn forest at all in Patay, thus suggesting the possibility that Villon is dealing again (as he so often does in the *Lais* and the *Testament*) in his favorite currency of fictitious gifts.

Voicing a familiar refrain, Villon again laments his poverty, stating that he would even, out of sheer desperation and destitution, sell a portion of his health to a Lombard usurer if doing so could improve his impoverished condition. Claiming that his money pouch is absolutely empty, the poet visualizes the missing coins; these coins in turn lead to an interesting chain of images:

> Biau Sire Dieux, je m'esbahis que c'est,
> Car devant moy croix ne se comparest
> Sinon de bois ou pierre, que ne mente;   (26–28)

> [Dear God! I marvel how it comes about
> That there appears before me not a cross
> Except of wood or stone (I tell no lie)]

The second verse of the passage refers to the image of the cross that appears on the reverse of side of coins of the period. The crosses of wood and stone, of course, represent markers, occasionally visible even to the modern traveler in parts of rural France. The *Testament* offers a similar association between the coined imprint of the cross and traveling:

En cheminant sans croix ne pille   (98)

[Tramping the roads without a coin].

The image of stone and wood crosses reminds us of the itinerant nature of the poet's existence (which he makes no attempt to conceal) and thus offers little assurance of the stability that will be needed to pay off his debt. The invocation of God's name at the outset of the passage cannot be totally separated from the image of the cross, and in the last of the three references, the cross is restored to its proper religious context:

Mais s'une foiz la vraye s'apparest,
Vous n'y perdrez seullement que l'attente   (29–30)

[But if the true one shows itself just once,
All you will lose will be the waiting time.]

Another stipulatory clause has been added to the contract. If the true cross happens to appear to the wandering poet, then he will promptly pay his debt. In other words, the paying of the debt now depends on the salvation of the debtor, a man who has already squandered the last generous gift he received from his patron, offers to perjure himself in a court of law by swearing to a promise he cannot possibly fulfill, and would sell his very health in order to make a little money. Nor is it clear how the figurative appearance of the true cross would ensure the payment of the debt. Are we to see here the hope for divine intervention, or rather a conversion that will result in the renouncement of sin, including the sin of borrowing money without the intent of repayment?

The fiction of the borrower who sincerely intends to make good on his debts, having served its comic purpose, ultimately degenerates as the true purpose of the poem reasserts itself in the *envoi:*

Que pensés vous comment il me desplaist
Quant je ne puis venir a mon entente.
Bien m'entendez; aydés moy, s'il vous plaist   (32–34)

[Just think to what a point I am distressed
When I cannot achieve what I desire.
You understand me well; then help me, please.]

Now that the pretense of the loan has been dropped, the poem takes on a more casual tone. The message, after all, is a simple one, and there is almost a hint of complicity toward the end: *Bien m'entendez.* The ballade ends with an unadorned, straightforward plea for money, phrased in terms whose directness and simplicity contrast sharply with the somewhat rarefied tone of the opening verses. A curious addendum follows the ballade proper, preceded in one of the manuscripts by the notation "Au doiz de la letre" [On the back of the letter]:

Allés, letres, faictes ung sault;
Quoyque n'aiez ne piés ne lengue,
Remonstrez en vostre harangue
Que faulte d'argent si m'assault.   (36–39)

[Go on, you letter, skip along;
Although you've neither foot nor tongue,
Tell it out in your harangue:
It's lack of cash assails me so.]

The quatrain is actually a separate poem, although it picks up a phrase from the preceding ballade, "faulte d'argent" (23). It is possible that one of the copyists may have taken the poem from the actual letter, hence the marginal notation "Au doiz de la letre." The addendum reinforces the status of the poem as *escripture*, not a legal document to be sure, but as a missive with a specific mission. The postscript forms a true *envoi*, reminiscent of the *envoi* of the *chanson d'amour* in which the *trouvères* of the thirteenth century bid their songs to quickly depart and deliver their intended message (hence the term *envoi*, from *envoyer*). We know of at least one other letter containing a request that Villon wrote in versified form, the ballade asking for a three-day extension to his banishment

from Paris in January 1463. Although Villon could have put his request
for money into prose, or chosen to deliver it verbally, the ballade as a
performance constitutes in itself a justification for the generosity the
poem seeks to inspire, especially if it was written (as many critics now
believe) to Charles d'Orléans, from one poet to another.

Epitre a ses amis

Scholars generally believe that Villon composed the ballade known as
Epitre a ses amis during his imprisonment at Meung-sur-Loire in the
summer of 1461. As in the case of the Requete au prince, the circumstances surrounding the composition of the poem, reconstructed from
internal evidence, remain somewhat cloudy. Whereas the Requete was
obviously written and delivered for a specific purpose (the solicitation of
financial support), the mission of the Epitre is more mysterious. It
appears, on the surface, to be a plea for help, and one verse in particular
suggests a specific intervention that may rescue Villon from his unpleasant fate. But how did Villon intend to communicate his message? Virtually cut off from the rest of the world in his dungeon cell, his contacts
limited to prison guards (for whom he has no kind words in the Testament), how did the poet expect to convey the plea to his distant friends
in Paris? It is possible, of course, that through resourcefulness and
bribery, Villon actually succeeded in smuggling the message out of
prison. It is equally plausible that although Villon directs the poem's
specific request to his acquaintances, he never succeeded (or even
attempted) to send the versified message. In this case, the ballade would
have been recopied (or written from memory) sometime after his release
from Meung-sur-Loire in October 1461.

The poem opens with a reference (practically a verbatim citation) to
the Book of Job:

Aiez pictié, aiez pictié de moy,
A tout le moins, s'i vous plaist, mes amis.   (1–2)

[Have pity, do have pity upon me,
You at least, if you please, who are my friends]

This echoes the words of Job, "Pity me, pity me, you that are my
friends."[4] It is significant that Villon omits the second verse of the cita-

tion, "For the hand of God has touched me." Job's plea for pity is based not only on the intensity of his suffering, but on the fact that his suffering is the result of divine will. Villon somewhat tempers the harshness of this concept:

> En fosse giz, non pas soubz houz ne may,
> En cest exil ouquel je suis transmis
> Par Fortune, comme Dieu l'a permis.   (3–5)

> [In a pit I lie, not under holly or may,
> Within this prison where I am consigned
> By Fortune, with permission had from God.]

In the *Testament*, Villon minces no words in placing the blame for his imprisonment squarely on Thibaut d'Aussigny. Whereas Job sees in his misfortune the hand of God, Villon at the outset of the *Testament* claims that all his recent troubles were received "Soubz la main Thibault d'Aucigny" (2). In the ballade addressed to Villon's friends, on the other hand, Thibaut and those more directly involved in Villon's imprisonment are never mentioned, nor can we find even oblique references to their presence. In fact, the poem gives no indication, not even the subtlest hint, that Villon has been unjustly punished. In the only passage concerning the circumstances of his imprisonment, Villon ascribes his misery to Fortune, who has acted, as always, with divine sanction, "comme Dieu l'a permis." Given the biblical subtext of the poem and the concession that the plight of the poet results, at least indirectly, from the hand of God, the ballade presents a view of the Meung-sur-Loire experience that differs fundamentally from the one presented a few months later in the *Testament*. Did Villon have reason to conceal what he perceived to be the true reasons for his unjust imprisonment, or does the ballade reflect a penitent point of view that he subsequently renounced after his liberation?

The dark and silent confinement of the *fosse* (prison cell) contrasts sharply with the joyful freedom of the persons to whom the poem is addressed:

> Danceurs, saulteurs faisans les piez de veaux,
> Vifs comme dars, aguz comme aguillon   (7–8)

[Dancers, tumblers doing the calf step,
As swift as darts, as sharp as cattle goads]

The motif of music runs through the poem, carrying connotations of joy, liberation, laughter, and sexuality, all the elements of life the *povre Villon* lacks. After the dancers come the singers:

Gousiers tintans clers comme gascaveaux   (9)

[Your gullets tinkling clear as little bells].

The freedom of the singers knows no limits:

Chantres chantans a plaisance, sans loy   (11)

[Singers singing as you like, no rules].

Next come those who compose songs:

Faiseurs de laiz, de motés, et rondeaux   (16)

[Composers of lays, motets, and rondeaux].

Contrapuntal to the themes of joy and freedom runs the theme of death. The reference to the Book of Job, a text filled with death and loss, immediately establishes a dark tone that will prevail to the end of the poem. The reference to the poet's *fosse*, designating a grave as well as a cell ("autour de ma fosse," *Testament*, 1876), immediately picks up this thematic strand. Envisioning his death as a consequence of the neglect of his friends, Villon cites a proverb (in slightly altered form):

Quant mort sera, vous lui ferez chaudeaux!   (17)

[When he is dead, *then* you'll send him hot soup]

Villon compares the walls of his cell to *bandeaux*, strips of cloth used to enshroud a corpse:

Ou gist, il n'entre escler ne tourbillon;
De murs espoix on lui a fait bandeaux   (18–19)

[No lightning or whirlwind enters where he lies;
Of these thick walls they've made him swaddling bands]

The verb *gist,* appearing for the second time in the poem (it first appears in verse 3, "En fosse giz . . ."), again connotes death (as it does in modern French).

Despite the grim conditions of Villon's imprisonment, the physical hardship he is forced to endure, and the thoughts of death that darken his hopes, a certain resilient spirit of humor surfaces occasionally. Villon describes his constant state of hunger in these terms:

Jeuner lui fault dimenches et merdiz,
Dont les dens a plus longues que ratteaux;
Aprés pain sec (non aprés gasteaux)
En ses boyaulx verse eaue a groz boullon.   (25–28)

[He has to fast on Sundays, Tuesdays too.
So that his teeth are longer than a rake's;
After dry bread (not after any cake)
He pours a deal of water in his gut.]

The days normally set aside for fasting were Wednesday, Friday, and Saturday, but it is clear that Villon's fervent "fasting" represents a break with tradition. Although the final verse obviously designates the liquid element of Villon's prison diet, the reference to consuming large amounts of water leads by association to the water torture inflicted on the prisoner, a treatment that he bitterly recalls in the *Testament:* "Qui tant d'eau froide m'a fait boire" (738). Granted, in the passage quoted above the prisoner describes the drinking of water as a voluntary act, but that he also describes his prison diet as fasting (another voluntary act), especially when taken in conjunction with the obviously humorous context, should raise doubts about the role of the prisoner's volition in the act of ingesting copious quantities of water.

The *envoi* contains two specific requests. One is that the persons to whom the poem is addressed raise the prisoner out of his cell in a basket:

Et me montez en quelque corbillon   (33)

[And in some basket or other hoist me out]

Although some scholars find allusions to St. Paul or Virgil on this verse, a more prosaic reading is possible given that prisoners were sometimes lowered into (and raised from) underground cells by means of a pulley.[5] Whereas the *corbillon* seems to refer to the mechanical means by which Villon will ultimately be removed from his cell, the second request sheds some light on the means by which he hopes to actually effect his release:

Impetrez moy graces et royaulx seaulx   (32)

[Get pardons for me, get me royal seals].

Royal pardons had, of course, saved Villon on at least one previous occasion, after the death of Philippe Sermoise. Just as Villon composed a poem around the request for six *écus* from an unnamed patron, and another poem building to the plea for a brief delay in the poet's 10-year banishment, it is possible to find in the request for a royal pardon the specific purpose assigned to this particular poem, placing it in the category of Villon's "functional" ballades. Indeed, one could argue that the poet's request for intervention would make sense only if the poem was intended for readers capable of carrying out this action.

La question que fist Villon au clerc du Guichet

At some point shortly after January 5, 1463, the date on which the court of parliament commuted Villon's death sentence (following the Ferrebouc affair) to a 10-year exile from Paris, Villon wrote the last of his surviving poems, one addressed to parliament, the other to Etienne Garnier, the *clerc du guichet*, or keeper of the door at the Châtelet prison. Although both ballades concern the commutation of the death sentence, their style (and, of course, their audience) differs radically. The poem addressed to parliament, *La Louenge que feist Villon a la Court,* employs ornate and highly rhetorical language to express the prisoner's gratitude for the annulment of the death sentence:

Or la langue seule ne peut souffire
A vous rendre souffisantes louanges   (7–8)

[The tongue all by itself cannot suffice
To render unto you sufficient praise]

The court is addressed in hyperbolic terms of praise, elevated even to a quasi-celestial status:

Si parlons tous, fille du Souverain Sire,
Mere des bons et seur des benois angles.   (9–10)

[So we all speak, child of the Soverign Lord,
Mother of good men, sister of the angels.]

The reason for this laudatory tone becomes obvious, of course, by the conclusion of the poem, in which Villon makes his plea for a brief delay in order to put his affairs in order before the impending departure.

Critics would certainly agree that *La Question que fist Villon au clerc du Guichet* does not represent one of Villon's greatest poetic efforts. It cannot be listed among his most artistic or most profound works. Shorter than most of the other ballades, both in verse length and total number of verses, the poem was probably composed hurriedly, at a time when Villon was undoubtedly preoccupied with more pressing concerns. On the other hand, we know more about the circumstances related to the poem's composition than we do for any other poem by Villon—the date and place of the poem's genesis, the identity of the person to whom the poem is addressed, and the events to which the poem refers. Thus, as a literary and biographical artifact, the poem clearly deserves attention. It demonstrates the exceptional degree to which Villon's poetry often incorporates and reflects biographical circumstances. Equally important, it allows us to study the dynamics of poetry intended for a specific audience (an audience that in this case can be readily identified), and to extrapolate from this specimen to the relationship between the poet and his audience in the case of longer, more complex poems, especially the *Lais* and the *Testament*.

The ballade addressed to Etienne Garnier speaks of the commutation in a triumphant, even boasting tone. The *clerc du guichet* held a fairly responsible position among the personnel charged with administering the prison of the Châtelet. He registered all new prisoners, indicating their name and clerical or secular status in the prison register. He also oversaw the transfer and release of prisoners and could be held

accountable for the escape of prisoners under his control. Prior to his
position at the Châtelet, Etienne Garnier had served as a jailer in the
prison of the Conciergerie, where he had been charged with dereliction
of duty resulting in the escape of a prisoner and had consequently lost
his position. Later, charged as a secondary accomplice in a theft, Garnier found himself a prisoner at the Châtelet. Granted an official pardon for the crime, Garnier somehow succeeded, despite his criminal
record and poor performance as a jailer in the Conciergerie, in securing
the position of *clerc du guichet* at the Châtelet in October 1459. It
should be noted that Garnier, for unknown reasons, did not hold his
new appointment for very long; he was replaced in 1464 by another
jailer from the Conciergerie.

Although we know nothing of Villon's relationship with Etienne Garnier, it is evident that the two men became acquainted during Villon's
two brief stays in the prison in 1462 and 1463. Given Garnier's own
criminal record, and that he had experienced life on both sides of the jail
door, one can surmise that his relationship with the prisoners under his
care often extended beyond the simple formalities associated with regis-
tration and release. From the tone and content of Villon's ballade and
even from the fact that Villon, upon learning of his release, would choose
to write a poem for Garnier's benefit, it is evident that the two men were
at least casual acquaintances. It is even possible, as Champion suggests,
that a friendship could have developed from this brief period of acquaintance, although this hypothesis cannot be proven.[6] While discussing the
appeal to parliament, Garnier had apparently advised Villon against what
the jailer perceived as a futile enterprise. This fact explains the gloating,
even sarcastic tone of the opening verses:

Que vous semble de mon appel,
Garnier? Feis je sens ou folye?   (1–2)

[What do you think of my appeal,
Garnier? Did I do well or not?]

The smug note of triumph in the rhetorical question is unmistakable.
Explaining his decision to appeal as an instinctual act of self-defense,
Villon reminds Garnier that

Toute beste garde sa pel   (3)

[Each animal defends its skin].

As further justification of his decision, Villon cites the injustice of the death sentence that was originally pronounced. Here we hear the familiar refrain of the *povre Villon* protesting against the unjust treatment of which he is again the victim. Whereas in other cases we can only speculate about the legitimacy of Villon's claim of victimization, knowing the details of the Ferrebouc affair, we can readily understand his protest against the harshness of the sentence. Without referring specifically to the judges who condemned him to death, Villon's implied assessment of parliament contrasts sharply with the "Souveraine Court . . . seur des benois angles" [Sovereign Court . . . sister of the angels], whom he literally praises to the skies in his *Louenge:*

Or quant par plaisir voluntaire
Chantée me fut ceste omelie,
Estoit [il] lors temps de moy taire?   (6–8)

[So when, by arbitrary law,
That homily was sung to me,
Was that the time to hold my tongue?]

The characterization of the capital sentence as *omelie* could reflect a familiar penchant for sarcasm—the idea of using death as a homily, a warning against future transgressions. It could also represent an accurate reading of the intention underlying the sentence, imposed perhaps as a warning both to the participants in the Ferrebouc affair (two of whom were subsequently given lighter sentences) and to others who might be tempted to follow the brawlers' example, that the mistreatment of politically powerful men would not be tolerated.

Villon claims that if he had been a member of the elite class that controlled the administering of justice, a descendant of Hugh Capet, for example, the poet would have been spared the hardships and indignities that he has just experienced. The reference to Hugh Capet, commonly believed to have descended from a line of men who made their living as butchers, leads into a characterization of the Châtelet torture cell as an *escorcherie* (slaughterhouse):

On [ne] m'eust parmy ce drappel
Fait boire en ceste escorcherie   (11–12)

[They wouldn't have forced me to drink
Through that cloth, in that slaughterhouse]

As he did in the prison at Meung-sur-Loire, Villon once again experienced the water torture that seems to have been widely popular as an instrument of torture and interrogation during this period. Pierre de la Dehors, the jailer charged with administering torture in the Châtelet, was—appropriately enough—also a master butcher (his name appears on the official register listing those of his trade). The reference to the *escorcherie* thus carries special meaning for persons who are able to read the presence of de la Dehors between the lines, and Villon alerts Garnier to the hidden irony:

Vous entendez bien joncherie.   (13)

[I'm confident you catch my drift.]

The term *joncherie* is jargon for "deceit" or "a deceitful joke." At one level, then, the verse signals the ironic use of *escorcherie* in the preceding verse. But the complicity between poet and reader probably goes deeper. To seize the meaning of this term presupposes some familiarity with the criminal milieu from which it originates, and Garnier, from his criminal associations (both as doorkeeper and prisoner), undoubtedly possessed the requisite knowledge to decode the hidden meaning of the verse in question. At a deeper level, the assumption that Garnier understands *joncherie* implies that Garnier is himself well versed in the art of deceit, having practiced it extensively.[7]

Following the parenthetical comment concerning Garnier's ability to understand *joncherie*, Villon again protests what he considers to be the arbitrary and excessively harsh nature of the original sentence, claiming that the *peine arbitraire* (15) was imposed *par tricherie* (16). Villon implies that to refuse the opportunity for appeal, the course of action (or inaction) apparently advised by Garnier, would be an act of madness or stupidity:

Cuidez vous que soubz mon capel
N'eust autant de philozophie
Comme de dire "J'en appel"?   (17–20)

[Do you think that beneath my cap
Was not enough philosophy
To make me utter "I appeal"?]

The tone of the passage, especially given the initial question to Garnier in verse 2 ("Feis je sens ou folye?") suggests a personal challenge rather than a rhetorical question. The implied message to the doorkeeper appears to be along these lines: How stupid do you think I am? Even an animal defends itself against the threat of death. Did you really think I would sit back and say nothing? The use of legal jargon (which we have seen Villon manipulate so deftly in the *Testament*) gives an edge to his sarcasm:

Oÿl, je le vous *certiffie*
(Si est il fol que trop s'i fye).
Quant on me dit, *present notaire*,
"Pendu serez," je vous *affye*   (20–23)

[Oh yes, there was, I promise you
(Though he who counts on it's a fool).
When they said, before a notary,
"You will be hanged," I swear to you]

Villon concludes the poem by spelling out for Garnier the disastrous consequences that would have been brought about by a failure to appeal the capital sentence:

Pieça [je] fusse ou est Clotaire,
Aux champs, debout comme une espye.   (26–27)

[I'd be where Clothair is, long since,
Like a lookout, upright, in the fields.]

Suspended from the gallows at Montfaucon, just outside of Paris, the bodies of hanged criminals were often left as a grim warning to those who might be tempted to follow their example.

We do not know for certain which of the two ballades, the one written to Etienne Garnier or the one addressed to parliament, was the last

recorded poem composed by Villon. In some anthologies, the former is
placed last, while others present the *Louenge* as the final poem. One may
argue that, because of the urgency of the situation (the period of exile was
originally ordered to take effect immediately), it is probable that Villon
wrote his request for a three-day reprieve first, then wrote the triumphant
poem to Etienne Garnier as an afterthought. There is a certain element of
logic to this hypothesis, but the question remains open to conjecture. At
any rate, we can safely state that one of the last (and quite possibly the
very last) images that we find in Villon's poetry is one in which the poet
visualizes himself among the bodies hanging at Montfaucon.

The Jargon Ballades

In addition to the fifteen ballades classified as *poèmes divers,* eleven ballades written in the jargon of the Coquillards are also ascribed to Villon.
Because only six of these appear in the first published edition of Villon's
poetry in 1489, the authenticity of the other five is open to question.
Scholars sometimes cite the poems written in jargon as evidence attest-
ing Villon's membership in the criminal society of the Coquillards. In
fact, there is no evidence to support this supposition, other than the
poems in question. Various Coquillards with whom Villon was
acquainted could easily have taught him the secret jargon of the criminal society, providing him with material for his poems.

Originally formed from the remnants of roaming soldiers who terror-
ized and pillaged the countryside during the Hundred Years' War, the
Coquillards formed a loose criminal association with chapters in Bur-
gundy (the Coquillards), the Loire Valley (the Caymans), and in the
southwestern part of France (the Rufians). The organization had contacts in Paris, and two of Villon's acquaintances, Colin de Cayeux and
Regnier de Montigny, both of whom died on the gallows, are believed to
have been Coquillards.

The poems in jargon present special problems to Villon's modern
readers. Given the inaccessibility of the poems' language, even to scholars well acquainted with the subtleties of Middle French, the jargon ballades have been understandably relegated to a position of secondary
importance and are rarely read or studied by students of Villon's poetry.
However, the ballades do raise some intriguing and important questions. For whom were these poems written? Who, other than persons
with close ties to the Coquillards, would be able to understand the
poems' language? To what degree does the audience of these ballades

overlap with the audience to whom the *Lais* and the *Testament* are directed? What is the meaning of the parallels between the *Testament* (particularly in its warnings to men who make their living by crime) and the poems written in jargon?

One of the untitled ballades opens with a clear indication of the identity of the persons to whom the poem is addressed:

> Coquillars enaruans a ruel
> Men ys vous chante que gardes
> Que ny laissez et corps et pel   (1–3)

> [Coquillards on your way to Rueil,
> Myself I sing to you: take care
> So's not to leave there body and hide]

Rueil is a town near Paris, but *aller à Rueil* is slang for "to attack" or "to murder." Here Villon announces the warning that will echo through all of the poems written in jargon, the grim reminder that all who persist in a life of crime are destined to end their lives on the gallows. The warning quickly moves from abstraction to concrete example, citing the case of Colin de Cayeux, Villon's unfortunate accomplice in the Navarre affair who was eventually hanged for his crimes:

> Quon fist de collin lescailler
> Devant la roe babiller
> Il babigna pour son salue
> Pas ne savoit oingnons peller
> Dont lamboureux luy rompt le suc   (4–8)

> [For they made Colin the Shell-man
> Chatter away before the bench;
> He made up tales to save his life
> But couldn't cry convincingly,
> And so the hangman breaks his neck.]

Colin's interrogation and his unsuccessful attempt to save himself with a show of penance are presented in comic terms, using the coarse language of hardened criminals, but there is nothing comic to temper the brutality and violence of the act depicted in the final verse, which serves as the refrain of the ballade. Although we cannot pin down the date of composition for this poem, it is certain that the ballade was written no more than several years after the hanging of Colin de Cayeux in September 1460. By citing the fate of a mutual acquaintance whose death by hanging occurred in the fairly recent past, Villon forcefully brings home to his audience the point of his lesson. To reinforce the first example, Villon reminds his readers of the tragic fate of a second acquaintance, Regnier de Montigny, who died the same way several years earlier, in September 1457:

Montigny y fut par exemple
Bien ataché au halle grup
Et y iargonnast: il le tremple
Dont lamboureux luy rompt le suc   (13–16)

[Montigny, by way of example,
Was well fixed and hoisted high,
Whatever tremolo he sang,
And so the hangman breaks his neck.]

The poem in question could almost serve as a paradigm for much of Villon's poetry, in particular the *Testament*. Villon frequently refers to people (such as Colin de Cayeux and Regnier de Montigny) well known only to himself and the small circle of readers to whom the poetry is addressed. Furthermore, although the majority of Villon's verse is not actually written in a secret language, it is often charged with irony and multiple meanings that can be comprehended and appreciated only by the initiated reader. Thus, just as poems in jargon must be deciphered by a reader familiar with the language, numerous sections of the *Lais* and the *Testament* must be decoded according to hidden meanings, the keys to some of which have been lost, causing portions of the poem to remain forever encoded.

The ballade concludes with a final warning, or rather a final version of the same warning repeated in various forms throughout the poem:

Prince erriere du ruel
Et neussiez vous denier ne pluc

Quau giffle ne laissez lappel
Pour lamboureux qui rompt le suc   (25–28)

[Prince stop short of violence
Even though you've got no pickings left,
Lest your cry should stick in your throat
Because of the hangman who breaks one's neck.]

The *envoi* picks up a string of images involving both the interior and the
exterior of the throat, especially related to the act of singing and speaking. The poem opens with a reference to singing, "Men ys vous chante,"
and proceeds to describe how Colin de Cayeux tried unsuccessfully to
talk his way out of a death sentence. In the next stanza, Montigny's
tremolo, "Et y iargonnast: il le tremple," fails to prevent his death by
the same means. The third stanza subjects the throat to two acts of violence. One is internal (the "leaden gag" or funnel used in water torture);
the other, external (the breaking of the neck by hanging). In the *envoi*,
the silencing of the voice and the breaking of the neck are conflated
in the final two verses. In each case, the voice act ultimately fails to
achieve its purpose. Colin's loquacious confession fails to save his life.
Regnier's tremolo meets with the same fate. Likewise, the cry of the
Coquillards to whom the poem is addressed will stick in their throats,
strangled by the tightening noose. As for Villon's song ("Myself I sing to
you . . ."), it is up to his listeners to decide whether or not this voice will
ultimately succeed or fail.

Ballade des pendus

The image of the hanged man, which appears in various poems by Villon,
attains its fullest development in the ballade that is undoubtedly the
most famous and most frequently anthologized of all Villon's poems. The
speaker of the *Ballade des pendus* (also known as *L'Epitaphe Villon*) is one of
the hanged men whose bodies were left (for public edification) suspended
from the gallows. Although not the only gallows, Montfaucon, just
beyond the walls of Paris, served as the main execution site for the city.
Montfaucon's enormous gibbet was capable of hanging 30 men at a
time.[8] The bodies of those executed by various means at other sites were
sometimes hung for display at Montfaucon.[9] The process of hanging did
not always go smoothly, and unforeseen complications occasionally pro-

vided entertainment to the spectators who invariably gathered to witness the grotesque scene. The author of the *Journal d'un Bourgeois de Paris* recounts one such incident, involving a certain nobleman, Sauvage de Fremainville, who was publicly executed on December 15, 1427:

> So he was brought to the gallows accompanied by the Provost of Paris and several other men, also by one Pierre Baillé . . . This Pierre Baillé, when Le Sauvage wanted to make his confession, refused to let him live so long but made him climb the ladder at once and climbed two or three steps up after him, shouting at him.

Angered by Sauvage's reply, Baillé struck him with a stick, then proceeded to strike the executioner five or six blows, impatient because the latter (following the proper protocol for an execution) was speaking to Sauvage about the salvation of his soul. Unnerved by Baillé's violent anger, the executioner failed to give proper attention to the task at hand, with disastrous results:

> The hangman, seeing Baillé's ill will, was afraid he might do something worse to him, and so, being frightened, hurried more than he ought to have done and hanged Le Sauvage; but because of his haste the rope broke or came undone and the condemned man fell and broke his back and one leg. Yet he had to climb up again, suffering as he was, and was hanged and strangled.[10]

The author later states (providing a piece of information that will be especially relevant to our reading of the *Ballade des pendus*) that the body of Sauvage de Fremainville was removed from the gibbet on September 10, 1428, having been left to decay for nine months after the execution.[11]

Among the richest and most profound of all Villon's works, the *Ballade des pendus* opens itself to multiple readings, and the few pages devoted here to its analysis can hardly do justice to its artistry and complexity. Commentaries on the poem often point to its grotesque realism, its moralistic tenor, and its relationship to the *danse macabre*. Although these features of the poem are obviously important, another aspect of the *ballade* that deserves equal attention is the conflict between the physical and the spiritual world. The opposition of material and spiritual values, an opposition with strong Christian underpinnings, pervades medieval thought and literature and surfaces periodically throughout the *Testament*. The poem opens with a plea spoken by one of the corpses suspended from the gallows invoking the compassion of an all-inclusive

Freres humains. The voice describes the state of decay to which the bodies of the hanged have been reduced:

> Quant de la chair, que trop avons nourrie,
> Elle est pieça devoree et pourrie,
> Et nous, les os, devenons scendre et pouldre.
> De nostre mal personne ne s'en rie
> Mais priez Dieu que tous nous vueille absouldre.   (6–10)

> [As for the flesh, which we nourished all too well,
> It's fallen apart and rotted long ago
> And we, the bones, now turn to ash and dust.
> Let no one make sport of our misery,
> But pray to God He may absolve us all.]

Thus the poem opens with a contemplation of the flesh, and the word *chair*, rich with religious and moralistic connotations, sets the tone for the subsequent contemplation of the human body in all its frailty and vulnerability. Although the flesh has long since disappeared from these bodies, they are still identifiable as human remains, and the speaker of the poem initially defines himself and his companions in terms of their physicality, the tangible remnants by which they establish their presence in the material world. The word *mal* (9) is somewhat ambiguous. It may refer generally to the misfortune of the hanged men, the tragic destiny that brought their lives to an end on the gallows, or (as Sargent-Baur's translation suggests) *mal* may refer to physical suffering. Even if *mal* is taken as "malheur" (as it is rendered in some modern French translations of the poem), the word cannot be totally separated from a notion of physical suffering. That the speaker of the poem is capable of experiencing pain is perfectly consistent with the physical terms in which he defines himself and his unfortunate companions.

In the second stanza, the speaker, anticipating a sense of alienation and repulsion on the part of his "human brothers," appeals to the compassion of his listeners, admitting that he and his comrades have used poor judgment. Their salvation, however, can be purchased only at the price of intercessory prayer:

> Excusez nous, puisque sommes transis,
> Envers le filz de la Vierge Marie,

Que sa grace pour nous ne soit tarie,
Nous preservant de l'infernale foudre.   (15–18)

[Make intercession since we ourselves are dead,
On our behalf before the Virgin's Son,
That his grace toward us may not be dried up,
Preserving us from the infernal fire.]

The speaker now defines himself in spiritual terms. The voice issues
from an indeterminate purgatorial region, perilously close to the thun-
der of hell. The souls of the hanged men, suspended between salvation
and damnation, form a spiritual parallel to the bodies dangling between
sky and earth. The *mal* of the first stanza, with its overtones of physical
suffering, now cedes to a deeper form of anguish as the spiritual destiny
of the speaker and his companions hangs in the balance.

In the third stanza, the physical dimension of the dead men reappears; exposed to the forces of nature, the corpses have undergone a
gradual but dramatic transformation:

La pluye nous a debuez et lavez
Et le soulail deceschez et noirciz.
Pies, corbeaux nous ont les yeulx cavez
Et araché la barbe et les sourcilz.   (21–24)

[The rain has soaked us and washed us clean
And the sun dried us up and turned us black.
Magpies and crows have hollowed out our eyes
And plucked away our beards and eyebrows too.]

Modern readers who bring their twentieth-century sensibilities to the
stanza tend to find this passage a grotesque, if not repulsive, image of
decay. There is, however, a more positive element that should not be
ignored. The stripping away of the flesh represents, above all else, a
restructuring of values, an acknowledgment of mortality, and hence the
futility of a life driven by the pursuit of physical gratification, the worth-
lessness of the "chair que nous avons nourrie" (6). Thus, in the washing
action of the rain, and even in the natural process of decay accelerated
by the sun and scavenging birds, there is an element of cleansing or

purification as the hanged men are finally freed of the flesh that corrupted their values and ultimately led them to their shameful deaths. Indeed, the phrase *debuez et lavez* would even seem to suggest a baptismal washing, an ablution that liberates these sinners from the burden of the flesh that throughout their lives they have carried (and nourished) to the detriment of their souls.

The stripping of the flesh leaves only the bone, the essence of the human body that gives it its distinctive form. Now the poem is brought to closure as the spiritual message of the *pendus* is also stripped to its essence:

Prince Jhesus, qui sur tous a maistrie,

Gardez qu'enfer de nous n'ait seigneurie.   (31–32)

[Prince Jesus, you who are lord of all,

Keep Hell from having power over us.]

The only hope for salvation is through divine grace, but grace can come only at the price of intercessory prayer. In asking their human brothers to pray for the salvation of those who have died for their crimes, the dead men are also asking their living counterparts to take an active role in their own salvation, because the measure of compassion the living give will determine the measure they will receive on the day of their own judgment. To what degree does Villon, who confesses an awareness of his sins more than once in the *Testament*, identify with the *pendus*? According to one tradition, Villon composed the poem while awaiting his own execution by hanging, and in the absence of any evidence to the contrary, it is tempting to believe that the poem was in fact written under these circumstances. Although the source of inspiration for the ballade cannot be conclusively established, it is obvious that the poet clearly does not lack reasons to identify, at least partially, with the voice of the poem. Although we may search in vain for an acrostic designating the poet, it is worth noting that the word *povre*, which Villon applies to himself at least 10 times in his poetry, appears in the third verse of the poem:

Car se pitié de nous *povres* avez . . .   (3)

[For if you have pity on us, poor men . . .]

How can we not read Villon's signature here?

Chapter Eight
The Biblical Subtext

One of the features that adds subtlety, depth, and complexity to Villon's poetry is the way in which he inscribes selected biblical passages within his text for a variety of purposes. When praising Louis XI, whom Villon with good reason views as his benefactor and liberator, biblical allusions heighten the tone of the encomium:

> Auquel doint Dieu l'eur de Jacob
> Et de Salmon l'onneur et gloire   (*Testament*, 57–58)

> [To whom may God give Jacob's luck
> And Solomon's honour and glory]

By liberating Villon from his tomblike cell, Louis actually gave the poet a new life: "Et que vie me recouvra" [And restored to me my life] (84). Given that Louis indirectly rescued Villon from confinement under especially harsh conditions, a confinement that could have continued for an indefinite time, there is no reason to search for hidden irony in this unusually strong laudation, nor is there cause to read the expression of gratitude as hyperbole rather than sincere thankfulness. The same is true of the third biblical personage with whom Louis is compared:

> Afin que de lui soit memoire,
> Vivre autant que Mathusalé.   (63–64)

> [So that his memory last, God grant
> He live long like Methuselah.]

By juxtaposing Louis XI with two patriarchs and a Hebrew king renowned for his wisdom, Villon elevates his benefactor to a quasi-legendary status. The use of biblical analogy to heighten the tone of eulogistic verse is common practice in medieval literature. Writing for a

134

biblically literate public, writers could rely on their audience to grasp the subtle nuances of even indirect references that may strike a modern reader as somewhat obscure. When Villon refers to the biblical admonition to pray for one's enemies, he is evoking one of the best-known passages of the New Testament:

Et l'Eglise nous dit et compte
Que prions pour noz annemys!   (29–30)

[And the Church tells us and repeats
That, for our enemies, we're to pray!]

Even the reader possessing no more than a superficial acquaintance with the Bible will readily discern in these verses an echo of Luke's Gospel:

Love your enemies; do good to those who hate you; bless those who curse you, pray for those who treat you spitefully.[1]

Equally apparent is the ironic twist that Villon creates by inserting an unmistakable exhortation for love and forgiveness into a bitter denunciation of Thibaut d'Aussigny, whom Villon clearly has no intention of ever forgiving. The command to love one's enemies ends with a warning: "for whatever measure you deal out to others will be dealt to you in return."[2] By condemning Thibaut, then, Villon is condemning himself. Thus, the evocation of the biblical injunction, wielded as a weapon against Thibaut d'Aussigny, ultimately (through a portion of the subtext not apparent in the immediate reference) implicates the accuser as well as the accused.

In a related passage of the *Testament,* after attacking the gluttony and hypocrisy of certain monks, Villon returns to the text from Luke's Gospel, claiming that he will not presume to judge another:

Je ne suis juge, ne commis
Pour pugnir n'assouldre meffait:
De tous suis le plus imparfait.   (259–61)

[I am not a judge, nor am I charged
To punish or absolve misdeeds.
I'm the least perfect one of all]

These verses clearly represent a paraphrase or an apparent personalization of the injunction against judgment and condemnation:

> Pass no judgment, and you will not be judged; do not condemn, and you
> will not be condemned; acquit and you will be acquitted.[3]

Villon's claim of neutrality, however, is a transparent travesty. Having just passed judgment in no uncertain terms on Thibaut d'Aussigny and other members of the clergy for whom the poet has no great respect, he now pretends to renounce all these harsh judgments. The biblical subtext that underlies Villon's references to judgment and forgiveness raises certain fundamental problems that commentators on the *Testament* often fail to signal. To say that the poet is simply manipulating scripture for ironic purposes does not do justice to the complexity of the issue. At the same time that Villon is acknowledging certain sacred injunctions, he is deliberately (flagrantly, one might even say) refusing to abide by them. Thus, Villon not only reacts against the hierarchical authority of the church by attacking a bishop and certain monastic orders, but also—at least on one level—refuses to submit to the authority of church doctrines. He clearly cites the doctrinal position of the church ("L'Eglise nous dit et compte") and then blatantly refuses to implement the church's teaching, precisely in the personal case to which the doctrine most aptly applies. Without going so far as to characterize Villon's attitude as heretical, one may rightfully question whether the refusal to forgive one's enemy in the face of unequivocal awareness of a biblical injunction to the contrary does not constitute an act of willful disobedience.

The problematic nature of Villon's position becomes even more apparent in the closure of the stanza:

> Que par moy leur soit satisfait.
> Ce que j'ay escript est escript.   (263–64)

> [Let this make my amends to them.
> What I have written, I have written.]

The final verse provides a verbatim transcription of Pilate's reply to those who objected to the phrase "King of the Jews" displayed above the cross on which Jesus was crucified: "Quod scripsi scripsi." If the phrase is taken out of context, it would seem simply to represent an adamant refusal to retract any position already committed to writing. As such, it would convey a somewhat cavalier and even arrogant disdain for the consequences of the written judgments that have just been presented. The remark by Pilate cannot, however, be dissociated from its context. Moreover, the Pilate speaking here is not perplexed and bemused, the responsible government official attempting to appease a dangerous mob while sparing the life of an innocent victim, but a Pilate who has just ordered the slow and torturous death of a man whom the Roman procurator has tried unsuccessfully to save, who now wishes to abdicate responsibility for the whole affair. The identification with Pilate, coupled with the conscious refusal to obey the Christian duty to forgive one's enemies, deepens the resonance of the admission of sin that we find early in the *Testament*: "Je suis pecheur, je le sçay bien" (105).

Mortality

Sermons, both medieval and modern, rely heavily on scripture to provide concrete examples and lend a note of authority to the homiletic voice. Alain de Lille, a medieval scholastic, gives this advice to those who write sermons:

> Le prédicateur . . . doit entreprendre l'exposé du texte qu'il propose et le faire servir tout entier à l'instruction de ceux qui l'écoutent. Il ne doit pas émettre un texte obscur ou difficile, de crainte de dégoûter ou de provoquer un manque d'attention.[4]

Well trained in theology, scholasticism, and the art of writing sermons, Villon chooses his scriptural texts carefully, skillfully integrating them into his own text for purposes of illustration and eloquence. The poet usually makes the connection between the biblical quotation and the personal context of the *Testament* readily apparent. In the prologue of the poem, as the narrator speaks of the follies of a misspent youth, he cites a relevant passage from Ecclesiastes:

> Le dit du Saige trop luy feiz
> Favourable (bien en puis mais!)
> Qui dit: "Esjoïs toy, mon filz,
> A ton adolessence." . . .
>
> (209–12)

[Ecclesiastes' words I took
Too favourably (much good it's done!)
Which say, "Enjoy yourself, my son,
In your youth." . . .]

Villon's quotation represents an accurate, although truncated, version of
the advice to a young man that appears toward the end of Ecclesiastes:

Delight in your boyhood, young man, make the most of the days of your
youth; let your heart and your eyes show you the way . . .[5]

In the preceding three stanzas the narrator alludes to wasted money,
unsuccessful relationships with women, and a refusal to take his studies
seriously, all classic symptoms of a *jeunesse folle* (202) experienced by so
many medieval (and modern) students. Judging by the portion of the
text quoted above, one would conclude that the advice given to the
young man basically represents a hedonistic exhortation to profit from
the pleasures of youth. However, the writer of Ecclesiastes is not simply
expounding on the carpe diem theme. The verse (of which Villon presents only a partial citation) ends with a serious warning: "but remember that for all these things God will call you into account." This somber
observation leads into a final piece of advice:

Banish discontent from your mind, and shake off the troubles of the
body; boyhood and the prime of life are mere emptiness.[6]

Villon paraphrases the latter part of the verse in the second half of the
stanza:

. . . Mes
Ailleurs sert bien d'un autre mes,
Car "Jeunesse et adolessance,"
C'est son parler, ne moins ne mes,
"Ne sont qu'abuz et ygnorance."   (212–16)

[On the other hand
Elsewhere he serves a different dish,
For "Youth and adolescence too,"

So he says, neither more nor less,
"Are but abuse and ignorance."]

The second quotation from Ecclesiastes resonates with a note of regret that we have already heard in the portion of the *Testament* immediately preceding the biblical text: "Je plains le temps de ma jeunesse" (169), "helas" (174), "A peu que le cueur ne me fent" (208). The most significant portion of the scriptural text, however, is totally absent from Villon's reconstruction. The thrust of these verses from Ecclesiastes relates not so much to the intrinsic meaningless of human pleasure, as Villon's spliced version of the passage might lead us to believe, but rather to the need to center one's life on the eternal, that is, the presence of God, before whom all will one day be held accountable. The author of Ecclesiastes picks up this thematic thread and develops it immediately after the verse concerning the emptiness of youth, which Villon paraphrases in verse 216. In an eloquent and impassioned discourse, the writer warns his young listener to remain constantly mindful of God's presence, knowing that earthly pursuits, ambitions, fears, and concerns are all quickly rendered meaningless by death:

Remember him [God] before the silver cord is snapped and the golden bowl is broken, before the pitcher is shattered at the spring and the wheel broken at the well, before the dust returns to the earth as it began and the spirit returns to God who gave it.[7]

This admonition leads into the most famous quotation from Ecclesiastes: "Emptiness, emptiness, says the speaker, all is empty."[8] To fully understand the depth of Villon's regret, the profound nature of his contrition, it is necessary to resituate the partially quoted text within its proper context. A straightforward reading of the portion of the *Testament* in question finds no hint of a spiritual conflict. Indeed, any overt reference to spiritual concerns is totally missing. The reader would seem justified in interpreting Villon's words as nothing more than the thoughts of a man—somewhat older, wiser, and more experienced as a result of all the hardship he has recently endured—who looks back sadly, and perhaps a little wistfully, at youthful pleasures that have disappeared so quickly into the past. Louis Thuasne, who includes in his commentary a brief synopsis of each *huitain* of the *Testament*, summarizes one of the stanzas immediately preceding the reference to Ecclesiastes in this fashion: "Villon regrette sa jeunesse perdue, qui s'est évanouie sans lui laisser le moindre don."[9] Many other readers through the years have followed Thuasne's example, finding in this portion of the *Testament* a nostalgic glance at a rapidly receding youth. In fact, one might argue that Villon intends this reading. In editing the text from Ecclesiastes, omitting the section concerning divine judgment, Villon has in effect created a new text, one that stresses the brevity and fragility of human existence, especially of youth, in a purely temporal frame of reference. On the other hand, if we contextualize the quotation, supplying the missing portion of the text and giving attention to the meditation on mortality that immediately follows in Ecclesiastes, then we discover a spiritual dimension to the passage that inevitably colors a rereading of the preceding stanzas.

From Ecclesiastes, Villon moves on to the Book of Job, where he finds another commentary on the brevity of human life:

> Mes jours s'en sont alez errant
> Comme, Job, dit, d'une touaille
> Font les filetz, quand tixerrant
> En son poing tient ardent paille;
> Lors, s'il y a nul bout qui saille,
> Soudainement il le ravit.   (217–22)

> [My days have gone speeding away
> Just as, says Job, do the loose threads
> Of woven cloth, when a weaver holds
> In his fist a bit of burning straw;
> If there's an end then sticking out,
> He takes it off immediately.]

The text on which the image is based reads somewhat differently:

> My days are swifter than a shuttle
> and come to an end as the thread runs out.[10]

Barbara Sargent-Baur has commented extensively on this passage, advancing several possible explanations for Villon's variant on the original, including a lapse of memory or a misreading.[11] The variation, as

Sargent-Baur points out, could also represent a conflation of the biblical quotation with an observation of actual weaving practice, the burning of stray threads. At any rate, Villon is now engaging in more than simple editing. Reworking a metaphor supplied by the biblical text, he has radically altered the original image. Whereas the words of Job stress the rapidity (and perhaps the tedium) that marks the passage of his daily existence, Villon emphasizes the destructive force of time. Although the weaver is absent in the first image, he is prominently featured in the second. The burning of the thread appears to represent a purposeful act rather than gratuitous violence. Given the equation between the stray thread *(bout qui saille)* and the poet's life *(Mes jours)*, and the deliberate design implied in the motion of the weaver's hand (which is both an act of destruction and an act of creation), Villon's image, far more graphic and violent than the original, takes on a well-defined spiritual dimension.

The trilogy of biblical texts relating to mortality culminates with a last reference from the Old Testament. Having just evoked Jacques Coeur, who had died in 1456, and whose name was synonymous with wealth, Villon calls to mind an appropriate verse from one of the psalms:[12]

> Seigneur, lasse! ne l'est il mais?
> Selon ce que David en dist,
> Son lieu ne cognoistra jamais. (290–92)

> [Lord, alas! Is he one no more?
> According to what David said,
> His place he nevermore will know.]

The reference to the biblical passage is again somewhat elliptical:

> Man's days are like the grass;
> he blossoms like the flowers of the field:
> a wind passes over them, and they cease to be,
> and their place knows them no more.[13]

It is curious, and perhaps significant, that Villon omits the most striking portion of the text, or at least the most visual portion of the image, in favor of the final verse, which is virtually void of imagery. The image of the burning thread presents a graphic depiction of the violence of time and the fragility of human life. The passage from Psalms 103 to which Villon alludes provides another graphic representation of mortality, the flowers in the field quickly and easily dispersed by the first wind. By selecting the last verse of the text, however, Villon draws the reader's attention to the absence of life rather than its ephemeral presence. The first text (Ecclesiastes) of the trilogy concerns youth. The second text (the variant on Job) focuses on the destructive force of time, a process that becomes increasingly apparent once youth has disappeared. In the third text of the trilogy, attention shifts to absence, nothingness, that which remains after death.

Lazarus and the Rich Man

One of the longest and most important biblical references comes at the end of the lengthy prologue, immediately before the opening of the will proper in the *Testament*. A theological digression on the harrowing of hell prompts Villon to introduce the parable of Lazarus and the rich man:

> C'est de Jhesus la parabolle
> Touchant du Riche ensevely
> En feu, non pas en couche molle,
> Et du Ladre de dessus ly.   (813–16)

> [It comes from Jesus' parable
> Of the Rich Man who was entombed
> In fire, not on any soft couch,
> And of the Leper high above.]

This story, one of the best known parables in Villon's day, was a popular subject of cathedral art, and can be found (among other sites) in the stained glass of the Bourges cathedral. As a dramatic warning against the dangers of sin, and a poignant reminder of the finality of divine judgment, the parable carried a particular appeal to the medieval imagination:

> There was once a rich man, who dressed in purple and the finest linen, and feasted in great magnificence every day. At his gate, covered with sores, lay a poor man named Lazarus, who would have been glad to satisfy his hunger with the scraps from the rich man's table.[14]

After their deaths, the fates of Lazarus and the rich man are reversed. The latter finds himself enduring the torments of hell. Looking up, he sees far above him Abraham with Lazarus at his side. Suffering from extreme thirst, the rich man calls out for compassion:

> "Abraham, my father," he called out, "take pity on me. Send Lazarus to dip the tip of his finger in water, to cool my tongue, for I am in agony in this fire." But Abraham said, "Remember, my child, that all the good things fell to you while you were alive, and all the bad to Lazarus; now he has his consolation here and it is you who are in agony.[15]

The rich man then pleads that he at least be allowed to return to his family to warn his brothers of the terrible fate that awaits them if they follow his example. Abraham denies this request, pointing out that they have Moses and the prophets to instruct them. The rich man, having now given up on his own salvation but desperately attempting to save his family, pleads again with Abraham, but to no avail. The didactic thrust of the parable is quite clear. Villon, however, finds a somewhat different meaning in the story:

> Se du Ladre eust veu le doyz ardre,
> Ja n'en eust requis reffrigere
> N'eaue au bout d'icelluy doiz aerdre
> Pour raffreschir sa machoüire.   (817–20)

> [If he'd seen the Leper's finger burn,
> He'd not have sought to cool himself
> Nor to get water from its tip
> In order to refresh his jaw.]

Rather than move from the rich man's eternal thirst to a meditation on sin and penance, the natural connection that one would expect, Villon instead returns to the motif of drinking that is prominently displayed throughout the *Lais* and the *Testament*:

> Pÿons y feront macte chiere,
> Qui boyvent pourpoint et chemise.
> Puis que boicture y est si chiere,
> Dieux nous en gart, bourde jus mise!   (821–24)

[Boozers will pull long faces there,

Who here drink up doublets and shirts.

Since there a drink's so hard to buy,

God keep us from the Devil's grip.]

Despite the scant attention this passage has drawn from Villon's commentators, it deserves close attention for a number of reasons. This is the only one of the New Testament parables to which Villon explicitly refers in the *Testament*. Why does he select this particular story? Moreover, Villon places the parable in a privileged position, immediately before the will proper. (In one manuscript, the scribe has even written between this stanza and the next, "Cy commence le testament.") The parable thus sets the stage for the fiction of the testament, the formal will of the dying testator. A second look at Villon's use of the Lazarus story will reveal that the selection of parable does not represent an arbitrary choice, but in fact foreshadows one of the major thematic preoccupations of the *Testament*.

To fully appreciate the meaning of the passage in question, the reader must remain cognizant of the fact that almost every portion of the *Testament* carries some personal signification, even if it is not always immediately apparent. In the story of Alexander and Diomedes (129–68), for example, Villon follows the anecdote with an exegetical explanation, indicating that he identifies with Diomedes (the pirate and criminal) and that the poet's fate would have been different had he encountered

Ung autre piteux Alixandre

Qui m'eust fait en bon eur entrer   (163–64)

[Another kindly Alexander

Who would have steered me toward good luck].

In this case, there is no doubt concerning Villon's identification with Diomedes, nor the personal significance the story carries when contextualized within the poet's life. In the Lazarus parable, however, the questions of identification and significance are less explicit. Rereading the opening of the parable reveals that the salient and defining characteristic of Lazarus is his poverty: "lay a *poor* man named Lazarus." All his suffering—his hunger, his physical ailments, and his humiliation—result directly from his poverty. As we have already seen, Villon defines himself repeatedly in terms of his own poverty, and the word *povre* even becomes one of his signatures. Dependent on the charity of others, Lazarus and the *povre Villon* share a common bond. The issue of identification, however, is not quite as simple as it might appear at first glance. Villon turns the parable of Lazarus and the rich man into a story about thirst and drinking, which leads the poet to reflect on the plight of drinkers in hell. The rich man is thus assimilated into the mass of thirsty sinners who populate the hottest regions of hell. Villon has announced his own thirst only recently:

> Je congnois approucher ma seuf;
> Je crache blanc comme coton (729–30)

> [I recognize my thirst's approach,
> I spit white as cotton is].

Roger Dragonetti finds in the *Testament* an elemental thirst that Villon shares with Jean Cotart, which (in the verses cited above) may even carry religious overtones:

> En somme, pour le fond, la soif inapaisée, inapaisable de Cotart n'est guère différente de celle du poète dont les paroles d'agonisant victime de l'amour, rappellent dans le *Testament* la soif du Christ expirant sur la croix . . .[16]

An even more explicit identification follows. The *pÿons* to whom Villon refers in verse 821 drink themselves into a state of total destitution and are forced to leave behind their very clothing in lieu of payment: "Qui boyvent pourpoint et chemise." Is it mere coincidence that Villon speaks on several occasions of possessions such as a dagger and an undergarment that he has left in various taverns to cover his debts (*Lais*, 83, 102) and alludes more than once to debts he owes the tavern keeper Robin Turgis (*Testament*, 774, 1015, 1054)? Thus, both the rich man and the *povre Villon* are eventually assimilated into the thirsty *pÿons,* none of whom, regardless of the resources they may have possessed while in the realm of the living, can now afford the price of a drink: "Puis que boicture y est si chiere."

Unlike the story of Alexander and Diomedes, the parable of Lazarus and the rich man entails a degree of ambiguity. If Villon can see himself or a part of himself in the beggar at the rich man's gate, the poet can also see another part of himself sharing the eternal thirst of the damned souls in hell. The ambiguity of his position, caught between Lazarus and the rich man, reflects a profound conflict underlying the spiritual implications of the *Testament*. For the medieval will fulfills not only a legal but also a religious function, as Philippe Ariès points out:

> Donc, à la fin de sa vie, le fidèle confesse sa foi, reconnaît ses péchés et les rachète par un acte public, écrit *ad pias causas*.[17]

The hour of death, which provides the temporal framework for the *Testament*, is a moment fraught with spiritual importance, as attested by an iconographic tradition dating from the late medieval period, showing various angels and demons fiercely struggling for the soul that is about to be released from its bodily confinement.[18] It is within this intensely dramatic moment, when the fate of the human soul hangs precariously between salvation and perdition, that the *Testament* unfolds.[19] Given the spiritual dimension of the medieval will, and of the *Testament* in particular, it is entirely appropriate that Villon should place over the portal of his poem the parable of Lazarus and the rich man.

Violence and Betrayal

As we have seen, an undercurrent of violence runs throughout much of Villon's poetry. Accordingly, it is not surprising that the largest group of biblical references relates in some way to violence and death. The texts in question run from mutilation to rape and incest to execution, suicide, and outright murder. In the *Double Ballade*—a bitter and cynical denunciation of love (or more accurately, the pursuit of lust) occurring fairly early in the *Testament*—Villon includes a cluster of biblical texts, each involving a degree of violence and violation. Leading the parade of victims are Solomon and Samson:

> Folles amours font les gens bestes:
> Salmon en ydolatria,
> Sanson en perdit ses lunectes.   (629–31)

> [Foolish love makes people fools:
> Solomon turned to idolatry
> And Samson, for love, lost his eyes.]

Solomon, toward the end of his life, blinded by his feelings toward the 700 wives and 300 concubines who made up his harem, betrayed his religious faith by building shrines to the gods worshipped by his foreign wives.[20] The blinding of Samson, by contrast, was painfully literal. Villon's facetious use of *lunectes* cannot conceal the extraordinary violence involved in this act of mutilation.[21] The parallel between Solomon and Samson extends beyond the figurative and literal blinding respectively exemplified in each case. In both cases, the damage (physical in one instance, spiritual in the other) results from an act of betrayal. Solomon's idolatry clearly represents an act of willful disobedience, for which he is held directly accountable, and the consequences of which will be borne by succeeding generations. Samson, of course, suffers more directly from the consequences of betrayal. Moreover, both Solomon and Samson are men of strength and virtue who are to some degree implicated in the betrayal whose consequences they are forced to suffer. Solomon, after all, had requested and had been granted the divine gift of wisdom, "a heart with skill to listen," and the ability "to distinguish good from evil."[22] Thus Solomon, of all people, was morally and intellectually equipped to fully understand the significant implications of his spiritual betrayal. Samson, endowed with a certain cunning and resourcefulness, as well as exceptional physical strength, clearly sensed Delilah's intent to betray him, and therefore purposefully misled her when she attempted to discover the secret of his strength, pretending first that he could be bound only by fresh bowstrings, then (when this method of restraint proved unsuccessful) advising her to use new ropes, then a rope woven from the locks of his hair. Ultimately, however, in the the case of both Solomon and Samson, love (or at least the power of seduction) proves to be the operative element in the betrayal. Solomon chose to renounce his gift of wisdom, the ability to discern good from evil, not out of any malicious intent, but in response to a stronger force within himself: "King Solomon was a lover of women."[23] Transgressing the taboo against marrying foreign women, Solomon demonstrated more loyalty to his wives than to his religion: "But Solomon was devoted to them and loved them dearly."[24] Delilah holds the same power over Samson, and when all her attempts to discover his secret fail, she finally resorts to her most powerful weapon: "How can you say you love me when you do not confide in me?"[25] In both cases, two factors contribute to the betrayal. First, and most obvious, the seductive power of women proves a formidable force. The betrayal could not take place, however, without the collaboration of the victim. A careful reading of the texts reveals that Solomon and Samson both are endowed with the capacity to resist the temptation to which they ultimately succumb.

The references to the two biblical figures set the tone at the end of the ballade for the poet's reflection on his own experience with women:

> Mais que ce jeune bachelier
> Laissast ces jeunes bachelectes?
> Non! et le deust on vif brusler   (665–67)

> [But do you think that this young man
> Would ever leave these girls alone?
> Not were he to be burned alive]

In the previous stanza, Villon complains of the physical punishment in which Katherine de Vausselles and Noël Jolis are somehow implicated, but the poet refrains from stating that he was the victim of an outright injustice. His anger seems motivated not so much by any perceived inequity but rather by the fact that his misdeed was discovered and that he was consequently apprehended. Katherine and Noël, although mentioned as participants in the unknown escapade, quickly disappear from the poetic train of thought. Instead of ending with a flat and vehement condemnation of those persons who may have collaborated in the betrayal, Villon closes the ballade with a reflective examination of his own role in affair, situating the incident in a broader personal context. The force that ultimately has been the source of so many problems, so much hardship, is to be found not in external circumstances but within the poet himself, within the lust-driven *bachelier* who cannot leave the *bachelectes* alone, even at the risk of dangers he knows all too well. Now the *jeune bachelier*, Solomon, Samson, and all the other unfortunate lovers of the ballade are united by their common flaw:

> Mais toutesfoys fol s'i fya   (670)

> [Yet he who trusted them's a fool]

The passion of lust lies at the ultimate source of all the betrayals cited in the *double ballade,* and sometimes both the recipient and the perpetrator of the crime become the victims:

Amon en voult deshonnorer,
Faignant de menger tartelectes,
Sa seur Thamar et defflorer   (649–51)

[Amnon, for love, willed to dishonour
(Pretending to eat little tarts)
And to deflower his sister Thamar]

Amnon, overcome with desire for his half-sister Thamar, and acting on the advice of a friend, took to bed, pretending to be ill, and requested that Thamar prepare a meal in his presence. Having dismissed all others from his quarters, Amnon then bid Thamar to bring the food to his bed, whereupon he seized and raped her. When Thamar's brother Absalom discovered what had happened, he patiently plotted his moment of vengeance. Two years later, during a family celebration, Absalom instructed his servants to kill Amnon when Absalom gave the command. Once his half brother was suitably drunk, Absalom gave the signal and thus finally avenged his sister's dishonor.[26]

Accounts of violent death make up a significant portion of the biblical texts embedded in Villon's poetry. As in the reference to Amnon, the account may not be explicit. Villon sometimes refers to a single moment of a particular story, relying on his biblically literate audience to supply the missing portion of the text. Thus, the poet refers eliptically to the story of David and Bathsheba:

David ly roys, saiges prophetes,
Crainte de Dieu en oublia,
Voyant laver cuisses bien fetes.   (645–47)

[And that wise prophet, David the king,
Quite forgot the fear of God,
Seeing shapely thighs get washed.]

Attracted by Bathsheba's beauty as he watched her from the roof of his palace one evening, David sent messengers to summon her, and she promptly obeyed. She subsequently sent word to David that she was pregnant by him. Having learned that Bathsheba was the wife of Uriah, a soldier, David instructed Uriah's commander to send the soldier into battle precisely at the point of fiercest combat, then fall back with his own men, leaving Uriah without support. Following the orders of his king, Uriah's commander sent Bathsheba's husband to his death. According to his plan, David was now free to marry the widow, after the appropriate period of mourning had passed. The story does not end here, however, and the closure of the episode is suggested by Villon's observation that David, in all his careful planning, overlooked one essential element: "Crainte de Dieu en oublia" (646). Bathsheba gave birth to a son, who shortly fell ill and, despite the fasting and prayers of his father, eventually died.

References to biblical violence, however, are usually more explicit than in the reference to David and Bathsheba. The violent death of Absalom is twice cited. In the *Ballade contre les ennemis de la France*, possibly written in honor of Louis XI, Villon includes the death of Absalom in a list of unpleasant fates that the poet wishes upon the enemies of France:

Ou aux cheveux comme Absolon pendus   (19)

[Or hanged by his own hair like Absalom]

In the *Ballade de Fortune*, in which the personified figure of Fortune recites a litany of destructive acts that she has performed (suggesting that the poet, whom she familiarly addresses by his first name, take consolation in the illustrious examples of persons whose fate is worse than Villon's), the name of Absalom occurs again:

Absollon, quoy? En fuyant le pendis.   (35)

[And Absalom? I hanged him as he fled.]

When Absalom, in revolt against his father, David, found himself caught in the branches of an oak tree, hanging by his long hair, his brother, Joab, taking advantage of Absalom's helplessness, had him beaten to death. Learning of his son's death, David was grief-stricken. As in many of the other biblical stories appearing in Villon's poetry, violence is linked to betrayal. David had given specific instructions to all of his commanders, including Joab, to spare the life of Absalom. Joab's decision to murder Absalom constitutes a triple transgression, as Joab takes the life of his own brother, orders the death of a helpless soldier, and violates his father's command.

The murder of Holofernes by Judith, also cited in the *Ballade de Fortune*, represents an act of heroism rather than betrayal, but continues the undercurrent of violence:

> Holofernés l'diolastre mauldiz
> Qu'occist Judic (et dormoit entandiz)
> De son poignart dedens son pavillon. (32–34)

> [I cursed Holofernes the idolater
> Whom Judith killed (he sleeping at the time)
> With his own dagger and inside the tent.]

The murder of Holofernes, although perhaps not especially well known today, represents one of the bloodiest episodes in the Bible. Having invited Judith into his tent for the purpose of seduction, the Assyrian commander eventually fell into a drunken sleep. Taking the scimitar that she found hanging above his bed, and praying for the strength to carry out her intention, Judith decapitated Holofernes with his own weapon. She then gave the head to her maidservant, who placed it in a sack. Once Judith returned to her town of Bethulia, she displayed the gruesome trophy to the astounded citizens.[27]

The most famous beheading of the Bible, the decapitation of John the Baptist, also appears in Villon's poetry, but again in a highly abbreviated form:

> Herodes, pas ne sont sornectes,
> Saint Jehan Baptiste en decola
> Pour dances, aulx et chansonnectes. (653–55)

> [Herod (this isn't idle talk)
> Had John the Baptist's head struck off
> For dances, skips, and little songs.]

The connection between violence and betrayal, although perhaps more subtle here than in some previous examples, can still be discerned. Herod had arrested John the Baptist and was holding him in prison, but refused (against the wishes of his wife Herodias) to execute the prophet, "knowing him to be a good and holy man."[28] The ruse by which Herodias obtains the decapitation of John the Baptist is, of course, well known. Herod is in effect blackmailed into ordering John's execution, and his reaction ("The king was greatly distressed, but . . . could not bring himself to refuse her") makes it clear that he orders the execution with the greatest reluctance.[29] As in the case of Solomon, Samson, and the *povre Villon*, Herod, perhaps sensing the deleterious consequences of his decision, carries out the action against his better judgment.

The other explicit allusion to the New Testament relates to the suicide of Judas Iscariot. The reference occurs in the *Ballade contre les ennemis de la France:*

Ou com Judas fut [pendu] par Desesperance   (20)

[Or else be hanged, like Judas, by Despair]

The connection here between violence and betrayal is by far the strongest of all the biblical episodes to which Villon alludes. Seized with overwhelming remorse, and realizing the enormity of his sin, Judas, in a state of unbearable despair, hangs himself.

What then are we to make of these biblical texts related to violence and betrayal that Villon inscribes within his poetry? At the very least, these texts extend, deepen, and enrich a thematic strand woven through much of Villon's verse. At the same time, they invite a closer look at Villon's refrain claiming that he, the *povre Villon*, is a victim—a victim of circumstance, injustice, society, and betrayal. As we have seen, some of the illustrious victims with whom Villon explicitly or implicitly juxtaposes his own story are, in the final analysis, victims of themselves.

The Crucifixion

The Old Testament dominates the biblical allusions found in Villon's poetry. With a few notable exceptions (the parable of Lazarus and the rich man, the execution of John the Baptist, and an enigmatic reference to Emmaus [*Testament,* 100]), Villon makes remarkably few references to the New Testament. In the closing ballade of the *Testament,* however, a cluster of images evokes the final moments of Christ on the cross. That the image of the crucified Christ has eluded Villon's commentators for so long may be explained by the comic tone of the ballade, a burlesque funeral eulogy for the *povre Villon*. Nevertheless, a careful reading of the poem reveals the presence of another, unnamed victim.[30]

Although none of the constituent pieces of evidence may be considered compelling when taken individually, together they form a composite image of the crucified Christ whose lines, however faint, are clearly discernible beneath the tone of self-mockery. The first clue consists simply of a color, bright red or vermilion, which literally and figuratively colors our reading of the remainder of the poem:

> Venez a son enterrement,
> Quant vous orez le carillon,
> Vestuz rouge com vermeillon,
> Car en amours mourut martir   (1998–2001)

> [Come to attend his burial
> When you hear the carillon,
> Dressed in red like vermilion;
> A martyr did he die, in love]

Red vestments would be appropriately worn during the feast days commemorating the death of religious martyrs. The *com vermeillon* intensifies the redness and serves as a reminder that the scarlet color of the vestments is intended to evoke the blood shed by the martyrs.[31] Thus, through a layer of well-established religious symbolism, the color red leads directly to the blood of martyrs. Moreover, the verse "Car en amours mourut martir" suggests a sacrificial death, a death in the name of love. Until this point in the poem, nothing points conclusively to the Crucifixion, but the indirect allusion to martyr's blood and the reference to a martyr who died for love certainly set the tone for the image that will gradually take shape in the following verses.

The clothing of the *povre Villon*, according to the narrative voice of the poem, can be found torn and scattered all the way to Roussillon:

> Tant que, d'icy a Roussillon,
> Brosse n'y a ne brossillon
> Qui n'eust, ce dit il sans mentir,
> Ung lambeau de son cotillon   (2007–10)

[So that from here to Roussillon,
There is no brushy patch nor bush
That didn't get, he truly said,
A fragment shredded from his smock]

The shredding of the martyr's tunic may be taken, in the context of related images, as a parallel to the division of Christ's clothing among the Roman soldiers. Another more subtle parallel may also be found here. The *brosse* (2008) and *brossillon* (a diminutive coined by Villon) are the equivalent of the modern French *broussaille* (thornbush or brambles). The word *lambeau* (2010) can be used to designate either a shred of cloth or a torn strip of flesh. Without referring explicitly to the crown of thorns, the juxtaposition of thorns and torn flesh (again, in the context of the entire network of allusions) evokes certain imagery related to the Crucifixion.

The death of the martyr bears more direct resemblance to the death of Christ:

Il est ainsi et tellement:
Quant mourut n'avoit q'un haillon.
Qui plus, en mourant, mallement
L'espoignoit d'Amours l'esguillon   (2012–15)

[The way of it's exactly this:
He died with nothing but a rag;
What's more, as death approached, the goad
Of Love pricked him most painfully]

The *haillon* (rag) represents the only clothing of Christ on the cross in virtually all late medieval paintings of the scene. The *esguillon* (or *aiguillon* in modern French) is a cattle prod consisting of an iron tip fastened to a long stick. The parallel between this image and the piercing of Christ's side by the soldier's lance is readily apparent. That the piercing takes place immediately after the victim's death in one case, and immediately prior to his death in the other, is of less importance than the proximity between the event itself and the death.

The final act of the dying martyr is recounted at the end of the ballade:

Sachiez qu'il fist au departir:
Ung traict but de vin morillon,
Quant de ce monde voult partir.   (2021–22)

[Here's what he did on taking leave:
He drank a draft of dark-red wine
When just about to leave this world.]

Culminating the series of allusions to the Crucifixion, the last recorded act of the *povre Villon*, like the last recorded act of the dying Christ, is the drinking of wine. Granted, in one case it is a cheap and sour wine, and in the other case it is a *vin supérieur*, but again we should not be thrown off by minor discrepancies. The act itself, rather than the quality of the wine, deserves attention.

Despite certain parallels (their age, their disputes with ecclesiastical authorities, the fact that both moved in a milieu considered dangerous by the social establishment), it does not necessarily follow that Villon deliberately presents himself as a Christ figure in the concluding ballade of the *Testament*. It would be more accurate to say that, with a little effort and imagination, the reader may detect a figure of the crucified Christ, however faintly and subtly outlined in the background, emerging from the end of Villon's masterpiece. Thus, recalling the figure of Thibaut d'Aussigny blessing the crowded streets of Orléans, we can see that the *Testament* opens and closes under the sign of the cross. We should not allow the tone of the passages in question—the bitter resentment of the poem's prologue and the self-deprecating irony of the poem's closure—to detract from the sacred character of the sign itself. After all, Villon warns us implicitly and repeatedly to mistrust the surface of the text, training us to remain in a heightened state of vigilance, always prepared to search for the hidden truth that may lie beneath the apparent meaning of a verse. Paradoxically, embedded in the closing ballade, with all its elements of obscenity, self-caricature, and merciless mockery, lies an image charged with the deepest spiritual meaning of any to be found in the medieval imagination.

Chapter Nine
The *Danse Macabre*

Background

Although the theme of death is prevalent throughout medieval art and literature, it becomes especially prominent in the late Middle Ages. Living in prolonged period of war, civil disturbance, plague, and famine, most residents of fifteenth-century France had an intimate acquaintance with death. The artistic motif of the *danse macabre* makes its first appearance in the early part of the fifteenth century. The earliest known representation of the *danse macabre* is a mural painted on one of the interior walls of the Parisian Cemetery of the Innocents in 1424. Throughout Europe, many other examples soon followed in cemeteries, chapels, convents, and monasteries in London (1430), Dijon (1436), Bâle (1440), Strasbourg (1450), and Rosslyn, Scotland (1450). The wall containing the original French mural was destroyed in 1669 (as part of a project during the reign of Louis XIV to widen public roads), but the design of the original is preserved in the 1485 edition of the *Danse Macabre*, published by the Parisian printer Guyot Marchant. The volume contains woodcuts copied from the mural as well as the text of the poem originally inscribed beneath the painting.

The Cemetery of the Innocents, as previously mentioned, ranked among the most popular sites of Paris in Villon's day. Thus the mural of the *danse macabre*, with its juxtaposition of the living and the dead, was especially well placed in this cemetery, where gravestones and charnel houses could be found interspersed with the booths of merchants selling books, cloth, ironware, and other articles. Virtually any male visitor could find himself among the group of figures included in the painting. Beginning with those of highest rank and then gradually descending, intermingling clergy and laity, the *danse* includes a pope, an emperor, a cardinal, an archbishop, a knight, a bishop, an abbot, a merchant, a monk, a usurer, a doctor, a lawyer, a minstrel, a friar, a laborer, a child, and a hermit, among others. This is not so much a dance of death as a dance of the dead. Each living figure is paired with a dead partner, representing the condition of the former after death. Thus the living, or *vif*, is presented with a posthumous image of himself. Guyot Marchant, obviously inspired by this aspect of the *danse macabre*, subtitled his edition *Le Miroir salutaire*. The dead (resembling mummies more than skeletons), grin gleefully, tugging at the arms of their reluctant partners, who wear expressions ranging from resignation to mild surprise to total disbelief.[1] The dead, reduced by decay to their universal human element, still retain traces of individuality, as Alberto Tenenti points out:

> Ainsi, sur le plan iconographique, la personnification de la mort s'émiette en s'individualisant à plusieurs reprises; chaque cadavre est caractérisé par un geste, un instrument de musique, un outil de fossoyeur, et même par un insigne ou une partie de l'habillement de sa victime.[2]

There is almost a playful element to the dance, the figure of the *mort*, one leg lifted in a dance step, tugging simultaneously at the arm of the startled cardinal and dignified king, who certainly do not seem ready to join in the dance. Although perhaps historically related to the representation of death found in Italian art of the previous century, the *danse macabre* departs from the more abstract and symbolic character of the Italian model and emphasizes not so much the figure of death but rather the encounter between the living and the dead, an encounter fraught with philosophical and spiritual implications.[3]

The following excerpt of the text from Guyot Marchant's *Danse Macabre*, a transcription of the poem inscribed on the cloister wall of the Innocents beneath the images of the mural, will provide some idea of the tone of the work:

Le Mort

Pelerin, vous avez assez
Aller en pelerinage.
Travelle estez, et lassez:
Bien appart a vostre visage.
C'est cy vostre derrenier voyage.
Que bon vous soit, faictez devoir:
La fin coronne tout ouvrage;
Selon euvre payement avoir.

Le Pelerin

En tout temps, yvers et esté,
Voyager estoit mon désir.
Or suis je par mort arresté:
J'en loue dieu quant c'est son plesir
Et luy prie qui me doint loisir
De tous mes péchés confesser
Pour mon ame en repos gésir.
Ung jour me fallait tout lesser.

[The Dead Man

Pilgrim, you have
Made enough pilgrimages.
You are tired and weary:
It's apparent from your face.
This is your last journey.
Let it be a good one; do your duty:
The end crowns every work.
Payment is made according to the work.

The Pilgrim

In every weather, winter and summer,
To travel was my desire.
Now I am halted by death:
I praise God since it's his pleasure
And I pray that he give me time
To confess all my sins
In order that my soul may rest in peace.
One day I would have to abandon it all.]⁴

The corresponding image depicts the pilgrim, dressed in a traveling robe and sandals, carrying a small pouch and a long staff, his hands folded in a gesture of submission. The dead man, wearing only a cloth wrapped around his loins, is positioned next to the pilgrim, one hand resting on his shoulder, one foot slightly raised as if to lead his companion off in a new direction. The reaction of the pilgrim, revealing resignation, acceptance, and perhaps even a note of relief, contrasts with the reaction of some of the dance's other living participants, who react with disbelief or regret. The pilgrim's ability to accept death may be ascribed, no doubt, to the life of religious devotion that has prepared him for this dramatic moment. By observing the various reactions of those who are drawn into the dance, the medieval spectator could witness the broad gamut of the *danse macabre,* embracing men of all social conditions and inspiring a wide range of emotion from horror and incredulity to peaceful and obedient acceptance.

The *Danse Macabre* as a Frame for the *Testament*

The prevalence of death in Villon's poetry is well established. Italo Siciliano devotes a lengthy chapter to the theme of death in his *François Villon et les thèmes poétiques du moyen âge.*[5] In order to better understand and appreciate Villon's treatment of death, however, it is necessary to look beyond the long medieval tradition stressing the constant need for penance and contrition in the face of impending death, and to look specifically at the images of the *danse macabre,* which literally give death a new face and a disturbingly intimate proximity to life. The *danse macabre* represents, among other things, an actual dance, and the movement of the dance is evident in every image. The motion of the dance, paradoxically, is generated not by the living, who remain in rigidly fixed postures, but by the dead, whose bodies prove surprisingly agile and supple. Death in the *Testament,* as in the *danse macabre,* generally appears not as an abstract or distant threat but as a tangible presence intimately connected to the living.

The strong imagery of the *danse macabre* underlies many of Villon's references to death. The passage in which the dance of death is most readily apparent comes early in the *Testament.* Following a meditation on his own mortality, Villon broadens the scope of his reflection:

Je congois que pouvres et riches,
Sagez et folz, prestres et laiz,
Nobles, villains, larges et chiches,
Petiz et grans, et beaulx et laiz,   (305–8)

[I know that the poor and the rich,
Wise men and fools, priests, laity,
Nobles, peasants, the liberal and mean,
The small, the great, the ugly and fair]

The conclusion of the stanza is already obvious. All the living are headed for the same end. The distinctions separating these men in life will soon become meaningless. In a remarkably skillful act of compression, Villon condenses the essence of the *danse macabre* into four verses, embracing all financial conditions (*pouvres et riches*), the entire range of human intelligence (*Sagez et fols*), the basic distinction between clergy and laity (*prestres et laiz*), class distinctions (*Nobles, villains*), fundamental character traits (*larges et chiches*), and defining physical characteristics (*Petiz et grans, et beaulx et laiz*). The second half of the stanza continues to widen the scope of inclusiveness, bringing women into the dance:

Dames a rebrassés colletz,
De quelconque condicïon,
Portans atours et bourreletz,
Mort saisit sans excepcïon.   (309–12)

[Ladies with collars folded back
(Whatever their status may be)
Having lofty headgear on,
Death seizes, no exceptions made.]

The graphic and exceptionally strong verb used to depict the act of death—*Mort saisit*—fits perfectly into the images of the *danse macabre*, in which we see the figures of the dead tugging, prodding, leading, coaxing, and grasping their reluctant living companions.

The parallels between this stanza and the *danse macabre* are self-evident and thus do not require extensive commentary. Another possibly more significant parallel that has barely received any critical commentary comes a little later in the poem, connected to a context that ostensibly has nothing to do with death. Villon, declaring that he is formally renouncing love, reinforces his claim by citing a proverb (italicized):

Ma vïelle ay mis soubz le banc,
Amans ne suiveray jamaiz.   (717–18)

[My fiddle's put beneath the bench,
I'll follow lovers nevermore.]

Villon, like other fifteenth-century French poets, frequently incorporates popular proverbs into his verse.[6] In this particular proverb, however, something more complicated may be taking place, for the verse in question rephrases (almost verbatim) a verse contained in Guyot Marchant's *Danse Macabre:*

J'ay mis sub le banc ma vielle,
Plus ne corneray sauterelle
N'autre danse: mort m'en retient.[7]

[I've put my fiddle beneath the bench,
I won't pipe any more jigs,
Or any other dances: death forbids me to do it.]

The quotation is from the *ménestral,* who appears relatively low on the social ladder, below the lawyer and above the parish priest. Of all the figures appearing in the *danse macabre,* it is without doubt the *ménestral* to whom Villon most closely corresponds. Claude Thiry has collected compelling textual evidence indicating the importance of music in Villon's poetry—musical terminology, references to music, and the musicality of his verses—and one of the many masks worn by the narrator of the *Testament* is that of the *ménestral.*[8] That the one intertextual reference tying the *Testament* to the *danse macabre* leads us precisely to the point on the cloister wall where Villon would be most likely to see a mirror image of himself can hardly be explained as mere coincidence.[9] By symbolically inscribing himself within the *danse macabre,* Villon broadens the scope of the *Testament,* giving his own struggle with mortality a universal dimension, situating it in the perspective of a profoundly human conflict. At the same time, he personalizes the *danse macabre* by inserting himself into the dance at the appropriate juncture.

Death in the *Testament* sometimes takes an abstract form, as in the trilogy of ballades beginning with the *Ballade des dames du temps jadis,*

where the poet reflects on the brevity of human life. Here, death takes
the form of an absence rather than a presence, as we see in the *ubi sunt*
refrain of each *ballade:*

Mais ou sont les neiges d'anten?   (336)

[But what's become of last year's snows?]

Mais ou est le preux Charlemaigne?   (364)

[But where's the worthy Charlemagne?]

Autant en emporte ly vens.   (392)

[All such, the wind carries away.]

At other points in the poem, however, death takes the form of a personal
and highly dramatic encounter. The stanza immediately preceding the *Ballade des dames du temps jadis* presents an extraordinarily graphic and violent
account of the last moments of an *agonisant*, dying in unbearable pain:

La mort le fait fremir, pallir,
Le nez courber, les vaines tendre,
Le col enffler, la chair moslir,
Joinctes et nerfz croistre et estendre   (321–24)

[Death makes him tremble and turn pale,
His nose grow hooked, his veins distend,
His neck swell up, his flesh turn soft,
His joints, bones, sinews grow and stretch]

The extreme suffering of the *agonisant* expresses itself through a concentration of forceful verbs—*fremir, pallir, courber, tendre, enffler, moslir,
croistre*, and *estendre*. This is not a peaceful and painless death, a passive
acceptance of the inevitable. Instead, Villon shows us the disturbing
image of a body struggling to live, futilely fighting against an insupera-
ble force that is torturously crushing the breath out of its victim:

Telle qu'il pert vent et alaine;
Son fiel se criesve sur son cueur
Puis sue, Dieu scet quelle sueur!   (315–17)

[He can no longer get his breath;
His bile bursts and spreads to his heart,
And then he sweats, God knows what sweat!]

The graphic violence of the deathbed presents a striking contrast with the somewhat ethereal representation of death found in the three ballades that follow. In effect, the description of the *agonisant* and the *ubi sunt* theme woven through the subsequent trilogy of *ballades* represent two distinct but complementary medieval attitudes toward death. On one hand, there is a recognition of things eternal (especially the eternal dimension of human existence, the soul and the afterlife), compared to which the body and all physical existence—with their attendant pain, pleasures, desires, and fears—pale into insubstantiality. The material world, which appears so solid and present, is nothing but an extremely compelling illusion:

Le monde n'est qu'abusïon.   (374)

[Naught but illusion is this world.]

This is the constant refrain of the sermons that Villon and his contemporaries could hear preached continuously in the Cemetery of the Innocents and in other public sites, and it is a theme that Villon occasionally preaches himself. In asking us what has become of the beautiful, seductive, or powerful women named in his famous ballade, Villon is asking us to reflect not only on their absence in the physical world but on their continuing presence in the eternal order that rules the universe.

On the other hand, the medieval imagination reveals a fascination with the physical act of death, the dramatic moment of encounter between life and death. While Villon and his contemporaries were listening to wandering friars speak eloquently about the fate of saints and unrepentant sinners, they could simultaneously study the mural of the *danse macabre* (a popular and effective backdrop for these sermons), in which the viewer could witness men of every conceivable social station literally coming to grips with death. Thus the *Testament* is inspired by both visions of death—the *ubi sunt* and the *danse macabre*. The trilogy of ballades about death, with all its mystery, poetic beauty, and haunting questions, follows directly on the heels of one of the most grotesque, violent, and disturbing passages in all of Villon's poetry.

The *Testament* is framed within the same moment depicted in the *danse macabre*, the point of encounter between life and death. The narrator of the *Testament* reminds us at several points of his impending death. There is a note of urgency as the dying testator begins the dictation of his will:

> Je sens mon cueur qui s'affoiblist
> Et plus je ne puis papïer.   (785–86)

> [I feel that my heart's weakening
> And that I can no longer speak.]

Toward the end of the will, the testator, exhausted by the effort and overcome with pain, prepares for his imminent death:

> Trop plus me font mal c'onques maiz
> Barbe, cheveux, penil, sourcys.
> Mal me presse, temps desormaiz
> Que crye a toutes gens mercys.   (1964–67)

> [Much more than ever I feel pain
> In beard, hair, private parts, and brows.
> Ills weigh me down; the moment's come
> To ask pardon of everyone.]

By contrast, the *Lais*, more closely aligned to the genre of the satirical testament, never claims to have been composed in the face of death.[10] In fact, references to the circumstances of the poem's composition, although uncorroborated, prove entirely consistent with the conditions under which the poem was probably composed, making such references realistic if not provably authentic. Thus the narrator of the *Lais* tells us that the poem was completed at night in the poet's chilly room, under the light of a dying candle, with the bells of the Sorbonne ringing in the distance. The *Testament*, by contrast, is dictated from the fictitious deathbed of the testator, and if the fiction serves obvious humorous purposes, it also situates the poem within a metaphysical context shared by the *danse macabre*.

There are moments in the *Testament* when the humor of the literary device, the mock will, virtually disappears, effaced by the gravity of the issues it raises, such as that of the poet's mortality:

> Item, mon corps j'ordonne et laisse
> A nostre grant mere la terre;
> Les vers n'y trouveront grant gresse,
> Trop luy a fait fain dure guerre.   (841–44)

> [Item, my body I bestow
> Upon our great Mother, the Earth,
> In it, the worms won't find much fat,
> For hunger's war has been too hard.]

Any humor in these dark verses is overshadowed by the morbid imagery reminiscent of the partially decayed corpses that parade through the *danse macabre*. Nor does the location of the passage, situated immediately after a stanza filled with sacred allusions in which the narrator commends his *povre ame* to the care of the Virgin, argue for any hidden ironic intent. Here the device of the satirical will (unlike the *Lais*, which reveals a very different state of mind), although perhaps initially chosen as a vehicle for humorous intentions, eventually entails reflection upon death, and the poet's own death in particular.

Having commended his bodily remains to the Earth, the poet continues to meditate on his mortality and the fragility of corporeal existence:

> Or luy soit delivré grant erre;
> De terre vint, en terre tourne.   (845–46)

> [Let it be given her in haste;
> From Earth it came, there let it return.]

Here biblical subtext, the artistic motif of the *danse macabre*, and the narrator's contemplation of his own death all intersect.[11]

Late in the *Testament*, in a passage we have already studied from a different angle in chapter 4, Villon reflects on the heaps of disarticulated bones in the charnel galleries of the Innocents. The entry into the cemetery is prepared by the poet's bequest of his spectacles to the blind:

Pour mectre a part, aux Innocens,
Les gens de bien de deshonnestes.   (1734–35)

[To sort out, at the Innocents,
Good people from dishonest ones.]

The joke is a cruel one, to be sure, but it leads to an abrupt change of tone. Now that we are inside the cemetery walls, in the realm of gravestones, bone heaps, and the *danse macabre*, all attempts at humor quickly disappear, and the narrator warns us that we are now entering a world where laughter has no place:

Icy n'y a ne riz ne jeu.   (1736)

[There is no laughing matter.]

As Sargent-Baur points out, the verse translates literally as "There is neither laughter nor play here."[12] The abrupt transition from humor to dead seriousness, and the poet's implied awareness of the transition, point to the tonal complexity of the *Testament*. To what degree the poet maintains control over the creative process we can only speculate, but the poem often at least gives the impression of creating its own momentum, following its own direction, occasionally taking the poet on a course he may not have anticipated. Thus, having wandered into the Innocents with the intention of leaving a mocking gift to the blind beggars who congregate here, the poet's attention now falls on the grim reminders of mortality that are plentifully strewn throughout the cemetery.

Whereas the site of the Innocents provides one transitional link between the facetious bequest of the spectacles and the somber meditation on death that follows, the poet also effects this transition in a subtler fashion by building on the theme of blindness. The blind beggars are given spectacles so that they might distinguish "Les gens de bien de deshonnestes" (1735). The joke of giving spectacles to the blind is compounded by the fact that even if they were gifted with sight, the beggars would be unable to judge moral distinctions, separating the honest from the dishonest, merely on the basis of appearance. But now, in a strange reversal, the joke rebounds, and it is Villon who has become blind, unable to make out any moral or social distinctions that will allow him to differentiate among the human remains with which he is presented:

Car d'evesques ou lanterniers
Je n'y congois riens a reddire   (1750–51)

[For, as to bishops or to lamp-men,
I can't tell any difference.]

Now that time has effaced even the most basic differences that separated these men in life, they all appear the same to the poet, just as all passersby might appear the same to a blind beggar. Moreover, the passage implies a third level of blindness. This is the fixation on earthly values that prevents one from perceiving the true spiritual values on which all eyes should be constantly focused. It is the blindness of the living figures in the *danse macabre*, a blindness that causes them to pursue earthly glory, material wealth, and physical gratification at the expense of spiritual enlightenment, a blindness that is finally and harshly broken by the sudden appearance of the living's dead counterparts. It is the spiritual darkness that deludes persons in positions of power into believing that they are inherently superior to those they command, leading the powerful to forget the basic humanity that binds us all together, and the loss of physical identity to which we will all one day be reduced:

La les voys toutes assouvies,
Ensemble en ung tas pesle mesle;
Seigneuries leur sont ravies,
Clerc ne maistre ne s'i appelle.   (1756–59)

[I see them there, all at an end,
Together in a heap, pell-mell;
All rank is snatched away from them,
No one's called clerk or master there.]

The ultimate lesson of the *danse macabre* is not, as one often reads, the inevitability of death, or that death, the great leveler, will eventually render meaningless all distinctions of human invention. More fundamental still, and a point that religious literature of the medieval period hammers home again and again, is the reminder that the essence of human existence resides not in the body but in the soul. The reactions of shock, disbelief, grief, and terror variously exhibited by the living figures of the *danse macabre* stem from a failure to grasp this fundamental truth. When the body dissolves, rendering meaningless all pursuit of physical gratification, only the essence of an individual's existence remains, and the eternal destiny of the human soul hangs in the balance:

> Et les os declinent en pouldre,
> Ausquels ne chault d'esbat ne riz.
> Plaise au doulx Jhesus les assouldre!   (1765–67)

> [And the bones are all becoming dust
> Without concern for sport and laughter.
> Please gentle Jesus to absolve them.]

Conclusion

The great paradox of Villon's work, a paradox that contributes significantly to his unique status among French poets of all periods, resides in the remarkable combination of universality and specificity that characterizes his poetry. On one hand, his work embraces certain fundamental aspects of the human condition—love and sexuality, suffering and violence, time and the aging process, mortality, and sin and redemption. Generations of readers from six centuries have found a beauty and timelessness in his work, particularly in certain ballades, thus assuring Villon a permanent place of honor among the greatest French poets. On the other hand, as this study has attempted to demonstrate, much of Villon's work remains firmly grounded in its historical context, tightly attached to specific sites, people, and events. The better acquainted we are with the historical and biographical circumstances that frame Villon's poetry, the richer our reading will be.

Our knowledge of François Villon is severely limited, based on a few archival records, internal evidence from the poetry itself, and extrapolation from various historical sources that touch tangentially on the poet's life. Yet, despite the numerous lacunae that prevent us from grasping the meaning of many portions of Villon's verse, we can at least appreciate the degree to which the poet incorporates aspects of his daily life into his poetry, embracing the rich and diverse human element of the city of Paris. Of the salient features that define Villon's poetry, perhaps the single most important element is the poetry's vitality. The energy of Villon's work, particularly the *Testament*, reflects the energy of the city that the poetry so frequently mirrors. Villon is very much a poet of the city, and he fills his poetry with the urban scenes he knows so well—streets, house signs, shops, taverns, brothels, schools, monasteries, convents, churches, prisons, gallows, and cemeteries. His poetry is populated by citizens of Paris from every walk of life—low-ranking and high-ranking members of the clergy, monks and nuns, bureaucrats, judges and lawyers, police and jailers, prostitutes and pimps, blind beggars, prosperous shopkeepers, wealthy money changers, members of the nobility, students, unemployed clerics, drunkards, innkeepers, barbers, petty thieves, and professional assassins. Thus, on one hand, Villon's poetry is very much a personal creation, reflecting the concerns, preoccupations, memories, and experiences of its creator. However, his poetry is also a reflection of the milieu in which he lives, and his own existence is to a large extent inseparably intertwined with the city of Paris.

We must remember, however, that the Paris we see reflected in Villon's poetry is actually the poet's *vision* of the city. While the *Lais* and the *Testament* offer a window through which the modern reader can catch occasional glimpses of fifteenth-century Paris, some of which are exceptionally well defined, we are allowed to view only the scenes that Villon chooses to show us. From thousands of possible sites and inhabitants, he selects those that, for personal reasons that may or may not be clear to us, he wishes to include in his work. In the final analysis, the thread that ties together all the images taken from the city is none other than the poet's memory. Of the hundreds of taverns in Paris during his day, why should Villon give prominence to the Pomme de Pin above all others? Clearly this particular tavern and its proprietor, Robin Turgis, hold a special place in Villon's past. Whereas our understanding of Villon's poetry would be undeniably enriched by a broader acquaintance with the historical milieu from which the poetry grows, the personal significance attached to every site, character, and event ultimately endows Villon's work with its true meaning. After isolating many of the historically based references in Villon's poetry, as we have done in several chapters of the present study, we are still left with the task of determining how those references all fit together to form a coherent picture.

In spite of all the guidance that can be provided to the uninitiated reader, all the explanatory notes, glosses, and commentaries, the final and most important phase of interpretation still rests with the reader. The image associated with the poetic voice of Villon will vary considerably from one reader to another. In classes on medieval literature, Villon typically elicits stronger reader responses than any other writer. Student reaction ranges from deep admiration for Villon's obvious poetic talent to blatant contempt for a perceived inability to accept responsibility for his mistakes. Even readers who claim to reject the lifestyle or values they find represented in Villon's poetry can find moments of the *Testament* that resonate with thoughts and feelings that the readers themselves have experienced.

Perhaps the most important point to keep in mind when reading Villon is that the separation between the poetic *je* and the people to whom it relates is not always as clear-cut as it may appear. The "other" is often a projection of the poet himself, or at least a fragment of the poet's personality. There is an element of Villon in the prayer that he presents to his mother. His voice blends with hers in the recitation of the prayer, and we find his acrostic signature in the closing verses of the ballade. But there is also an element of Villon in the *Ballade pour la Grosse Margot*, and although we know nothing about the woman who appears in the poem, only the most naive reader could dismiss Villon's intimate portrayal of his relationship with a prostitute as a pure fabrication bearing no connection whatsoever to reality. Again, we find Villon's acrostic signature at the end of the ballade. These signatures represent more than merely gratuitous additions. They are a signal to the reader that the poet's presence is everywhere in his poetry—sometimes open, sometimes cleverly concealed beneath a mask. To grasp the totality of this presence, we must search for fragments of the poetic personality not only in self-referential passages but in segments of the work that appear to deflect our attention from the poet. It would be a mistake, therefore, to dismiss as extraneous, superfluous, or inconsequential the large portions of his verse that do not appear to bear any immediate relation to the speaker. Villon reveals elements of his character not only in what he says about himself, but through his relationship to others.

Notes and References

Chapter One

1. See Barbara Sargent-Baur, "Communication and Implied Audience(s) in Villon's *Testament*," *Neophilologus* 76 (1992): 35–40; Yvan Lepage, "Villon et ses masques," in *Villon hier et aujourd'hui: Actes du Colloque pour le cinq-centième anniversaire de l'impression du Testament de Villon*, ed. Jean Dufournet (Paris: Bibliothèque Historique de la Ville de Paris, 1993), 161–74; David A. Fein, *François Villon and His Reader* (Detroit: Wayne State University Press, 1989).

2. Barbara Sargent-Baur, trans. and ed., *François Villon: Complete Poems* (Toronto: University of Toronto Press, 1994). All subsequent quotations and translations from Villon's poetry are from this edition. Reprinted by permission of University of Toronto Press Incorporated. © University of Toronto Press Incorporated 1994.

3. See Robert D. Peckham, *François Villon: A Bibliography* (New York and London: Garland, 1990).

4. Pierre Champion, *François Villon*, 2 vols. (Paris: Champion, 1913).

5. Louis Thuasne, ed., *François Villon: Oeuvres*, 3 vols. (Paris: Picard, 1923).

6. Paul Zumthor, *Langues et techniques poétiques à l'époque romane* (Paris: Klincksieck, 1963).

7. David Kuhn, *La Poétique de François Villon* (Paris: Armand Colin, 1967).

8. Nancy Freeman Regalado, "Effet de réel, Effet du réel: Representation and Reference in Villon's *Testament*," *Yale French Studies* 70 (1986): 63–77.

9. Dufournet, *Villon hier et aujourd'hui*, 315.

10. Pierre Michel, ed., *François Villon: Poésies complètes* (Paris: Livre de Poche, 1972), vi.

Chapter Two

1. Janet Shirley, trans., *A Parisian Journal* (Oxford: Clarendon Press, 1968), 356.

2. See Bronislaw Geremek, *Les Marginaux parisiens au XIVe et XVe siècles* (Paris: Flammarion, 1976), 175–84.

3. See Pierre Braun, "Les Lettres de rémissions accordée à François Villon," in Dufournet, *Villon hier et aujourd'hui*, 53–67.

4. For a perceptive commentary on this passage, see Jean Dufournet, *Recherches sur le Testament de François Villon*, vol. 1 (Paris: SEDES, 1971), 251–57.

5. In his *François Villon* (Paris: Fayard, 1982), Jean Favier suggests that Marie's entrance into Orléans may have freed Villon from a death sen-

tence, in which case his expression of gratitude should be read literally rather than as mere hyperbole: "Il semble qu'il soit déjà en prison lorsque, le 17 juillet 1460, la jeune princesse Marie, fille de Charles d'Orléans et de Marie de Clèves, fait dans Orléans son entrée solennelle. Il y a un défilé, un bal. Les prisonniers sont élargis. Sans doute Villon est-il des quelques malandrins que la joyeuse entrée de la petite princesse remet en circulation. Comme il se sentait en passe d'avoir la corde au cou, il lui paraît convenable d'exprimer sa gratitude" (389).

6. Several critics have also wondered whether certain verses in the *Testament* might be read as oblique references to the bishop's homosexual orientation, or perhaps to acts of forced homosexuality. See, for example, Yvan G. Lepage, "François Villon et l'homosexualité," *Le Moyen Age* 92 (1986): 69–89. "Villon n'aurait-il pas été la victime des appétits sexuels de l'évêque . . . ?" (82). The hypothesis, although one that has attracted interest from several commentators, is based at best on tenuous linguistic evidence.

7. Favier, 488.

8. According to one hypothesis, the channel of intercession may have been Robert Thibout, a judge in the Parlement, who had ties to Saint-Benoît-le-Bétourné, the church with which Guillaume de Villon was affiliated.

9. Favier, 495.

Chapter Three

1. In a lengthy commentary on the dating of the *Lais*, Jean Rychner concludes: "De toute façon il faut abandonner l'image romantique d'une "nuit de Noël" partagée entre la composition solitaire du *Lais* et le vol du Collège de Navarre . . ." (Jean Rychner, *Les Lais Villons et les poèmes variés*, vol. 2 [Geneva: Droz, 1977], 7–9).

2. See Winthrop H. Rice, *The European Ancestry of Villon's Satirical Testaments* (New York: Corporate Press, 1941). For examples of actual fifteenth-century wills, see Alexandre Tuetey, *Testaments enregistrés au Parlement de Paris sous le règne de Charles VI* (Paris: Imprimerie Nationale, 1880).

3. Jean Dufournet has advanced the hypothesis that Villon's rival may be Ythier Marchant, which would explain the appearance of Marchant immediately after the reference to Villon's mistress. Dufournet, *Recherches*, 259–74.

4. M. J. Freeman, " 'Faulte d'argent m'a si fort enchanté: Money and François Villon," in *Romance Studies* 24 (1994): 64.

5. For example, Jean Dufournet, *Nouvelles recherches sur Villon* (Paris: Champion, 1980), 89–96.

6. Champion, vol. 1, 128.

7. Dufournet, *Recherches*, vol. 1, 281.

8. It is in this sense that he later uses the word in lines 1501–2 of the *Testament*: "Mais, quoy que ce soit du laborieux mestier, / Il n'est tresor que de vivre a son aise" [But, however it may be with rustic chores, / No treasure matches living at one's ease].

9. Dufournet, *Nouvelles recherches*, 179.

Chapter Four

1. See, for example, Marcel Thomas, *The Golden Age: Manuscript Painting at the Time of Jean, Duke of Berry* (New York: Braziller, 1979), 54.

2. Tuetey, 302. A comparison with Villon's request reveals obvious parallels in phraseology. Other similar phrases in the *Testament* and the *Lais* reveal a familiarity with testamentary language used in the period. One plausible explanation is that Villon served for a period of time as an assistant or apprentice to a notary, copying or even helping to prepare a variety of legal documents.

3. Champion, vol. 2, 369.

4. Ibid., 370.

5. Favier, *François Villon*, 177.

6. Thuasne, *François Villon: Oeuvres*, vol. 2, 277.

7. Shirley, 230.

8. Ibid., 132.

9. For example, the will of Thomas l'Ecorché, a lawyer at the Châtelet, stipulates: "Et apres, il eslust sa sepulture en terre benoiste, et volt estre inhumé et enterré ou cymtiere des Sains Innocens, a Paris, en la grant fosse aux povres." Tuetey, *Testaments*, 427.

10. Quoted in Italo Siciliano, *François Villon et les thèmes poétiques du moyen âge* (Paris: Nizet, 1933), 253. (My translation.)

11. For further commentary on the question of Villon's imagery, see chapter 2, "Imagery," in my *François Villon and His Reader*. Sights similar to the *charniers* are rare today, but may still be found in certain ancient churches and monasteries in Greece and Italy, for example.

12. See Thuasne, vol. 2, 82–83.

13. Kuhn, *La Poétique de François Villon*, 428.

14. In *A Reading of Villon's Testament* (Birmingham: Summa Publications, 1984), I focus on the spiritual dimension of the *Testament*.

Chapter Five

1. Stéphane Gombertz, " 'Je' est un autre: Contradiction et méditation dans la poésie de François Villon," in Dufournet, *Villon hier et aujourd'hui*, 160.

2. Ibid.

3. Jean Frappier, "Pour le Commentaire de Villon, *Testament*, vv. 751–52," *Romania* 80 (1959): 191–207.

4. Thuasne, vol. 2, 311.

5. Ibid. Thuasne speculates that Villon may have in mind the work of Jean Gerson entitled *Le Livre de contemplacion*.

6. For a full discussion of this stanza see Dufournet, *Recherches*, vol. 2, 359–80.

7. See, for example, André Lanly, ed. and trans., *François Villon: Oeuvres* (Paris: Champion, 1978), p. 274, note 3.

8. Rychner, 194.

9. Thuasne, vol. 3, 353.

10. Pierre de Ronsard will continue to develop this symbolic dimension of the lute in the sixteenth century.

11. See, for example, Dufournet, *Nouvelles recherches,* 165–66, and Rychner, 248–49.

12. Sargent-Baur, *François Villon: Complete Poems,* 226.

13. "The 'rehabilitation' of the legatees is clearly meant to be ironic. Nonetheless, in the process of disguising their identity, Villon is reminding us, whether deliberately or inadvertently, that greedy old men were once carefree boys, prostitutes were once honorable women, and corrupt police agents at least have a capacity for goodness and honesty." Fein, *A Reading of Villon's Testament,* 44.

14. Pierre Champion, ed., *Charles d'Orléans, Poésies,* vol. 1 (Paris: Champion, 1924), 46. The translation is my own, taken from David Fein, *Charles d'Orleans* (Boston: Twayne Publishers, 1983), 26. "By fragmenting his personality into two distinct entities, one acting as an intermediary for the other, the poet partially dissociates himself from the emotional conflict represented by the *prison de Desplaisance"* (27).

15. "By the combination of the words *plus que pere* and *mere,* we feel, and we feel that Villon felt, the richness of the love and protection which the canon Villon gave or tried to give to his adoptive son." Evelyn B. Vitz, *The Crossroads of Intentions: A Study of Symbolic Expression in the Poetry of François Villon* (The Hague: Mouton, 1974), 56.

16. Champion, vol. 1, 112.

Chapter Six

1. Sylvia Huot, "From Life to Art: The Lyric Anthology of Villon's *Testament,"* in *The Ladder of High Designs: Structure and Interpretation of the French Lyric Sequence,* ed. Doranne Fenoaltea and David Lee Rubin (Charlottesville: University of Virginia Press, 1991), 26–40. "The versification clearly sets the ballades and rondeaux apart from the huitains, inviting analysis of these pieces as a special poetic program within the *Testament:* a small lyric anthology of fixed-form compositions embedded within the larger quasi-narrative framework of the huitains" (26).

2. *François Villon,* 63.

3. Ibid., 63.

4. Pierre Le Gentil, *Villon* (Paris: Hâtier, 1967), 133.

5. For a more extensive commentary on this section of the *Testament,* see my "The *Belle Leçon,"* chapter 5 in *François Villon and His Reader.* "Although ironic overtones are always possible in passages where the poet speaks of himself, it is difficult to imagine how a reference to the fate of the unfortunate Colin, in the absence of any clues pointing to possible ambiguity, could signal humor" (91).

6. Pierre-Yves Badel, *Introduction à la vie littéraire du Moyen Age* (Paris: Bordas, 1969), 168.

7. For a commentary on this acrostic see Karl Uitti, "A Note on Villon's Poetics," *Romance Philology* 30 (1976): 187–92; Kuhn, *La Poétique de François Villon*, 59–60; David Fein, "An Unexplored Acrostic in Villon's *Testament*," *Fifteenth-Century Studies* 6 (1983): 115–19.

8. Italo Siciliano, for example, finds a tone of deep empathy in the poem: "Il est donc près de Villon, il est donc près de son cœur, il est non seulement dans sa gratitude, mais aussi dans sa profonde sympathie." Siciliano, *François Villon et les thèmes poétiques du moyen âge*, 481.

9. Quoted in Lanly, *François Villon: Oeuvres*, 198, note 1. The translation is my own. Lanly juxtaposes the Latin quotation with the quote from the popular French drinking song: "Si je meurs, je veux qu'on m'enterre / Dans une cave où il y a du bon vin."

10. Thuasne, vol. 3, 339. "Il n'en est pas moins vrai que ces vers barbares, comme il en existe tant au moyen âge, circulaient parmi les étudiants, dans les Universités d'Europe, sous forme de parodie."

11. Roger Dragonetti, "La Soif de François Villon," in Dufournet, *Villon: Hier et aujoud'hui*, 132–33.

12. Ibid., 132.

13. François Rabelais, *Pantagruel*, ed. Pierre Michel (Paris: Livre de Poche, 1968), chap. 1, p. 61.

14. Although Villon may well be invoking a biblical precedent ("Put your hand under my thigh: I want you to swear by the Lord, the God of heaven, that you will not take a wife for my son . . ." [Genesis 24:2]), the context of the verse (given the strong sexual overtones present in the rest of the ballade) clearly indicates that the verse should be taken exactly as it appears, as a patent obscenity.

15. See Rychner, 201–2, for a summary of interpretations, including this literal reading advanced by Gaston Paris.

16. Dufournet, *Recherches*, vol. 2, 471–72..

17. For an extended commentary on the relationship between these two poems, see David A. Fein, "Joined Hearts and Severed Tongues: An Illustration of Antithetical Juxtaposition in Villon's *Testament*," *Philological Quarterly* 66 (1987): 315–24.

18. Rychner, 206.

19. Huot, 37.

Chapter Seven

1. All 15 of the ballades included in the *poèmes variés*, of course, merit attention, but given the constraints of the present study, some editorial selection is required (as in the case of the 16 ballades included in the *Testament*). I have therefore limited myself to those ballades that I find especially significant, either owing to biographical connections, content, or (in the case of the poem

written in jargon) as the representative of a particular genre. The poems are given various titles according to the manuscript source. The titles by which I refer to these ballades are the titles chosen by Sargent-Baur for her edition.

2. Two important pieces of internal evidence support this theory. First, the royal lineage of the patron (cited in the second verse of the poem) applies more aptly to Charles d'Orléans than to Jean II, the former possessing a more direct link to the royal family. Second, the reference to the Forest of Patay would mean more to an audience located in Blois (60 kilometers from Patay) than to an audience located in Moulins, the residence of Jean II (225 kilometers from Patay). Rychner, *Le Lais Villon et les poèmes variés,* 80–81.

3. Thuasne quotes an example of this phrase found in a legal document of 1454: "esperons y donner provision par maniere que tout sera content et n'y perdra chacun autre chose que l'actente . . ." (Thuasne, vol. 3, 569).

4. Job 19:21. For an excellent study of the relationship between Villon's poetry and the Book of Job, see Barbara N. Sargent-Baur, *Brothers of Dragons: Job dolens and François Villon* (New York: Garland, 1990).

5. Rychner, 114–15.

6. Champion, vol. 2, 384.

7. This triple reading of *joncherie* is advanced by Claude Thiry in his edition of Villon's poetry, *Villon: Poésies complètes* (Paris: Librarie Générale Française, 1991), 318.

8. According to the *Journal d'un Bourgeois de Paris,* 30 robbers were hanged at Montfaucon on May 4, 1431 (Shirley, 258).

9. Champion, vol. 1, 318–19.

10. Shirley, 221–22.

11. Ibid., 226.

Chapter Eight

1. Luke 6:28, *New English Bible* (New York and Oxford: Oxford University Press, 1972). All subsequent citations are from this edition.

2. Luke 6:38.

3. Luke 6:37.

4. Quoted in Odette Petit-Morphy, *François Villon et la scholastique* (Paris: Champion, 1975), 461.

5. Ecclesiastes 11:9.

6. Eccles. 11:10.

7. Eccles. 11:6–7.

8. Eccles. 11:8.

9. Thuasne, vol. 2, 120.

10. Job 7:6.

11. Sargent-Baur, *Brothers of Dragons,* especially pages 86–87.

12. The home of Jacques Cœur, which conveys the wealth of its former owner, is located in the city of Bourges, where the house now serves as a museum.

13. Psalms 103:15–16.
14. Luke 16:19–21.
15. Luke 16:24–25.
16. Dragonetti, 133.
17. Philippe Ariès, *L'Homme devant la mort* (Paris: Editions du Seuil, 1977), 188. Jean Englemann, an expert on fifteenth-century wills, emphasizes the inherently religious character of these documents: "Les invocations pieuses si universelles et si développés qu'ils contiennent nous permettent de conclure, sans pouvoir être taxé d'exagération, qu'au point de vue purement formaliste, le testament du quinzième siècle est un acte religieux." Jean Englemann, *Les testaments coutumiers au xv* siècle* (Paris: Macon, 1903), 80.
18. For examples of this artistic motif see Alberto Tenenti, *La vie et la mort à travers l'art du xv* siècle* (Paris: Armand Colin, 1952).
19. "L'alternative du mourant médiéval était la suivante: ou bien ne pas cesser de jouir des *temporalia*, hommes et choses, et perdre son âme, comme lui disaient les hommes d'Eglise et toute la tradition chrétienne, ou bien y renoncer et gagner son salut éternel: *temporalia aut aeterna?*" (Ariès, 190).
20. 1 Kings 11:1–13.
21. Judges 16:21.
22. 1 Kings 3:9.
23. 1 Kings 11:1.
24. 1 Kings 11:3.
25. Judg. 16:15.
26. 2 Samuel 13:1–30.
27. Judith 13:1–16.
28. Mark 6:20.
29. Mark 6:26.
30. I first proposed this reading of the final ballade in "The Conclusion of the *Testament*: An Image in the Shroud?" *Fifteenth-Century Studies* 5 (1982): 61–66.
31. Thiry, 250.

Chapter Nine

1. Pierre Champion, in the preface to his edition of Guyot Marchant's *Danse Macabre* (Pierre Champion, ed., *La Danse Macabre* [Paris: Editions des Quatre Chemins, 1925], 4), provides an excellent description of the *le mort:*

Il est gai, se dandine, empressé à son office, le pic sur l'épaule, aimable, fraternel, goguenard . . . Non pas le squelette précis et mécanique, mais une étonnante figure, revêtue de lambeaux de chair, au torse musclé, à la panse trouée d'où coulent des vers, qui vous regarde de ses yeux vides et vous parle de sa bouche sans lèvres . . . C'est la Mort triomphante, ou plutôt la figure du vivant transfiguré, la mort qui sasit le vif; c'est nous-même, avec notre bel avenir!

2. Tenenti, 28.

3. The fresco of the Campo *Santo in Pisa*, for example, personifies Death in the form of an aged woman who has a merciless expression, long hair, black wings, and claws on her hands and feet and brandishes a scythe. A fresco in the monastery of Subiaco (painted at the end of the the fourteenth century) depicts Death as one of the Four Horsemen of the Apocalypse, a skeleton brandishing a sword.

4. Pierre Vaillant, ed., *La Danse Macabre de 1485* (Grenoble: Editions des 4 Seigneurs, 1969), 159–60. The translation is my own.

5. Siciliano, 227–79.

6. Jean-Claude Muhlethaler, *Poétiques du quinzième siècle* (Paris: Nizet, 1983). Muhlethaler's observation concerning Michault Taillevent, a lesser-known contemporary of Villon, could also apply to the latter: "le proverbe ne vient pas seulement renforcer l'énoncé de la strophe, mais il s'intègre en plus parfaitement au champ sémantique . . ." (88–89).

7. Vaillant, 157.

8. Claude Thiry, "Villon a-t-il réelement 'mis sa vielle sous le banc'?" in Dufournet, *Villon hier et aujourd'hui*, 73–91. "Villon est avant tout un adepte, voire un maître incontesté de la "musique naturelle," des *paroules métri-fiées* . . ." (91).

9. Moreover, it is interesting to note certain curious resemblances between the image of the *ménestral* in Marchant's *Danse Macabre* and the wood-cut of Villon appearing in the first printed edition of his poetry (published by Pierre Levet in 1489). Appearing almost 30 years after Villon's banishment from Paris, Levet's sketch can hardly be taken as a reliable portrait, but the sketch leads one to wonder whether the artist modeled the drawing on the famous musician that could be seen on the cemetery wall.

10. For a complete study of the genre of the satirical testament in its Latin, French, and non-French vernacular forms see Winthrop T. Rice, *The European Ancestry of Villon's Satirical Testaments* (New York: Corporate Press, 1941).

11.   You shall gain your bread by the sweat of your brow
         Until you return to the ground;
         from which you were taken.
         Dust you are, to dust you shall return.   (Gen. 3:19)

12. Sargent-Baur, *Complete Poems,* 226.

Selected Bibliography

EDITIONS AND TRANSLATIONS
Dufournet's edition includes an excellent modern French translation of all Villon's verse. Thiry's edition (available in a relatively inexpensive paperback) includes notes on the facing page for each page of text. At the present, Thiry's is the best edition of Villon's poetry available to students. Galway Kinnell's translation represents the work of an accomplished poet, and his translations often succeed admirably in recreating the poetic effects of the original. Readers should be cautioned, however, that Kinnell's work is based on a faulty text. The most accurate translation into English, and the one based on the best text, is that of Barbara Sargent-Baur. For these reasons, I have chosen to include excerpts of her translation in my book. The editions of Rychner and Henry offer a wealth of philological and historical information, as well as many insightful commentaries on Villon's poetry. They should be considered an essential source for any serious study of Villon.

Bonner, Anthony, trans. *The Complete Works of François Villon*. New York: Bantam, 1960.

Dufournet, Jean, ed. *François Villon Poésies*. Paris: Imprimerie Nationale, 1984.

Kinnell, Galway, trans. *The Poems of François Villon*. New York: New American Library, 1965.

Lanly, André, trans. *Francois Villon, Oeuvres*. 2 vols. Paris: Champion, 1969.

Mary, André, ed. *François Villon, Oeuvres*. Paris: Garnier, 1962.

Rychner, Jean, and Albert Henry, eds. *Le Testament Villon*. 2 vols. Geneva: Droz, 1974.

———. *Le Lais Villon et les poèmes variés*. 2 vols. Geneva: Droz, 1977.

Sargent-Baur, Barbara, trans. and ed. *François Villon: Complete Poems*. Toronto: University of Toronto Press, 1994.

Thiry, Claude, ed. *François Villon, Poésies complètes*. Paris: Librarie Générale Française, 1991.

Thuasne, Louis, ed. *François Villon, Oeuvres*. 3 vols. Paris: Picard, 1923.

SECONDARY WORKS
Jean Favier's *François Villon* offers the most complete historical background on Villon and the events and conditions of fifteenth-century France related to his poetry. Favier's book is meticulously accurate and

highly readable. Pierre Champion's lengthy *François Villon* also contains useful historical background, but tends to be more speculative and less rigorous in its historical approach than Favier's book. A wealth of studies, covering practically every aspect of Villon's work, is available to scholars who wish to explore specific areas of interest. The list provided here is highly selective and constitutes only a small fraction of the total bibliography. For a brief overview of Villon's life and work, I strongly recommend Pierre Le Gentil's *Villon*. For the most recent Villon bibliography, see Robert D. Peckham's *François Villon: A Bibliography*.

Books

Anacker, Robert H. *François Villon*. New York: Twayne Publishers, 1968.

Burger, André. *Lexique de la langue de Villon*. Geneva: Droz, 1957.

Champion, Pierre. *François Villon*. 2 vols. Paris: Champion, 1913.

Demarolle, Pierre. *L'Esprit de Villon*. Paris: Nizet, 1968.

————. *Villon: un testament ambigu*. Paris: Larousse, 1973.

Dérens, Jean, Jean Dufournet, and Michael Freeman, eds. *Villon hier et aujourd'hui: Actes du colloque pour le cinq-centième anniversaire de l'impression du Testament de Villon*. Paris: Bibliothèque historique de la Ville de Paris, 1989.

Deroy, Jean. *François Villon: recherches sur le Testament*. The Hague: Mouton, 1967.

Dufournet, Jean. *Nouvelles Recherches sur Villon*. Paris: Champion, 1980.

————. *Recherches sur le Testament de François Villon*. 2 vols. Paris: SEDES, 1971.

Favier, Jean. *François Villon*. Paris: Fayard, 1982.

Fein, David A. *A Reading of Villon's Testament*. Birmingham, Alabama: Summa Publications, 1984.

————. *François Villon and His Reader*. Detroit: Wayne State University Press, 1989.

Fox, John. *The Poetry of Villon*. London: Nelson, 1962.

Guiraud, Pierre. *Le Jargon de Villon ou le gai savoir de la Coquille*. Paris: Gallimard, 1968.

Kuhn, David. *La Poétique de François Villon*. Paris: Armand Colin, 1967.

Le Gentil, Pierre. *Villon*. Paris: Hâtier, 1967.

Mulethaler, Jean-Claude. *Poétiques du quinzième siècle. Situation de François Villon et Michault Taillevent*. Paris: Nizet, 1983.

Peckham, Robert D. *François Villon: A Bibliography*. New York and London: Garland, 1990.

Petit-Morphy, Odette. *François Villon et la scholastique*. Paris: Champion, 1977.

Rice, Winthrop H. *The European Ancestry of Villon's Satirical Testaments*. New York: Corporate Press, 1941.

Rossman, Vladimir R. *François Villon: les concepts médiévaux du testament*. Paris: Jean-Pierre Delarge, 1976.

Sargent-Baur, Barbara. *Brothers of Dragons: Job Dolens and François Villon.* New York and London: Garland, 1990.

Siciliano, Italo. *François Villon et les thèmes poétiques du moyen âge.* Paris: Nizet, 1933.

Vertone, Teodosio. *Rythme, dualité et création poétique dans l'œuvre de François Villon.* Rome: Lucarini, 1983.

Vitz, Evelyn B. *The Crossroads of Intentions: A Study of Symbolic Expression in the Poetry of François Villon.* The Hague: Mouton, 1974.

Articles and Book Chapters

Blakeslee, Merritt R. "Le *Lais* et le *Testament* de François Villon: Essai de lecture freudienne." *Fifteenth-Century Studies* 5 (1982): 1–8.

Calin, William. "Observations on Point of View and the Poet's Voice in Villon." *L'Esprit Créateur* 7 (1967): 180–187.

DuBruck, Edelgard. "Villon's Two Pleas for Absolution." *L'Esprit Créateur* 7 (1967): 188–196.

Edelman, Nathan. "A Scriptural Key to Villon's *Testament*." *Modern Language Notes* 72 (1957): 345–51.

Fein, David A. "The Conclusion of the Testament: An Image in the Shroud?" *Fifteenth-Century Studies* 5 (1982): 61–68.

———. "An Unexplored Acrostic in Villon's *Testament*." *Fifteenth-Century Studies* 6 (1983): 115–19.

———. "Joined Hearts and Severed Tongues: An Illustration of Antithetical Juxtaposition in Villon's *Testament*." *Philological Quarterly* 66 (1987): 315–24.

———. "Time and Timelessness in Villon's *Testament*." *Neophilologus* 71 (1987): 470–73.

Frank, Grace. "The Impenitence of François Villon." *Romanic Review* 37 (1946): 225–36.

———. "Villon's Poetry and the Biographical Approach." *L'Esprit Créateur* 7 (1967): 159–69.

———. "Pour le Commentaire de Villon, *Testament*, vv. 751–52." *Romania* 80 (1959): 191–207.

Frappier, Jean. "Paris dans la poésie de François Villon." *Romance Philology* 22 (1968–69): 396–407.

Freeman, Michael. " 'Faulte d'argent m'a si fort enchanté': Money and François Villon." *Romance Studies* 24 (1994): 59–70.

Hayes, Joseph J. "Gothic Love and Death: François Villon and the City of Paris." *Journal of Popular Culture* 11 (1978): 719–29.

Huot, Sylvia. "From Life to Art: The Lyric Anthology of Villon's *Testament*." In *The Ladder of High Designs: Structure and Interpretation of the French Lyric Sequence,* edited by Doranne Fenoltea and David Lee Rubin. Charlottesville: University of Virginia Press, 1991.

Lacy, Norris J. "The Flight of Time: Villon's Trilogy of Ballades." *Romance Notes* 22 (1982): 353–58.

———. "Villon in his Work: The *Testament* and the Problem of Personal Poetry." *L'Esprit Créateur* 18 (1978): 60–69.

Lepage, Yvan G. "François Villon et l'homosexualité." *Le Moyen Age* 92 (1986): 69–89.

Pallister, Janis L. "Attrition and Contrition in the Poetry of François Villon." *Romance Notes* 11 (1969): 392–98.

Payen, Jean-Charles. "Le coup de l'étrier: Villon martyr et Golliard ou comment se faire oublier quand on est immortel?" *Etudes Françaises* 16 (1980): 21–34.

Peckham, Robert D. "François Villon's *Testament* and the Poetics of Transformation." *Fifteenth-Century Studies* 11 (1985): 71–83.

———. "Textual Orality: Patterns of Ambiguity in François Villon's *Testament*." *Fifteenth-Century Studies* 17 (1990): 291–98.

Pinkernell, Gert. "François Villon, La Ballade des contrevérités: Aphorismes pour un public criminel." *Zeitschrift für Romanische Philologie* 101 (1985): 28–44.

Regalado, Nancy Freeman. "Effet de réel, Effet du réel: Representation and Reference in Villon's *Testament*." *Yale French Studies* 70 (1986): 63–77.

Sargent-Baur, Barbara. "Communication and Implied Audience(s) in Villon's *Testament*." *Neophilologus* 76 (1992): 35–40.

Speer, Mary B. "The Editorial Tradition of Villon's *Testament*." *Romance Philology* 31 (1977): 344–61.

Storme, Julie A. "Love in the *Testament*." *Romance Notes* 24 (1984): 270–76.

Terdiman, Richard. "The Structure of Villon's *Testament*." *Publications of the Modern Language Association* 82 (1967): 622–33.

Uitti, Karl. "A Note on Villon's Poetics." *Romance Philology* 30 (1976): 187–92.

Weinmann, Heinz. "L'Economie du *Testament* de François Villon." *Etudes Françaises* 16 (1980): 35–61.

Wilkins, Nigel. "François Villon, poète universel." *Romania* 103 (1982): 338–44.

Other Related Works

Ariès, Philippe. *L'Homme devant la mort*. Paris: Seuil, 1977.

Clark, James M. *The Dance of Death in the Middle Ages and the Renaissance*. University of Glasgow, 1950.

Shirley, Janet, trans. *A Parisian Journal: 1405–1409*. Oxford: Clarendon Press, 1968.

Zumthor, Paul. *Essai de poétique médiévale*. Paris: Seuil, 1972.

Index

INDIA AND THE WEST

HARVARD UNIVERSITY CENTER FOR THE STUDY OF WORLD RELIGIONS

Studies in World Religions

edited by
M. David Eckel

Studies in World Religions publishes monographs, translations, and collections of essays on the comparative study of religion, on religious traditions, and on methodological issues in the study of the world's religions, as well as proceedings of conferences and colloquia sponsored by Harvard's Center for the Study of World Religions.

Number 4 ⎯⎯⎯⎯⎯⎯⎯⎯⎯⎯⎯⎯⎯⎯⎯⎯⎯⎯⎯⎯⎯⎯⎯⎯⎯⎯⎯

INDIA AND THE WEST
The Problem of Understanding
Selected Essays of J. L. Mehta

INDIA AND THE WEST
The Problem of Understanding
Selected Essays of J. L. Mehta

Scholars Press
Chico, California

INDIA AND THE WEST
The Problem of Understanding

Selected Essays of J. L. Mehta
With an Introduction
by Wilfred Cantwell Smith

Library of Congress in Publication Data

Mehta, J. L. (Jaswant Lal), 1931-
India and the West, the problem of understanding.

   (Studies in world religions ; 4)
    1. Philosophy—Addresses, essays, lectures.
1. Title. II. Series.
B29.M453   1985   85-2050
ISBN 0-89130-826-1
ISBN 0-89130-827-X (pbk.)

Printed in the United States of America
on acid-free paper

To

John Braisted Carman

in friendship and gratitude

CONTENTS

FOREWORD

In a lecture that marked his last semester as visiting
professor in the Center for the Study of World Religions,
Professor Mehta remarked:

> I suppose it is this sense of a mysterious unity
> in all otherness as concretely experienced and
> enabling us to want to listen to the alien
> voice, that constitutes the Western preoccupa-
> tion with the other, as it does the non-western
> openness to winds blowing from the West.

In his own graceful way, Professor Mehta was commenting on
the complex currents that ran through his own scholarly
career and enriched the experience of all who worked with
him as students or as colleagues in his years at Harvard.
For many he seemed to embody the spirit of cross-cultural
philosophical and religious studies. Trained in India in
western psychology and philosophy, Professor Mehta was
able to stand in a creative sense on the margins of two
traditions. He not only could speak with authority from
both the western and Indian perspectives, but he could
reflect on the act of speaking itself, in a way that
continually sparked new insights for those of us who were
fortunate enough to work with him.

The essays in this volume were chosen by Professor
Mehta and the editorial staff of *Studies in World Religions*
to show both the range of his scholarly interests and the
way in which those interests developed during the major
portion of his career. The reader will find that the
essays are arranged in rough chronological order. The
first essay, "The Concept of the Subjective," was presented at the All-India Seminar at the Centre of Advanced
Study in Philosophy, Visva-Bharati University, in 1965,

ix

the year in which Professor Mehta became Professor of
Philosophy at Banaras Hindu University. The last seven
essays in this volume first appeared between 1968 and
1978, the period in which Professor Mehta's attention was
shifting to problems posed by the American academic
environment. In 1968 he began the series of visiting
appointments at Harvard that culminated in his full-time
presence on the Harvard faculty from 1973 to 1978. The
essays "Problems of Inter-cultural Understanding in
University Studies of Religion" and "Heidegger and
Vedanta: Reflections on a Questionable Theme" show the
interest in cross-cultural questions that came to play
such an important role in his thinking during his years at
Harvard. Both these essays were written during his years
as a visiting professor in this Center.

As editor of the *Series* I have the pleasant responsibility to acknowledge the help of many colleagues and
friends who have contributed to the production of this
volume. First, there is Professor Jane Smith, my pre-
decessor as editor, who presided over this project in its
early stages and whose editorial wisdom is evident in many
ways throughout the book. Professor Smith was ably assisted
by William Darrow, whose editorial and production skills
are so amply demonstrated in earlier volumes in this
series. More recently the jobs of editorial and production assistants have fallen to Mary McGee and Helen Schultz,
and with them the responsibility of overseeing the myriad
of steps necessary to bring a manuscript to completion.
To these four and to all others who have had a hand in the
production of this volume, I am deeply grateful.

Finally, I would like to express my gratitude to
Professor Wilfred Cantwell Smith, who agreed in the last
few months before his retirement from Harvard to add an
introduction to this volume. In his final lecture at the
Center, Professor Mehta spoke of Professor Smith's conception of human history as essentially religious history as

a concept that helped lead the discipline of the study of
religion out of its infancy and into maturity, a maturity
in which it could find "an integrative conceptual center
and a comprehensive, unifying perspective." Those words
describe the vision that Professor Mehta was seeking in
his own essays. It is appropriate that Professor Smith
should add his own voice to this volume, and for that we
are very grateful.

Harvard University   M. David Eckel
January 1985

INTRODUCTION

To any thinker pondering the intellectual problems of
the modern world, the reward will surely be great from
studying these uniquely illuminating pieces. They are
the work of an acute intelligence, philosophically expert.
That is obviously an important point; yet equally significant, and underlying the adverb "uniquely" just used, is
that the author furnishes us with the insights of a highly
qualified and sensitive participant observer. Only as we
learn to observe that in which we participate do we move
towards enhanced understanding.

Religious pluralism is beginning to be taken seriously
by religious thinkers; cultural pluralism by thinkers
about our own as well as others' cultures; philosophic (or
"worldview") pluralism has been less attentively developed
as yet, but is surely coming. A first step in each case
in one's becoming carefully aware of other positions,
vision, views, accurately delineated by outsiders; a
second, increasingly recognized, is becoming aware of them
as they appear to those within. I have pled that a third
step, now possible and requisite, is a becoming construc-
tively aware of how one's own appears to outsiders.

Not that the author of these chapters is an outsider.
He helps us all with the desired fourth step: becoming
consciously self-critical of our own orientation, and
critically self-conscious of the pluralism that subsumes
our separateness and today characterizes our being.
Professor Mehta has appropriated modern Western Philos-
ophy--especially, of course, Heidegger, on whom he is
recognized in the West as an authority--more deeply and
with more acuity than have most Westerners. He is a

salient and admirable example of the present-day univer-
salism of "modernity" in its meaning of the Western-
generated modern outlook. Yet he comes to it not from the
West but from India; and modernity cannot be fully understood unless recognized as Western-derived but global-
become, and unless understood as, once global, therein
more complex than before. The outlook serves those--
Westerners--for whom it is continuous with, however
aberrant from, their past; and also now those--for
instance, Indians--for whom it is discontinuous, however
inescapable, or however even preferred. We cannot, any of
us, understand that in which we participate unless we
understand the other co-participants.

Even our own criticism of modernity is firmer if we
discern more sensitively how it appeals to, and how it is
seen by, our fellows around the world.

Yet even apart from the pluralism issue itself, we are
helped much more fully to understand our thinking by the
assistance offered in the penetrating work of a close
participant observer.

Readers will find in these pages illumination on many
matters in which they are already engaged. Let me mention
a few that I personally have found of moment. To comparativists, striving to understand cultures other than their
own, there is reward in, for instance, the paper "Understanding and Tradition" proffered here. It was given
originally as the presidential address to the Metaphysics
and Epistemology section of the Indian Philosophical
Congress; and it therefore shows an Indian expounding to
fellow Indians current European analyses of the concept of
"understanding" (chiefly Dilthey, Husserl, Gadamer,
Heidegger), and their relevance to modern (modernized,
Westernized) Hindu intellectuals' apprehension of the
centuries-long Indian tradition to which they are in some
ways heir and from which in some ways distanced. For the
Western student of India--especially the English-speaking

Western student, whose familiarity with recent Continental thought may not be firm; yet for any Western student--the paper's significance lies not only in the substantive contribution to the problem of a modern understanding of India's past, a problem in which a Westerner is also engaged, but further, in its illuminating of a major aspect of India's present-day transitions.

Comparable is the piece on the Western idea of progress and on the important recent Western criticisms of that idea. This may be taken both as substantively interesting in itself, and as an outsider's comment, addressed in the first instance by an Indian to Indians.

Another matter that I myself, as a religionist, found illuminating is the author's changing attitude to religion, an attitude whose development can be traced here by a careful chronological reading. Mehta is a philosopher, by profession and by temperament. At one point he explicitly affirms, of course, that the philosophy/religion duality rests on a specifically Western view of things, and has to be left behind if the Indian tradition is to be seriously appreciated. Once again he was here speaking originally to Indians, while the observation is of course relevant to Western attempts to understand that tradition. To use these categories, and particularly the distinction between them, in interpreting what has been going on there, is to impose, and inevitably to distort. Various of us who are comparative historians of religion have come through our historical studies to the same conclusion, of course, and have written about it. Yet it is one thing to see this, however sharply, and another--given our modern condition, and our modern language and our modern thought-patterns and our social realities--to be able to speak or to think or to work or to live in terms of discernment.

Mehta himself, with his fundamental philosophic interests, and in his highly modern, highly Westernized, spirit and awareness and education, for long paid no attention to

religion, explicitly. He grew up in India, but in its modern phase, feeling like many intellectuals there in our day quite negative about religion, he has said; and he remarks in a recent paper not here published that for him the first lecture on religion "that made sense" he heard in his fifties (from a Western academic). Nevertheless in the latter part of his life, and this is slightly evident in the later papers gathered here, he seems gradually to have become a little less distant from Western religious thought, at least to the point of taking serious note of recent developments, and seeming to sense that a philosophic analysis should take such note.

Is this perhaps related to the fact that comparative religionists have of late taken primary interest in Indian thought, even its "philosophic" thought (and even in him as a humane thinker)? (One of the world's leading Chinese scholars of Chinese thought, himself a contemporary thinker of substance and originality, mentioned to me recently that he had had occasion to remark to his fellow philosophers in a recent [Western] philosophic congress that Western academic thinkers in philosophy, supposedly universal, are in fact strikingly less, and in religion, reputedly narrow, in fact strikingly more, hospitable to and interested in Chinese thought.

However that may be, there is reward in observing how a mind like Mehta's has been attracted by the philosophic thought of continental Europe in this century more than by the Anglo-Saxon; and especially, by the thought of Heidegger. Has the affinity for Heidegger something to do with that thinker's profound critique of the rest of the Western philosophic tradition? Indeed, one might find oneself speculating as to whether Heidegger's inherent significance, in turn, may have something to do with the point that the received distinction between philosophic and religious is idiosyncratic and not finally valid. Yet if one is to think in terms of that distinction,

Continental philosophy in the twentieth century, not least
Heidegger, has been on the whole rather closer to what is
meant by religious than has Anglo-Saxon. No doubt it is
an over-simplification, but perhaps not in the end a
misleading one, that Mehta's choice of Continental
thinkers for close study may have that sort of
significance for the comparative religionist.

It is perhaps unfair to raise this issue about a
writer who has himself made only a little of it. The
short piece "Beyond Believing and Knowing" here is,
however, germane; and in a paper published elsewhere Mehta
has written that "For an Asiatic, the fascinating thing
afoot in Heidegger's work is the appropriation of the
religious" into philosophy. (Admittedly, that sentence is
but one among a hundred, and is not developed.) I venture
to raise the matter only to illustrate my contention that
readers will indeed find stimulus in Professor Mehta's
writings for many a question in which they are interested,
as well as illumination of the topics directly addressed.

Perhaps I may close by noting, as illustrative of the
riches here, that in one footnote to one paper (n. 24 of
the final essay here) is propounded in passing a precious
new idea potentially richly productive: a number of doc-
toral dissertations are suggested in this one provocative
insight. I may also add that I find myself shedding a
tear that the author and the editors have, no doubt for
compelling reasons, had to omit from the collection
certain other essays of this enormously intelligent writer
that I personally have found helpful.

Harvard University   Wilfred Cantwell Smith
June 1984

THE CONCEPT OF THE SUBJECTIVE

Speaking of the rise of modern philosophy, Hegel
remarks in his *Lectures on the History of Philosophy*, "Now
we come for the first time properly speaking to the
philosophy of the new world and begin with Descartes....
Here we can say that we are at home, and, as sailors after
a long voyage upon stormy seas, we can cry 'land.'"
Hegel's reference here is to Descartes' discovery of the
realm of the subjective, the solid ground on which
philosophy treads henceforth, triumphantly marching to its
consummation in Hegel's own theory of the Absolute Spirit.
From the perspective of developments in recent European
philosophy, such as Phenomenology and Existential
Philosophy, it may indeed be said that the entire history
of modern philosophy since Descartes is in a sense the
history of the explication and development of a theory of
subjectivity. The conception of the subjective has varied
according to the metaphysical, epistemological or ethical
preoccupations of the philosophers from Descartes to Hegel
and according to their rationalistic or empiricistic
preconceptions. Whether the subject is conceived as the
ego cogito of Descartes, as the Leibnizian monad, as the
Transcendental Ego of Kant, as Fichte's Infinite Ego, as
the Absolute Spirit of Hegel, or as Freedom, with
Schelling, whether we follow the line of thinkers who
pursue the Cartesian *cogito* or of those who followed
Locke's "way of ideas", in each case, the realm
which is being directly or indirectly explored is the
field of human subjectivity.

Originally published in *Visva-Bharati Journal of
Philosophy* 2 (1966): 40-57.

The subjective, as opposed to the objective, may be understood in the sense of the "merely subjective", the false or the irrational. It may mean, secondly, the merely private and solipsistic as against the inter-subjectively, universally valid. This is the contrast which Heraclitus brings out in Fragment 92: "So we must follow the common, yet though my word is common, the many live as if they had a wisdom of their own," and again in Fragment 9: "The waking have one common world, but the sleeping turn aside each into a world of his own." The subjective may be understood, thirdly, in the sense of the psychological, following the Cartesian metaphysics of the dual realms of *res extensa* and *res cogitans* and his conception of the latter as a kind of container swarming with ghostly *cogitans*. This is the sense of the subjective in which it has been subjected to detailed scrutiny and scathing criticism by the later Wittgenstein, by Ryle and by Sartre. But, again since Descartes, the subjective has also been understood in the sense of the transcendental, as the ground and source of all objective validity and of the intelligibility of all that is objec- tively given. Far from constituting the realm of the false, of what merely seems, of that which encapsulates me within my own self and of the psychological, subjectivity in this sense refers to that transcendental sphere in man which alone can provide an absolute foundation to our experience and in which is grounded the "objectivity," i.e., the truth, of all that is. Subjectivity in this sense is the *subjectivum veritatis*, the *hypokeimenon*, the ground and fundament of all truth and of all that is. And it is in this sense of the term that modern philosophy may be regarded as consisting of a series of contributions towards a theory of the subjective.

Wherein lies the subjectivity of the human subject? What is its constitution? How is it related to the objec- tive sphere? The traditional textbook account of the doc- trines of the modern philosophers is largely dominated by

the perspectives of the theory of knowledge, whereas the
attempt to answer these questions in recent philosophy, in
particular by Husserl and Heidegger, goes beyond the
merely epistemological conception of the subjective and
seeks to reopen the question on the ontological level.
The theory of subjectivity, in other words, is an ontological inquiry into the nature of the subjective, in the
sense in which, according to Kant, the question, "What is
man?" is already implied in the three central questions of
metaphysics: "What can I know? What shall I do? What may
I hope for?" The main purpose of this paper is to present
this new perspective on the problem of subjectivity that
has been opened up in recent Continental philosophy. Not
more than passing reference will be made here to the
doctrines of Descartes, Kant, or Hegel, much less an
attempt to re-interpret their views from the perspective
of present-day developments. A great deal of the thought
of Husserl, Sartre and Merleau-Ponty constitutes a criticism and re-interpretation of the Cartesian *cogito* and
Hegel's dialectical theory of consciousness, with its
central doctrine of negativity, undergoes an existentialistic re-interpretation in the philosophies of the last
two. Heidegger offers a re-interpretation of Kant's
Transcendental Analytic in studied opposition to both the
Hegelian and Neo-Kantian schools and yet incorporates
Kantian and Hegelian themes, annulled and sublated, into
his own critical inquiries into the subjectivity of man
from the perspective of the question of the sense of
Being. The task of tracing these developments and transformations, however fascinating, cannot be attempted here.
Husserl's Phenomenology, with its claim to set aside all
metaphysical and epistemological presuppositions, provides
the starting-point and the setting for contemporary
inquiries into the nature of the subjective, but here too
we can do no more than use it as such, leaving it to
others to explore this primeval forest and expound the
Husserlian theory of the subjective in detail. Nor is it

possible to enter here into the details of Sartre's theory of consciousness and explain how the for-itself, or existence conceived as a creative void, as freedom and as a perpetual transcending of the given, ceaselessly liberates itself from the empirical self, the other and the in-itself, and how it is engaged in the interminable labour of an active transformation of both the self and the objective world regarded as the product of man's work. In Kant's and Hegel's theory of the subjective, in Schelling and in Kierkegaard and above all in Sartre, freedom is conceived as the very being of the subject. For Heidegger also the subjectivity of the subject lies in freedom and the little that he has written on this topic marks a significant advance over the thought of his predecessors. This, too, would require a paper by itself to develop and will not therefore be further touched upon here.

Modern philosophy has been widely characterized as a philosophy of subjectivity but in recent times it has become more and more apparent that the deeper we dig into the subjectivity of man, the further are we carried beyond a conception of the subject in the sense of the traditional subject-object dichotomy. Husserl's quest of transcendental subjectivity eventually took him into a region which can hardly be called subjectivity in the traditional sense, as Ludwig Landgrebe has pointed out. Sartre's absolute consciousness has, as he himself remarks, no longer anything of the subject in it. But it is above all in the thinking of Heidegger that we see how the most sustained effort to lay hold of the essence of subjectivity eventually leads to the annulment of the concept of the subjective and to its most radical criticism in the history of philosophy. For this reason, this paper will concentrate on an exposition of Heidegger's views and criticism of the subjective, dealing with other thinkers only as they lead up to it or are relevant in this context.

For Husserl, the wonder of all wonders is the pure ego and pure subjectivity or consciousness. Like Descartes, Husserl is primarily concerned with "a complete reforming of philosophy into a science grounded on an absolute foundation, with a radical re-building that satisfies the idea of philosophy as the all-inclusive unity of the sciences, within the unity of such an absolutely rational grounding." For, as he remarks, "With the Cartesian discovery of the transcendental ego, a new idea of the grounding of knowledge also becomes disclosed: the idea of it as transcendental grounding." As with Kant, his concern is with apodicticity and objective validity in the sciences, and his philosophizing a quest for absolute foundations. Like both he discovers these foundations in transcendental subjectivity. For Kant, transcendental consciousness constitutes the structure of pure reason, not itself experienced but inferred, not given in direct, lived experience but deduced. Unlike Kant, however, Husserl seeks, with Descartes, for the ground in the "fundamental fact" of the experienced "I am". But, unlike Descartes, Husserl is not content merely with the bare identity of the "I am" as the only thing given as indubitable in transcendental self-experience. Nor does he attempt, like Descartes, "to use the *ego cogito* as an apodictically evident premise for arguments supposedly implying a transcendent subjectivity." The phenomenological epoche (the bracketing of the world as directly experienced in the natural attitude), "lays open an infinite realm of being of a new kind, as the sphere of a new kind of experience: transcendental experience." Husserl plunges into the task of a laying open of this infinite field of transcendental experience and through his method of successive reductions, aims at bringing into existence "a science of concrete transcendental subjectivity, as given in actual and possible transcendental experience, a science that forms the extremist contrast to sciences in the hitherto accepted sense."

The phenomenological reduction is a reversal of the naive, natural attitude of an unquestioning acceptance of the world, the sum of all that is given to me in experience, and brings me to an awareness of the activity of my own consciousness as the source and ground, along with other consciousnesses, of all such givenness. The sphere of immanence or subjectivity in which these activities of world-constitution occur, however, cannot itself be any given entity or part of the world. It cannot be anything but is a pure, transcendental subject, beyond the world, itself not a thing and yet the ground of the givenness of all things. In classical Idealism, transcendental reflexion led from the world to a sphere of pure validity and ideality, to a sphere of pure *Principles*. In phenomenology, on the other hand, the reduction leads to a sphere of *experience*, equally pure, transcendental and grounding in character and yet a sphere of pure subjectivity of which it cannot be said that it is in the same sense in which all that is given to us is in the world. Husserl's attempt to ground the truth of the experienced in "the fundamental fact of the experienced 'I am'" and not in the sphere of pure principles thus immediately raises the question of the ontological status of pure subjectivity. This was pointed out by Heidegger in his letter to Husserl concerning the latter's draft of the article on Phenomenology for the *Encyclopedia Britannica*:

> There is agreement between us on the point that
> what is, in the sense of what you call "world",
> cannot be explained in respect of its transcen-
> dental constitution through a going back to an
> entity having the same kind of being. But this
> is not to say that what makes up the locus of the
> transcendental is not at all something that is.
> It raises rather the *problem*: which is the mode
> of being of the entity in which "world" is
> constituted?....It needs to be shown that the
> mode of being of a human being is totally
> different from that of all other entities and
> that precisely because it is such a mode of being
> that it contains hidden within itself the
> possibility of transcendental constitution.
> [This] is a central possibility of the factually

> existing self....The constituting subject is not
> nothing, hence it is something and has being--
> although not in the sense of something given.
> The inquiry into the mode of being of the
> constituting source is not to be evaded.

Such an inquiry, Heidegger adds, is precisely the task of
Being and Time. To be accessible even in pure experience,
this constituting source must *be*, but what is is part of
the world. The only alternative left for Husserl--since
for him to be was to be objectively given--was to think of
it as the sphere of absolute being as against the
conditioned being of the world. And this is no answer to
the question raised by Heidegger.

Reading the Cartesian starting-point from an experienced *cogito*, Sartre took the logical way out of this
difficulty by eliminating the transcendental ego and conceiving of pure, impersonal consciousness as a nothingness, a nihilating field of the for-itself forever constituting the "I" as well as the world and forever liberating
itself from them. Transcendental consciousness is for
Sartre "a fact which is absolute," "a first condition and
an absolute source of existence," whereas the Cartesian
cogito is a fully reflexive, positional or thetic
consciousness in which it becomes its own object; Sartre's
transcendental consciousness is non-thetic, immediate and
pre-reflexive consciousness of itself. Such unreflected
consciousness or consciousness in the first degree constitutes the transcendental sphere, the sphere of *absolute*
existence, i.e., a sphere of pure spontaneities which are
never objects and which determine their own existence.
Sartre is enabled thus to attain to a transcendental
grounding sphere without introducing into it anything of
the world.

Heidegger chooses another way out of the difficulty.
In Sartre, the series of phenomenological reductions is
transformed into a single act of pure consciousness
tearing itself away from the world, from the whole sphere
of objects, through a movement of nihilation rather than

reflection. Heidegger, on the other hand, completely by-passes the whole notion of reduction in his conception of the phenomenological method. How then does he go back from the world as given to the transcendental sphere in which its ground is to be disclosed? He does this by reopening the entire problem on the ontological level and unfolding it from the perspective of the question of Being. He makes an explicit and radical distinction between beings and their being, between the ontic and the ontological, where what is, the ontic, is the grounded, and the being of what is, the ontological, is the ground. He holds fast to the insight that the ground of what is cannot be found in anything that itself is a being and that the being of what is cannot itself be a being. Heidegger also realised that any inquiry into Being, any ontological inquiry into the ground of beings, must be rooted in an investigation of the being of man in whom alone the sense of Being manifests itself. This investigation of man's being or of subjectivity is therefore designated as fundamental ontology by him. In inquiring into man's being, Heidegger looks for something more basic than the transcendental ego or consciousness, for an ontological level deeper than the level of consciousness, in terms of which one can understand what it means to be consciousness itself. The subjectivity of the human subject lies solely, according to Heidegger, in the transcendence which is inherent in him. As he puts it (WGIS): "Transcendence denotes the very essence of the subject; it is the fundamental structure of subjectivity....To be a subject is to be a being in and as transcendence." Consciousness, the transcendental ego self-hood, the subject-object-relation are all secondary concepts and pre-suppose the basic fact of transcendence, in terms of which they can all be defined. "It is only through an elucidation of transcendence," Heidegger declares, "that we can seize the possibility of a determination of what 'subject' and 'subjective' mean.

Transcendence can be disclosed and grasped not by a flight into the objective (as in Platonism) but solely through a continuously renewed ontological intepretation of the subjectivity of the subject, an interpretation characterised as much by its opposition to 'subjectivism' as by its refusal to subserve 'objectivism' of any kind." The term *Dasein*, which Heidegger uses in place of consciousness, the transcendental ego or subject, is meant to convey this reference to man in terms of the transcendence inherent in him. What precisely is the *Dasein*, or as he alternatively puts it, the *Dasein* in man? Literally, it means the being or happening (*Sein*) of the "there" (*Da*), of overtness or opening up and it aptly describes the being of man, for he is a being who *is* as having to be his own overtness, clearing or illumination. Man is this there-ness of himself, of the world and of other beings, some like himself, others unlike. The name *Dasein* was chosen for the ontological sphere in which man stands as man, Heidegger explains, in order to seize in one word the relation of Being to the essential nature of man as also the essential relation of man to the openness of Being as such. In using this term "being there", he does not merely substitute a traditional term by a new one. As he has said, "It is not merely the word *Dasein* that takes the place of the word 'consciousness' and neither is it the fact designated as 'being there' that takes the place of what we call by the name of 'consciousness'. 'Being there' names rather that which should first of all enter into our ken and then appropriately be thought about, as the place, namely of the location of the truth of Being." In *Being and Time*, the essence of being-there is said to lie in its existence and this term too is meant to designate man's unique mode of being, i.e., his openness to Being or rather the fact of his being this openness itself. "The existential nature of man is the reason why he can represent being as such and why he can be conscious of them. All consciousness presupposes the ecstatically

understood existence as the *essentia* of man, where
essentia means that which enables man to be man. But
consciousness does not itself create the openness of
beings, nor is it consciousness that makes it possible for
man to stand open for beings." Consciousness is not an
entity itself but the mode of being of the entity called
man or, alternatively, in Quentin Lauer's words, "the mode
of being which things have when we are conscious of them."
For these reasons, the inquiry into the structure of
transcendence in man is called by Heidegger the Analytic
of *Dasein* or existential analytic rather than a theory
of consciousness.

Central to Husserl's theory of consciousness is the
conception of its intentionality, the view namely, that
"all consciousness is consciousness of something and that
as a *cogito* it bears within itself its own *cogitatum*."
The "of" is inseparable from consciousness. It is not a
merely static relation connecting two entities, however,
for consciousness is here conceived as activity and
orientedness towards. Consciousness as intrinsically
intentional does not merely objectivate its data, refer
them to poles of identity and synthesize them but also
constitutes the object through its own "achievements." We
may describe it as a dynamic field generating meaningfulness in things, "constituting" them as also itself as a
stream of acts through its innermost time-building depths,
characterized by Husserl as "absolute subjectivity."
Consciousness is not an entity or region of inwardness
standing by itself, not a container and not a mirror; it
neither causes the world of objects to come into being nor
is it made up of representations of these objects. The
conception of consciousness "as intentionality" implies
the rejection of the notions of an object in itself, of a
consciousness closed in on itself and producing the world
out of itself, out of the subject-object dualism of
traditional ontology. The merit of intentionality, it has
been remarked, is to explode idealism by projecting

consciousness towards the world by placing it in the
world. The world is tied to consciousness as ever already
giving itself to it and consciousness is tied to the world
as always having to give sense to it. By emptying
absolute consciousness of all content and transforming it
into a nothingness to which the world (i.e., everything,
including the "I") is wholly external, Sartre has given a
more radical sense to intentionality. Consciousness is
now itself defined by intentionality, by the movement
towards the object by virtue of which it transcends
itself. As he says, "Consciousness is purely and simply
consciousness of being consciousness of that object. This
is the law of its existence." Far from being a disinterested spectator, however, consciousness is engaged in a
ceaseless struggle with the brute-in-itself, with all
those "things" which can be objects for it, constituting a
meaningful world out of them, becoming ensnared in the
world because it is itself a lack, tearing itself away
from it by virtue of its absolute freedom, an emptiness,
in the massive fulness of being. Sartre has even charged
Husserl with misunderstanding the essential character of
intentionality. Pure subjectivity is not something that
can be given prior to the act by which it goes out of
itself to posit the given. As he says, "For consciousness
there is no being outside of that precise obligation to be
a revealing intuition of something, i.e., of a transcendent being." In other words, to say that consciousness is
consciousness of something is to say that it must produce
itself as a revealed-revelation of a being which is not it
and which gives itself as already existing when consciousness reveals it. Consciousness has no other being than
that of being a nihilating presence both to itself and to
things. Intentionality thus implies on the one hand that
consciousness in its very mode of being is embedded in a
world, that in Heidegger's words, it is a being-in-the-
world, or in Merleau-Ponty's, that we are subjects "wedded
to a world." On the other hand, the intentionality of

consciousness implies that its essence lies in transcending itself, going out of itself on existence or just
openness. It is precisely to refer to this openness
characteristic of man that Heidegger uses the term being-
there (*Da-sein*) and declares that the essence of *Dasein*
lies in its existence. As in the case of consciousness,
Heidegger finds intentionality itself rooted in something
more basic, namely, the transcendence inherent in *Dasein*.
As he remarks, "If all relating oneself to beings is
characterized as intentional, then intentionality is only
possible on the basis of transcendence; it cannot be
regarded as being identical with transcendence, far from
being itself the condition that renders transcendence
possible." (WGI5) It is thus that the theory of subjectivity, which Husserl developed in terms of consciousness,
the transcendental ego, intentionality and reduction, is
at the same time taken up and radically transformed in
Heidegger's philosophy in which these concepts find no
place. Sartre and Merleau-Ponty retain the traditional
term consciousness to designate human subjectivity, though
not without radical alteration in their ways of conceiving
its essence and structure. Consequently they retain also
the notion of intentionality, whereas in Heidegger this
basic directedness of man's being-there towards the world
is transformed into care, which is itself to be understood
in terms of temporality, and which represents man's
specific way of being open to Being.

The inquiries into the nature of subjectivity
conducted by Husserl, Heidegger, Sartre and Merleau-Ponty
are phenomenological rather than speculative and their
concern is with analysis of the structure and foundations
of experience rather than with metaphysical construction.
It will therefore be useful if a brief mention is made
here of some of the consequences for the phenomenological-
existential theory of subjectivity which follow from this
approach. We have already seen that according to the view
heralded by Husserl, consciousness is not a worldless

entity, unrelated to the world to begin with and in its
essence. Its very being lies, as Heidegger was to say
later, in being-in-the-world and it is the structure of
this concrete subjectivity with which, following
Heidegger's systematic attempt in *Being and Time*, Sartre
and Merleau-Ponty are concerned. In its basic intention,
therefore, this view seeks a radical overcoming of the
classical alternative of Realism and Idealism and of the
subject-object dichotomy; it may in fact be considered as
an attempt to carry reflection about subjectivity to a
deeper level than was accessible to traditional
"epistemology." The transcendental ego or pure consciousness of Husserl is neither a disembodied *res cogitans* nor
a detached "I think" but is inserted and involved in the
world; it is an engaged consciousness and its life is
"life-experiencing-the-world."

In the second place, subjectivity in this view is not
conceived as "*Bewusstsein überhaupt*," consciousness in
general, but as a particular, individual locus of awareness and spontaneity, not as an abstract principle but as
a concrete structure. The transcendental ego in Husserl
is a particular ego, "my own transcendental ego," a
solipsistically reduced ego. It is for this reason that
the constitution of the alter ego in me, i.e., the problem
of intersubjectivity assumes cardinal importance in his
theory of consciousness. In the fifth of the Cartesian
Meditations, he even speaks of "the total nexus of that
actual and potential intentionality in which the ego
constitutes within itself a peculiar ownness." Heidegger
makes this notion of ownness even more basic and
incorporates into it the Kierkegaardian conception of the
single, existing individual, responsible and free,
infinitely concerned about his own being and anxiously
taking upon himself the either-or of his own being. The
Analytic of *Dasein* in *Being and Time* opens with a
statement of this principle of Ipseity (*Jemeinigkeit*,
each-his-ownness, in-each-case-mineness), where Heidegger

pointedly remarks that the entity to be analysed is not
just an indifferent, anonymous being-there or man in
general but we ourselves. The being of this entity is *in
each case mine.* In its very being it is related to its
own being, is delivered over to its own being, as something it has to be and as that which is "at stake" for it.
"The being which is at stake for this entity in its very
being is in each case mine." Similarly, consciousness for
Sartre constitutes "a synthetic and individual totality
entirely isolated from other totalities of the same type."
It is an individuated spontaneity, even though impersonal
in the sense that there is no transcendental ego to own or
inhabit it. And yet, inasmuch as consciousness exists as
a presence to itself, a certain selfness or ipseity
characterizes all consciousness; as a privation or nihilation also each for-itself is defined as this particular
consciousness by being a particular privation or nihilation of a particular in-itself and not of being in
general. The plurality of consciousness, realized in the
form of a double reciprocal relation of exclusion, is for
Sartre a "primary fact," "a scandal which no logical or
epistemological optimism can cover" and which even
ontology can only seek to describe without being able to
overcome it.

A third feature of the subjective as developed in
existential thought is the conception of its facticity and
finitude. Husserl, it will be recalled, takes as his
starting-point the *fact* of the experienced "I am", though
it was not until the closing phase of his career that he
was led to reflect on the implications of this factuality,
basically different from the factuality of all other types
of entity in the ontological sense. This he calls the
faciticity of man's being and it lies in the sheer "that"
of his being thrown into existence, in being delivered
over to the "that it is and has to be" of his *Dasein.*
Man's existence is qualified by his thrownness, by his
finding himself already there in the world and left to

himself to be what and how he can in the midst of
entities, upon which he is dependent. The projects of
understanding with which man, as already existing in and
as the openness of Being, seeks to grasp the world, are
always thrown projects just as he himself in his being is
a thrown possibility, already conditioned by a past. They
are determined by all the factual particularities of the
situation in which such projects are made, not excluding
the historical. All knowledge or disclosure of truth is
thus factitious and hence imperfect, coloured and shot
through with concealment. Man has no other "essence"
except his existence, by virtue of which he ceaselessly
runs ahead of himself and projects himself upon the
future. Existence is conditioned by its facticity and
thrownness and is thus determined by the past, the
has-been. Another character of man's way of being is
termed fallenness or forfeiture by Heidegger. This is the
tendency to exist as abandoned to and taken up with the
world, as scattered among the things of the world, as not
being himself and disowned, as caught up in the present
and so faced with the task of disengaging himself from it
and winning his selfhood. Existentiality, facticity and
forfeiture together constitute the full structure of man's
being. This Heidegger defines as care, to be understood
not in the sense of a psychological process or fact but in
the ontological sense of being the condition of the
possibility of all such processes and indeed of all
experience. And care itself, i.e., the being of man, his
subjectivity, is intelligible only in terms of temporality
as its ultimate ground.

Hegel's conception of the subject as Absolute Spirit,
which can assimilate everything to itself through the
exercise of total reflexion and to which nothing can in
principle remain alien or opaque, was the culmination of
the Platonic striving to bring all that is factual under
the transparency of essence. Against this reduction of
the subject to pure and absolute thought, against this

supremacy of the concept, Kierkegaard, Marx, Feuerbach,
Dilthey and others brought forward cogent criticisms which
all tended, despite the diversity of their approaches and
interests, to affirm the finitude of the human subject,
its irreducibility to pure reason and its concreteness and
historicity. The later Schelling in particular, showed
that spirit or reason in its ceaseless self-meditation
experiences the sheer "that" of its own activity as a
"that" which resists the transparency of reason and so
cannot be conceived as a pure "what". In contemporary
existential thought, this critical reaction against
Idealism has developed into a phenomenology of the
concrete subject and in Heidegger this takes the form of
an ontology of man and so also in Sartre. The human
subject, instead of being conceived as a detached
spectator engaged in universal reflection, is shown to be
rooted in the irreducible "that" of existence. The
subjectivity of this subject is not to be found in a
timeless essence but in the finitude of man's factual
existence in a particular historical situation. It is
true that man's subjectivity lies in freedom and transcendence, but this freedom and transcendence are finite
and conditioned by the sheer contingency of man's givenness to himself as a possibility to be realized, his being
given over to himself, as well by his dependence upon
entities other than himself. The givenness of entities
and the occurrence of himself as such transcendence does
not lie in the power of man; as transcendence, man exists
as grounding in character, but he himself is powerless
over both the sheer "that" of being a ground and of that
which he grounds through his creative projects.

Heidegger is at great pains to show that the being of
man cannot be determined on the basis of traditional
epistemology which regards man as essentially the subject
of knowledge and conceives the latter as a relation
between subject and object. Knowing is itself a derivative mode of *Dasein*'s being-in-the-world and is grounded

in a prior being-already-with-the-world which is
essentially constitutive of *Dasein*'s being. As a way of
being, knowing represents a modification of the primordial
being-in of *Dasein* and of the disclosure of a world that
goes with it. "Knowing does not in the first instance
produce a *commercium* of the subject with a world, nor does
it arise from an action of the world upon a subject.
Knowing is a mode of *Dasein* founded upon being-in-the-
world." Man's being or subjectivity therefore cannot be
identified with a cognitive subjective in the narrow
sense. Similarly, when subjective is understood in the
sense of the *a priori*, the subject means not an entity
which at first is unrelated to a world but subject in the
"ontologically properly understood" sense of *Dasein* as
constituted by its being-in-the-world. Apriority has in
fact nothing to do with inherence in an ideal, worldless
subject, as Scheler and Hartmann had demonstrated even
before Heidegger, nor is it confined to knowledge as such
and to the categorical structure of the known. Apriority
extends to the ontological and existential sphere of the
whole of experience and refers primarily to the factual
subject, *Dasein*, and to its being-in-the-world. One of
the basic aims of Heidegger in *Being and Time* is to
demonstrate that the conception of Being implicitly taken
for granted in all ontology up till now has been that of
an entity simply there, present at hand, objectively given
or *vorhanden* and that in consequence the being of man also
has so far been understood in the light of that conception. Man's unique mode of being, however, is radically
different and therefore inaccessible to the traditional
ontology of the *Vorhanden*. It cannot be determined in
terms of the categories which are applicable only to
substantially given, *vorhanden* entities. Unlike all other
entities, man exists, i.e., he *is* as transcendence, as
being-in-the-world, as comprehending being, as concerned
with his own being, as sheer possibility, thrown into
being and yet always ahead of himself towards his own

future, in short, as care. The true character of human subjectivity is describable only in terms of existentialities, not categories, and these are to be thought of not as properties qualifying it but as ways of being of the factual *Dasein*.

The traditional ontology, the "I" or the self is regarded as the true *subjectum*, the underlying ground, as that which remains the same through the multiplicity of its experiences. But in this way one still conceives the "I" or self as something *vorhanden*, present-at-hand and substantially given, whereas the "substance" of man lies, not in any ideally constructed or inferred entity that is presumably unchanging and abiding but in his existence, in the factual way of his being-in-the-world as *Dasein*. If the "I" and selfhood are essential determinations of *Dasein*, they must be given an existential meaning, for it is as existing that we can gain or lose our selfhood, can realize ourselves or fail to do so. In our average, everyday mode of being, we go out into and are merged in the world of our preoccupations, including our being-with-others, and are thus not "ourselves". The "who" of this everyday being-with-others is the anonymous "they", the everyman, where each man is the other and nobody his own self, where the self of *Dasein*, or that of the other, has not yet found (or lost) itself, being dissipated in the "they" and the world of its practical concerns. Disengagement from this mode of being and disclosure of selfhood always occurs first as a sweeping away of all that veils and darkens it, as a pulling down of the fence of dissimulation which man raises up against his own self. Thus "the self-sameness of an authentically existing self is divided by a wide gulf from the identity of an 'I' that remains the same in the midst of a diversity of experiences." The ontological concept of the subject characterizes the sameness and permanence of something that is all the time substantially present and not the selfhood of the "I" *qua* self and hence to determine the

"I" ontologically as subject in this sense is to regard it
as a *vorhanden* entity. The self as ontologically constituted, in other words, cannot be derived either from an
"I" substantially conceived or from a subject and neither
is it the permanently *vorhanden* ground of care as the
being of man. It must rather be understood existentially
in terms of man's authentic potentiality of being himself,
i.e., in terms of the authenticity of *Dasein* as care. The
permanence of the self lies, in this view, not in the
persistence of an abiding subject but in the constancy and
steadfastness of the *Dasein* that has achieved authentic
existence. And since, according to Heidegger, the being
of *Dasein* (i.e., care) is itself grounded in temporality,
the subject in the ontological sense of the existing
Dasein is temporal through and through. Neither timeless
nor worldless, human subjectivity is yet not something
"in" time or "in" the world. Such a mode of being belongs
to substantial, objectively given entities alone, whereas
Dasein, the non-substantial factual subject, is in its
very ontological constitution worldly and timeish. With
care as its being, it is itself rooted in a primordial
temporality, of which time as an unending succession of
"nows" is a derivative and degenerate manifestation and
which is the ultimate condition of the possibility of the
being-there of man as being-in-the-world. This is also
the reason why historicity is an intrinsic constituent of
the subjectivity of man and of world as an existentiality
of *Dasein*.

"Everything that is," Heidegger has remarked, "*is,*
independently of the experience, the cognition and the
comprehending through which it is revealed, discovered,
and determined. But its being "is" only in the understanding of that entity to whose being there belongs such
a thing as an understanding of Being." Idealism is right
in emphasizing that Being and Reality are only "in
consciousness," i.e., that they manifest themselves only
within man's understanding and that Being, ever

transcending the entity of which it is the being, cannot
be explained in terms of beings. But does this mean that
man is the ultimate subject or ground of all that is?
Man's true subjectivity lies, as explained above, in the
Dasein in man, but does this mean that *Dasein* constitutes
a subject in relation to the being of all beings or to
Being as such? *Subjectum* is the Latin translation of the
Greek *hypokeimenon* and means literally what underlies,
what lies at the bottom and constitutes the basis, that
which already by itself lies before and presents itself.
Before the modern period in philosophy was ushered in by
Descartes, not merely man but every entity, in so far as
it has being, was conceived as *subjectum*, both in the
ontological sense of anything that is as well as in the
logical sense of the subject of all predication. It is
only since Descartes that man, the human ego, has come to
mean in a predominant manner the "subject" as that which
lies at the ground of everything that is taken as being.
Torn from the Medieval security of faith in the salvation
of the individual immortal soul, man has since then been
thrown back upon himself, to seek within himself the certainty and assurance of what he can know, aim at and have
in his grip. It is Heidegger's merit to have shown how
the history of modern Western philosophy since Descartes
constitutes the story of the unfoldment and rapid
acceleration of a subjectivism in which not only does man
become the ground and measure of everything but in which
there is a complete transformation of what it means to be
measure and ground, of what it means to be true and of
what it means to *be*. The modern quest of objectivity, in
science and in philosophy, is itself a manifestation of
this subjectivism, for here everything that is is
conceived as being an object for a subject and as being
grounded in a subject. As he says,

> At the beginning of modern philosophy stands the
> sentence of Descartes: "I think, hence I am."
> All consciousness of things and of the totality
> of what is is traced back to the self-

consciousness of the human subject as the
unshakable ground of certainty. The reality of
the real is determined henceforth as objectivity,
as something that is conceived as projected and
held over-against and confronting it, *by* a
subject and *for* it. The reality of the real
means representedness *by* the representing subject
and *for* it.

The objectification of all that is is accomplished through
the activity of re-presentation which aims at so bringing
entities before itself that man can count on them,
ascertain and certify them, hold them fast and catch and
possess them in his grasp through his conceptualizing
thought. When man is regarded as subject, his being thus
emerges as of the nature of pure willing and his relationship to what is an assault on his being.

In defining man as *Dasein* and his substance as existence, Heidegger sought to overcome this conception of man
as subject, though at the stage of writing *Being and Time*
he was still enmeshed in the idiom of the subjectivistic
tradition. The core of human subjectivity lies in its
openness to Being, not merely in his standing out of
himself, i.e., his ek-sistence, but in his insistence, in
his standing within the light of Being. In this sense man
is no "subject", neither within Reason nor as Spirit, but
himself subject to the happening of that primordial
un-hiddenness which carries him, needs and uses him and
which Heidegger calls the Truth of Being itself and not
merely the truth of beings with which metaphysics has so
far concerned itself. Man's relationship to others, to
things and to himself rests, as indicated earlier, on his
openness to Being and on the projective and interpretative
understanding of Being inherent in him. In this sense and
to this extent only man is grounding and a subject. But
once it is realized that man's relationship to these is
itself rooted in the way Being reveals itself in man and
in the way it at the same time conceals itself from him,
that neither the being of beings nor the Truth of Being
itself is a construct of man and his understanding and

that the relationship of man and Being is entirely governed from the side of Being, everything turns round, as it were, and it becomes necessary to determine man's nature in the light of Being rather than in terms of an eternal essence intrinsic to man as such alone. Man is seen now as no longer a subject, the self-grounding ground of all that is, for his own nature is found to be grounded in the Truth of Being as such. He is neither a subject as conceived substantially and categorically, as a *vorhanden* entity, in the metaphysical tradition nor, in the ultimate instance, a subject in the existentialistic sense dwelt upon earlier in this paper. The existentialities of man, his being-in-the-world as existence, his facticity and forfeiture, care itself as the being of man, have now to be understood as being grounded in the Truth of Being in which man has his dwelling. For man, as Heidegger puts it in the non-conceptual language of a thinking that is no longer representational, is not the lord of what is; man is the shepherd of Being.

> Man is rather "thrown" by Being itself in the Truth of Being so that, ek-sisting in this manner, he may keep watch over and tend the Truth of Being, in order that in this light of Being, what is may manifest itself as it is. Whether and how it manifests itself, whether and how God and the gods, history and nature enter into the clearing or luminosity of Being, present or absent themselves, does not stand under the decision of man. The arrival of what is depends on the destiny of Being. For man, the question that remains is whether he can find that appropriate and adequate function of his own nature which is in correspondence with this destiny; for it is in conformity with this that man, as one who ek-sists, has to guard the Truth of Being. Man is the shepherd of Being.

The understanding of Being, both the being of things and his own, is inherent in man as his very essence and specific virtue. But how he understands it and in what terms he conceives it does not depend so much upon man's will to conceive as on the way Being reveals itself to and conceals itself from him. "The understanding of Being,"

Heidegger says, "does not mean at all that man as subject possesses a subjective representation of Being and that Being is a mere representation....Understanding of Being means that man by nature stands in the openness of the project of Being and endures the understanding as thus meant. When the understanding of Being is conceived in this way, the representation of man as subject is, to speak with Hegel, brushed aside." The conception of man as subject is a consequence of man's erroneous way of *being* in relation to Being and of understanding this relationship accordingly. But this "error" is a fateful one not only in the sense that it determines henceforth all his dealing with himself, with others and with all that is, but in the sense that it is not so much man's doing as something fated and brought to pass by Being itself. In the second place, the conception of man's being as subject is itself rendered possible on the basis of an *a priori* conception of the being of what is as itself the *hypokeimenon*, the underlying ground, prevailing throughout in the entire metaphysical tradition of the West. The subjectivity of man is only the modern form, and a consequential modification of what Heidegger calls the subjectivity of Being in this tradition. How the concepts of subject, ground and enduring presence, in terms of which Being has been conceived since Plato, are utterly inadequate to the truth of Being itself cannot be dealt with on the present occasion.

THE PHILOSOPHICAL NECESSITY OF EXISTENTIALISM

Existentialism as a movement of thought is not limited to the academic field of philosophical scholarship but embraces the wider sphere of cultural activity: literature, political writing and popular philosophy and religious thought. It has been widely assailed by critics as the effervescence of a passing mood, as a phenomenon of decadence or as symptomatic of the spiritual malaise which has overtaken the world today. As a philosophy it has been decried as a merely transitory outbreak of irrationalism, romanticism and as a futile gesture of despairing revolt against the time-honoured classical tradition of western metaphysics. And yet it would be a mistake, as I shall try to show in this article, to treat it as one of the "isms" that blossom for a while in the intellectual field, spend their force and wither away. Like its counterpart in the Anglo-American world, Logical positivism, it has few adherents today. It has already become part of the history of philosophy and contemporary European thought is moving into fields which cannot be designated with the title of Existentialism. Of the living philosophers who fathered this movement few are agreeable to being called existentialists. Even Jean-Paul Sartre, who was, is now more concerned with assigning limits to this type of thought than claiming for it a place comparable to the great philosophies of the past. We must not, however,

---

Two lectures given at the University of Delhi in 1966, originally published under the title "Existential Philosophy" in *Proceedings of the All-India Seminar* (2), Centre of Advanced Study in Philosophy, Banaras Hindu University, 1967, pp. 85-107.

on this account lose sight of the seriousness of intellectual purpose behind the strictly philosophical core of the
movement nor neglect to take stock of the abiding contribution to philosophy that this movement has made. In the
course of this essay I shall try to give an idea of the
historical background and philosophical necessity of
existentialism, say something about the general features
of existentialist thought as represented by Jaspers,
Heidegger and Sartre, and conclude with remarks aimed at
assessing the enduring philosophical worth of this new way
of thinking.

Existentialism, in the first place, is the expression
of a peculiar historical situation in the spiritual condition of the man of today. If, as Hegel said, philosophy
is its time grasped in thought, then existentialism is the
characteristic manifestation of the spiritual climate of
the present age. It is a philosophy of crisis, giving
voice to a situation in which established certainties have
broken down, values and forms of bygone order no longer
experienced as binding. Such situations of homelessness
and spiritual insecurity are a recurring feature of man's
historical life on earth. Classical expression of such
moods can be found in the Old Testament as well as the
New, in Greek tragedy, in Socrates, the Stoics, Saint
Augustine, Pascal, Jacobi and Hamann. In modern times, it
is above all the Danish theologian Soren Kierkegaard,
generally called the father of this movement, who has
contributed massively to the breakdown of inauthentic and
false securities and who has laid down the basic pattern
of a new mode of philosophical reflection. He has laid
bare the implications of spiritual crisis and insecurity
and opened up a new area of philosophical exploration, the
field of concrete, individual subjectivity. But even
Kierkegaard dwelt in the security of faith and as a true
Christian had an eternal God standing unshaken in tne
midst of a world gone to rack and ruin. Since Friedrich
Nietzsche, who gave for our era the definitive expression

to the final breakdown of past values and of the Platonic-Christian framework within which western man lived till then, even this last refuge of religious certainty has gone. The secularized faith in Reason and Progress which marked the buoyant optimism with which the present century opened was finally uprooted by the two world wars and the time was ripe for poet and philosopher to lament, to herald and to depict the desolate landscape of a world-wide wasteland and look for a hidden seed or gem from which a new spiritual life could blossom or a new ray of light could go forth into the future. If existentialism is a philosophy of crisis, it is one which has arisen in response to the deepest extremity of man's intellectual condition in the course of his historical existence. And to the extent to which human spiritual life has an aspect of perennial crisis, the insights of existentialism constitute an essential supplement to the classical *philosophia perennis*.

But existentialism, far from being a passing fad, vogue or malady, supplements traditional metaphysics even in a more far reaching sense than the one mentioned above. The central characteristic of the founders of western philosophy and science, the Greeks, was their attitude of pure, detached contemplation, their pursuit of reality as objectively given, their quest of an unchanging conceptual order which would correspond to it and enable us to grasp it. This attitude and approach to reality, beyond the opposition of rationalism and empiricism, is responsible for the development of metaphysics as a scientific discipline along with that of logic as its principal instrument. But this pursuit of objective, rationally ascertained knowledge left out of account the concrete reality of the thinker himself, with his hopes and fears, his aspirations and cravings, his concern with his own self and its relation to the world. The realm of the subjective and of the soul's destiny, of all that matters

in life, of life itself, one may say, was left to literature, art and religion. It is only with the discovery of
man as an individual since the Renaissance and of the
realm of the subjective since Descartes that the way has
been paved for the appropriation of this realm by
philosophy. Cartesian subjectivism, however, was itself
linked up with its inseparable counterpart, rationalistic
objectivism, and it was not until recently that philosophers have been able to reach beyond the subject-object
dichotomy to a deeper conception of human subjectivity.
All existentialist thinkers are united in their rejection
of objectifying thought, following Kierkegaard's declara-
tion that subjectivity is truth. Says Kierkegaard,

> when the question of truth is raised in an objec-
> tive manner, reflection is directed objectively
> to the truth, as an object to which the knower is
> related (as another objectively given entity).
> Reflection is not focussed upon the relationship,
> however, but upon the question of whether it is
> the truth to which the knower is related....When
> the question of truth is raised subjectively,
> reflection is directed subjectively to the nature
> of the individual's relationship; if only the
> mode of this relationship is in truth, the
> individual is in the truth even if he should
> happen to be thus related to what is not true.
> [Further,] the only reality to which an existing
> individual may have a relation that is more than
> cognitive, is his own reality, the fact that he
> exists; this reality constitutes his absolute
> interest. Abstract thought requires him to
> become disinterested in order to acquire know-
> ledge; the ethical demand is to become infinitely
> interested in existing....The real subject is not
> the cognitive subject...but the ethically
> existing subject....The ethical lays hold of each
> individual and demands that he refrain from all
> contemplation, especially of humanity and the
> world; for the ethical, as being the internal,
> cannot be observed by an outsider.

Kierkegaard took recourse to paradox, irony and devious
modes of indirect communication. Jaspers warns constantly
and explicitly against taking the basic terms of his
philosophy as referring to objectively cognizable entities

and wishes his philosophizing to be understood as appeal
rather than as a series of statements, from one existing
individual to another. Heidegger has struck the hardest
blow against the traditional ontology of objective
presence and regards genuine thought as a response to the
call of Being, an evocative gesture of thanksgiving and
surrender. Sartre's concern is with the *cogito* but not in
the Cartesian form of thought confronting an object. The
starting-point of philosophy for him is the pre-reflexive
cogito, prior to the emergence of the subject-object
dichotomy and its immediate aim is not detached contemplation of a pre-given reality but thinking in the
perspective of a possible change, change towards greater
freedom, inner as well as outer. Marcel distinguishes
sharply between problem and mystery, the former calling
for a universally valid answer, the latter eluding all
objectification because here the subject is involved in
what it is trying to understand and therefore cannot stand
over against it. In Marcel's words,

> My effort can be best described as an attempt to
> establish (an ontology) which precludes all
> equation of being with *Ding*....My aim [is] to
> discover how a subject....is related to a reality
> which cannot in this context be regarded as
> objective, yet which is persistently required and
> recognized as real....The undertaking [has] to be
> pursued within reality itself, to which the
> philosopher can never stand in the relationship
> of an onlooker to a picture.

It is in this sense that existentialism must be regarded
as a completion, a corrective and necessary supplement to
traditional metaphysics. Unlike the latter, it does not
aim at laying down universally valid and necessary
propositions about what is the case but develops a new
mode of reflection more adequate to that dynamic
unobjectifiable reality in which the thinking subject is
inextricably involved and which is of the utmost moment
and concern for it.

What then is existentialism and what, if we consider
only the central philosophical core of its doctrines, are
the philosophically relevant and serious influences that
have gone into its making and the issues and disciplines
that have emerged from it? It has often been remarked
that existentialism cannot be defined in one sentence,
that it is not a single, well-defined movement within
philosophy possessing a common set of ideas, that it is
not a philosophy but a mood embracing a number of
disparate philosophies, the differences among them being
more basic than the temper which unites them. There is
consensus among textbooks as to the principal representatives of this philosophy: Nietzsche and Kierkegaard are
commonly included as forerunners but an important
anthology also includes selections from Heraclitus, the
Old and the New Testaments and Meister Eckhart, from
Nicolas Berdyaev, Jacob Boehme and Pascal, from Hasidism,
from Schelling, Feuerback and Karl Marx, from Hermann
Melville and Dostoevsky. Among contemporary thinkers,
Karl Jaspers, Martin Heidegger, Jean-Paul Sartre and
Gabriel Marcel are generally included, but also sometimes
the Spanish thinker, Ortega y Gasset, Maurice Merleau-
Ponty, Jacques Maritain, Martin Buber, Albert Camus,
Rainer Maria Rilke, Franz Kafka, Paul Tillich, Franz
Rosenzweig and Edmund Husserl. To this list may be added,
among forerunners, the psychoanalyst Sigmund Freud, and
Henri Bergson and Wilhelm Dilthey as representatives of
Lebensphilosophie; amongst contemporaries, Protestant
theologians like Karl Barth, Brunner, Bultmann, Gogarten
etc., and Catholics such as Guardini, Przywara, Hacker and
Peter Wurst. Among psychiatrists, we may also include
Binswanger, Boss, Strauss, May, Fraenkel, Moreno, Rogers,
Laing and Cooper. What is common to all of these is their
concern with man in the depths of his being, either in
relation to a transcendental reality, or in relation to
other men, or in his own Promethean self. These writings

may be regarded, from their different perspectives, presuppositions, points of departure and approach, as contributions to the discipline of philosophical anthropology,
which must be sharply distinguished from psychology and
all other empirical sciences of man. As Jaspers has said,
"Existence-philosophy is the way of thought by means of
which man seeks to become himself; it makes use of expert
knowledge while at the same time going beyond it. This
way of thought does not cognise objects, but elucidates
and makes actual the being of the thinker." It is a way
of thought, not a set of doctrines; what it says is
neither made up of definitions nor of factual assertions
but is meant to persuade, awaken, appeal and alter. Its
subject is man, but man as he may become, man in his
height and depth, man as necessarily involved in a
non-empirical reality. In intention at least, it is an
attempt to answer the question, "What is life?" without
metaphysical or theological presuppositions. It
investigates man not as a thing or an objectifiable
reality but as *existence*.

What does this term mean in the usage of the principal
existential thinkers? The term "existence" refers, not to
everything that is, but to the mode of being peculiar and
proper to man, to which he may fully attain or from which
he may fall away. For Kierkegaard, existence refers to
that inwardness of subjective life in which the man of
faith goes out towards God and by thus becoming a pure
Christian realizes his own self. This is an inwardness
which can never be made the object of knowledge; in
Sartre's words, "This subjectivity rediscovered beyond
language as the personal adventure of each man in the face
of others and of God--this is what Kierkegaard called
existence." It is a state of being, moral and religious,
rather than one of knowing, and so involves choice and
commitment. Jaspers takes over this Kierkegaardian
concept but de-theologizes it. For him existence is

> that which can never become an object, the source
> from which my thoughts and actions spring....
> Existence is that which is in relation to itself
> and thus to its transcendence. Man is more than
> his empirical being, more than consciousness in
> general, more than reason and spirit. As the
> condition and enlivening source of all these,
> man's existence is the dark ground of his
> becoming a self, the hiddenness from which I
> encounter myself as emerging and for which alone
> transcendence becomes actual.

Man is potential existence and takes his life from a
primal source that lies beyond mind. He fulfills this
potentiality of existence in relation to transcendence and
in communication with others. In Marcel also the concept
of existence includes the notion of becoming oneself,
through relation to transcendence. In *Being and Time*,
Heidegger has explained, with greater precision and
clarity, what he means by existence and has also made a
number of valuable distinctions which have been ignored by
other existentialist thinkers. Unlike other beings, which
merely are there as objects or things, man exists, i.e.
his mode of being is such that it cannot be stated through
the categories of objective being. Further, to say that
man exists means that he *is* in such a way that he
understands himself in his being, is concerned with this
being, that for each man his own being is at stake. In
the next place, each man understands himself not only in
what he *is* but in terms of what he *can be*, he understands
himself in terms of his possibilities, in terms of his
ability to be and of a future towards which he is
anticipatively oriented. Man's being, he asserts, is
care. To go out beyond himself to the possibilities of
his being and be aware of himself in relation to them is
the unique way of being which Heidegger calls existence.
Man's essence, Heidegger remarks, lies in his existence as
thus described. Heidegger has repeatedly insisted that
his use of this term is meant in a radically different
sense than that in the Existence Philosophy of Jaspers or

the Existentialism of Sartre. The interests of
Kierkegaard and Jaspers are largely focussed on the
existentiell, i.e., on the description of factual
experience, whereas Heidegger seeks to inquire into the
conditions of the possibility of such experience and
therefore concerns himself exclusively with the analytic
of existence in the manner of Kant--his inquiry is
existential. For Heidegger, man's supreme feature lies in
his ontological awareness.

> Without the comprehension of Being inherent in
> man, man would never be the entity that he is,
> even if he were to be equipped with the most
> wonderful faculties. Man is a being who is in
> the midst of other entities in such a way that,
> in this being, the entity that he is not, and the
> entity that he is, have become simultaneously
> manifest. This mode of being of man we call
> existence. Only by virtue of the understanding
> of being is existence possible.

In order to indicate his distance from the Kierkegaardian
concept of existence--which is also in essentials that of
Jaspers-- and from that of Sartre in particular, which is
derived from the Medieval contrast between *essentia* and
existentia, Heidegger later spells it as ek-sistenz, and
characterizes it as the ecstatic standing within the
illumination of Being. Man stands out of himself and
stands within the light of the truth of Being--he ek-
sists, and it is this that makes him a man and not any
sort of actualization of an essence or possibility. The
basic tenet of existentialism as formulated by Sartre
says, existence precedes essence. In doing so he takes
existentia and *essentia* in the sense of traditional
metaphysics which since Plato says: *essentia* precedes
existentia. Sartre only converts the sentence. But the
converse of a metaphysical statement still remains
metaphysical. As such a statement, it remains oblivious,
like all metaphysics, of the truth of Being.

Heidegger's criticism of Sartre implied in the above,
however, is not quite fair and shows some lack of understanding. It is strange that Sartre, with whose name the
existentialist movement is more closely associated than
with anyone else, does not use the term "existentialism"
in his properly philosophical books and articles up to and
including *Being and Nothingness*. It was only later, in
his polemical writings, that he unwillingly took up the
label. As a competent critic points out, existence in
Sartre does not have its classical meaning, i.e., the
actualization of a being, the reality of a being, as
opposed to its simple logical possibility, the fact of
existing. It is no longer the "complement" of essence but
appears as the transcendental condition of the possibility
of essence. Nor does it have the "existential" meaning of
lived existence (as we find in his literary works) or the
Kierkegaardian meaning of separation, of interiority or
relation to transcendence. It designates solely
consciousness, in all its simple purity, translucency,
negativity, spontaneity and freedom. As Sartre explicitly
states in his biographical work, *Saint Genêt*, "This
authentic subjectivity which he touches beyond and within
being, within and beyond the possible, is *existence*."
Again, "And this particularity which is no longer an
object for any one, not even for himself, which is not,
which is in the making, is situated beyond being and language...this creative consciousness is: existence...a
faceless freedom...beyond the empirical self." About the
philosophical background and details of Sartre's concept
of existence, however, I shall enlarge in a subsequent
essay devoted entirely to this thinker.

As the above examination of the concept of existence
has made clear, existential philosophers differ from one
another in a far-reaching sense in their views. This
arises from the fact that neither Kierkegaard nor
Heidegger and Sartre, neither Jaspers nor Marcel, is a

mere existentialist in the ordinary sense. Each is
concerned with something more than man's peculiar mode of
being, each has a different starting-point, each a
different philosophical end in view. Kierkegaard, from
whom almost all basic existentialist concepts derive, was
inspired by a primarily theological or religious passion.
Heidegger's main problem is the question of Being and his
systematic working out of the structure of existence in
Being and Time is only incidental to that. Sartre's
concern is with human freedom, inner as well as outer and
social, and like Heidegger he derives from the school of
Husserl's Phenomenology. So does Maurice Merleau-Ponty.
Jaspers is in the line of the classical thinkers of the
perennial philosophy and has striven to build up a system
in which the new and revolutionary insights of Kierkegaard
and Nietzsche have been used to supplement, synthesize and
re-write the contributions of the great classical
philosophers in a Kantian and broadly religious framework.
Marcel is a Catholic engaged in analysing the relations
between man and man in terms of the Christian concepts of
faith, hope and charity, and of fidelity, transcendence
and the all-enveloping mystery of Being. We may aptly
conclude, therefore, with the words in which O.F. Bollnow
characterizes the significance of this type of philosophy:

> Existentialism, viewed historically, is the
> beginning of a philosophy which places man, with
> his real tasks and problems, finally and uncondi-
> tionally, in the centre of philosophical thought.
> Systematically considered, existentialism is an
> enduring limb of philosophy, which keeps its
> entire body in a state of perpetual unrest by
> virtue of its polar relation with the whole. But
> existentialism can never become itself the whole
> of philosophy. There is no such thing as a pure
> existential philosophy.

It remains, therefore, to see how existential thinking
joins hands with, and itself exists in the medium of, an
intellectual concern that is deeper and more comprehensive.

Existentialism is something more, it must be repeated, than a merely popular philosophy and deserves serious attention, even though only as a part of a comprehensive and constructive philosophical endeavour. In the writings of Martin Heidegger, Jean-Paul Sartre and Merleau-Ponty, it has been developed on the firm basis of a sober philosophical discipline like Phenomenology. In the process, Phenomenology itself is being creatively developed in directions hardly envisaged by its founder, Edmund Husserl. At the hands of men like John Wild in the United States and Paul Ricoeur in France, not to speak of a host of less known thinkers, a new branch of this discipline is emerging under the name of Existential Phenomenology. It is impossible for any student of Existentialism to make headway in the study of existential classics such as *Being and Time, Being and Nothingness* and Merleau-Ponty's *Phenomenology of Perception* without a sympathetic understanding of the aims, method and terminology of Phenomenology. It is hardly possible to give, within the short space at my disposal, even a rough idea of what Phenomenology is and how it has developed since it was launched as a new, serious philosophical discipline with the publication of Husserl's *Logical Investigations* in 1900-1901. Suffice it to say that, like analytical philosophy in the English speaking countries, Phenomenology has provided on the Continent during the past few decades not merely a school or trend in philosophy but also the language, the medium, in which philosophizing has been carried on there and is now radiating to other parts of the world. Terms and phrases like intentionality, intuition of essences, consciousness, phenomenon; the eidetic, phenomenological and transcendental reductions; the epoche, the bracketing or suspension of belief common to the natural attitude, transcendental field and transcendental experience; constitution, subjectivity, the transcendental ego, the *Lebenswelt*--all these constitute the everyday jargon of

the philosopher schooled in Phenomenology. And they are
used, it must be remembered, not in the service of
developing a system of speculative metaphysics in the
traditional manner but in the interests of what Husserl
called an as yet non-existent discipline which is both a
first philosophy and a radical empiricism. The approach
is descriptive and concrete, seeking to avoid presuppositions deriving from metaphysics or from scientific
knowledge and yet striving to get to the bed-rock of
experience. Its subject-matter is the Cartesian *cogito*,
but the *cogito* freed of its metaphysical accompaniments,
re-enforced by Kantian transcendentalism and avoiding the
pitfalls of both realism and idealism in the traditional
sense. Instead of enlarging further, however, I refer the
student of existential philosophy who wishes to inform
himself about Phenomenology to the excellent introductions
provided e.g. by Pierre Thevenaz in *What is Phenomenology?*
and by John Wild in his recent writings. The early works
of Sartre on Imagination and on the Emotions, his
Transcendence of the Ego, all directly in the line of
Phenomenological writings, can acquaint the reader with
this type of thought and prepare him for the study of his
magnum opus, *Being and Nothingness*, which bears the sub-
title "An Essay on Phenomenological Ontology". Heidegger's
Being and Time contains an introductory explanation of
Phenomenology as he himself interprets it, and the
"Preface" in Merleau-Ponty's *Phenomenology of Perception*
is devoted entirely to giving, in a few compressed pages,
an answer to the question, what is Phenomenology? The
serious student will be well-advised to grapple with the
texts themselves rather than spend his time reading
popular expositions, either of Phenomenology or of Existentialism. I may add here a word on the use of the term
"ontology" in Phenomenology and by existentialists
influenced by it. For the Phenomenologist, the phenomenon, that which appears or manifests itself, is all that

is, without a noumenon hidden behind it, of which it is
the appearance, illusory or otherwise. The study of
phenomena is, therefore, for him the study of what is, of
Being and the time-hallowed Aristotelian name for such a
study is Ontology. Husserl employs the term freely,
though his concern is not so much with what he calls the
"formal ontology" of traditional metaphysics but with the
material or regional ontology of the different realms of
being. Sartre only follows him in this, though in an
original fashion. Heidegger even identifies all
philosophy with ontology and remarks in this connexion
that "ontology and phenomenology are not two distinct
philosophical disciplines among others. These terms
characterize philosophy itself with regard to its object
and its way of treating that object." The whole of *Being
and Time* is devoted to what Heidegger calls "fundamental
ontology", i.e., to an investigation of the structure of
man's being, as preparatory to the inquiry into the nature
of Being itself. We see already how Existentialism,
seriously studied, leads to Phenomenology and that in turn
into the central realm of philosophy, from the Greeks down
to the present day.

Another point to which I may refer briefly here is the
religious or theological background of Existentialism. In
the case of Kierkegaard we have already seen that his concern was primarily the religious one of defending the possibility and the necessity of Christian faith in a world
which had suffered the breakdown of the Christian doctrine
of Creation. His immediate impact was first felt in the
field of contemporary dialectical theology, on Karl Barth
and his school and only later on philosophers such as Karl
Jaspers and Martin Heidegger. From the latter then
Rudolph Bultmann derived the conceptual tools for carrying
into effect his programme of demythologizing in New
Testament interpretation. The fact that the Christian
certainty of faith has become more and more problematic

since the first Copernican shock, and as proclaimed, e.g.
dramatically in Nietzsche's words about the death of god,
has been at the bottom of the recent crisis both in
theology and philosophy and must be regarded as one of the
roots of Existentialism. It represents, from this point
of view, the twentieth-century philosopher's response to
the crisis of faith and the loss of revealed certainties.
In the west, it was left to Biblical religion to answer
the basic questions about the nature and destiny of man
and about his status in the universe; it was in terms of
the Christian revelation that he was provided with the
understanding that he had of himself. As a result of the
gradual secularization that has been going on since the
Renaissance, philosophy, as founded by the Pre-Christian
Greeks, has come to occupy itself more and more with
matters which formerly fell within the scope of revealed
religion. The discerning student can observe this
happening from Descartes down to Hegel; Existentialism
represents only the final stage in the attempt to reappro-
priate philosophically, i.e., in secularized form and
without needing the warrant and the guarantee of religious
faith, insights into human nature which religious faith
had sustained so far. These insights it now seeks to
derive immanently, from within the depths of man's
subjectivity alone and from this perspective one can speak
of all existential thinking as being in its basic motivation religious, irrespective of whether the philosopher
concerned subscribes to any creed, whether he is theistic
or atheistic. In Gabriel Marcel, a professed Catholic,
the preoccupation with religious problems is, of course,
obvious. But even in his case most of this original
analysis of the human condition owes nothing to revealed
religion. As he himself admits, the revelation of Divine
Grace is something that philosophy "cannot demand or
presuppose or enhance nor, to say it outright,.can it even
comprehend it." At the most philosophy can prepare for

its acceptance and in turn its prior awareness may prepare
philosophy to unfold in a dimension which otherwise would
have remained closed to it.

Sartre's case may seem to contradict our thesis, for
he is an avowed atheist. His position is, and is meant to
be, utterly unacceptable to a theist of any complexion,
Christian or otherwise. But why is it then equally
unacceptable to the orthodox Marxist, as his controversies
with Marxist thinkers show? In the second place, Sartre's
consuming passion for human freedom is not merely the
contemplative passion of the philosopher for depicting
reality as he finds it. He writes, first and foremost,
"in the perspective of a possible change," and in this he
is a true follower of Marx, who was not content with
describing the world but thought that the time had come
when philosophers should take upon themselves the task of
changing it. Sartre wants primarily to change, through
his writings, philosophical and literary, man's conception
of himself as well as of the world in which he lives.
This makes him uncompromising and adopt extreme positions
and express thoughts calculated to shock and hurt, in
particular, the respectable upholders of the established
order. But his driving passion is nonetheless religious,
no less than Nietzsche's. He is neither a metaphysician
nor a theologian but he cannot be denied the title of a
man of good and great faith. No longer living in a world
for which the God of revelation has reality, nor having
any use for the constructed God of the philosopher, he yet
finds in man the profound need to achieve this fullness of
Being which he projects in the idea of God. As he remarks,

> God is dead, but man has not for all that become
> atheistic. Silence of the transcendent joined to
> the permanence of the need for religion in modern
> man--that is still the major thing, today as
> yesterday....God is silent and that I cannot
> deny.--Everything in myself calls for God and
> that I cannot forget....As a matter of fact, this
> experience can be found in one form or another in
> most contemporary authors: it is the torment in

Jaspers, death in Malraux, destitution in
Heidegger, the reprieved being in Kafka, the
insane and futile labour of Sisyphus in Camus.

Sartre has renounced God and sets out from the postulate,
God does not exist. The only Absolute he recognizes is
Consciousness and all his piety is laid up in man's
ability to liberate himself by work, by the work which
consciousness performs upon itself and by the productive
work which changes the world, material and social.
Writing about Andre Gide, Sartre says,

He *lived* his ideas, and one, above all--the death
of God....The problem of God is a human problem
which concerns the rapport between men. It is a
total problem to which each man brings a solution
by his entire life, and the solution which one
brings to it reflects the attitude one has chosen
towards other men and towards oneself. What Gide
gives us that is most precious is his decision to
live to the finish the agony and death of God.
He could well have done what others did and
gamble on his concepts, decide for faith or
atheism at the age of twenty and hold to this for
his entire life. Instead, he wanted to put his
relationship with religion to the test and the
living dialectic which led him to his final
atheism is a journey which can be repeated after
him, but not settled by concepts and notions....
He allows us to avoid the traps into which he has
fallen or to climb out of them as he did. Every
truth, says Hegel, has become so....Gide is an
irreplacable example because he chose to *become
his truth*. Chosen in the abstract, at twenty,
his atheism would have been false. Slowly
earned, crowning the quest of half a century,
this atheism becomes his concrete truth and our
own. Starting from there, men of today are
capable of becoming new truth.

All Sartre's writings, and his life, constitute a massive
thought-experiment, very much in the manner of Nietzsche,
to draw out the implications for man of the lived
postulate that God does not exist. Perhaps it still
remains to be realized how all the riches of the
religious consciousness can be drawn without loss into the
new image of man that Sartre, as much a pilgrim of the
Absolute as any one, is helping to fashion, into the new
truth that man can yet become.

Let us next take Jaspers and see how the religious question stands in the background of his philosophizing and even explicitly forms the content of much of his thought. Jaspers, it was suggested earlier, is a philosopher with a backward glance, summing up, like Hegel, all that he finds worthwhile in the philosophy of the past and seeking to develop a thought-structure in which the insights of past thought, Western and Eastern, find a place. The thinking of Kierkegaard and Nietzsche are for him events which require a reformulation of the *philosophia perennis*, a rewriting of the history of philosophy in the world and a re-assessment of the Christian claim to lay down the archetypal pattern of religious thinking. He seeks in short to develop a philosophy, in terms of what has already been thought, which is synthetic and comprehensive, which incorporates within itself *all* wisdom, religious, metaphysical or critical, Greek, Medieval or Modern, Eastern or Western. But what is very much more interesting, in the second place, is the process of secularization, the transformation of religious and theological notions into philosophical, to which reference was made earlier. This amounts, in fact, to a transformation of philosophy itself in such fashion that it takes up within itself matters of ultimate concern which so far have been the preserve of warring religions. We can find the same process at work in the thinking of Heidegger, and in reverse in the theological work of a Tillich or a Bonhoeffer. We may describe this alternatively as the quest of a unity of religions on the philosophical level, but a level on which philosophy itself is transformed in its nature, no longer remaining merely contemplative but becoming a challenge and an invitation, an instrument of self-knowledge and self-realization. Jaspers expresses this hope for philosophy in these words:

> By the side of traditional church religions and
> in polar relation to them, philosophy will
> become, as in (pre-Christian) antiquity, a form
> in which men will discover their unconditioned
> earnestness, in stillness and without noise. In
> many countries of Europe today, a kind of
> thinking about a common conduct of life is
> developing under the name of existence philos-
> ophy, differing from each other even to the
> extent of mutual foreignness but perhaps
> springing up out of a related impulse. This
> philosophizing has been growing here since the
> later Schelling, decisively set in motion by
> Kierkegaard, stimulated by pragmatic thought,
> tested in time's exigency. It recognizes itself
> mirrored in the older philosophizing, which was
> ever existence philosophy, but which today knows
> itself as determined by destiny through the
> extremity of the utter breakdown of earlier laws
> and validities....Is existence philosophy mere
> dreaming and wild fancy? If this is dreaming, I
> dare to answer, then it is one of those dreams
> from which is born, from time immemorial, all
> that is human and which makes life worth living.

For Jaspers, philosophy itself is capable of taking over
the place of religion, not as mere theory but as inner
action and realization, for Transcendence speaks directly
to individual men in the shape of truth and of the freedom
which enables him to become himself. Not only does
Jaspers conceive philosophical thinking as a form of
praxis which, as he says, springs up from that depth of
life where eternity meets time. He also seeks to overcome
the traditional alternative of revealed faith or nihilism
by conceiving philosophy as something one can live by.
Faith is no longer restricted to religion but becomes an
integral part of philosophy itself. To the elucidation of
his conception of philosophical faith Jaspers has devoted
an entire book and another, more recently, in which he has
examined such faith in relation to revelation. Philosophical faith, for Jaspers, however, never hardens into a
creed or dogma, for it is not grounded in anything objective and finite in the world. Such faith is life out of
the Comprehensive, that being which is neither subject

alone nor only object but encompasses both; it is guidance
and fulfillment through the Comprehensive. It has its
source in the non-objectifiable Comprehensive and because
it is not tied to any finite thing that has been made into
an absolute, it is free. The religious problem thus not
only forms the background of Jaspers' Existentialism but
constitutes the very core of its subject matter.

In the case of Heidegger, too, the preoccupation with
the religious question and with theology cannot be
neglected if we wish to understand his thought in its true
import. Unfortunately, however, Heidegger has not himself
explicitly discussed in his writings the precise details
of the role which religious and theological thought has
played in shaping and motivating his philosophy, barring a
few hints. This has led to grave misunderstandings in
various quarters, which are being only gradually removed.
The question is complex and I can only offer here a few
comments suggesting the necessity of keeping this aspect
of his philosophy in view. It is well-known that
Heidegger received his earlier education at a Jesuit
seminary where he acquired a thorough knowledge of the
Catholic doctrine. It was during these years in the
gymnasium that he got to know Franz Brentano's work, *On
the Multiple Meanings of Being in Aristotle*. Referring to
this early theological education, Heidegger has remarked
that without this theological origin he would never have
arrived on the way to thinking, adding that it is our
origins that determine what we become in the future. It
is also well-known that in Thomistic theology, the
Aristotelian doctrine of Being is developed within a
Christian framework. Later, during the years Heidegger
spent at Marburg, he came into intimate contact with, and
stimulation through, Protestant theology. His *Being and
Time*, in fact, grew out of this fruitful contact, a
contact which was not without conflicts and tensions of
the most intense type. It has even been asserted that

Being and Time grew out of a lecture delivered at a
gathering of Marburg theologians. It is not so well-known
that during his pre-*Being and Time* years Heidegger gave
lectures and held seminars on religious subjects. Among
these may be mentioned a lecture course on "The philosophical foundations of Medieval mysticism," another
entitled, "Introduction to the phenomenology of religion,"
one on "Augustine and Neoplatonism," a colloquium on "The
theological foundations of Kant," a seminar on Scholasticism, not to speak of the Addresses and Seminars he has
held with theologians in recent years. Some of his older
pupils have written works on Plotinus and Meister Eckhart
and his own extensive preoccupation with Kierkegaard, with
Hoelderlin and with Nietzsche amounted largely to a
wrestling with religious issues. Evidence of all these
influences lies scattered not only in *Being and Time* but
also in his other writings. From Kierkegaard he took over
directly many of the topics discussed in *Being and Time*,
such as existence, anxiety, situation, resoluteness and
choice, death, authenticity, repetition, possibility,
anonymity, the "moment". Even the definition of
philosophy given there has reference to a concept derived
from theology. As Heidegger defines it, both at the
commencement of the inquiry and at the end, philosophy is
universal phenomenological ontology, taking its starting-
point from the hermeneutic of *Dasein* which, as an analytic
of existence, has made fast the guiding-line for all
philosophical inquiry at the point where it *arises* and to
which it *returns*. The term "hermeneutic" used here comes
originally from the theological field and refers to the
art of interpreting and explicating the meaning of the
Holy Book. Its scope was expanded by the theologian
Schleiermacher to include the theory and methodology of
interpretation in general and applied by Wilhelm Dilthey
in the field of the humane and historical studies.
Heidegger uses it in a still wider sense in *Being and Time*

to interpret and explicate the being of *Dasein*, i.e., to
man in the aspect of his openness to Being. Because of
the historicity inherent in *Dasein* and because of its
facticity, such intepretation, even though ontological,
takes on the character of hermeneutic. The sheer "that"
of man as *Dasein* finding himself in the midst of the
world, along with others, in the particularity of his
situation, constitutes man's facticity, his thrownness,
which affects and determines all his projects of understanding. The explication of the being of man or of his
existence requires, therefore, not mere conceptual
analysis but an analysis which is interpretive in character, as in the case of a historical or literary document.
As has been shown by Heidegger scholars recently, this
basic conception of the historicity and facticity of
Dasein was derived from Heidegger's study of the structure
of religious experience in early Christianity. Many other
concepts of *Being and Time* can be traced back to Biblical
or theological sources. About the central notion of
"care", for example, Heidegger explicitly admits, "The way
in which 'care' is viewed in the foregoing existential
analytic of *Dasein* is one which has grown upon the author
in connexion with his attempts to interpret the
Augustinian (i,e., Hellenic Christian) anthropology,
having regard to the basic principles reached in the
ontology of Aristotle." Even his most original conception, that of historicity and temporality, can be traced
back to the eschatological *kairos* of Christian life-
experience as expressed in the New Testament.

Instead of multiplying examples, let us for a moment
try to understand what Heidegger is seeking to accomplish
with his analysis of existence, and indeed in all his
philosophical work, and why religious experience and
theology have been of so much significance to it. *Being
and Time* is devoted to an analysis of human existence. It
is not an empirical or *existentiell* analysis but

existential or ontological, for it seeks to arrive at the
most general and formal structure of man's being which
would constitute the condition of the possibility of any
concrete, actual experience whatever--whether scientific
(to which Kant restricted his analysis in the First
Critique), historical or religious, whether cognitive or
affective. Such an analysis of the ultimate ground-
structure of human experience may in fact be said to be
the aim of all his writings. To the extent to which it
has succeeded, it should be possible to derive from it any
and every form of concrete, particular experience as its
specification and especially those aspects of human
experience which have been dealt with by the various
religions. It would thus be in a position to provide the
most basic, the most neutral and the most comprehensive
language in terms of which the life-experience embodied in
these religions can be expressed, in terms of which the
nature and destiny of man, his place in the world, his
ultimate hopes and aspirations can be described. This, of
course, opens out the prospect of a "unified language of
the religions," to use an expression common amongst
logical positivists. But it also opens out the prospect
of an eventual "secularization" of religion in the sense
of enabling the translation of every religious concept
into a philosophical one, without absorbing, like Hegel,
the facticity of religious experience completely into the
concept. This is no loss to religion in so far as it is
an integral part of human experience, an ineluctable
dimension of man's being and the source from which his
existence derives its ultimate meaningfulness. And it is
a distinct gain to philosophy, to any philosophy which is
careful to guard the purity of experience and which,
instead of willfully imposing its categories upon
experience and thus falsifying it, remains loyal to its
humble task of seeking the adequate and disciplined word
which can depict and chart out, unveil and evoke the truth

of experience, without giving up its prerogative of ceaseless questioning and its basic stance of openness and
inquiry. The piety of thought lies in questioning,
Heidegger says; such asking may be folly in the eyes of
faith but it is in this folly that the essence of
philosophy lies. For it is only thus that philosophy,
like poetry in a different way, enlarges the area of the
communicable and brings men of diverse persuasions nearer
together. That in this process, philosophy transforms its
own nature, as suggested earlier, and itself takes on
something of the sacredness of the religious quest is no
mean gain for it.

I should like, in what follows, to say a few words
more about existentialism in general and how each of the
above mentioned existential philosophers is more than a
mere existentialist. This will also give an idea of the
kind and extent of philosophical knowledge presupposed in
the serious study of any of these. Phenomenology and
Christian religious doctrines have already been mentioned.
For the study of Sartre, a knowledge of Hegel is an
inescapable additional presupposition, for it is on
Hegel's *Phenomenology of Mind* and his *Logic* that Sartre's
dialectical theory of consciousness and his ontology are
based, as also his theory of interpersonal relations.
Marx is there always in the background and in the later
Sartre very much in the forefront. As the author of a
Critique of Dialectical Reason, not to mention the
contribution to thought made in his strictly literary
writing, Sartre is more than just an existentialist. For
Jaspers and Heidegger, close familiarity with the entire
range of European philosophy is essential, in particular
with Kant. The general framework of Jaspers' thinking is
Kantian and the grand synthesis of the thought of the
great philosophers of the past that he attempts is
effected within this framework. His delimitation of
knowledge, objective and universally valid, to the field

of science, his conception of Transcendence and his
condemnation of absolutizing and objectifying what we
learn in other fields are well-known Kantian themes. For
him Kant is *the* philosopher, a very prototype of this
calling. Kierkegaard and Nietzsche contribute powerfully
to his thought and provide the immediate challenge to his
work of synthesis, in which, of course, all the great
figures come in one by one. For Jaspers, author of a
three-volume work, *Philosophy*, of an enormous volume on
Philosophical Logic entitled *On Truth*, and of an equally
bulky first volume of a history of world philosophy, not
to speak of numerous monographs on individual philosophers, existence philosophy is identical with philosophy
or metaphysics itself. In addition, there is his work on
Psychopathology, with which he made his intellectual
start, and his *Psychology of World Views* in which his own
philosophy germinated. And during recent years he has
written extensively on matters which are of topical
urgency, like Bertrand Russell, and applied his wisdom to
matters which are relatively of the moment. This is true,
in even greater measure, of Sartre.

In the case of Heidegger, it is even more emphatically
true that he is more than an existentialist philosopher.
His *Being and Time*, which alone is concerned with
existence, is only a propaedeutic to the only question
that moves Heidegger: the question of Being. It does not
even aim at providing a comprehensive ontology of man and
analysis of existence but only so much as is essential for
the pursuit of the question of Being. In his other
writings it is not only ignored but explicitly disavowed
as the sole or proper task of the philosopher. In
reopening the question of the sense of Being, Heidegger is
led to a searching examination of the whole body of
Western metaphysics, emphasis being mainly laid on the
Greek founders, from the Pre-Socratics to Aristotle, on
the heralds of the modern age, Descartes, Leibniz, Kant

and Hegel and on Nietzsche, standing at the end of one
whole era and proclaiming that end, in agony and joy, as
the result of life-long wrestling with the attempt to
comprehend the inner metaphysical foundation and destiny
of the western intellectual tradition. No one without a
thorough and imaginative grasp of this history can even
begin to understand "the more than existentialist"
in Heidegger.

In a sense these existentialist thinkers are antimeta-
physical, but in another sense they provide us with a profounder glimpse into the realm of the invisible, opening
new perspectives and dimensions of experience and bringing
them within the scope of philosophical reflection. Each
of them carries us in his own unique way, beyond the
preoccupation with man, into realms largely untrodden
hitherto and in ways of thinking which are novel yet
undisciplined and on which we may safely wander, in
delight and unexpected gain--Sartre to a comprehensive
philosophy of freedom, Jaspers to Periechontology,
Heidegger to a new conception of Being. If this is found
of some relevance to the task of constructive philosophizing in this country and in building on the traditions
which are inescapably ours, the serious study of this type
of thought will have served its proper purpose in the
context of the present state of philosophy here.

THE EXISTENTIALISM OF JEAN-PAUL SARTRE

As a philosopher and man of letters, Jean-Paul Sartre is "with those who want to change both man's social condition and the conception which he has of himself." Even though he takes as his point of departure the Phenomenology of Edmund Husserl and is deeply indebted to the analyses of existence in Heidegger's *Being and Time*, he is very far from viewing it as the task of philosophy merely to disclose, intuit and contemplate what is as such already given in an implicit manner. The driving power behind all his work, philosophical no less than literary, is freedom, and action born of freedom and in the service of freedom. His writings are stations on the way to this sole quest and if his reader is not to miss the continuity and unity of his thought, he must not overlook the itinerary for the destination, as Sartre warns.

Sartre's earliest philosophical works exhibit a marked preoccupation with the method and doctrines of Phenomenology. In them Sartre seeks not only to apply the phenomenological method to an investigation of such mental functions as Imagination[1] and Emotion,[2] as ways in which man relates himself to his world, but also subjects Husserl's phenomenology to searching criticism.[3] In doing so he at the same time foreshadows some of his later concerns, thus giving indications of the process by which

---

Lecture given at the University of Delhi in 1966, published under the title "Existential Philosophy: Jean-Paul Sartre" in *Proceedings of the All-India Seminar* (3), Centre of Advanced Study in Philosophy, Banaras Hindu University, 1967, pp. 119-133.

Phenomenology became transformed, in his major work[4], into a phenomenological Ontology of human existence. The descriptive phenomenology of the work on imagination, the imaginary and the emotions is not merely of psychological interest but is of considerable relevance to the basic philosophical issues about the nature of consciousness, its nihilating power, its freedom, its possible surrender to the "magic" of the emotions and its capacity to refuse being enmeshed in the world of causality. It is, however, in *The Transcendence of the Ego* that we find Sartre putting forward, in critical modification of a central doctrine of Husserl's, his own remarkable theory of consciousness, a theory which he later uses as the foundation of his own philosophical system in *Being and Nothingness*. This essay may indeed be characterized as pivotal in the making of Sartre's whole philosophy, for it is here that he achieves, through a radicalization of the Husserlian "reduction" and of the Cartesian *cogito*, what he calls "the liberation of the transcendental field and at the same time its purification." The second stage in Sartre's philosophical development is represented by *Being and Nothingness*, which goes on to exhibit, at great length, the structure of man's involvement in the world and the complex dialectic of the relationship between his own free subjectivity and all forms of objective being, including the empirical ego as well as other people and things. In these philosophical works and in his novels, plays, biographical and literary essays, Sartre has attempted to explore human subjectivity to its limit, depicting man's consciousness as free and yet captive in the world, endangered by the world of meanings it builds up and yet capable of winning its liberation in the midst of it. His latest philosophical work,[5] voluminous and as yet incomplete, seeks to explore the objective aspect of human reality to its limit in the hope of an ultimate synthesis of the two sides. Here Sartre investigates

man's social, collective and historical existence with a
view to building up an historical, philosophical
anthropology which can incorporate into itself both the
insights of existentialism into human subjectivity as well
as the objective, historical approach of a reformed
Marxist philosophy.

In *The Transcendence of the Ego*, Sartre wholeheartedly
accepts Husserl's notion of the intentionality of consciousness but proposes a more radical phenomenological
reduction than Husserl carried through. In Husserl, only
the psychological Ego fell before the *epoche*, while a
transcendental I was retained within consciousness as a
principle of unification, constitution and meaning.
Sartre points out that since in phenomenology consciousness is defined by its intentionality, it can by itself do
everything for which Husserl requires a transcendental
ego. The role of such an I within consciousness is not
only superfluous but is actually incompatible with the
phenomenological conception of consciousness as intentional. In addition, Sartre claims, such an *I* is even
"harmful", a "hindrance" to the pure lucidity of consciousness, an opaque blade within consciousness which
would divide and destroy it. "The transcendental *I* is the
death of consciousness." Even such an *I* is an object *for*
consciousness and must, therefore, fall before the stroke
of phenomenological reduction and go over to the side of
the world. With the rejection of this last vestige of
"opacity" from consciousness, the latter becomes completely pure, emptied of all content, sheer translucency.
Consciousness, though always consciousness *of* an object
transcendent to it, is at the same time immediate
consciousness of itself and requires no act of reflection
to be aware of itself. Its very existence is hence
absolute. Unreflective self-awareness is the very mode of
being of consciousness and it is such non-positional,
non-thetic consciousness or the prereflexive *cogito*, as

Sartre later called it, that renders possible the positional or reflexive consciousness in which consciousness becomes an object to itself. Pure unreflected consciousness is for Sartre a non-substantial absolute, a "phenomenon" in the special sense in which "to be" and "to appear" are one. It is, further, an impersonal spontaneity which "determines its existence at each moment" and is thus pure freedom. Pure consciousness is existence and prior to essence since all essences are "intentions" or projects of consciousness. The Cartesian *cogito* is reflective consciousness and it is on this reflective level that the Ego really appears. The subject and the object, the *me* and the world are both "objects for absolute, impersonal consciousness, and it is by virtue of this consciousness that they are connected." Why then does the ego arise at all? Its essential function, Sartre suggests, is not so much theoretical as practical: "Perhaps the essential role of the ego is to mask from consciousness its very spontaneity...as if consciousness hypnotized itself before this ego which it has constituted, absorbing itself in the ego as if to make the ego its guardian and its law."

In the course of developing his conception of transcendental consciousness as impersonal spontaneity, Sartre points out that this "monstrous" freedom is something more fundamental than the freedom of the will, for the will itself "is an object which constitutes itself for and by this spontaneity" and presupposes it as its ground. What Sartre calls "existence" is identical with this transcendental consciousness, is itself nothing else than pure spontaneity, pure freedom, the utterly lucid principle of subjectivity which confronts and goes out towards all that is objective, "thingly" in character, "constitutes" it and gives it meaning. Because this pure spontaneity or freedom lies deeper than the *I*, it can happen that it suddenly manifests itself on the reflective, empirical

level and overwhelms the ego. Then consciousness is
overtaken by its own vertiginous freedom, and becomes
anguished. According to Sartre, this fear of itself is
constitutive of pure consciousness; it is an anxiety, he
says, "which is imposed on us and which we cannot avoid:
it is both pure event of transcendental origin and an ever
possible accident of our daily life." This view of
consciousness as anguished before its own freedom explains
why we ever come to move away from what Husserl calls "the
natural attitude" and perform the phenomenological
reduction, thus rising up to the transcendental level of
reflection. In the phenomenology of Husserl, Sartre says,
the *epoche* appears as a miracle. But if the "natural
attitude" is itself understood as the consequence of "an
effort made by consciousness to escape from itself by
projecting itself into the *me* and becoming absorbed there
and if this effort is never completely rewarded, and if a
simple act of reflection suffices in order for conscious
spontaneity to tear itself abruptly away from the *I* and be
given as independent, then the *epoche* is no longer a
miracle, an intellectual method, an erudite procedure.
Unfortunately, Sartre has not developed these ideas
further nor clarified the deeper philosophical issues
involved here. May it not be that this second, mediated
movement away from projection and absorption into the *me*
and the world occurs, as it must, in the full lucidity of
consciousness, the latter is experienced as the pure
freedom that it is but no longer as essentially anguished.
For a consciousness that comes home to itself and its
freedom, fear of itself cannot be constitutive.

It should be borne in mind that in this essay and in
Being and Nothingness, Sartre writes from a point of view
which is phenomenological rather than metaphysical. The
consciousness of which he speaks is not consciousness in
general but this or that particular consciousness, a
spontaneity which is impersonal and yet *individuated*, and

which as pure intention is always in the midst of the
world. Sartre liberates and purifies the "Transcendental
Field" by emptying it of everything that can be an object
to it (the ego, "all physical, psychophysical, and psychic
objects, all truths, all values") and shows this absolute
consciousness to be "quite simply a first condition and an
absolute source of existence." But he does this in order
to pass on to his main task, viz., the return to the
world, to "the level of humanity" at which the *I* has
already appeared and man "plunged back" into the world.
It is on this level that *Being and Nothingness* deals with
the human reality, analyses man's concrete experience as
moulded by the dialectic of his relations with himself,
with others, and with things. Transcendental
phenomenology is now transformed into a phenomenology of
human existence.

In *Being and Nothingness*, Sartre goes on to develop a
"phenomenological ontology" on the basis of the theory of
impersonal, non-substantial and prereflective consciousness given in the earlier essay. Since every thing is
exterior to pure consciousness, consciousness itself is in
a sense *nothing*, as Sartre said there. In the later work,
this conception of consciousness as something negative and
negating, barely hinted at in earlier writings, emerges
fully developed and plays the central role in Sartre's
dialectic of experience. Consciousness is pure transparency, spontaneity and intentionality; but it is also
pure negativity, not only itself a nothing but an essentially nihilating presence. This is the first of the two
regions or modes of being in Sartre's ontology and is
designated as "being-for-itself." The second is the
region of "being-in-itself," the sphere of pure
positivity, sheer thinghood, opaque and self-identical,
encompassing the entire realm of the mental, the bodily
and the physical, with which consciousness ever stands
confronted and in dialectical relation with which it

ceaselessly wrestles. Like Heidegger, Sartre also
criticizes Husserl for not inquiring into the mode of
being of consciousness: his own answer to this question
is, as mentioned above, that consciousness *is* as
transparency, spontaneity, negativity, as for-itself. But
in *Being and Nothingness*, the nihilating character of
consciousness looms so large that Sartre identifies
consciousness (i.e., existence) with Nothingness, as
opposed to the in-itself which is then simply designated
as Being. Sartre rejects both realism and idealism. Consciousness, the for-itself, and what it is consciousness
of, the in-itself, together constitute a structure in
which neither of the two can be reduced to the other.
They are bound together by the internal relation of
negation: "the for-itself constitutes itself outside the
in-itself as negation of the latter."

Being-in-itself is the intentional object of
consciousness and is transcendent to it. It is sheer
objectivity, opaque and massive. The principles of
Identity and Noncontradiction apply to it. "Being is,
being is in itself, being is what it is," as Sartre puts
it. It has no becoming, is untouched by otherness, is
non-temporal. It has neither possibility nor necessity
but simply *is* and thus utterly contingent. It is that
which consciousness itself is not but of which
consciousness is a revealing intuition as the other than
itself. Being-for-itself is the very opposite of all
this. For Sartre the basic "Ontological Difference" is
not the difference between Being and beings, as with
Heidegger, but the difference between consciousness and
being (i.e., the in-itself), between existence, as the
pure spontaneity of consciousness, and essence, which,
though projected by existence, threatens to enslave it and
congeal it into a thing. Echoing Heidegger, Sartre says
that consciousness is a being which in its being questions
its own being and it does so, he adds, because that being

implies a being other than itself, i.e., the object *of*
which there is consciousness. Such questioning
presupposes negativity, an implicit comprehension of
non-being and itself a manifestation of the nihilating
character of consciousness. Non-being, the "other" to the
positivity of being thus lies like a worm coiled in the
heart of being, like a hole or fissure in being, a
haunting presence in us and outside of us, in Sartre's
picturesque language. It is because consciousness is
essentially nihilating, a "decompressing" of the
in-itself, and able to "secrete a non-being which isolates
it," that it can disengage itself from the in-itself and
manifest itself as freedom.

Consciousness is self-nihilating, perpetually escaping
the causality of the past and spontaneously going out
towards and intending a world. It is wholly "project" of
the *world*, however, and its freedom is always "situated",
i.e., freedom relative to a situation and *in* a situation.
The freedom of consciousness, further, is a project of
freeing, an unending task for consciousness, not something
that *is* already there, once and for all. This abyss of
freedom, anchored to nothing, is revealed in moments of
anguish in relation to our past or future possibilities,
in moments when we are forced to assume responsibility for
choosing one way or the other. Unable to bear this
anguish and this freedom of which it is an index, we take
recourse to various strategies of escape: flight into the
"spirit of seriousness" (i.e., seeking reasons for action
in the nature of things or in the values supposedly
"attached" to them), belief in psychological determinism,
projecting the freedom of consciousness on the ego,
conceived as the agent of actions, and, finally, "bad
faith," a kind of self-deception by which we dissociate
ourselves from our own mental states. We live mostly in
bad faith, trying not to be what we are. Sartre goes even
so far as to assert that to realize absolute sincerity

towards oneself, to be what one is, is an impossible task, for this would be to abrogate the negativity of the for-itself and to convert consciousness into an in-itself.

Consciousness is not what it is and it is what it is not, as Sartre paradoxically formulates the inherent negativity of Consciousness, in contrast with the in-itself, which is what it is, which wholly *is*. Consciousness, as a pure spontaneity, can never be turned into an in-itself, into a self-identical block of being. It is always ahead of itself, escaping itself; positing its own unity, it constantly evades identity. Consciousness is merely present to itself as not being itself. The law of being of the for-itself, Sartre says, is to be itself in the form of presence to itself. Such presence implies not *being* itself and "supposes that an impalpable fissure has slipped into being," but it is a fissure which is wholly negative, for consciousness as presence to itself is separated by itself, *by no thing*. The principles of Identity and Non-contradiction do not obviously apply to the peculiar mode of being of the for-itself. But consciousness has also in "something of which it is not the foundation--its presence in the world" and to the sheer contingency of the in-itself. Free to give meaning to its situation, consciousness cannot create it and cannot, therefore, give a foundation to itself. In addition, since it is always possible that a particular for-itself as such could also not be, it shares all the contingency of the in-itself. This is what Sartre calls the facticity of consciousness; consciousness is both consciousness of its own nihilating freedom as well as of its facticity and "complete gratuity." Because of his practical concern with the destiny of "the human reality" in the world of things, Sartre philosophizes on what we may call the level of the Sāṁkhya, a level on which the plurality of consciousness and their several possibilities of being enslaved and liberated are all real. Sartre is

not interested in the analysis of concepts nor is he concerned primarily with the question of ultimate reality. Hence it may be confusing and perhaps not quite legitimate if criteria belonging to the level of the Vedānta are applied to his thought.

The for-itself posits itself as not being the in-itself and thus there arises its internal relation with the in-itself which the for-itself experiences as a lack. Being-for-itself is awareness of a lack of being, of the concrete plenitude of the in-itself; consciousness hence is a perpetual striving to make good this lack by achieving a totality of being-for-itself-in-itself. The attainment of such an ideal value is clearly impossible and yet this ideal haunts human consciousness in the form of the concept of God. In straining after this mode of being, in appropriating into itself the positivity of the in-itself, consciousness projects values, through his acts of choice, and pursues them as his goals. Such pursuit of values, according to Sartre, is both a necessity for man and yet a task impossible of achievement. Consciousness, further, is always projected toward its particular possibilities, transcends itself toward them, and is hence necessarily involved in the structure of temporality. In this structure, the past, as *my* past, is not sheer nothing but stands to my present in the relation of an in-itself to which I may go on giving fresh meaning but which I am powerless to change. The present is the presence of consciousness to the in-itself and, as perpetually vanishing, it is a perpetual flight before the in-itself. The future is that towards which consciousness, as not being what it is, projects itself in a vain effort to complete its own lack. "The future is the ideal point where the sudden infinite compassion of facticity (past), of the for-itself (present), and of its possible (a particular future) will at last cause the *Self* to arise as the existence in-itself of the for-itself." This is an

impossibility and the for-itself keeps pressing on towards the future as pure project; what is realized slips back into the past as an in-itself and consciousness moves on as something always *to be*. Inasmuch as consciousness assumes its past as *its* past, is present as a lack to an in-itself and is of the nature of a project, always ahead of itself, temporality constitutes, in the unity of its structure, the very mode of being of consciousness: its perpetual escape from being sucked in by the in-itself as well as its ceaseless striving to incorporate the in-itself within itself as for-itself. The in-itself simply is and has neither a past, nor a future, nor a present.

Sartre, as mentioned earlier, philosophizes on the level of concrete experience. On this level there is not only a plurality of consciousness but each consciousness is at the same time a being for-itself as well as for-others and is aware of itself in the constant dialectical interplay of the I and the other. Sartre gives credit to Hegel and to Husserl for the importance they attached to the phenomenon of subjectivity but criticizes them both for treating the relation between two consciousnesses as one of knowing rather than of being. We have "knowledge" of objects, of the in-itself, not of our own subjectivity which is immediately and pre-reflexively apprehended. The other as proved or known can only be another object. Heidegger saw that this relation is not one of a knowing subject to a known object but a relation between being and being. But according to Sartre, by characterizing this relation as that of being-with, Heidegger has failed to provide a real bridge between me and the other or to how I encounter the other and enter into concrete relation with him. What is needed here is, in Sartre's words, that "In my inmost depths I must find not *reasons for believing* that the other exists but the other himself as not being me," the other not as an object but as another for-itself. Such a revelation of the other occurs when I am looked at

by another who, by this very act, constitutes himself as a
subject against me and makes me aware of myself as being
an object for another. Feelings like shame -- when I am
caught by the other's glance -- show that as being-for-
myself, I am also for-others as centres of independent
subjectivity. Normally, I tend to regard the other as an
object in the sense of an autonomous centre of reference
within *my* world and "my relations with the other as object
are made up essentially of ruses intended to make him stay
an object." As a result of the "look" of the other,
however, I myself become objectified as an autonomous
centre of reference within *his* world and so feel compelled
to acknowledge the other as for-himself. The relation
between two consciousnesses is thus one of reciprocal
negation in which both affirm themselves as incompatible
absolutes. The dialectical relation between one-for-
itself and another, being based on the nihilating
character of each, is one of unresolved conflict, an
unending game of mirrors in which each is thrown back and
forth between being-for-himself and for-another. On the
plane of being, subjectivities "remain out of reach and
radically separated;" if at all some kind of harmony is to
be achieved, it can only be on the level of action, of a
common aim directed towards the accomplishment of tasks in
the world.

Sartre's philosophy is basically a philosophy of
action rather than of contemplation. The nihilating
tearing away of consciousness from the world is not a
flight into itself but only a moment in its engagement
with the world. Consciousness is wholly intention of the
world and wholly project; recovering its freedom, it
returns to the world with the intention of transforming
both the self and the world through its freely chosen
projects. Its freedom too is nothing else but pure
project or task, the task of *freeing* itself through
action. "To say that the for-itself has to be what it is,

to say that it is what it is not while not being what it is, to say that in it existence precedes and conditions essence...is to say one and the same thing, i.e., that man is free." Freedom is never a possession and never empirically given. It is transcendental and total, without any limits except that man is not free to cease being free. Anguish in the face of such freedom may make me try to hide it from myself by incorporating the in-itself as the true mode of being of my consciousness but even such escape is of my own choosing. As a nihilating power, consciousness tears itself away from its past and, projecting itself into goals in the future, returns to itself in the present, the moment of presence and freedom. Sartre rejects all forms of determinism, including the whole psychology of passions, pushes and pulls, conscious or unconscious. As against Freudian psychoanalysis, which explains my present behaviour and attitudes as being determined by my childhood experiences and the causality of unconscious forces within me, Sartre sees in the pattern of an individual's life the working out of a "fundamental project" freely adopted at an early age. In *Being and Nothingness* Sartre outlines a method, which he calls existential psychoanalysis, by which we may decipher and interpret the observable behaviour patterns of a man in terms of the fundamental project and the categories of being, doing, making and having. In his biographical studies of Baudelaire and Genêt, Sartre has demonstrated how much this approach can contribute to our understanding of man. Our fundamental projects are ordinarily not objectively "known" to us because we *are* that, but in so far as we achieve reflective awareness of them in moments of anguished crisis, we are even free to abandon it for a new one. I may cause that "liberating instant" to arise in which I escape the former project by relegating it into the past as an in-itself and take up a new one, thus bringing about a total conversion in myself. "The

extraordinary and marvellous instant", says Sartre, "when
the prior project collapses into the past in the light of
a new project which rises on its ruins and which as yet
exists only in outline...these have often appeared to fur-
nish the clearest and most moving image of our freedom."

Sartrian freedom is absolute but it is the freedom of
man abandoned in the world, freedom in the midst of
facticity. Our freedom meets obstacles all round: the
resistance of things, the particular place I happen to
occupy, the particular past that I happen to have, the
things or tools that I find around me, the presence of
others--each with his own freedom--and, finally, death.
Each of these except the last constitutes an internal
limit or condition of freedom, just as the in-itself is
the necessary correlate or object of consciousness. They
provide the medium in which freedom operates, *for* which it
can be freedom. Whether anything presents itself to me as
an obstacle or not depends, in fact, upon the ends I
choose and hence freedom is presupposed in the experience
of anything as an obstacle. My situation, far from being
an external limit to my freedom, is defined as an obstacle
by my freedom itself. There is no freedom outside of a
situation and no situation except to a consciousness free
to give it a meaning and make it his own. Death alone,
depriving me of all possibility of choice, is utterly
absurd and falls completely *outside* of my life, my
consciousness and my freedom. It is the radically
external limit to my freedom and in no way affects its
absoluteness so long as I am alive. Sartre's doctrine of
the freedom of the for-itself, condemned to choose its
projects and to structure the world, to make itself and to
create values by its acts of choice, has a far-reaching
ethical consequence. It places overwhelming moral
responsibility on man, a responsibility which is no less
absolute than his freedom. "I carry the weight of the
world by myself alone without anything or any person being

able to lighten it," for it is I and nothing foreign that has decided what I have made of myself and of my world.

Sartre's ontology recognizes, as we have seen, being-for-itself and being-in-itself, pure consciousness on the one hand and all objectivity on the other, as together encompassing the entire realm of being. A theory of pure consciousness as the absolute of existence, as pure creativity and sheer negativity, leaves no room for either pre-given essences or God in the ordinary sense. Since consciousness is utterly void of any content, no hint can be found in it of any other reality transcending it and constituting its foundation; nor is anything more basic required or indeed even conceivable. God, as Nietzsche said, is dead. And yet, as an absence he subsists, Sartre holds, integrally in our humanity as the "intention" of man, as the ideal value of a for-itself which is at the same time in-itself. "The ideal of a consciousness which would be the foundation of its own being-in-itself by the pure consciousness which it would have of itself" corresponds to the notion of God as *ens causa sui* and the realization of this ideal, Sartre says, is man's fundamental project. Man is fundamentally the desire to be God, an ideal value forever drawing him on and forever incapable of being realized. Sartre's philosophy is a humanism, a philosophy for which there is only man in his world. But by anchoring his humanism to the conception of a pure consciousness, Sartre achieves a breakthrough into a dimension which is far removed from a crude "atheism" as well as from the type of subjectivistic humanism so sharply condemned by Heidegger.

In all his writings, Sartre's sole quest is for the truth of man. But he has gone to school with Hegel and realized that all truth is truth that has become so and that it is a whole, though not as Hegel believed a whole that could be conceptually possessed at any point of time. The foundations of this truth lie in the dimension of

human subjectivity examined in the earlier phases of his
writings. But man's subjectivity is only one moment in
the whole; it is immersed in society and its group
structures, in the whole fabric of culture and history.
Man fashions these through his work but he is himself
fashioned by the way he responds to them and understands
them. It is towards the articulation of such a total
truth about man, synthesizing the subjective and the
objective moments, that Sartre addresses himself in his
most recent works. In *Saint Genet*,[6] which may be regarded
as marking the transition from his earlier to his later
Marxist phase, we already find the original scope of ideas
widened, so that the story of this poet-dramatist's
liberation is told not only in terms of "existential
psychoanalysis" and the other categories of *Being and
Nothingness* but also takes into account the dialectical
interplay between the individual and the groups,
institutions, and class to which he belongs. In *The
Search for a Method*, we finally see the emergence of a
total framework, a kind of a philosophical macro-anthro-
pology in which the investigation of individual subjectivity becomes one element in a larger whole comprising
the entire sphere of work and culture, the life of the
group and the movement of history. The one question with
which Sartre is concerned in this work is "whether we have
the means today to constitute a structural, historical
anthropology," a comprehensive science of man in which the
insights of both Existentialism and historical materialism
can be reconciled and synthesized. Sartre believes that
the most comprehensive framework or "totalization" as he
calls it, within which we can think of man today is
Marxism, but a Marxism purged of its present-day
dogmatism, its mechanistic determinism and "dialectic of
nature" and incorporating within it the human dimension of
freedom and creativity.

The most ample philosophical "totalization" to have
been given in the recent past was Hegelianism and its
great merit was to have recognized the dialectical
relationship between knowing and being and nature of truth
as perpetually in process as History. But as Kierkegaard
saw, the rationalism of Hegel assimilates the *existing*
man, his unique subjectivity and lived experience, into a
system of ideas. Pure subjectivity can never be made the
object of knowledge and it was the merit of Kierkegaard to
have pointed out, "against Hegel and thanks to him," this
incommensurability of the real and knowledge. But while
Kierkegaard contents himself with an empty subjectivity,
Hegel reaches forward through his concepts to the
"veritable concrete," ever enriched by the constant
process of mediation, to the concrete man in his objective
reality. Marx agrees with Kierkegaard in asserting the
irreducibility of human existence to an idea and with
Hegel in his concern for the concrete objectification or
externalization of man in the world. But he reproaches
Hegel, quite correctly according to Sartre, for not taking
notice of the fact that self-externalization in the world
does not simply remain there as something to be contem-
plated as the product of man's creativity but results in
an alienation between man and his products so that his
externalization turns back against man and enslaves him.
For liberation from such alienation what is required is
not the work of the concept but "*material* work and
revolutionary *praxis*" which can bring about an objective
change in the world and enable man to live in greater
harmony with himself and with nature. Marxism thus
constitutes for Sartre a synthesis of the living truth in
Hegel and Kierkegaard and in that sense it remains "the
philosophy of our time," beyond which it is impossible to
go. Present-day Marxism, however, does not any longer
have the openness and the heuristic approach which are
essential to any living philosophy and hence Sartre
subjects it to trenchant criticism.

According to him, even original Marxism needs a more adequate theory of knowledge than Marx or Lenin have been able to provide. It will not do either to eliminate subjectivity altogether or to reduce consciousness to a simple reflection of the objective order. "Subjectivity," Sartre points out, "is neither everything nor nothing. It represents a moment in the objective process (that in which externality is internalized) and this moment is perpetually eliminated only to be perpetually reborn." In this process, both the internalization of the external and the externalization of the internal are necessary. Subjectivity or consciousness, as pure spontaneity and revealing negativity, represents the moment of freedom and *praxis*, the passage from objectivity to objectivity through internalization and choice of a personal project. This subjective or existential moment is one of immediate awareness or "comprehension," not of objective knowledge, which always presupposes it. Marxism as a system of knowledge must incorporate into itself, as its very core and foundation, this existential awareness, Sartre insists. So long as it does not provide an existential foundation for its anthropology by re-integrating man into it and by re-integrating "comprehension" into knowledge as its non-theoretical foundation, existential philosophy will continue to go its own separate way and attempt the task of constructing a philosophical anthropology in which the human reality is not forgotten. But, Sartre adds, "from the day that Marxist thought will have taken on the human dimension (i.e., the existential project) as the foundation of anthropological knowledge, existentialism will no longer have any reason for being. Absorbed, surpassed and conserved by the totalizing movement of philosophy, it will cease to be a particular inquiry and will become the foundation of all inquiry." It is not possible to attempt here anything beyond this bare hint at the direction Sartre's thought has taken in recent years.

The *Critique de la Raison Dialectique*, of which *The
Problem of Method* forms only the Introduction, has not yet
been translated into English, though expositions which are
already available[7] give some idea of the depth, range and
originality of this difficult work.

NOTES

1. *L'Imagination*, 1936; *L'Imaginaire*, 1940 (*The
Psychology of Imagination*, 1949).
2. *Esquisse d'une Théorie des Emotions*, 1939 (*Outline of
a Theory of the Emotions*, 1948).
3. *La Transcendance de l'Ego*, 1936-37 (*The Transcendence
of the Ego*, 1957).
4. *L'Etre et le Néant*, 1943 (*Being and Nothingness*, 1956).
5. *Critique de la raison dialectique*, *I*, 1960; serving as
Introduction in this work is the essay entitled, *Question
de Method* (*Search for a Method*, 1963).
6. *Saint-Genêt: Comedien et Martyr*, 1952 (*Saint
Genêt*, 1963).
7. Laing, R.D. and Cooper, D.G.: *Reason and Violence*
(1964); Odajnyk, Walter: *Marxism and Existentialism*
(1965); Desan, Wilfred: *The Marxism of Jean-Paul Sartre*
(1965); Cumming, R.D.: *The Philosophy of Jean-Paul Sartre*
(1965), which also contains translated extracts from *The
Critique of Dialectical Reason*.

THE CONCEPT OF PROGRESS

The ideas of self-fulfillment and freedom, as possible
ends of human worldly endeavour, have provided the dominant terms in which Western man has sought to understand
himself and his place and destiny in the world since the
Renaissance. In individual life and in the collectivity,
in social and economic spheres, in political affairs, in
the pursuit of scientific knowledge and in philosophical
thinking, these ideas have formed and sustained what we
call the modern world. Both these ideas, inter-linked and
mutually dependent, presuppose a new awareness of time,
not found in classical antiquity, and a changed relationship of man to time largely determined by the process of
secularization that has marked the shaping of the modern
mind. The first of these crystallized into the idea of
progress in the eighteenth century and is very much with
us still, despite vicissitudes in the way it has been
conceived and evaluated. The second has been a moving
force of incalculable power in human affairs and
reflection on it has constituted the core of modern
philosophical thinking about man and society.

Man's new awareness of time, oriented towards a wide
open future big with infinite possibilities of fulfillment, led to the rise of the historical consciousness and,
eventually, in the last two centuries to the recognition
of historicity as a basic dimension of human experience.
In this connection, names of thinkers such as Vico and
Herder, Hegel and Croce, Dilthey and Heidegger immediately
spring to mind. The conception of human history as moving

Originally published in *Indian Philosophical Annual* 3
(1967): 20-29.

towards a worthwhile and cherished goal, as against all
cyclic theories of history, is generally traced back to
the eschatological outlook of the Jewish Prophets and of
early Christianity. Referring to the secularization of
sacred history that occurred later, Karl Loewith has
pointed out that the attempt to understand the past and
the present in terms of a future *eschaton* is at the root
of belief in progress. As he remarks, "The future is the
true horizon of history....And while the West still
remains a Christian Occident, its historical awareness of
itself is also eschatological: from Isaiah to Marx, from
Augustine to Hegel, from Joachim to Schelling." This is
also true of historical practice. The English, French and
Russian Revolutions would never have happened without the
belief in progress, and there would have been no worldly
belief in progress without the original belief in an
other-worldly or supra-mundane goal of life. In the words
of Friedrich Schlegel, "the revolutionary desire to
realize the Kingdom of God is the buoyant point from which
springs all progressive culture and the origin of modern
history." Paul's Epistles to the Thessalonians constitute
a *locus classicus* of the Christian principle of hope, of
trustful waiting and working for a future that will save
and fulfill. In recent years, Ernst Bloch, the "Marxist
Schelling" of today and no Christian believer in the idea
of Providence, has offered a monumental version of a
secularized "Principle of Hope" as the foundation of a
complete philosophical system. The theory of lived time
as developed by Bergson, Husserl, and above all,
Heidegger, provides now an adequate ontological foundation
for a conception of history of which the true element is
seen to be in the future. History is meaningful only in
the perspective of future possibilities.

The idea of secular progress emerged as a fully
developed doctrine of humanity's triumphant march towards
Utopia in the writings of eighteenth-century French

scholars Turgot and Condorcet, who lived in the sunrise of the modern scientific spirit and, inspired by its confident optimism, saw the Golden Age "not behind us, but before us" and almost round the corner. Turgot spoke of the successive progressions of the human mind, in which "the human race, considered from its beginnings, appears to the eyes of a philosopher to be one immense whole that, like every individual, has its infancy and its progress." Following him, Condorcet wrote his famous *Sketch of a Historical Survey of the Progressions of the Human Mind*, aptly described as the canonical eighteenth-century French text on the idea progress. For Condorcet, the cumulative effect of scientific knowledge assures an irreversible but indefinite advance to a condition in which men will be ever healthier and happier, more developed in sensibility and reason, more equal in wealth and opportunity, more human and rational in their conduct. This Enlightenment idea of inevitable and infinite progress in rationality was supplemented and enlarged in the first half of the nineteenth century and given a more determinate goal in the writings of Saint-Simon and his followers and of Auguste Comte. Man was seen to be more than abstract reason and an honourable place was given to the activist and emotional elements of his whole nature. Progress in the Saint-Simonian view is linear and continuous and the law of perfectibility is absolute. It is also organic, a harmony of complex parts, not confined to rationality but involving an actualization of all human capacities and held together and animated by the power of love, expanding and diffusing through humanity in an ever-widening circle. The final, systematized formulation of the ideas of perfectibility and progress was given by Auguste Comte, with whom the religion of humanity became at the same time the religion of progress. A disciple of Condorcet and a great admirer of Catholicism for its principles of order and organization, Comte elaborated and gave definitive

shape to the thoughts of the French school in his system
of Positive philosophy. "The fundamental march of human
development," as he presents it here, is governed by the
supreme "law" of progressive evolution according to which
humanity advances from the theological to the metaphysical
stage and achieves adulthood in the final scientific or
positive stage of Western civilization. No longer sharing
Condorcet's "chimerical and absurd expectations," Comte
pleads for promoting the triumph of positive philosophy by
completing the vast operation begun by Bacon, Descartes
and Galileo, thus "reconstructing the system of general
ideas which must henceforth prevail amongst the human
race." Believing firmly in man's natural goodness and
rationality and focussing his attention on the socio-
political aspect of collective humanity, he looked forward
optimistically to the immediate future as one in which
human society will be scientifically organized and wars
"inevitably" eliminated.

For Hegel, history exhibits the progressive self-
realization of the Spirit or reason through the dialectic
of its successive incarnations in individual cultures. As
the sovereign reality of the world, reason brings about,
through its "cunning," the accomplishment of rational,
universal purposes and, eventually, of the ultimate purpose, the justification of God in history and the realization of His Kingdom on earth. Secular history becomes
identical with sacred. Marx seeks to go beyond Hegel in
his concern with the task of truly realizing reason in the
realm of material and human reality and therefore issues
the call for a radical break with the traditional philosophy of pure contemplation and for a revolutionary transformation of the world through *praxis*. He sees the
history of all hitherto existing society as the history of
class-struggles, of conflict between the oppressor and the
oppressed and of man's alienation from himself and his
labour. In this struggle a messianic role is henceforth

assigned to the proletariat, which will redeem and transform the world, once it has been made conscious of itself
and has become organized and politically active, and usher
in a period in which the "realm of freedom" will be
realized on earth. Marx is inspired by an eschatological
faith and his historical materialism is, as Loewith
remarks, "essentially, though secretly, a history of fulfillment and salvation in terms of social economy." In
the writings of the Jesuit paleontologist Pierre Teilhard
de Chardin we find a recent expression of this trust in a
religion of science, in which the positivist belief in
progress, the Bergsonian doctrine of Creative Evolution,
and the Pauline expectation of the coming of the Kingdom
of God and the mystical body of Christ are combined in a
strange synthesis. Condorcet, Saint-Simon, and Comte
erred not in their conception of a religion of science and
progress but in failing to see that their cult of humanity
depended upon a reinstatement, even though in a modified
form, of the very same forces of faith from which they
imagined themselves to be emancipated. And they could not
anticipate the eventual extinction of life, the destruction of the earth itself, which, modern science tells us,
must one day inevitably occur. According to Teilhard, the
basic error of all forms of belief in progress, as they
find expression in the positivistic confessions of faith,
lies in their inability to exclude death finally. Of what
use is the attainment of a centre and focal point at the
peak of evolution, when this centre must one day crumble
into dust? "Omega," the far-off, divine event, must be
independent of the collapse of the forces of evolution, a
supernatural fulfilment, beyond space and time, a
cosmo-christological metamorphosis, must occur when the
earth and mankind reach this terminal point of the
evolutionary process.

The notion of progress as a secularized eschatology
sketched above has been found unacceptable on many

grounds. Events and trends in European and world history since the eighteenth century have, in the first place, shaken that simple faith and its optimistic outlook on the future. The actual consequences of the French and later revolutions, the two world wars, the rise of new despotisms and the purges and concentration camps that accompany them, the atom bomb, all of these have more than justified the gloomy forebodings of Flaubert and Baudelaire, Dostoevsky and Tolstoy, Kierkegaard and Nietzsche. Crisis, catastrophe and extinction have over-taken civilizations and cultures in the past. This can happen again, as we learn from Spengler and Toynbee, who take, like Vico and Herder before them, a cyclic view of history. Who can predict with assurance that the complex, highly-strung civilization of today will not meet with sudden annihilation tomorrow or die of hunger a slower but more ignominious death? It is such doubts as these that have led in recent years to crises within theological and philosophical thinking and to a more deepened awareness of the difference between what humanity can achieve in its historical course, possibly but not necessarily, and what man is called upon to realize individually within the brief span of life allotted to him. The advance of scientific knowledge and technology during the last hundred years has opened out vistas of human achievement beyond the dreams of the Enlightenment thinkers of progress. But humanity is nowhere nearer perfection, materially or morally, and it has become evident that such advance, precious in itself and indispensable in the solu-tion of problems that face mankind, nevertheless, itself gives rise to further problems and threats which show up and expose man in all his finitude and neediness.

Secondly, the development of the historical conscious-ness itself has made philosophical historians more wary and critical, more sceptical of *a priori* constructions of history and speculation about last things. Historical

thinking, it was realized, must not be governed by norms
extraneous to it nor seek for a *telos* borrowed from
without. Already in the late eighteenth century, Herder
had shown that "each historical age and each people as
well as each age of the individual has the centre of its
blissfulness in itself," rejecting the Enlightenment idea
of inevitable progress from a primitive to a perfect stage
in humanity as a whole, either in respect of moral or of
rational perfectibility. As he remarked mockingly, "The
growing perfection of the whole might be an ideal that
refers to no one in particular. Well, perhaps it exists
only in the mind of God, in the Spirit of the Creator.
Now what would He be wanting with that kind of toy?" An
awareness of the illusory character of progress in world
history, of what Buckle called "moral progress," and
scepticism with regard to the validity and usefulness of
philosophical or theological interpretations of history,
in terms either of progress or providence, is clearly reflected in Burckhardt's *Reflections on History*. Attempting, like Dilthey, to comprehend the historical process in
a purely immanent manner, the only guiding principle he
insisted on was the principle of continuity, which gives
to finite man, "as he is and was and ever shall be," an
awareness of tradition and frees him in relation to it.
Continuity of historical awareness constitutes tradition
and its breakdown and replacement by a new barbarism would
be for the historical view of the world not just a
catastrophe within world history but, as Gadamer remarks,
the end of this history itself.

R.G. Collingwood has distinguished sharply between
historical progress and progress in nature or evolution
and has pointed out how the nineteenth-century conception
of progress as a law of nature was based on the misinter-
pretation of the historical process of nature. It also
failed to distinguish, as we have seen, between processes
within history and eschatological notions derived from

faith on the one hand and speculative notions concerning
the cosmos or the totality of beings on the other.
According to Collingwood, "Historical progress is only
another name for human activity itself, as a succession of
acts each of which arises out of the last...the accomplished act gives rise to a new problem...which the new
act is obliged to solve." But such progress is possible
only on the basis of historical knowledge, i.e., the
re-enactment of past experiences in the mind of the
present thinker, of a past experience known as past but
re-enacted here and now together with a development of
itself that is partly constructive and partly critical.
For Collingwood, historical knowledge is the mind's own
knowledge of itself as purposive and reflective, the
knowledge of what mind has done in the past, and at the
same time it is the redoing of this. Historical progress
is thus progress in self-knowledge. Such progress,
however, is "not a mere fact to be discovered by historical thinking: it is only through historical thinking that
it comes about at all," i.e., by the retention in the
mind, at one phase, of what was achieved in the preceding
phase in such fashion that the two phases are related not
merely by way of succession, but by way of continuity.
Whether Collingwood has said the last word on the precise
nature of this continuity is arguable but there is no
doubt that he has taken a first step that carries us
beyond Burckhardt's scepticism and beyond Loewith's Stoic
withdrawal from the historical consciousness within which
alone progress can be a meaningful concept.

There emerges thus a purely empirical view of history
for which progress presupposes a tradition of culture,
kept alive by unbroken awareness and carried foward by
incessant endeavour from generation to generation and
through continuous renewal and re-interpretation in the
light of possibilities and tasks to which the future
beckons us. For this empirical concept of progress, of

progress as fact, historical teleology is finite, intra-
mundane and dependent upon the human will to progress, be
it in the sphere of science and technology, be it in the
solution of those social, economic and political problems
where progress is both hindered and made possible, both
demanded and discouraged by the far greater pace of the
advance of science today. From the point of view of the
tradition, viz., the Western, which has generated the
concept of progress, progress in this sense is the very
condition on which the survival of that tradition depends.
And in so far as the rest of the world has become either
enveloped in that tradition or has consciously assimilated
it, it is also under the compulsion of progress, facing
the future in hope and determination and with a glimpse
into it which is content to be *ex parte, per speculum, in
aenigmate*. On the empirical level, thus, progress is
possible and necessary, in respect of both material
attainments and of man's historical understanding of
himself, as also of the freedom which is their basis as
well as conditioned by them, as Hegel and Croce, Marx and
Sartre have amply shown. In the oft-quoted words of
H.A.L. Fisher, "The fact of progress is written plain and
large in the page of history; but progress is not a law of
nature," and, as Karl Popper adds, "To progress is to move
towards some kind of end, towards an end which exists for
us as human beings. 'History' cannot do that; only we, the
human individuals can do it...progress rests with us, with
our watchfulness, with our efforts, with the clarity of
our conception of our ends, and with the realism of their
choice. Instead of posing as prophets we must become the
makers of our fate." The massive attack on the superstition of "historicism" by Karl Popper and against
notions of historical inevitability by Isaiah Berlin have
laid, once for all, the ghost of determinism and
prophetism in historical thinking.

To come back to our criticism of the religion of progress, the eschatological conception of progress derived from an experience of faith, in the next place, has not only no direct relevance to scientific or philosophical thinking about the future prospects of man's worldly life; by transferring it from the religious to the secular sphere it impoverishes and falsifies the meaning of that Biblical experience itself. Burckhardt saw genuine Christianity as essentially "ascetic" and otherworldly, with its hope and expectation in another world; a religion of suffering and renunciation, in permanent conflict with the *saeculum*, with a transcendent faith in a future redemption. "The crux of the modern religion of progress is not," Loewith remarks, "that it forgot the spiritual 'centre' of its secular 'applications' but that it applied an idea of progress which is anti-religious and anti-Christian both by implication and by consequences." The "pilgrim's progress" is very different from humanity's progress to perfection. The permanent centre of history where all meaning is realized is after all the human individual, suffering, striving, acting. The religious progress of the individual man, as temporally structured in his existence, converges on an ever possible moment in *his* future, in which time is fulfilled and history comes to end for him. "In every moment slumbers the possibility of being the eschatological moment," as Rudolf Bultmann remarks, and the irreligion of progress arises because the future of authentic existential time and the future of world-time, derived from it in the manner shown by Heidegger, are confused and, in consequence, the former is understood in terms of the latter. The very process of secularization which, as Loewith himself brilliantly demonstrates, led to the cult of progress, can also liberate us into the ability to re-think and reformulate the truth about time that lies hidden behind the mythical conception of eschatology, the metaphysical concept of

eternity and the understanding of time in the historical
consciousness. For secularization is nothing but the
continued and critical appropriation of tradition in the
language of the present, the demythologizing of the
utterance of faith in the attempt to comprehend its truth.
Loewith fails to notice this hermeneutic significance of
the existential interpretation of religious experience and
of the historicity that clings inexorably to the human
endeavour of self-understanding and its articulation. It
is this that makes him seek comfort in a revival of the
cosmological thinking of the Stoics, escaping both the
truth embodied in myth and religion and its faltering and
imperfect but progressive comprehension through the
historical consciousness.

The idea of continuous material, social and cultural
progress has generally been rejected by such contemporary
religious thinkers as Berdyaev, for whom it is the
seductive teaching of a modern anti-Christ and who thinks
of the redemption as a redemption from history, Niebuhr,
who thinks of it as a new idolatry, and Dawson, for whom
it is a failure to see the corruption inherent in all
things. Paul Tillich admits that the "law" of universal
progress as well as the circular theory of history are
myths, religious symbols as he calls them, and their
employment in understanding secular history is due to a
confusion of dimensions. He also accepts what we have
called "progress as fact," mainly within the spheres of
technology, the sciences, education, and the "increasing
conquest of spatial divisions and separations within and
beyond mankind," each of which, however, has a non-
progressive element which sets a limit to it. There is no
progress in realms where individual freedom is decisive
as, for example, in the moral act, the arts, philosophy,
the principles of personality and humanity and the
religious consciousness, though here, again, each of these
has a dimension to which the concept of progress is

appropriate. Beyond these "indisputable facts," as he calls them, progress is a "symbol beyond reality," a quasi-religious symbol defining the meaning and end of history itself. From the Christian perspective, the appropriate symbol for this is the "Kingdom of God" which, as a committed theologian, Tillich works out in all its implications for a theological interpretation of history, wondering yet whether this concept can provide a framework wide enough to cover the outlook of the Asiatic religions, particularly Buddhism. But, as Paul Weiss has incisively remarked, "A philosophy which fails to provide for all religions (even from the standpoint of the religion it favours) can be only an apologetic; the religion which fails to instance an independently achieved and grounded philosophy must (even from the standpoint of the philosophy it favours) be arbitrarily subjective." The empirical concept of progress is not limited, further, to the facts of progress, as in Tillich's view, and it must seek for a general explanatory principle immanent in the historical process itself. Theological interpretations of history as a whole, such as Tillich offers, depend upon experience illumined by faith and comprehended metaphysically through a presupposed notion of Being. Metaphysical interpretations of progress, affirming it in the form of a cosmic or divine evolutionism, or rejecting it in some form of non-Hegelian Absolutism or Greek and Nietzschean circularism, are all concerned with the truth of what is in its totality, with the truth of beings as such, and not with the truth of Being itself, as Heidegger has been at pains to point out. It is only in the context of an inquiry on this ultimate level, the level of what Heidegger has called the history of Being, that the true significance of progress or its absence, of the whole of what is or within it, can be laid bare. Here we can only give a brief indication of what Heidegger has to say in this regard.

Just as religious thinkers have seen behind the
outward occurrences, deeds, and ends pursued on the stage
of history the hidden hand of God, so many philosophers
have sought to formulate that hidden movement of reality
of which the externals of history can be understood as so
many manifestations. In his *Phenomenology of Mind* Hegel
has given an account of this real, hidden history behind
history as the progressive movement of mind towards
absolute self-consciousness. For Collingwood metaphysics
itself is the study of the history of the "absolute
presuppositions" upon which external progress and decline
depend and from which they flow. Nietzsche looked more
deeply, searchingly and realistically into this inner
movement of Western history and saw in it the approach of
that "uncanniest of all guests," Nihilism. Following him,
Heidegger has traced the lineaments and genesis of this
basic movement of which the outward manifestations
constitute what we cheerfully call progress and which is
no longer confined to the Western world. Accompanying
"progress" as its chill and deadening shadow is the
spiritual night falling on mankind, "the darkening of the
world, the flight of the Gods, the depradation of the
earth," as Heidegger describes it. Man has become the
subject of history, in this age of technology, objectifying the real and having it in his grip, calculating,
planning and ordering, seeking to enlarge his domain over
the realm of events by conceptualizing and representing
them. He has forgotten that in his essence he is not the
Lord of beings but the shepherd of Being and in consequence he has become enslaved and forfeited to beings.
The dimension of the Holy, in which alone Divinity can be
real to him, has vanished; Nature has turned into a mere
play of forces predictable and controllable by man; things
have become mere objects, and history the narration and
grasping of the factual and objectifiable, instead of that
invisible happening that has brought world-history to

pass. This is the price, as Karl Jaspers puts it, that
the West has paid for its "progress," the price which the
whole of mankind must pay in so far as it is also
enveloped in this process of "civilization," i.e.,
Europeanization. To be aware of this bleak and cold wind
blowing in the midst of "progress" is to inquire into the
genesis of both; it is to inquire into the Truth of Being,
into that happening of Truth from which both man and being
derive their essence. It is to realize that the Western
"metaphysical" tradition of thinking, conceptualizing,
objectifying and being concerned with the truth of beings,
is at the root of the present world-night as also of the
"progress" behind which it hides itself. For, as
Nietzsche saw, Nihilism is the basic happening behind
Western history, its "inner logic" and, as Heidegger has
laid bare in all its implications, Nihilism is only
another name for metaphysics as the history of the truth
of beings as such. The oblivion of the truth of Being
can, however, enter into our awareness; the impoverishment
and threat behind all "progress" can be experienced as
such and the oblivion experienced as oblivion. While
revealing beings to us *as* beings, Being conceals itself as
such. But once this withdrawal of Being is realized as
its way of recalling us to it, the possibility is opened
for our entering into its truth again, provided only that
we recognize ourselves as claimed by Being, at its
disposal, and subject to its destiny. Only if we let
Being in its truth be as the ultimate Identity in which we
are united with all that is, is it possible to save
ourselves, from the danger of "progress"; not by rejecting
it or putting a stop to it but by a resigned and tranquil
acceptance of it as a derivative and consequential
phenomenon. Its mastery can be broken only by opening
ourselves to a deeper truth lying concealed at the root of
the hidden metaphysical history behind the outward history
of "progress".

BEING AND NON-BEING

The basic words and ultimate concepts in which, about
which and around which the philosophizing of a people or
culture is carried on are not merely matters of remote
academic concern, and neither are the issues raised by
them resolvable through purely formal argumentation and
dialectical maneuvering. A deeper concern is at work
here, which we may seek to comprehend, even though without
the apparent conclusiveness of a logical demonstration.
For, these words and concepts are fatefully determinative,
in the last resort, of the way of being, seeing and doing
characteristic of a people's life and their historical
existence, as also of their experience of and relationship
to other cultures. Their thinking in general, not alone
their philosophical thinking, is generated from and
rendered possible on this basis; it is a culture's
characteristic response to what reveals itself in these
groundwords and concepts, and is no less limited and
restricted by them. Myth and ritual, poesy and music,
dance and holy image lay down the basic pattern of our
experience of that reality. But it is only with our
thinking response to this reality through our primordial
words that our historical existence as a cultural entity
is launched, a continued, collective life of dialogue,
conflict and self-criticism, of triumph and failure, but
also of a growing self-awareness. Such awareness then may
eventually enable us to transcend the limitation of these
formative "prejudgments," without loss of their liberating
power, and so open ourselves thinkingly to the challenge

Originally published in *Visva-Bharati Journal of
Philosophy*, 5 (1968): 15-34.

of other cultures and of other times and be prepared for
the task of freely determining our own historical life.
The term "being," with its correlate "non-being," is one
such groundword in the history of Western thought, indeed
the central directive concept of Western philosophical
thought. Its basic discipline, metaphysics, is therefore
primarily an inquiry into Being or Ontology, an inquiry
which is itself rendered possible by the fact that reality
revealed itself to the founders of this culture and this
philosophy under the aspect of Being, *as* Being. The
primordial experience which dominated and determined their
questions as well as the manner of their questioning was
the experience of this wonder of all wonders, that things
are, that they have being and are grounded in it. In what
does the being of a thing consist? What is Being itself?
How is it known and how is it related to thinking? What
are its possible modes and against what must it
be delimited?

Things come into being and pass away. Is there a
common ground from which they spring up and into which
they return? Is this ground, boundless and undifferen-
tiated, itself a thing, or is it rather the non-existent
principle (*arche*) through which each thing comes to be a
thing? All things in their totality are held within this
whole of beings. Does this whole itself have a ground
transcending it, in which case this ground cannot also *be*,
or is this whole, having nothing outside it, to be
understood entirely in terms immanent to itself as a
universal, the "beingness" that is common to all beings?
Is the world-ground to be thought of as the Being of all
that is in its totality but itself not a being? In what
terms then must this Being be conceived or spoken about,
so that one way of speaking is more adequate than another?
Or shall we speak of it as the One, beyond Being
(Plotinus) or, better still, as the Nothing (Pseudo-
Dionysus, Eckhardt), Abyss and *Ungrund* (Boehme), from

which Being itself emerges? Is it to be conceived as pure light which causes everything as such to emerge out of darkness and be, or as the primordial I, Reason or Spirit, certain and secure in possession of itself as the originative ground of everything? But, then, is this not to conceive the ground of what *is* in terms of something that also is, though not in the form of a substantial entity? Perhaps there is a way of raising these questions in a manner which is more radical, less metaphysically "loaded" and which might enable one to incorporate all the genuine insights of our experience of the ultimate, in the West or East, into this questioning, yet without presuming to adopt a position unconditioned by one's point of departure within a tradition of thought and absolute in its divine elevation above the finitude that attaches to all human thinking.

This is the way taken by Martin Heidegger, for whom the notion of Being constitutes the basic, but also the most problematic, gift handed over as a task for thought in the Western tradition. His point of departure therefore is the question about the sense of Being, but his field of exploration and interrogation is the entire landscape of the Western spiritual adventure. On his way back to the destination, he brings to bear upon this notion and his questionings about it the full weight of the philosophical and religious thinking, metaphysical or otherwise, in this tradition, aware that his own search may have relevance for the planetary thinking of the future, and for the dialogue between different traditions necessary for that. His inquiry is hence emphatically not one into a dessicated logical abstraction but into a notion that is comparable, in its plenitude, to the Heraclitian *Logos*, the ideas of God and *Gottheit* in the high tide of Medieval Scholasticism, or the Absolute of Hegel, consummate with a richness of content derived from both the Platonic-Aristotelian and the Judaeo-Christian

streams of the Western tradition. What Heidegger seeks
and offers is not a "conceptual analysis" of "being" but a
topology of Being, an attempt at charting a region from
which all lines of meaningfulness can be seen to emanate,
including the meaninglessness, the Nihilism, as Nietzsche
called it, in which mankind seems to be enveloped today.
For any attempt to investigate this place is bound to come
up against Not-being and the *Nihil* and to experience the
closeness of the Negative in the very Being of things,
just as, seeking to demarcate the realm of beings, one
must reckon with non-being, at the edge of the one whole
of all that is. As Heidegger has remarked,

> It is true that the Nothing appears to be utterly
> null and futile, so that even so much as men-
> tioning it by name is to do it too much honour;
> but this insignificant and common Nothing is
> nevertheless so uncommon that we encounter it in
> very unusual experiences. And what is common or
> vulgar about Nothing is only this, that it has
> the seductive power of letting itself be
> seemingly disposed of and eliminated, as a sheer
> nullity, through mere chatter. The Nothing of
> beings follows the Being of things as the night
> follows the day. Could we ever see and exper-
> ience the day as day if there were no night?
> Hence it is the hardest, but also the most
> unerring touchstone for the genuineness and power
> of thinking in a philosopher, whether he is
> aware, forthwith and from the bottom, of the
> nearness of the Nothing in the Being of what is.
> He who is denied this remains, for ever and
> without hope, banished from philosophy. [1]

It is for this reason that in approaching the question of
Being, Heidegger begins, following Hegel's admonition, by
looking Negativity squarely in the face, so that eventually he is enabled to incorporate it into the topology
of Being itself. The raising and answering of questions
pertaining to Being and Non-being, in varying perspectives
appropriate to its different periods, constitutes the
history of Western philosophy and Heidegger has only
sought to delve into the foundations of this ontological
history and point forward to a new way of thinking about

its presupposed basis. In this paper I shall be concerned
neither with this total history nor with Heidegger's
thinking on this topic directly. On the basis of the
perspective opened out by him and guided by his own treatment of the question, I attempt instead an elaboration and
discussion of Kant's views on this subject. I shall begin
with a brief examination of what Kant has to say about
Non-being and Nothing, pass on to his view of Being and
conclude with a reference to Heidegger's views on Nothing,
in so far as they are relevant to a critical appropriation
of Kant.

In the *Critique of Pure Reason*, Kant has given a table
of the division of the concept of nothing. His summary
remarks on "nothing" are attached, it may be recalled, to
the Appendix on "The Amphiboly of Concepts of Reflection"
with which the Transcendental Analytic comes to a close.
Kant appends them not because they are of any importance
in themselves but as "requisite for the completeness of
the system." That he did not altogether regard them as
unimportant is shown by the fact that in the *Prolegomena*,
he draws pointed attention to the distinction between the
concepts of "something" and "nothing," this most abstract
of ontological divisions, as he calls it, and to the table
he has constructed in the *Critique*. Kant, however, again
makes it clear that his main purpose is to exhibit the
completeness of his system of categories and how it can
provide unfailing guidance in the task of knowing with
completeness any object whatsoever of a pure concept of
the understanding or reason. Kant takes the concept of an
object in general as the higher concept and divides it
first into "something" and "nothing." "Nothing" is then
divided, "according to the order and under the guidance of
the categories"--since the categories are the only
concepts which refer to objects in general--as follows:
The first species of nothing is the *ens rationis*, an empty
concept without object. This is nothing in the sense of

"none," of the object of a concept to which no assignable intuition whatsoever corresponds and is opposed to the concepts of all, many and one. The second is the *nihil privatum*, the empty object of a concept or, as Kant also puts it, a concept of the absence of an object. This is nothing in the sense of the negation of reality (one of the categories of quality) as *something*. The third is nothing in the sense of an imaginary entity, the *ens imaginarium*, just an empty intuition without object. This is the mere form of intuition, without substance, itself no object, but the merely formal condition of an object. The fourth kind of nothing is the *nihil negativum*, an empty object without concept. This is the object of a concept which contradicts itself and, since the concept itself is nothing, this object is without content and so nothing in the sense of the impossible.

It may be of some interest to inquire whether this account, aimed at "the distinguishing of an object, whether it is something or nothing," is exhaustive of all possible meanings of "nothing" and whether Kant's thinking is not determined by a preconceived notion of being which is never explicitly stated and examined. Kant's remarks on "none" imply that our concepts of all, many and one remain mere *Gedankendinge* or thought entities and so without objective reference, unless they bear upon something given to us in intuition. We have the idea of an All or totality of things and of the unity possessed by this. As finite beings dependent upon something being *given* to us in intuition, we are in thought at least open to the Infinite. And yet, for Kant, this totality, either as the whole or as the unifying ground of all that is, remains a mere *ens rationis* to which there corresponds-- nothing. The rational entity, Kant says, is not to be counted as possible, for it is not supported by any example from experience, but it must not for that reason be declared also to be impossible for it can be

entertained in thought without self-contradiction. And
yet, the *ens rationis* is itself a form of "nothing," a
mere fiction, i.e., itself nothing, in the first of the
four senses distinguished by Kant. The third kind of
"nothing" is the imaginary entity, also positively
characterized by Kant as an *ens*. It is exemplified by
pure space and pure time, which are indeed something, Kant
admits, but as merely formal conditions of intuition, are
not themselves objects which are intuited. Both the empty
concept and the empty intuition are forms of nothing,
though the former must not be declared to be impossible
and the latter is a necessary condition of any object
being given in experience. The *nihil privatum* is the
negation of something determinate given to the senses.
But as Kant repeatedly asserts, all true negations are
nothing but limitations. Reality, or that which
corresponds to a sensation in general, when combined with
negation gives rise to limitation, i.e., to "something,"
which is thus inclusive of the limiting negation, as Plato
declared, even if we understand reality to mean, with
Kant, the "what," the *Sachheit* of anything. Reality and
negation are taken by Kant as concepts representing being
and non-being, respectively, in time. Further, negation
here is to be understood not as logical negation, which
does not properly refer to a concept but only to its
relation to another concept and is therefore quite
insufficient to determine a concept in respect of its
content. The negation is transcendental, for it refers to
such content as can be thought *a priori* as belonging to a
predicate, and it signifies the not-being in itself of
this content. Reality, on the other hand, is transcendental affirmation, "which is a something the very concept
of which in itself expresses a being." The *nihil negativum*, finally, is total nothingness, an *Unding*, because
the impossible object of a self-cancelling concept. That
of which the concept contradicts itself, for Kant, *is not*

and not a something, as yet indeterminate, but awaiting
conceptualization. Kant also completely disregards the
possibility, later envisaged by Hegel, that contradiction
may inhere in the content of the concept itself or that
the self-contradictory concept may, instead of being
totally self-annulling, be the positive indication of a
more adequate determination. Here then would be a nothing
incorporated within being itself and a negativity inherent
in "the labour of the concept."

Kant's views on "something" and "nothing" are derived
from and based upon his conception of knowledge as
resulting from a combination of intuition and concept;
where one of these is lacking we get a form of nothing.
Further, "anything" and "nothing" are conceived as sub-
classes of the concept of an "object in general," taken
problematically, as opposites *within* this wider class. An
object is a thing as "represented" in an intuition and as
conceived in relation to a subject which "represents" it
in a concept. For Kant only that counts as something
which can be in the mode of an object. But this leaves
open the possibility of a nothing as the other to all
"objects" as not a sheer nothing and yet not an object.
This becomes obvious in Kant's treatment of the imaginary
entity and the rational entity, as has been adumbrated
above. Pure space and pure time are imaginary entities
intuited in pure intuition. They are nothing in the sense
of not being objects, but as given in such intuition they
are still something. Although what pure intuition
discloses is not intuited thematically in the manner of
our apprehension of something that is simply given and
actually there, such intuition is not altogether vacuous.
What is intuited in pure intuition is the pure, unthe-
matic, unobjectifiable "look" or aspect which constitutes
the horizon within which empirical intuition can operate
and have objects disclosed to it. The "derivative
intuition" of finite beings has this in common with the

intuitus imaginarius of a divinity that, through the
activity of pure imagination, it can creatively project
the horizon within which a particular entity given by
sense may then be taken up. Human intuition is dependent
upon something given to it, whereas Divine intuition is
itself creative of what is apprehended in such intuition.
What the formative giving of pure finite intuition itself
gives is not a thing and yet not nothing, something and
yet a nothing. It may be argued in like manner that an
empty concept without object, i.e., the *ens rationis,* is a
nothing also in another sense than that meant by Kant.
The mere concept, to which no assignable intuition
corresponds, is a representation nevertheless and what is
represented in it is unity in a multiplicity, a rule and
the way it functions. Nothing in this sense is also a
something, though not as an object which can be given
directly in intuition.

In two passages in the *Critique of Pure Reason*, Kant
speaks of this something-nothing as an X and calls it an
"object":

1. All representations have, as representations,
their object, and can themselves become objects
of other representations. Appearances are the
sole objects which can be given to us immediately, and that in them which relates
immediately to the object is called intuition.
But these appearances are not things in themselves; they are only representations, which in
turn have their object--an object which cannot
itself be intuited by us, and which may,
therefore, be named the non-empirical, that is
transcendental object = X. [2]

2. All our representations are, it is true,
referred by the understanding to some object; and
since appearances are nothing but representations, the understanding refers them to a
something, as the object of sensible intuition.
But this something, thus conceived, is only the
transcendental object; and by that is meant a
something = X, of which we know, and with the
present constitution of our understanding can
know, nothing whatever, but which as a correlate
of the unity of apperception, can serve only for

the unity of the manifold in sensible intuition.
By means of this unity the understanding combines
the manifold into the concept of an object.[3]

The X is "object in general," not a general object,
entity or essent confronting us. Other than all essents
and constituting the horizon of objectivity as such,
within which any essent can be apprehended thematically as
an object standing over against us (*Gegen-stand*), this X
is, as sheer horizon, a nothing that transcends all
essents. It cannot be "known," as objects are known in
direct apprehension, and yet it is disclosed as that
through which essents become manifest. It is for this
reason that Kant calls such disclosure "transcendental
truth," for it is a form of knowledge of which the truth
lies in letting things be encountered and "known" in
experience as "objects." "All our knowledge," Kant says,
"is contained within this whole of possible experience,
and transcendental truth, which precedes all empirical
truth and renders it possible, consists in this general
relation to that experience."[4] The "nothing' transcending
all possible objects, it must now be obvious, is no other
than the being of these essents themselves and what Kant
calls "transcendental truth" refers to this ontological
domain, "an island enclosed by nature itself within
unalterable limits." No wonder he goes on to speak of
this realm, this "land of truth-- enchanting name!" as
being "surrounded by a wide and stormy ocean, the native
home of illusion."[5] What first seems to be a "nothing,"
when "to be" is to be given as an object, exhibits itself
as the very being of objects and the transcendental ground
of our knowing them. But this very Being, as Kant's
doctrine of Transcendental Illusion teaches, turns again
into a "nothing" when it is taken apart from all relation
to our knowledge of these objects, as subsisting
independently in the fashion of *a* being or essent.

Our knowledge of beings (essents), ontic knowledge,
depends upon a prior comprehension of their being. Kant
abandons "the proud name of an Ontology"[6] in favour of the
title "transcendental philosophy" because he rejects the
claim of traditional ontology to have, through pure
reason, direct and unconditional knowledge of the realm of
Being. Man is dependent upon something being *given* in
intuition, but knowledge of what is thus given (i.e.,
ontic knowledge) is possible only through the *a priori*
"knowledge" of Being, which transcends all beings. This
is ontological knowledge, but it has only an "empirical
use," for it is knowledge of the being of all beings as
encounterable in experience and hence "relative" to
experience. Pure intuition, pure imagination and pure
apperception in their unity constitute, as Heidegger has
remarked, "the pure act of objectification (*das Gegen-
stehenlassen von...*) which thus first makes manifest such
a thing as the horizon of objectivity in general. And
because pure knowledge in this way first opens up the free
space necessary for a finite being, i.e., the space in
which 'all relation of being and non-being'[7] occurs, this
knowledge must be termed ontological."[8] This was also the
concern of "the transcendental philosophy of the
ancients."[9] The *Critique of Pure Reason,* however, is "a
treatise on method, not a system of the science itself,"
as Kant expressly says, and what it accomplishes is the
exhibition of the inner possibility of Ontology or
metaphysica generalis. There is little that is directly
said about Being, that nothing-something in the light of
which beings are known. What was his conception of Being
and what were the limitations within which his conception
moved? The best known of his somewhat episodic remarks on
Being occurs in the course of his discussion of the
arguments for the existence of the *ens realissimum,* in the
section entitled, "The impossibility of the ontological
proof of the existence of God." Kant says here:

> "Being" is obviously not a real predicate; that
> is, it is not a concept of something which could
> be added to the concept of a thing. It is merely
> the positing (*Position*, from Lat. *positio* and
> equivalent in Kant's use to the German *Setzung*)
> of a thing, or of certain determinations as
> existing in themselves.[10] In logical usage, it
> is merely the copula of a judgement. The
> proposition, "God is omnipotent" contains two
> concepts, each of which has its object--God and
> omnipotence. The little word "is" adds no new
> predicate, but only serves to posit the predicate
> *in its relation* to the subject.

What is of primary significance here is the onto-
theological context in which Kant offers his view of
Being, here as well as in the pre-Critical essay, "The
only possible principle for the demonstration of the
existence of God." This may serve to remind us that in
the tradition of Greek-Christian metaphysics, the
Aristotelian question, "What is being (*ti to on*)?"
necessarily takes the two-fold form of an inquiry into
beings as such (*on he on*) as well as an inquiry into the
highest being (*to theion*). The metaphysical inquiry into
the being of what is (the essent) is, in other words,
simultaneously ontology, which is concerned with beings in
general, and theology, which deals with what can be said
to be in the highest, most complete sense. In both cases,
the being of all that is (beings or essents) is conceived
as the ground of essents, whether as the underlying basis
by virtue of which the essent is as such, or as the
highest being which causes everything to come into being.
For Kant also the ideas of the *ens necessarium, ens
originarium, ens summum, ens realissimum, ens entium*
constitute the theological background of what he has to
say about being (*ens*). Although, according to Kant, "the
ideal of the supreme being is nothing but a *regulative
principle* of reason, which directs us to look upon all
connection in the world *as if* it originated from an all-
sufficient necessary cause,"[11] yet he also speaks of such
ideas as "unsubstantial and baseless for the merely

speculative reason," which "feels indeed no loss in allowing them to vanish entirely."[12] And although the objective reality of the supreme being cannot indeed be proved and "it remains a mere ideal, it is yet *an ideal without a flaw*, a concept which completes and crowns the whole of human knowledge."[13] It is a fiction, an illusion which nevertheless is "indispensably necessary if we are to direct the understanding beyond every given experience (as part of the sum of possible experience), and thereby to secure its greatest possible extension, just as, in the case of the mirror-vision, the illusion involved is indispensably necessary if, besides the objects which lie before our eyes, we are also to see those which lie at a distance behind our back."[14]

As Heidegger has observed, the need to think that "God is" is the secret spur that drives the thinking of the *Critique* and subsequent works of Kant. Is God a being? Or is God the same as Being? Is Being itself also one more being or is it rather the other to all possible beings, in the light of which all beings are revealed as such? Is "to be" the same as to be an "object" for a knowing subject? How far can we conceive a supreme being as the existing ground and substratum of everything? Can Being itself be conceived, in the last resort, as ground? Kant's intense awareness of the unresolved problematic character of this notion--which he rejects for pure speculative reason, and for that alone--is vividly expressed in this passage in the first *Critique*:

> Unconditioned necessity, which we so indispen-
> sably require as the last bearer of all things,
> is for human reason the veritable abyss.
> Eternity itself, in all its terrible sublimity...
> is far from making the same overwhelming
> impression on the mind; for it only *measures* the
> duration of things, it does not *support* them. We
> cannot put aside, and yet also cannot endure the
> thought, that a being, which we represent to
> ourselves as supreme amongst all possible beings,
> should, as it were, say to itself: "I am from
> eternity to eternity, and outside me there is
> nothing save what is through my will *but whence
> then am I*?" All support here fails us.[15]

How problematic indeed the whole situation, in respect of
Being as supreme being and ground of things, must have
been for Kant can be realized when we recall that he was
confronting a legacy of thought which combined in itself
the Eleatic-Aristotelian notion of Being and the Christian
conception of God as Creator *ex nihilo* and, more
immediately, the legacy of an Aquinas, for whom, as for
Augustine, God and Being were the same. As Gilson has
remarked, in good Christian doctrine the first or proper
name of God is Being and this name denotes His very
essence, in such fashion that in Him essence and existence
are identical. The further view of St. Thomas that God as
Being is the pure act of existing, the conception of being
as act, being understood in the verbal sense of being, is
so foreign to Kant's subjectivistic way of thinking and to
his view of being as the "objectivity" of objects that it
is completely disregarded by him, and we have to wait
until Hegel and Heidegger to take serious note of the
dynamism inherent in the notions of Being and Non-being.
In terms of Kant's "transcendental theology," if we ask

> whether there is anything distinct from the
> world, which contains the ground of the order of
> the world and of its connection in accordance
> with universal laws, the answer is that there
> *undoubtedly* is. For the world is a sum of
> appearances; and there must therefore be some
> transcendental ground of appearances, that is, a
> ground which is thinkable only by the pure under-
> standing....[But] what this primordial ground of
> the unity of the world may be in itself, we
> should not profess to have thereby decided, but
> only how we should use it, or rather its idea, in
> relation to the systematic employment of reason
> in respect of things of the world....This idea is
> thus valid only in respect of the *employment* of
> our reason *in reference to the world.* If we
> ascribe to it a validity that is absolute and
> objective we should be forgetting that what we
> are thinking is a being in idea only.[16]

Kant clearly perceives that being is such only in relation
to beings, and that is the great insight of transcendental
philosophy. But like Aquinas he conceives Being as an

individual, as a being--and only as such can God be
conceived--and he is therefore forced to reduce it to a
demand of reason, a mere nothing. Thinking within the
Christian framework, he never allowed himself the
possibility of raising the question of Being in
independence of the theological problem of God. For the
same reason, he missed the insight that Being *as* Being,
independently of the notion of God, may be power and act
in relation to beings, without itself being conceived as *a*
being. For Kant, the activity is all on our side and
consists in our "employment" or "use" of reason; what
alone bothers Kant is how *existence* can belong to this
primordial ground, not how, if this ground "undoubtedly
is," as he admits, it must be conceived as generative, in
some sense, of both existence and *our* manner of comprehending it, and how if the ground is the ground of all
that is (exists), it cannot itself be an existing ground.
Kant is not only insensitive to the notion of Being as
pure act but does not question how the being of all beings
can itself be a being. In European thought the demand for
conceiving an ultimate ground in terms of a being beyond
substantial being (*epikeina tes ousias*) and of not-being
has been persistently felt and voiced by the protagonists
of apophatic or negative theology, from Plotinus to
Nicolas Berdyaev and Henry Dumery in our day, by the
German speculative mystics and by thinkers such as Jacob
Boehme and Schelling. Kant had a lively and deep sense of
the abyss before which reason stands and could not shake
it off, for deep calls unto deep, *abyssus invocat abyssum,*
as the old saying has it. But he was too much the
prisoner of his own Enlightenment presupposition as to the
nature of pure thought as "critical" and as "reason" to
have any use for these speculations. He could only shrink
back in horror from this shadow thrown by his own rationalistic, subjectivistic prejudice and make room for faith
as the repository of all that proved recalcitrant to
thinking conceived as reason.

To come back to Kant's statement of his "thesis," as Heidegger has described it.[17] Kant denies here that "being" is a real predicate, not that it is a predicate; and he asserts that it is mere or pure positing (*Position*). Kant here repeats what he already wrote, about twenty years earlier, in the pre-Critical essay mentioned before, except that the denial refers now, not just to a predicate, as in the earlier essay, but to a "real" predicate. A "real" predicate is one that belongs to the *res*, the content or the "what" of a thing, which can be represented in a concept. But such representation by itself does not imply that the thing is or exists nor, if it does exist, does its "what" or concept come to include any additional attribute thereby. Being is not real, in Kant's sense, i.e., does not pertain to the "what" of anything. But though to say of a thing that it *is* does not give us any further information about the thing as such or about its "what," it does tell us *that* this thing, this something as an object, is or exists. Being as pure position cannot be spoken about in terms of the 'what' or concept of an entity, for it is not part of the object, but means the positedness of something in an act of representation which is positing in character. Kant goes on to speak of "the logical use" in which being is merely the copula in a judgment, which only posits the predicate in its relation to the subject. Where, however, it is not merely the relation between subject and predicate that is posited but the thing itself is posited in itself, "being" is used in a different way from its logical use and means existence as, for example, in the sentence, "God is." Being in this use is described by Kant as the "Absolute positing of a thing," in which, as he puts it, "I go beyond the concept, not to another predicate not contained in the concept, but to the thing itself with just the same predicates, neither more nor less; only the absolute position beyond the relative is

thought in addition."[18] It should, however, be noticed
that even in "absolute position," i.e., in the objective
or ontic use of being (as Heidegger calls it to
distinguish it from the logical use), a relation is
posited, giving to the "is" the character of a predicate,
even though not a "real" one. This is the relation
between the positing subject and the object, with the
subject-predicate relation interposed across that, as
Heidegger puts it. Thus the copula "is" has a richer
meaning in the objective use than in the purely logical.

In the pre-Critical essay, Kant declared that the
concept of "is" was so simple that nothing could be said
towards explicating it and that in this case "the nature
of the object in relation to the faculty of our understanding does not also allow of a higher degree" of
clarity than that provided by the determination of being
as position. In the *Critique*, however, he sees that "to
be" *can* be explained further but that to do so we must not
consider being and existence solely in their "relation to
the faculty of our understanding." This further elucidation is given in connection with a discussion of
possibility, existence and necessity as modes of being.
So long as we seek their definition, Kant says, solely in
pure understanding, they cannot be explained save through
an obvious tautology and that if all sensible intuition,
the only kind that we possess, is removed, not one of
these concepts can be shown to be really meaningful.[19]
"To be" is indeed to be posited by an operation of the
understanding but such positing requires that something
should be *given* through sense affection, on which the
positing can catch and so set it up as an object standing
over against us. Being thus is positedness, but it is the
positedness of an affection. In order, however, that the
streaming multiplicity of presentations given in sensible
affection should find a halt and come to a stand in the
form of objects standing over against us, it is necessary

that it be ordered and connected together. This connecting can only be accomplished by the faculty of understanding, which is characterized by a mode of representation which Kant calls "synthesis." Such synthesis is
positing (*Position*) in the manner of a proposition, i.e.,
a judgment, through which alone thus what is given in
affection is known as an object. The "is" as copula here
means something more than "the representation of a
relation between two concepts," in which, according to
logicians, the nature of a judgment truly consists. As he
himself declares, Kant could never find this view satisfying, for its leaves undetermined the nature of this
"relation" and says nothing about the basis on which the
predicate is posited of the subject. The subject of the
proposition can be this basis only when it is at the same
time an object for a knowing subject. Kant, therefore,
says, "...a judgment is nothing but the manner in which
given modes of knowledge are brought to the 'objective'
unity of apperception. This is what is intended by this
little word of relation 'is,' employed in it to distinguish the objective unity of given representations from
the subjective."[20] The copula "is" is now seen to include
in itself the sense of unity, of a gathering and binding
together, that inter-relatedness of being and unity which
was already noticed by Parmenides and Heraclitus in the
first Western speculations about Being.

The "is" signifies a combination of the propositional
subject and predicate in the object and, along with that,
the unity which combines the given manifold. This unity
does not itself arise from a combination. Kant says,
therefore,

> This unity, which precedes *a priori* all concepts
> of combination, is not the category of unity...
> the category already presupposes combination. We
> must therefore look yet higher for this unity,
> namely in that which itself contains the ground
> of diverse concepts in judgment, and therefore of
> the possibility of the understanding, even as
> regards its logical employment.[21]

Upon this primordial synthetic unity of transcendental apperception rests the very possibility of understanding and therefore, as Heidegger puts it, it is that *hen*, the *Logos* of which Heraclitus spoke, from which arises all *syn* (together) of every *thesis* (positing). In this "principle of the original *synthetic* unity of apperception" lies, according to Kant, "the first pure knowledge of understanding," through which the being, i.e., the objectivity, of the essent regarded as object is rendered possible. Consistently with his premises, however, the location of this primordial unity is shifted to the "I" as subject and being, with its different modalities, is determined in terms of its relation to the understanding. For Kant, being as positedness is the positedness of something given and hence the objectivity of objects as disclosed to a thinking subject; it is with reference to such a subject that being derives its meaning as position.

A glance at Kant's treatment of those principles of pure understanding which he calls "Postulates of empirical thought in general" will show that this conception of being as positedness is also borne out in the case of the modalities of being. The three postulates, referring respectively to possible being, actual being and necessary being, are as follows:

> 1. That which agrees with the formal conditions of experience (in respect of intuition and concepts) is *possible*. 2. That which is bound up with the material conditions of experience (sensation) is *actual*. 3. That of which the connection with the actual is determined in accordance with universal conditions of experience, is (exists as) necessary.[22]

In conformity with Kant's thesis that "being" is obviously not a real predicate, the modalities of being also say nothing about *what* the object is but, as Heidegger puts it, only give information about the *how* of the relation of the object to the subject, for which reason they are called modalities. As Kant himself says, "The categories

of modality have the peculiarity that, in determining an object, they do not in the least enlarge the concept to which they are attached as predicates. They only express the relation of the concept to the faculty of knowledge," i.e., to understanding in its relation to affection.[23] The predicates of modality posit "certain determinations" of the object, for they tell us something about the object in itself, i.e., about the object as such, though not in respect of its "what" or reality. Being as possible, actual or necessary, in other words, is not a real or ontic predicate but a transcendental or ontological predicate. "Agreeing with," "being bound up with," and "connection with" are the relations posited by the various modalities as requirements for the possible, actual and necessary existence of objects. Being, as positedness, thus, is the pure relation of the objectivity of objects to the subjectivity of the knowing subject and possibility, actuality and necessity signify the position of the various modes of this relation. The pure synthesis of transcendental apperception is the primordial act of thought as an element in knowledge, the original "thesis" of human subjectivity from which arise the various modalities, determining what "to be" means, along with its different modes.

Why must we distinguish between possibility and actuality and what is the basis of this distinction? Towards the close of the *Critique of Judgment*, Kant remarks in a Note (Sec. 76), "It is for the human understanding inescapably necessary to distinguish between the possibility and actuality of things. The reason for this lies in the subject and the nature of his faculty of knowledge." The need for this distinction lies in the fact that for knowing anything we require two quite disparate functions, understanding for concepts and sense intuition for objects which correspond to them; were our understanding intuitive, it could have no objects as

actual, and concepts (which concern only the possibility
of objects) and sense intuition (through which alone
something is given, but without being determined as an
object) would both become superfluous. In regard to the
basis of the distinction, Kant goes on to say, "Now, all
our distinctions of the merely possible from the actual
rests on this that the first signifies only the positing
of the representation of a thing in respect of our concept
and of the faculty of thinking in general, whereas the
latter means the positing of the thing in itself (beyond
our concept)." This not only confirms that for Kant being
is positedness and possibility and actuality different
modes of positing but shows that in the very nature of the
being of things, as Kant conceives it, there inheres this
necessary distinction between possibility and actuality.

Kant "explains" being as pure position and thus
"locates" its meaning in positing as an activity of human
subjectivity. That from which, or in terms of which,
being gets its meaning is its location and to ask about
the geography of this location (*Ort*) is to attempt to
determine the context from which "positing" itself derives
its meaning.[24] "The crossbearings" of this region have
been traced by Kant, as Heidegger has pointed out, in the
Appendix to the *Transcendental Analytic* entitled "The
Amphiboly of Concepts of Reflection" to which attention
has already been drawn earlier. Being as position, i.e.,
as the positing and the positedness of objects, has been
explained with reference to the different relations to the
faculty of knowledge. These relations are reflexive
relations, for they refer to "the act by which I confront
the comparison of representations with the cognitive
faculty to which it belongs," which Kant calls "transcendental reflection" and which is concerned, not with
objects directly, but with the experiencing subject.
Being, in other words, has been explained in terms of that
location to which reflection is the appropriate cognitive

response. The further exploration of this region consists of an examination of the "concepts of reflection," in a reflection on reflection which constitutes for Kant the ultimate *locus* (*topos* or place) of human subjectivity as defined by its relation to what is given in sense affection. The principal concepts of reflection mentioned by Kant are those of identity and difference, of agreement and opposition, of the inner and the outer and of the determinable and the determination (matter and form) and hence the final location of the sense of being must be found in terms of the distinctions contained in them. Amongst these transcendental concepts of reflection, the contrasting pair of matter and form is the most basic. As Kant himself declares, "These two concepts underlie all other reflection, so inseparably are they bound up with all employment of the understanding. The first (matter) signifies the determinable in general, the second (form) its determination."[25]   And it is in terms of these that Kant has "explained," as we have seen, the meaning of "possible being" and "actual being," the one referring to the formal, the other to the material conditions of experience. "Form" is determination, depending upon the spontaneity of the understanding, and "matter" the determinable, presented through the receptivity of sense-perception. Thus, for Kant, "to be" means to be posited and the latter itself gets its meaning from the innermost core and location of human subjectivity, i.e, from a thinking of thinking which is intrinsically bound up with sense-perception.

Western speculation about Being has taken a great stride forward in Kant's reflections on Being, for he has demonstrated that the being of things is not itself a thing and not objectively given, that it belongs to a non-objectifiable realm of its own; he has seen something of the complex structure of this realm and in particular its character as unifying and enabling, but he has also

exhibited how all talk of Being is meaningful only in the
context of our experience of beings. We have "knowledge"
of beings but only in the light of a prior conception of
their being. Kant has also stated his "thesis" about this
prior conception and told us that being and non-being lie
in the objectivity of beings, i.e., in their being experienced as objects and also that such experience is grounded
in the depths of our own subjectivity, i.e., in our own
being, conceived as *subject*. But Kant does not inquire
into the basis of this prior conception itself, does not
ask as to the presupposed sense of being which makes it
possible for being to be determined in terms of position,
positing and positedness. He has made it evident that the
being of things gets its sense from beyond it, i.e., from
what he calls its "transcendental location," the thinking
of thinking as conditioned by sense. But he does not ask
why, in Heidegger's words, "in determining the positedness
of what is posited, the former emerges as subject in a
two-fold form, once as subject in relation to a predicate
in a proposition and again as I-subject in its relation to
the object. What does it mean for being to be determinable in terms of the *subiectum* or, to use the Greek
expression, of the *hypokeimenon*?" Heidegger's own answer
to this question is that the sense of being tacitly
presupposed in all "metaphysical" thought, including that
of Kant, is that of constant presence, which is then
interpreted as what lies in front (*hypokeimenon*), as what
has been laid down, put down, represented and posited.
Once it has been seen that positedness and objectivity are
themselves derived from being understood as constant
presence, it becomes also clear that being in this primary
sense cannot be explained in terms of and through
reflection (thinking of representational thinking), nor
can it be located as to its origin and meaning in the
human subjectivity.

The specific interpretation of being, including man's being, as subject, presupposes being as presence. Is it possible to think about, or locate the sense of, being and non-being, presence and absence, not in terms of human subjectivity nor indeed in terms of any essent but in themselves? Is it possible to think about and determine the sense, not of beings as beings, but of Being itself as Being? To ask this, as the metaphysical tradition of the West has never done, is to raise, with Heidegger, the question of Being and so inquire, beyond the truth of beings, into the truth of Being itself, from which all presence and absence flow and are sustained as such.

The history of ontology begins with Parmenides' sharp *krisis* or separation between being and non-being, with his assertion that only being is and that non-being is not and with his prohibition to let thought travel on the way of nothingness. Plato laid unfilial hands on the pronouncement of "father Parmenides" by taking this way and sought to "establish by main force that what is not, in some respect has being, and inversely that what is, in a way is not." In his account of the "great refusal,"[26] Whitehead follows him, in this century, in insisting that every event is decisive in proportion to the importance (for it) of its untrue propositions, and that each eternal object which is synthesised *qua being* is also synthesised *qua* not-being. The Platonic perplexities over being and non-being, handing over to posterity the logical problems of negation and existential judgment, and his characterization of the sensible world itself as *me on* (non-being, not utter nothing) did nothing, however, to overcome the dualism of Being and Non-being generated by Parmenides' delimitation of Being against Non-being. The dark shadow of Non-being, looming as the unthought and unthinkable Other to Being in the background, deepened with the arrival of Christianity. The idea of creation *ex nihilo* added to the notion of non-being (*genesis* and *phthora*,

change and otherness) the dimension of Nothingness in the
interpretation of world and man, giving rise to the need
for justifying the very existence of things in their
totality. The Spanish philosopher Xavier Zubiri has
described this happening in the following words:

> The Greek is alienated by the world because of
> its *changeability*. The European of the Christian
> era is alienated by its nullity or, better still,
> its *nihility*....For the Greek, the world is
> *something* that changes; for the man of the
> Christian era it is a *nothingness* that seems to
> be or exist....With this change of perspective
> being comes to mean something *toto caelo*
> different from what it meant in Greece: for a
> Greek, being means to be there, at hand; for the
> Western European, being means, first of all, *not
> being nothingness*....In a certain sense, then,
> the Greek still philosophizes *from the point of
> reference of being*, and the Western European
> philosophizes *from the point of reference of
> nothingness.*[27]

It is against this theological background that we must
understand the notion of Non-being as Nothingness, like
the problem of Being, if we are to make sense of the
question raised by Leibniz, "Why is there something rather
than nothing?", later repeated by Schelling and taken up,
in our own day, but in a transformed sense, by Martin
Heidegger in the context of his inquiry into the sense
of Being.

While asking this question, Heidegger does not
inquire, like Leibniz, into the sufficient ground of
essents, itself essent, but into the Being of beings,
problematically and tentatively conceived as the
transcendental ground of beings. Leibniz's question
already presupposes the Christian answer, as also the
principle of sufficient reason, first explicitly stated by
himself as the central principle underlying all
metaphysical inquiry. Setting aside the testimony of
revelation as inappropriate to philosophical thinking and
seeking to discover the possibility and structure of
transcendence within man himself, Heidegger asks whether

and how man can reach out beyond himself and all essents, what it is that manifests itself to him in this act of transcendence and how far this is to be conceived as the ground of all essents. The "metaphysical" inquiry into the essent *qua* essent is an inquiry that seeks to comprehend the essent by going beyond it and Heidegger also begins his questioning with an examination of the nature of that transcendence. But though his question is posed in the manner of the metaphysical tradition, he answers it in a quite different way, for according to him, that *to* which we transcend in going beyond all essents is not God—Himself an essent, albeit the highest one—but that which is the other to, or the other of, all things, the nothing. But this nothing, far from being absolute non-being, is the "not" of beings only when regarded in terms of the latter; though it constitutes an experience necessary to make us aware of the limits of the meta-physical concern with essents, the nothing shows itself, once this insight is attained, to be only the veil of Being itself. Seeking to discover a transcendent ground for all that is, we find ourselves confronting the abyss of nothingness. For Heidegger this leads to the insight that this negativity of transcendental experience is an experience of non-being as the inescapable correlate of the subjectivistic will to ground beings, to go beyond them only to have beings all the more firmly in our grip. As he has remarked,

> Non-being as the "not" of beings is in sharpest opposition to mere nullity. Non-being is never sheer nothingness and it is as little a something in the sense of an object; it is Being itself, the truth (disclosure) of which is only then made over to man when he has vanquished himself as subject, i.e. when he no longer represents the essent as object.[28]

The encounter with the "not" of essents enables us to shed our self-will, to see things in their true being and the "not" itself as a manifestation of Being and integral to

it. The experience of this "not" is the surrender of the
"metaphysical" will to possess and ground, to secure and
certify; it is the abandonment of all hope and all desire,
the suspension of all willing and all knowing and hard as
cutting ourselves loose from the last shore, as the aged
Schelling saw. In the latter's words, "What is needed
here is to leave *everything*, not merely, as we are wont to
say, wife and child, but everything that *is*, God Himself,
for in this respect even God is an essent. He who would
place himself at the starting-point of a truly free
philosophy must hence lose God Himself. Here it is true
that he who wants to retain it shall lose it and he who
loses it shall find it."[29] With such surrender, the abyss
of non-being is seen to be a "not" clinging to Being
itself as its veil.

Neither of Being nor of Non-being can we say that it
is (for only beings are) and yet, as Heidegger puts it,
"It gives (*Es gibt*)" both.[30] We shall not ask here, with
Heidegger, how both derive simultaneously from the mystery
of truth and the mutual owning of man and Being in the
Ereignis, to which Heidegger is finally led in his
"topology" of Being. Instead, let us examine briefly the
notion of Non-being as the veil of Being. If Non-being is
not sheer nothing, it must belong to Being itself as a
negativity inherent in it. Its origin cannot lie
ultimately in human subjectivity, either as privation or
negation, as an illusory projection of thought or figment
of the imagination, as little as the way Being is revealed
to man can be regarded as his invention. The "not,"
Heidegger says, never arises from the no-saying of negation, for every "no," which does not misinterpret itself
as wilful presuming on the power of subjectivity to posit,
is really our response to the claim of the naughting that
resides in Being itself and which reveals itself as the
"not". Every "no" is only the affirmation of Non-being.

> Because the naughting occurs in Being itself, we
> can never perceive it as something clinging to
> the essent. But this impossibility is no proof
> that Non-being has its origin in no saying. This
> proof appears sound only when the essent is set
> up as the objective (counterpole) of subjec-
> tivity. From this alternative it is then con-
> cluded that every "not," since it is never mani-
> fested as something objective, must necessarily
> be the product of the act of a subject....The
> naughting prevails in Being itself and by no
> means in the human being, in so far as this is
> conceived as the subjectivity of the *ego cogito*.[31]

In the absolute idealism of Hegel and Schelling, negativity is for the first time taken up into the innermost
happening of Being, but it is conceived there as "negation" because Being itself is for them of the nature of
Will, a character which was soon to emerge to the surface
as the will-to-power, along with Being itself as the
Nihil, in the explicit metaphysical nihilism of Nietzsche.

Being, as presence, and Non-being belong together in
the same location *(topos)*, according to Heidegger, and
both are consequent on the "metaphysical" quest for
transcendence and ground. The "not" as absence, and as a
possibility inherent in presence itself, is the nihilistic
spectre lying in wait at the heart of all "metaphysical"
thinking as such, for such thinking is concerned solely
with the essent, and with *its* being only as it transcends
and grounds it, and not with Being itself in its own
truth. From the perspective of the latter, however,
"metaphysics" is not due to man's making but is one way in
which Being conceals itself as such from man in the
process of revealing the essent as such to him. The
unhiddenness or disclosure of the essent as such is the
happening of metaphysics. In this happening, Being itself
is disclosed as the being of beings, while staying away in
its own truth, remaining hidden as Being and denying
itself as such. Non-being as the veil of Being is not
another entity, as little as Being itself, with which
Being covers itself up; it is this staying away itself, as

which Being discloses and gives itself to us. This is the
negativity inherent in Being, the "not" which derives in
the ultimate resort from the nature of truth itself. For
truth in the primordial sense is unhiddenness rooted in
hiddenness, revelation anchored to concealment. Metaphysical thinking of every form, but especially the
Cartesian-Kantian variety of subjectivism, is rooted in a
disclosure in which what remains hidden is precisely this
"not," this contrariety in the truth of Being as such. In
Kant's conception of Being as positedness, the presupposed
view of being as constant presence, underlying the entire
metaphysical tradition, remains the basis. But if, as
Heidegger maintains, being and nonbeing are not simply
equivalent to presence and absence, if being is conceived
as rich with the opponency of refusal and bestowal
intrinsic to it, it can no longer be regarded as amenable
to "pure reason" and its concepts, nor can presentedness
in pure intuition exhaust the full richness of Being.
Further, if the primacy of the present in all presence is
presupposed, unquestioningly and unjustifiably, as
Heidegger insists, in the Greek experience of Being on
which the whole metaphysical tradition rests, Being as
thus inclusive of the "not" must also be regarded as
incorporating within itself the full reality of time as
the unity of the past, present and future. Finally, if
"to be" cannot be thought of as something apart from the
human essence but only as mutually related and ingressive,
as Heidegger has demonstrated, it necessarily evades metaphysical thought, whether conceived as *theoria* or as
reflexio, giving no promise of the assurance and certitude
in our thinking about Being so relentlessly pursued by Kant.

Transcendental illusion, Kant says, mocks us with a
reality where none is to be found.[32] According to him,
the illusion is natural and inevitable, and it rests on
subjective principles, which it foists upon us as
objective. As he declares in a well-known passage,

> There exists, then, a natural and unavoidable
> dialectic of pure reason—not one in which some
> sophist has artificially invented to confuse
> thinking people, but one inseparable from human
> reason, and which, even after its deceptiveness
> has been exposed, will not cease to play tricks
> with reason and continually entrap it into
> momentary aberrations ever and again calling for
> correction.

Where is the locus of this "entirely natural antithetic"?
Does it lie in the positing, thetic character of reason or
does it derive, more primordially, from the contrariety of
Being as such, or, in the last resort, from the revealing-
concealing mystery of truth itself? Is the transcendental
dialectic merely negative, or does it not rather lead to a
more positive location of this transcendental untruth
(illusion) within transcendental truth itself and at one
with it as its own disessence?

NOTES

1. *Nietzsche*, 1:460.
2. *Critique of Pure Reason*, A 108f.
3. Ibid., A 250.
4. Ibid., A 146, B 185.
5. Ibid., B 294f.
6. Ibid., A 247, B 303.
7. Ibid., A 110.
8. *Kant und das Problem der Metaphysik*, 82.
9. *Critique of Pure Reason*, B 113.
10. The translation is N. Kemp Smith's. In the original
the sentence runs: "*Es ist bloss die Position eines
Dinges, oder gewisser Bestimmungen an sich selbst.*" Max
Müller translates this as "It is merely the admission of a
thing, and of certain determinations in it." According to
Heidegger's commentary in *Kants These ueber das sein*,
"certain determinations" are the modalities of the thing
as it is in itself, i.e., as object.
11. *Critique of Pure Reason*, N.K. Smith's translation, 517.
12. Ibid., 513f.

13. Ibid., 531.

14. Ibid., 533f.

15. Ibid., 513.

16. Ibid., 565ff.

17. *Kants These ueber das Sein.* The discussion of Kant's view of Being in this paper is based on this essay by Heidegger.

18. *Kant's gesammelte Schriften, Akademieausgabe,* vol. ?, 73; see also vol. 18, no. 6276.

19. *Critique of Pure Reason,* B 302 and B 302a.

20. Ibid., B 141f.

21. Ibid., B 131.

22. Ibid., A 218f., B 265f.

23. Ibid., A 219, B 266.

24. For Kant's remarks on "transcendental location (topic)" and its difference from "logical location (topic)" see *Critique of Pure Reason,* A 265f., B 324f.; for his discussion of "definition" and "explanation," see A 730, B 758. Following him, Heidegger distinguishes between *Erklaerung* and *Erlaeuterung* and derives both from *Eroerterung.* For further elucidation of these distinctions, see Otto Poeggeler's *Der Denkweg Martin Heideggers,* 280-296 and the author's *The Philosophy of Martin Heidegger,* 58 and 387.

25. *Critique of Pure Reason,* A 266, B 322.

26. *Science and the Modern World,* Mentor ed., 143ff.

27. Quoted by Julian Marias, *History of Philosophy,* 105-196.

28. *Holzwege,* 104.

29. Schelling, *Ueber die Natur der Philosophie als Wissenschaft,* quoted in Walter Schulz, *Der Gott der neuzeitlichen Metaphysik,* 57f.

30. *Zur Seinsfrage,* 38.

31. *Humanismusbrief,* in *Platons Lehre von der Wahrheit,* 112-114.

32. *Critique of Pure Reason,* B 530, A 502.

33. Ibid., A 298, B 355.

PROBLEMS OF INTER-CULTURAL UNDERSTANDING IN
UNIVERSITY STUDIES OF RELIGION

The question of the study of religions in Indian
universities has to be raised within the context of the
cultural situation prevailing in the world today generally
and in this country in particular. And since the
religious tradition that constitutes the predominant
strand in the cultural fabric of India is Hinduism, I, as
a Hindu coming from the Holy City of Varanasi and from the
Banaras Hindu University, can only raise it from this more
particular and specific point of view. It is only when we
speak from such concrete *points* of view that we save our
talk from running into abstract generalities, evading the
real issues that confront us, and come to grips with the
actual and the problematic. Far from limiting or
narrowing our inquiry, or encapsulating us within the
particularity of our cultural horizon, such points of
view, along with the presuppositions and prejudices that
inevitably go with them, alone provide the vantage point
from which a problem can be seen as real and meaningful to
us. As a student of "understanding" (*Verstehen*), I am
aware that "all understanding, irrespective of whatever
object it refers to, is ultimately religious", as Van der
Leeuw puts it, and also that the modern phenomenon of
"comparative religion" can itself be profitably approached
as a species of such "understanding." In what follows, I
shall accordingly seek to explore the subject of inter-
cultural and religious understanding from the perspective

Originally published in *Ānvīkṣikī: Research Bulletin of
the Centre of Advanced Study in Philosophy*, ed. by N.K.
Devaraja. Banaras Hindu University 1 (1968): 78-93.

of philosophical hermeneutics in so far as it is relevant
to our present task and to our concrete situation. The
factors that enter into and condition the particular
situation in this country may be broadly divided into two
groups: those that involve the Indian's relation to his
own religious tradition and those that concern the
contemporary impact upon this of other world-religions and
traditions. As implied by our perspectivistic approach
and as I hope to show more explicitly in the course of
this paper, the first of these is the more basic task for
us in India and in consequence any intelligent formulation
of the question which concerns us must be sought in terms
of that rather than in terms of an abstract and general
comparison of different religious traditions. The primary
task which faces us in this country today is, I submit,
the task of a critical and creative understanding of our
own religious traditions. This is not a merely
"academic," ivory tower pursuit but a necessary effort at
self-understanding upon which depends not only the sense
we have of our own identity but also what we strive to
become in the future in a world in which barriers of time
and place, of memory and hope, are breaking down, in which
we are slowly becoming enveloped in a common destiny.
This is both a threat and an opportunity. Among the
leading Christian thinkers of the West, at least, one
finds notable examples of intense and searching efforts
towards such self-understanding. That these efforts are
inseparably linked with the general intellectual climate
of the present and with a sincere striving towards a
dialogue with other religious traditions is evident from
the emergence of the new discipline of Comparative
Religion. In this paper, I should like to dwell at some
length upon the self-criticism and reconstruction that go
hand in hand with it. I should also like to say a few
words as to why I think that we in this country must learn
from this pre-occupation of Western theologians and

religious thinkers and why, before undertaking to formulate a conceptual frame-work or formula for a possibly
universal religion, we must take upon ourselves the more
humble task of self-examination and self-understanding, in
explicit awareness of all that such a task involves.

Lest I may have given the impression of conceiving too
narrowly the objectives of instituting religious studies
in Indian universities, I hasten to add that I consider
the very first of these to be a better knowledge of "the
faith of other men" and of other religious traditions, a
knowledge which is not merely scientific but insightful
and an understanding awareness of what is other. The
second task before such studies here is a similar comprehending knowledge of religions that have, on the one hand,
taken root in India, e.g. Christianity, Islam and Zoroas-
trianism and, on the other, those that have grown from
within our own tradition, e.g. Hinduism in all its variety
of sect and cult, Buddhism, Jainism and Sikhism. The
third aim, referred to earlier as the primary task before
us, is that of self-understanding of a critical appropriation and reconstruction of our own religious tradition in
its unity, in the perspective of our present cultural
situation and of our participation in the secular, scientific and technological adventure of man in the present
day world. Only after this return movement to ourselves
can we, in the last place, go on to the task of constructing a broad enough frame of reference for all religions,
in terms of which we can comprehend their variety, and of
reawakening an understanding of the sacred as an ineluctable and basic dimension of our experience, of our very
being as necessarily involved in Divinity. A fifth task
suggested by the Education Commission refers to religious
instruction and I shall say nothing about it here.

It may appear that the fulfillment of the first task
is an easy matter, requiring only a study of readymade
textbook material on the religions of the world. But

obviously a study which seeks to *comprehend* from within
the faith and traditions of other men must go much further
than acquiring mere information *about* them. It must
strive to comprehend the other in its otherness, let it
speak to us in its difference from us and allow it to lay
hold of us in its claim to truth. I make bold to suggest
that such an approach to what is other is somewhat alien
to the genius of our entire tradition and the task
therefore correspondingly difficult and against the grain
for us; also that we cannot take the first steps towards
an understanding of other religious traditions unless we
first notice and acknowledge understandingly this more
basic difference at the root of the cultural traditions of
East and West. In its understanding of both itself and
the other, India has followed the way of growth through
absorption and assimilation, rejecting what could not be
appropriated without its own disintegration, accepting
from other cultures whatever could be suitably transformed
to become part of its living body. The Indian cultural
tradition thus has retained its identity and continuity
but it has at no time *defined itself* in relation to the
other, nor acknowledged the other in its unassimilable
otherness, nor in consequence occupied itself with the
problem of relationship as it arises in any concrete
encounter with the other. It is true that much of the
purely philosophical activity in this country has been in
the past concerned precisely with this task of analysing,
demarcating and defining the metaphysical presuppositions
of the principal religious trends that were of indigenous
origin here. But this led only to the fixation and
hardening of a number of rival "positions," to the emergence of an extraordinarily energetic analytical thinking
in which the logical implications of each were meticulously worked out, and to the development and co-existence
of independent "religions." The other was allowed to
live, mostly in peace, but without any effort at mutual

dialogue and understanding. In the second place, neither
in religious thinking nor on the strictly philosophical
level was there any explicit intellectual attempt within
our tradition, in the long history of its encounter with
Christianity and Islam, to understand them in their
difference or to let them address us in their truth. The
strategy was one of defense through insulation rather than
one of active grappling or dialogue and this was perhaps
made necessary by the exigencies of historical circumstance and, partly at least, by the very nature of these
alien incursions and their uncomprehending claims.

The Western approach, in this respect, has been
markedly different. As Karl Loewith has remarked: "The
experience of the essential difference between Orient and
Occident has laid the foundation of the entire history of
Europe and put its stamp on it." Ever since the Greeks
attained a sense of their own individual identity through
their encounter with the Persians, from whom they distinguished themselves as from their Barbarian other, this
process of delimitation and exclusion has been continuous.
The West's relationship to other cultures is determined by
its characteristic mode of thinking in concepts, that
"enormous power of the negative" of which Hegel speaks in
the *Phenomenology of Mind* and which constitutes that
"energy of thinking", the intellectual activity of making
distinctions, of dividing and separating, in which lies,
according to Hegel, "the most amazing and the greatest
power and work of the understanding." This negative,
separative intellect of the West does not leave the world
as it is, but works it over, changes it, analyses it into
its elements, puts them together again and in this manner
makes it its own. As the power of the negative, the
understanding also objectifies everything, and is thus
enabled to change and direct the course of the world. For
Hegel, the crucial mark of the European spirit, as against
the Oriental, is this capacity to turn everything into an

object standing over against it and thus to appropriate it
to itself as its own other. The peculiar freedom of the
European spirit lies, according to him, in "being with
itself in being different," as mediated by the negative
activity of the mind. Tne European spirit puts the world
over against itself, makes itself free from it, annuls
this opposition again and appropriates the other to
itself. In this mastery through objectification,
abstraction and conceptualization, there is nothing, as
Hegel proclaimed, which can present itself to this spirit
as a barrier that cannot be surmounted. Otherness is
overcome here through being grasped, comprehended, by the
objectifying concept.

It is not enough that we in this country should unreflectively assimilate, in our concern and need for participation in the economic, political and social efforts of
the modern world, this mode of thinking, indispensable as
the basis of all scientific and technological achievement.
Such assimilation, if it is not to insinuate into our very
being an alien force bound to disrupt and eventually
master it, must appropriate this other through the Western
way of conceptualization and in full awareness of its
otherness. A clear understanding of this peculiarly
Western attitude to the other is, more specifically, a
necessary first step towards an appreciation of its religious tradition and of the contrast between knowledge and
faith (*Wissen* and *Glauben*) which is characteristic of it.
The Western conception of knowledge and of faith have a
common origin in the mode of thinking peculiar to the West
which has been described above. To quote Loewith again:

> Both, scientific knowledge and faith, have before
> them a determinate object, and all determination
> is a delimitation or negation (*determinatio est
> negatio*), i.e. stating definitely that it is thus
> and not otherwise. We know something when we
> know something determinate and we have faith in
> something when we have faith in something
> determinate, e.g. in God's revelation in Christ.
> And we know something and have faith in something

> when we do *not* know something else or have faith
> in something different. The European perceives
> all that is indeterminate and unlimited as
> something *not yet* determined or indeterminable,
> which can always be grasped more definitely and
> more determinately.

This is how the West understands the other and this is how
it has in the main understood itself so far. To understand the religious traditions that have come to us from
the West, we must understand, not just their religions but
also, first and foremost, their way of understanding
themselves as well as others, the self-understanding of
their faith as well as the way in which it defines itself
and its aims in relation to other religious traditions.

Hegel has given classical expression to the West's
understanding of itself and its characteristic mode of
thought. His understanding of the "Oriental spirit",
however, summing up and making explicit the Western
approach to the Orient, is itself predetermined and
restricted by the limits imposed upon it by this very mode
of thought and of the way it understands itself. Judging
Eastern philosophy and religion in terms of the *not yet*
determined, he notices only a lack in the Orient. He
fails to see that this lack is at the same time, in the
words of Loewith, the Orient's great merit and its subtle
superiority, which consists in the fact that it acknowledges the undetermined and indeterminable *as such* and is
thus capable of taking it, in an attitude of natural
attunement and precisely in its indeterminateness, as the
starting point and goal of a complete and well-rounded
knowledge. Maurice Merleau-Ponty also refers to Hegel as
one "who contrasted the Western idea of truth as the total
conceptual recovery of the world in all its variety to the
Orient, and who defined the Orient as a failure *in the
same understanding*." He recognizes it as a prejudice to
treat all other modes of thinking as only distant
approximations of conceptual understanding and to force

every other type of thought to the alternative of
resigning itself to being a first sketch of the conception
or disqualifying itself as irrational. He admits, even as
a Westerner, that "the Orient's 'childishness' has something to teach us, if it were nothing more than the
narrowness of our adult ideas" and that in these cultures
can be found

> a variant of man's relationship to being which
> would clarify our understanding of ourselves, and
> a sort of oblique universality. Indian and
> Chinese philosophies have tried not so much to
> dominate existence as to be an echo or sounding
> board of our relationship to being. Western
> philosophy can learn from them to rediscover the
> relationship to being and the initial option
> which gave it birth, and to estimate the
> possibilities we have shut ourselves off from in
> becoming "Western" and perhaps reopen them.

But even Merleau-Ponty agrees with the Hegelian, Western
claim, reaffirmed by Husserl, that the "historical
entelechy" of the West requires and authorizes it to
understand other cultures and that it is "committed to the
onerous task of understanding others," not necessarily in
order to destroy them but to face up to the crisis they
are going through and to rediscover the source from which
they derive and to which they owe their long prosperity.

This whole enterprise of "understanding," it would
seem, is a characteristically Western one. It must be
added, however, that it is also a recent one, even in
Western history. If the Orient has followed the path of
pre-conceptual absorption and insulation, the Occident has
also, until recently, treated the other merely as its own
negation, without caring to determine it in itself or
seeking to understand it from within. May it be that the
emergence of "understanding" heralds a new mode of
thinking without objectifying, more appropriate to this
new venture in mutuality. What is significant of the
present situation, inter-culturally speaking, is that with
all our difference, and despite our long indifference to

the enterprise of mutual understanding, we are now
actually participants in a world-embracing process which
can become aware of itself through a dialogue which has
already started and in which the difference between East
and West is becoming growingly blurred. So far, we have
been mostly engaged in exploring other cultures and
religious traditions with a view to discovering points of
similarity, if not just confirmation of basic insights in
our own. In doing so we have been guided and impelled by
the inner genius of our own cultural tradition. It is
time that we opened ourselves to the differences now,
coming to closer grips with the truth of those other
traditions, and turn the monologue of the past into a real
dialogue. Perhaps the other may then present itself to us
a truer face, come nearer to us and help us in comprehending our own selves, somewhat differently perhaps but
certainly more deeply and truly. True dialogue is less a
telling each other than a questioning of each other and it
never leaves us where we were before, either in respect of
our understanding of the other or of ourselves.

Most of what has been said above applies to the second
task confronting religious studies in our universities,
the task namely, of understanding the other within the
complex fabric which is the heritage of the Hindu student
of religion, with which he must come to terms from the
vantage point of his own belongingness to his specific
religious tradition, in the process widening and correcting this perspective itself. The attempt to grapple
with this task has already over a century's history behind
it and most of the great leaders of this country's
national renascence have contributed to it. It still
remains, however, for our universities to take up the task
in an organised, systematic way and devote to it the
scholarly, dispassionate and patient labour that it
requires. Much of what has been accomplished in this
field has been done by Western scholars and there is no

reason why we should not also bring to bear upon this task the same detached and disciplined academic energy and attention. In Professor Murti's classical study of Madhyamika Buddhism we have already a model to inspire scholars here.

To come to the third and central point, the task of understanding our own religious and cultural tradition. It is obvious that as intellectuals living in the world of today, we are shaped not only by our own cultural heritage but by three other forces to which we cannot close our minds: the scientific and technological requirements of today, along witn the general outlook and way of thinking that sustain them; the pervasive secular cultural climate of thought, expressed by the single word modernity, in which we are enveloped; and the free encounter with other traditions, religious and cultural, which has not only become possible for us now but which constitutes an obligation and a challenge coming to us from humanity's new vision of a world community. It is in this new context, the context of present, contemporary life, that we are required to understand and re-appropriate our tradition and make it truly our own. And we have to do this not merely as scholars dedicated to the academic pursuit of a "subject," nor in the interests of any sort of a "traditionalist revival," nor indeed because any special sanctity attaches to the past as past, but out of a passionate concern with our present religious life. The attempt to recapture what once was, the voice that was once heard and the event that once happened, in the perspective of an open future that can be ours, is the only way in which we can be liberated into and for our true present and see our religious present for what it really is.

In the cultural history of Europe, the central problem of the modern age has been posed by the coming into existence of modern science, and since the seventeenth

century the principal task of its philosophy has been to reconcile this new power of knowing and making with the entirety of man's experience of life and his image of the world and of himself, to a ceaseless wrestling with the problem of revising his understanding of himself, including his relationship to the heritage of his own past, classical as well as Christian. What is important for us in this country to realize is that as an integral factor of our life now, scientific activity and outlook cannot be kept apart, in another compartment as it were, from our traditional culture, intellectual or religious, that the scientific way of thinking, if it is not to be a frail and superficial possession, must permeate all our intellectual activity and that in consequence we are placed under the obligation of a continued examination of the nature of this way of thinking as well as of revising and re-comprehending our tradition from the perspective of our altered awareness. An instructive example of such an experienced requirement in the field of recent religious thought is Rudolf Bultmann's wrestling with the mytho-logical elements in the New Testament and more radically projected, in Dietrich Bonhoeffer's programme of reinter-preting Biblical concepts. The self-comprehension of faith, this basic concept of Bultmann's theology, is different from the metaphysical concept of self-consciousness (as Gadamer has been at pains to point out), and refers to the historical and hermeneutical task of comprehending, in the context of the scientific temper of thought today, the encounter with unobjectifiable happening of revealed faith in the Christian tradition. The pursuit of science is not just the specialized preoccupation of a few professional scientists, nor a mere skill, nor a stocking of expert knowledge about the "material" world. It is a way of looking at things, an attitude of mind and a habit of thinking, leaving nothing unsubjected to its scrutiny, generating again and again

trends and movements exemplified by the Enlightenment of
the eighteenth century, criticising, debunking and
replacing concepts no longer capable of ordering our
experience in the manner demanded by its own inner logic
and commitments. The birth and death of gods, the rise of
new cosmologies, the criticism of superstitions--e.g. Pico
della Mirandola's attack on astrology during the Italian
Renaissance--a radical transformation of religious
concepts bearing on the forces which determine the affairs
of men and their regulation, all of these illustrate the
extent to which science transforms the whole of human
thought and existence. It is only when we have fully
opened ourselves to its impact and submitted to its
discipline that we can realise the magnitude of the task
of a renewed understanding and interpretation of our
cultural tradition and its special importance in this
country. No facile compromise or reconciliation,
miscalled "synthesis," but a relentless exposure to the
tension between the scientific consciousness and the
legacy of tne past is the way we can learn to address the
right questions to our religious tradition and be rewarded
by the answers truly adequate to our present situation.

Edward Shils, in his remarkable studies entitled, *The
Intellectual between Tradition and Modernity: the Indian
Situation* and *The Indian Intellectual*, has analyzed in
detail the whole nest of problems that face an ancient
tradition-bound society, such as ours, which seeks to
transform itself into a modern society. The pattern for
this has been laid down for our age by "Western civilization," with its educational, social, economic and
political thinking, its concepts of freedom, organization,
industry and rational administration, its scientific and
humanistic thought, its creative adventures in art,
literature and ideas. This complex of idea, sensibility
and practice has generated an international community of
intellectuals, a world-wide climate of opinion and a new

way of thought, expression and approach to our concrete worldly problems which is characteristic of what Shils calls the modern intellectual tradition, as against India's own "great tradition of Brahmin intellectuality." This modern tradition of intellectual work in literature, science and scholarship has not yet succeeded, Shils insists, in finding a firm foundation in India. Yet, in so far as we are pushing on towards the goal of modernization and thus sharing in its world-wide intellectual base, we are bound to experience the tension between the claims of our traditional culture and the impulsion toward modernity, as also a sense of alienation and distance from our cultural past.

Without such experience of alienation, the question of "understanding" could not have arisen and it is only when "religion" becomes, as Professor Wilfred Cantwell Smith has so well said, one aspect of life among others, merely one facet of life alongside many others, instead of being coterminous with human life in all its comprehensiveness, that the "study" of religion arises. This fragmentation of "an earlier cohesiveness or integrity of man's social and personal life, once religiously expressed and religiously sanctioned," generates the secular quest of religious "understanding," just as the rise of "the aesthetic consciousness," in Gadamer's sense, represents an alienation from that immediacy of living in which art was once man's way of experiencing the Divine and of his response to it. Understanding seeks to overcome this alienation by letting tradition speak to us once again in all its revelatory power, without any attempt at reviving a past mode or form of life, in the world of today, fragmented, secularized and "modern," and in its language. As a people striving to participate in the heightened, incredibly complex and differentiated consciousness of this world of today, we can neither go back to any epoch of our past nor regain the immediacy of a bygone form of

consciousness. It is therefore all the more incumbent upon us, if not indeed the only possibility open to us, to strive to recapture, from the perspective of our own station in time and place, the truth revealed and yet hidden in our religious tradition and express it for our time, for ourselves. Of the many elements in our religious tradition calling for understanding, i.e., for re-interpretation and reformulation, I may refer to two, by way of example. The worship of "the many gods" is in this country not just dead tradition or evocative poetry but part of the life of many, a living reality of their world, not yet overpowered by modernity. Does this so-called polytheism, this worship of the graven image, not have a profound truth of its own? Is there not here something to understand, something which we can make our own? Is not such understanding likely to make us more explicitly aware of those presuppositions or prejudgments which have been responsible for relegating such experience of Divinity to an inferior level of the religious consciousness? Can we not learn something, to this end, from the history of *Mythos-Forschung* from Schelling to Walter F. Otto and Karl Kerenyi, from Hoelderlin, from Cassirer and from Martin Heidegger's re-opening of the question of "God and the gods"? Another example is the place, authority and understanding of revealed truth, along with the role and significance of language in the happening of such truth. Both in the Indian and Western traditions there is a long history of logos-speculation which is profoundly relevant to the task of a mutual understanding, comprehensive of the very foundations of each. We can learn something here not only from the long tradition of the Christian doctrine of incarnation and the word that became flesh, of the logos-mysticism of men like Hamann and Boehme, Cusanus and Eckhart, but also from the approach to language inaugurated by Heidegger and taken up in the philosophical hermeneutic of Hans-Georg Gadamer and

in the theology of language as developed in the recent
Protestant thought of an Ebeling and a Fuchs. Revelation,
Incarnation, the Word, are root ideas in our own religious
tradition, though in respect of them we are not only more
"alienated" but have perhaps lost all living sense for
them, as also the language in which to think about them.
The recovery of the meaning of these for our present
religious consciousness, their re-appropriation through
understanding, is a major task for the study of our
religious tradition in our day. From the vantage point of
this renewed understanding we may then begin to inquire
whether, and in what respects, the Christian doctrine is
different, whether, and in what sense, the idea of
"historicity" constitutes the crux of this difference.
The rise and development of the historical consciousness
during the last two hundred years, I may add here in
passing, constitutes an integral element of modern intellectuality. This further contributes to the experience of
alienation mentioned above and forces upon us a reflective
relationship to the witness of past modes of life and
thought, thus enabling the adoption of a critical attitude
towards ourselves as taken up in a historical process.
Our relation to tradition can no longer be one of conser-
vation alone or determined by the rationalistic ideal of a
total assimilation of fact into the concept, much less of
an unreflective immersion in it.

In the third place, the free encounter with other
traditions made both possible and necessary in today's
planetary civilization provides an unparalleled opportunity to reawaken, in Whitehead's words, the sense of
vast alternatives, magnificent or hateful, lurking in the
background, and awaiting to overwhelm our safe little
traditions, which was lost by the moderns. We must
realize that every tradition "only presents one finite
aspect of the many-sided modes of importance which are
pressing upon the outskirts of human consciousness."

Such expansion of understanding is not merely a "prime
necessity" for the survival of civilization; it is the
only safeguard against the dogmatism which paralyses
self-criticism and halts the emergence of novelty in the
patterns of conceptual experience, congealing tradition
into a lifeless burden, a deadening deposit which hides
and chokes up the very wellsprings which bestow the
dimension of the Holy and the quality of piety upon our
experience. What is needed here is that spirit of joyous
adventure which boldly marches out into the unfamiliar and
the alien, without fear of self-loss, and returns to
itself with enhanced understanding of itself, changed and
yet the same. Like all understanding, the understanding
of our cultural tradition is inescapably dialectical in
character and presupposes a going out of oneself, the
encounter with the other and the strange, and a return to
oneself. The encounter itself has the structure of mutual
questioning, presupposing mutual openness and so an
acknowledgement of the other as question-worthy, not its
dismissal as questionable. And, as Heidegger has said,
the wandering out in the direction of what is different
and question-worthy is not mere adventure but a homecoming. The way to what is closest to ourselves is the
longest way back and into the remote, back to the
nourishing well-head and away to distant regions. Only
thus can we truly come home to ourselves, understand and
be ourselves, and enter into the legacy of a vision that
is neither distorted nor blurred. This nisus towards the
goal of a *world-community* cannot reach its end through any
sort of *Herschaftswissen*, or any sort of cultural and
conceptual conquest, nor merely through a peaceful
co-existence of religious traditions, but solely through
this reaching out to the other in active understanding,
and in the service of a Truth which will perhaps never
shed its mystery but to which each tradition bears witness
and is in this united with each other.

The basic principle of all interpretation is that we must understand a text from and out of itself and the hermeneutic rule for this is that the whole must be understood in terms of the parts and the latter in terms of the whole. And we understand the text not by transposing ourselves into the mind of the author but by sharing the meaning of what he says and allowing for the possibility of its being true. Its goal is reached when we arrive at some kind of understanding with the text (person or tradition), with respect to the matter or meaning, with its claim to be valid. Our understanding of this meaning is in the first instance distorted, but also made possible, by our preconceptions and anticipations. Only our openness for what the other says and our willingness to listen to him, can guarantee that the encounter will lead us to an awareness of these preconceptions and thus to understand it, without bias, in the otherness of what it means. This circularity in the movement of understanding (from whole to part and back and from text to reader and back, in regard to form and content respectively) is governed by the basic presupposition that only what really possesses a perfect unity of sense is comprehensible. This "anticipation of perfectness", as Gadamer calls it, grants to the text from the very first the possibility not only of expressing a meaningful whole but of uttering a truth that could deepen, widen or correct our own vision of the reality which is at bottom our common concern. The distance of time or cultural space is not a gulf over which understanding seeks to throw a bridge but is "the carrying ground of the process in which our present understanding is rooted" (Gadamer). This is what makes understanding a creative and unending processes. And it presupposes receptiveness for the other, preparedness for a radical suspension of our prejudgments, a spirit of questioning, i.e. of laying open and keeping open possibilities which were hitherto beyond

our ken, mindfulness of the historicity of our own way of understanding and an awareness of the fact that in our attempt to understand the past, history itself is effectively at work. He who seeks to understand, his own tradition or that of other cultures, can do so only from his own particular standpoint; his "prejudices" not only restrict his vision but enable it. In the act of understanding, this vision is both enlarged and corrected, at the same time making the seeker explicitly aware of these "prejudices," which are not just peripheral but constitute the very core of our particularity. The critical awareness of these prejudices alters, however slightly, this core itself and all understanding, therefore, changes us and presupposes a readiness for that. But all understanding, in the next place, also changes what is understood. We never understand either our own cultural past or that of other traditions as they understood themselves, but always differently and in the context of our present way of life, in terms of which understanding translates it. Understanding thus is never mere repetition or reaffirmation of what has been; it is itself a movement, an event in cultural history, generates true novelty and thus remoulds tradition. No culture is an island enclosed within its own horizon, though all cultures and traditions have their being within such horizons. It is of the very essence of the "hermeneutic experience," i.e., the explicit comprehension of the voice of the past and the other, that in it the horizons, within which both he who seeks to understand and what is understood exist, open out, move towards and fuse with each other, in however small a degree. This is a movement towards a higher generality, but it is an unending movement, and towards a universality which can emerge in the concrete only dimly, imperfectly, without foreknowledge of its true shape. The problem of intercultural understanding as a movement of living thought is not the problem of discovering a formula

for the "other" culture, or of grasping it in a concept, but of a mutual sharing of horizons, however slightly. Understanding in this context is not to be taken as a psychological process or occurrence but solely in terms of the matter or reality comprehended, with the fusion of horizons implied in it, and in this sense the movement of understanding is a movement in the very substance of this reality. The two partners in the dialogue of thought that is understanding, are not so much the agents of this process as themselves taken up in it and carried by this movement. "They do not so much lead as they are led by it," in Gadamer's words, and "mutual understanding or its failure is like something that has happened with us....The dialogue has its own spirit and the language which is employed and formed in it bears a truth of its own, i.e. discloses something, makes something emerge, which henceforth is." Understanding is thus a dynamic and creative process, and what is understood in it is this movement of truth towards novelty. Language is the medium in which this movement is accomplished, leading to the forging of a new and common language, which alone enables participation in a common meaning and a common truth in its actuality. For it is not we, but language that speaks. Self-understanding is thus inseparable from the understanding of the other, and it reaches its fulfillment only with the fashioning of a language which mediates us with the other and our present with our past.

The final task for religious studies in our universities is a purely theoretical one, in the narrow sense of the term, and its scope is covered by what is called the philosophy of religion. In so far as each religion is particular, concrete and individual, its study implies investigation of a mass of empirical material or factual information. The problem of conceptualizing this, in explicit comparison with and in the context of similar material in the other religious traditions and with other

human sciences such as psychology, sociology and anthropology, comes first. Next, we have the philosophical problem of analysing and systematising the most general religious concepts, of building up a framework allowing for all religions--showing how they are possible--and of examining the truth-claims of each. To the extent to which these problems are adequately solved, we have the promotion of inter-cultural understanding, if only on the plane of abstract conceptualization. Finally, there is the problem of examining our religious life and ideas on a level deeper than the "metaphysical," beneath or beyond the level of that objectifying, presentational thinking which has brought, if Heidegger's analysis is to be accepted, the spectre of Nihilism, that uncanniest of all guests, into our midst. This is the problem of seeking for a name for that which evokes piety in the men of today, of discerning the truth that bears it, of taking note of its remoteness and nearness from us, of learning to speak about it in a manner which will bring men of different faiths and traditions nearer and not divide them, which will make us sightful, not merely for "our" faith but for the reality to which we respond by faith or its lack, and which is ever with us, even when manifest only as its own absence. For, what we understand, in the last resort, is not men but, through their doings, feelings and sayings the matter or *Sache*, the truth that shines through these and to which they bear witness. The collaborative striving for seeing this truth is at the time the problem of finding a language that goes beyond the opposition of East and West, beyond the clash of cultures and the conflict of tongues. This is the encounter and dialogue on a level beneath the emergence of difference, insight into the true nature of these differences, and a step taken beyond them. It is a task to which our very finitude commits us, never terminating so long as the human spirit endures on earth.

I have dealt in this paper with four tasks for university studies in religion and I have tried to show how in each case the basic problem is one of "understanding." The fifth task pertaining to religious education is no exception to this. In all understanding, the moment of what may be called "application" is essential, i.e., the comprehension of a general utterance in terms of my own particular present. In such mediation of the religious tradition and the present consciousness lies precisely the function of religious education.

UNDERSTANDING AND TRADITION

Recent philosophical thought has been marked by a
growing awareness of the role of tradition in moulding our
experience of the world and of ourselves and in determining both the manner and content of philosophical
reflection on experience. Along with that has gone a
recognition of the particularity and uniqueness of
traditions and a quest for the hidden logic of their
historical development. Western philosophical thinkers
like Edmund Husserl, Martin Heidegger and Maurice
Merleau-Ponty, for example, all philosophize with an
explicit awareness of the fact that they stand within a
particular tradition of thought, the Occidental.
Furthermore, they not only reflect on the basis of this
tradition, so that the questions they raise and seek to
answer have a necessary reference to that tradition; they
also exhibit a relatively novel concern within philosophy
for this fact itself as being integral to that quest for
universality which is of the very essence of philosophical
thinking. What we call progress in philosophy depends in
large measure on the continued exposure and overcoming of
our naivety, of what is at any stage taken for granted and
remains implicit. Philosophical claims to universality,
not only in individual thinkers but also in entire traditions are themselves rooted in presupposed particularities
of vision and what was once regarded as an obvious,

Presidential address in the Metaphysics and Epistemology
section of the Indian Philosophical Congress, Dharwar,
1969, originally published in *Ānvīkṣikī*, *Research Bulletin
of the Centre of Advanced Study in Philosophy*, ed. by N.K.
Devaraja. Banaras Hindu University, 2 (1969): 117-136.

straightforward and absolutely valid affirmation turns out
to have been "rendered possible" by certain implicit
presuppositions. A significant advance in present-day
philosophical awareness consists in the growing sense of
such particularity and limitedness, in the asking of new
sorts of questions engendered by this and in the quest of
a wider generality of thought and utterance which is not
yet unmindful of the particularities it seeks to transcend
and of the fact that such transcendence always remains
relative to the particulars which constitute its point
of departure.

In his last work, *The Crisis of the European Sciences
and Transcendental Phenomenology*, Husserl speaks of the
"inborn telos" of European man, since the birth of Greek
philosophy, to desire to live as men inspired by
philosophical reason and be able to live only as such. He
asks whether this urge towards the infinite movement from
latent to manifest reason and this striving for self-
regulation through the presence in him of the authentic
truth of humanity itself is a mere historical-factual
delusion, a merely fortuitous acquisition of a type of man
accidentally emerging in the midst of other peoples and
races and of other historical developments, or is it
rather that in the Greek man there comes into view for the
first time what is intrinsic to humanity as such as its
very entelechy? What is at stake in the present-day
crisis in "the European sciences" is reason and
rationality, this specific entelechy of European man
itself, and upon its power to sustain itself and prevail
will depend, Husserl asserts, the decision "whether
European humanity carries within itself an absolute idea
and is not a merely empirical anthropological type like
'China' or 'India', and whether, furthermore, the
spectacle of the Europeanization of all other parts of
mankind reveals the sway of a significance which is part
of the meaning of the world itself, and not just an

unmeaning, historically accidental emergence." In the
Vienna Lecture on the crisis of European man and philosophy, out of which the larger "Crisis" volume developed,
Husserl speaks again in similar fashion of the uniqueness
of Europe and of the spiritual telos of European man.

> There lies (in our own Europe) something unique,
> which all other human groups, too, feel with
> regard to us, something that, apart from all
> considerations of expediency, becomes a
> motivation for them--despite their determination
> to retain their spiritual autonomy--constantly to
> Europeanize themselves, whereas we, if we
> understand ourselves properly, will never, for
> example, Indianize ourselves. I think that we
> feel (and with all its vagueness this feeling is
> not without its own justification) that in our
> European humanity there is an innate entelechy
> that thoroughly controls the changes in the
> European image and gives to it the sense of a
> development in the direction of an ideal of life
> and of being, as moving towards an eternal pole.

The term "philosophy" itself is for Husserl a proper name
denoting that "completely new kind of attitude of
individuals towards their environing world" resulting in a
"completely new type of spiritual structure, rapidly
growing into a systematically rounded cultural form that
the Greeks called philosophy."

In Heidegger's thought, philosophical reflection is
even more explicitly and prominently linked with the
specific Greek-European tradition, and the tradition-bound
character of thought itself, the cultural particularity of
its origin and historical unfoldment, emerges vividly and
sharply into view. Heidegger does not merely assert
dogmatically, "However and whatever we attempt to think,
we can only think within the bounds sketched out by tradition. Its presence reigns when it frees us from thinking
back to a thinking ahead which is no more planning. Only
when we turn thinkingly towards what has already been
thought, shall we be used for what has yet to be thought."
The whole movement of his thought, all along the way, is a
massive demonstration of this claim as well as a long

drawn out exercise in uncovering the facticity and historical particularism that has ever clung to the Western philosophical tradition. His thinking is thus basically a critique of this tradition, oblivious so long of its own particularism, and at the same time an attempt to develop a way of thinking for which that tradition will provide a liberative rather than a restrictive basis for future planetary thought. "Metaphysics" is for Heidegger only another name for "Occidental thought in the entirety of its essence" and his quest for the way back into the ground of metaphysics, his attempt to take the step back that leads out of metaphysics into its essence and source, his overcoming metaphysics, are all attempts at making explicit the particularistic, historically rooted presuppositions in which that specific mode of thinking has been based and thus at dispelling the illusion of its apparent universality and necessity. Philosophical thinking itself, as he analyses its nature, is a specific, historically conditioned mode of thinking about man, world and Being, Greek in origin and proper to the West, and not just thinking *simpliciter* about these ultimates. As he puts it in *What is Philosophy?*

> The word *philosophia* tells us that philosophy is something which first determines Greek existence. Not merely that--*philosophia* determines also the inmost distinctive feature of Occidental-European history. The phrase "Occidental-European Philosophy" which one so often hears is in truth a tautology. Why? Because "philosophy" is in essence Greek--Greek in the sense that in the origin of its essence philosophy is of the sort that it has first claimed the Greeks in order to unfold itself. To say that philosophy is in essence Greek is the same as to say that the Occident and Europe, and they alone, are in their inmost historical course originally "philosophical." This is proved by the rise and domination of the sciences. Because they originate from the inmost Occidental-European course of history, namely the philosophical, therefore they are today in a position to give their specific stamp upon the history of man on the whole earth....The word *philosophia* appears as it were

as the birth-certificate of our own history; we
might even say, as the birth-certificate of the
contemporary epoch in world-history which calls
itself the Atomic Age.

It is as an invitation to Western thought to shed its
particularism of tradition that Heidegger declares, "The
thinking of the future is no longer philosophy, because it
thinks on a level deeper than metaphysics, which term also
means the same."

I do not propose to discuss here either the contrasting assessments of the Western philosophical heritage
by Husserl and Heidegger or their differing evaluation of
the significance of the Oriental traditions, in the
perspective of our present and ongoing search for self-
understanding and of an ultimate framework of meaning upon
which that rests. Nor do I intend here to track down the
changing presuppositions behind Western thinkers' understanding of the significance of their own philosophical
tradition relatively to the Oriental, first explicitly
stated by Hegel, repeated by Husserl and subjected to
critical scrutiny more recently by Heidegger and Merleau-
Ponty. The views quoted above open out a fascinating and
challenging domain of questions, of central philosophical
importance and vital to our own self-understanding as
legatees of another heritage than the Western but as also
having an inescapable share, in the present and for
tomorrow, in what both Husserl and Heidegger call "the
Europeanization of the earth." Instead of discussing
these on the present occasion, I should rather like to
draw your attention to this basic fact, as it seems to me,
of the rootedness of philosophical thought in a cultural
matrix, to the fact that human reflection on the basic
problems of life and experience, the very fabric and
character of that experience itself, is always embedded in
a context of tradition. This gives it a factual and
historical dimension requiring what has been called
understanding (*Verstehen*) and interpretation in recent

thought on the foundations and philosophical significance of the human sciences (*Geisteswissenschaften*). Further, and principally, I should like to speak at some length on what understanding means in this context, leaving it for a future occasion to discuss what this conception of the role and significance of understanding implies for a more broadly conceived theory of experience itself. In what I have to say on these questions, I may add, I am indebted to the ideas of Martin Heidegger and Hans-Georg Gadamer, two contemporary thinkers who have contributed significantly to our knowledge of the place of understanding in that self-awareness of tradition which is so intrinsically a part of philosophy itself.

The human sciences are concerned with aspects of experience which in the main lie outside the scope of the exact sciences, and include, in Gadamer's words, the experience of philosophy, the experience of art and the experience of history itself. They deal, thus, with that dimension of experience in which a truth is disclosed to us and an awareness of reality is made available to us through the vehicle of tradition which is not accessible through the methods of the exact sciences and is not verifiable by them. Systematic reflection on the epistemological problem of the nature and validity of knowledge in the human sciences began with the reaction, during the last decades of the nineteenth century, against the prevailing positivism in philosophy and the claim of the exact sciences to be the model and norm of all knowledge whatsoever. Wilhelm Windelband and Heinrich Rickert of the South-West German Neo-Kantian School sought to justify the independent epistemological status of the cultural sciences as against the natural sciences by pointing out the differentiating features of the fields to which each kind addressed itself. The former, Windelband pointed out, are "ideographic" and concerned with individual happenings and processes, whereas the latter are

"nomothetic" and concerned with universally valid laws.
Rickert held fast to the dualism of natural and cultural
sciences, considered the individual and singular character
of the processes dealt with by the latter as being due to
the connection of facts with value-systems and in general
sought to ask, after the manner of Kant, how a science of
historical knowledge is possible and, conceiving historical knowledge after the pattern of knowledge in the
natural sciences, attempted to provide an epistemological
foundation for it. It was, however, Wilhelm Dilthey, the
philosopher of life, who saw vividly and clearly that
human life and thought are embedded in tradition and
history, who wrestled massively with the problems this
raised for the distinctive methodology of the human
sciences and who first grasped, even though in a fumbling
and groping fashion, that the philosophical foundations of
these sciences cannot be laid through a narrowly conceived
theory of knowledge, as it became prevalent with the "back
to Kant movement" in German philosophy. What he was
concerned with was the full and concrete movement of human
life, as expressed and embodied in literature and art, in
philosophy, religion and history, whereas, as he declared,
"in the veins of the 'knowing subject' constructed by
Locke, Hume and Kant runs no real blood." The decades of
hard work which Dilthey devoted to laying the foundations
of the *Geisteswissenschaften* (a term which became current
in German thought since the translator of Mill's *A System
of Logic* first mis-rendered the phrase "moral sciences" by
this term) represents, as Gadamer has pointed out, a
continuous effort to grapple with the logical demands
raised for these sciences by the famous last chapter of
Mill. Even though unable to liberate himself completely
from the hold of the natural science model of knowledge
and from the notions of method implied in it, he nevertheless saw that the dogmatism of Mill's insistence on
induction was the outcome of a lack of historical

awareness, that the key to the specific kind of knowing
involved in the human sciences lay precisely in the
historical dimension of life and in the fact that these
sciences were concerned with historical processes and with
the way our present consciousness is determined by what is
transmitted to us from the past. Keeping in view this
distinctive and essential dimension of human experience,
Dilthey sought to do for the historical human sciences
what Kant had done for the science of nature and for "pure
reason," namely to write a critique of historical reason,
and to formulate categories appropriate to "life," i.e.,
to human experience as determined by historical tradition
and man's own inner historicity, as against the abstract
categories of pure reason operative in the scientific
knowledge of natural processes. He went beyond the Neo-
Kantians in conceiving experience not in a narrow
"epistemological" framework but as part of the process of
living itself, as *Erlebnis* or felt and lived experience
and as that fusion of memory and expectation in the
present which is implied in the historicity intrinsic to
human living and experiencing as such.

Dilthey thought of life, along with its historical
expression and objectification, through which alone it can
be understood, as a text which must yield its meaning from
within itself and for which the appropriate cognitive
operation is understanding rather than explaining, as in
science, or subsuming conceptually the particular under a
universal. World-history is for him, in Gadamer's words,
a great obscure book, the collective work of the human
spirit composed in the languages of the past which has to
be understood, as one understands a text handed down from
the past. Dilthey, it should be recalled, was the
biographer of the theologian Friedrich Schleiermacher and
profoundly influenced by his work on Hermeneutics, "the
art of understanding" anything that exists in written form
and even what is orally communicated, not just the

interpretation of the Holy Bible, to which this term was originally restricted. By giving to the problem of understanding a central position in his work, Schleiermacher transformed this ancient auxiliary discipline providing a method to be applied by the philologist or the theologian, into the philosophical theory of the nature and scope of the activity of understanding itself and thus laid the foundations on which Dilthey, Heidegger and Gadamer have built. It is significant to note that according to Schleiermacher hermeneutics is the art not so much of producing understanding where there was none before as of avoiding misunderstanding. He believed that misunderstanding arises of itself and that "understanding has at every step to be deliberately desired and pursued." His conception of a universal hermeneutics or theory of understanding is based on the realization that the experience of strangeness and alienation and thus the possibility of misunderstanding, in respect of what is transmitted to us from the past, torn from the world to which it originally belonged, is universally present. The quest of understanding presupposes such a sense of alienation and remoteness from tradition and does not arise so long as we unreflectively live under its domination, or fail to see the novel present as it actually is and claims us. As for the phenomenon of understanding itself, Schleiermacher thought that it consisted in transporting ourselves into the psychology of an author, into the individuality of his frame of mind, tnrough the reproduction in our minds of his original act of creation, through a sort of reversal of the original process of composing, and in the last resort, through a congenial divination of his creative individuality.

This psychological interpretation of the nature of understanding in the sense of the re-creation of an original creation is open to the charges both of psychologism and of an inadequate conception of our

relationship to our past. The first, psychologism, has been a constant challenge to philosophers, so diverse in temper and approach as Bradley and Frege or Husserl and Wittgenstein, since its emergence in British Empirical philosophy and is by now a dead horse. In the present context, the problem is: when we understand a human document expressive of a thought, deed or experience, is that which is understood a particular, factual mental process, or is it a meaning, with the moment of ideality and impersonality attaching to it, that we comprehend and share? Do we understand a text, as a vehicle of meanings, or the mind of the author, the *mens auctoris*? Or, is the true object of understanding not even the text but, through the text, the truth it seeks to disclose to us? As in a conversation, do we not rather understand each other in respect of the subject matter talked about than pry into the subjective processes occurring within us? Where a considerable distance of time separates us from the author of a text, understanding aims, according to Schleiermacher, at equating ourselves with the *author* and putting ourselves in his position, to which the putting ourselves in the position of the original *reader* is a preparatory act. Is the latter not equally, even more basically part of the attempt to understand? Schleiermacher was not unaware of the fact that the reproduction can never amount to identification with it and he therefore laid it down as the aim of the hermeneutical enterprise to understand a writer better than he understood himself. This formula, which has been subsequently interpreted in a variety of senses, contains the core of the hermeneutical problem. It is obvious that the deliberate activity of reproducing the original creative act can bring into consciousness a great deal of which the author himself was unaware, as happens, for example, in literary criticism. To understand an author thus includes understanding his unconscious intention and

rendering explicit the implications of what he said. But is this superiority of the critic and interpreter to be understood in a psychological sense or in the sense of a better knowledge of the subject matter dealt with by the author? Is it legitimate, in other words, to take a text purely as a document expressive of the author's mind, in isolation from its claim to lay bare and communicate a truth? Is understanding a sort of psychoanalysis? The opposite extreme of such a psychological claim to understanding in the sense of knowing better, we may add, is frequently found in the practice of philosophers, from Aristotle to Wittgenstein, and is exemplified by the following assertion of Kant:

> I need only remark that it is by no means
> unusual, upon comparing the thoughts which an
> author has expressed in regard to his subject,
> whether in ordinary conversation or in writing,
> to find that we understand him better than he has
> understood himself. As he has not sufficiently
> determined his concept, he has sometimes spoken,
> or even thought, in opposition to his own
> intention.

In the case of the philosophical tradition as such, the emphasis is all on the subject-matter, the truth of a thought, and on conceptual clarity and consistency in dealing with it. Further critical analysis can always lead to new logical insights and a later thinker may be able to see what the earlier has said in the light of a truth hidden from himself. Some such principle is involved not only in the notion of philosophy as primarily critical and analytical and is itself determined by the rationalistic ideal of a total and supra-historical conceptual transparency. Even in a thinker like Heidegger, for whom philosophical reflection is itself a "hermeneutics of facticity", the understanding and interpretation of finite, tradition-centred thought, the principle of the unthought in what a philosopher has actually thought appears to be based on the assumption

that in some sense to understand an author is to understand him better than he understood himself. But "better," in this case, is historically meant and is an admission of the limits imposed upon a thinker by his temporal situation within a tradition; every great thinking, Heidegger asserts therefore, understands itself best within the limits marked out for it.

These considerations throw light also on the erroneous notion of understanding as reproduction. What is allegedly reproduced in understanding is never meaningful today in tne same way as it was when first produced, and when its original meaning is sought to be grasped in isolation from the historical process which has nourished it and kept it alive and from our own place in the present, it can only amount to the re-evocation and transmission of a dead meaning. Hegel had better insight into the futility of all attempts to restore the past and of the true task of the thinking spirit in relation to the past, for, as he saw, the nature of the spirit as historical, as which alone can it come to full awareness of itself, consists, not in the restitution of what is gone but in its reflective mediation with our present experience. The historical distance which separates an author and his interpreter introduces a necessary difference between what the author may have meant and what the interpreter understands. The author, Chladenius even roundly said, need not know the true meaning of his own text at all. In Gadamer's words, "Every age has to understand a text passed down to it from the past in its own way, for it is part of the totality of the tradition, in which that age is materially interested and within which it seeks to comprehend itself." The real meaning of a text need not be restricted to what the author "intended," nor to what the first readers understood, for it is also determined by the historical situation of the interpreter and thus by the entirety of the objective

process of history. The meaning of a text always
surpasses and overflows its author and understanding is
therefore never merely reproductive but always contains an
element of creative productivity. Understanding, strictly
speaking, is not understanding better but understanding
differently and with that excess of meaning which accrues
from the existence of a historical tradition itself.

Dilthey followed Schleiermacher in regarding understanding as the reproduction or re-experiencing of the
inner world of experience of another, but was led by his
own persistent questioning to overcome the psychologism
infecting the earlier view. According to him, the human
sciences owe their distinctive character to the fact that
their procedure is based on the systematic relation among
life, or lived experience, expression and understanding.
What is to be recaptured in understanding, through its
expression, is an *Erlebnis*, immediate and pre-reflexively
given, not as an object standing over against my apprehension but as an occurrence in which content, existence
and awareness are not yet distinguished. But as he saw
more and more clearly, what is significant in such lived
experience is not merely its subjective reality but the
fact that it represents a unit of meaning. As he
remarked, "That which in the stream of time forms a unity
in the present because it has a unitary meaning is the
smallest entity which we can designate as a lived
experience." It is these unities of meaning--conceived by
Dilthey as temporal, reaching out to the future in
anticipation and back to the past in recollection--which
we grasp in the act of understanding and which become
accessible to us not in introspection but only through the
interpretation of their expression and objectification in
history and tradition, and through an interpretation,
moreover, which is itself in terms of historical rather
than abstract and static categories. The knowledge of man
is the knowledge of everything in which the human spirit

has expressed itself, and the mode in which we have such
knowledge is understanding, which, as Dilthey said, has
its true object in the objectification of life itself.
According to him, "What man is and what he wills, he
experiences only in the development of his nature through
the millenia and never completely to the last syllable,
never in objective concepts but always only in the living
experience which springs up out of the depths of his own
being." Despite the fact that Dilthey conceived his quest
as one for objectively valid knowledge in the human
sciences, after the Neo-Kantian model, he could not fail
to realize that the knowing subject, the historian seeking
to understand, does not simply stand over against the
historical flow of life which is the object of his
inquiries but is himself also borne on the same movement
of historical life. But the implications of this for the
nature of understanding as itself shot through with
historicity were to be drawn only later by Heidegger and
Gadamer, thus exhibiting man's relationship to tradition
in a radically new perspective.

Dilthey asserted that universally valid synthetic
judgments are possible in historical knowledge because man
himself is essentially historical, in the very opaque
depths of his being, because here, as Vico said long ago,
man is both the maker and the investigator of history, and
subject and object in this case have thus a common nature.
But this does not yet answer the question how on the basis
of the experience of single individuals we can rise above
to historical experience. As Gadamer has remarked, the
fabric of inter-relationships in history must in the end
be understood as a systematic complex of meanings which
basically transcends the horizon of the lived experience
of individuals. History is concerned with structures
transcending what can enter into the experience of single
individuals or what others may understand through
reproduction in their own experience. The meaning which

is to be understood here is not only not objectively given
but is something that goes beyond the collective
experience of all possible subjects, and the question is
how such transsubjective meaning is at all knowable.
Erlebnis, regarded non-psychologically as a unity of
meaning, cannot provide the basis for historical understanding, and it cannot do this, moreover, because every
Erlebnis is itself already determined *a priori* by pre-
existing historical realities such as society, state and
the entire heritage of the past. Nor can the concept of
"expression," objectifying the structural inter-relations
of lived experience, provide the adequate field to which
understanding and interpretation may address themselves,
for if the movement of history exhibits an excess of
meaning, and discloses a truth, beyond all that can be
apprehended within the experience of individual human
beings, how and what does this express, and can it be
regarded as "expressed" at all, in Dilthey's sense, unless
we posit an ideal subject and a supra-individual *Erlebnis*?
It is not surprising, therefore, to find that Dilthey
extended Hegel's concept of the objective spirit to
include art, religion and philosophy itself, which were
for the latter constitutive of Absolute spirit. For
Dilthey, they were not immediately revelatory of truth but
forms in which life expresses itself, and the historical
consciousness therefore remained the only access to what
metaphysics so far had been the means of knowing, the
achievement of absolute and infinite self-transparency of
spirit. Can, however, historical understanding take the
place of the absolute self-knowledge of the spirit through
concepts? Contrary to the claims of Ranke, Droysen and
Dilthey, a historical consciousness aware of its own
historicity can never rise above history, nor shed its
linkage with the particularity of its place in the
movement of history. As pointed out above, for Dilthey
the object of understanding is the world of history

regarded as a text to be deciphered; everything in history is comprehensible, for it is all text, as Gadamer comments, and historical inquiry is a matter of decoding the alphabet of history and thereby acquiring objective and universally valid knowledge of the past rather than gaining historical experience aware of its own finitude. The epistemological Cartesianism in which he remained caught up and the vain aspiration after total clarity, rational transparency and de-mythologizing which he shared with the thinkers of the Englightenment, prevented him from seeing the true historicity of our experience of history itself, the finitude infecting it, and led him to conceive the act of understanding both subjectivistically and ahistorically.

We cannot deal here with the early Husserl's contribution to the phenomenology of understanding, including his doctrine of the intentionality of consciousness which deeply influenced Dilthey, nor with the implications of his theories of anonymous and implicit intentionalities, or horizontal intentionality and of the life-world, for the phenomenon of understanding in relation to the historical tradition and to human experience generally. Heidegger's own views, central to this topic, will be assumed as familiar and mentioned here in the most summary fashion. The radical critique of subjectivism in modern philosophy he launched, the temporal interpretation of Being and man and in general the re-opening of the ontological dimension in philosophical inquiry are all reflected in the conception of the nature and role of understanding. In his existential analytic of *Dasein* in *Being and Time*, Heidegger has laid bare the ontological structure of man, and this includes understanding as an intrinsic constituent of man's being-in-the-world. As thus conceived, understanding is not just one method of knowing but the basic mode of man's being-there itself, tne primordial cognitive openness to his being-in-the-

world or, in Kantian terminology, the condition of the possibility of all actual ways of knowing open to man and thus prior to them. According to this transcendental interpretation of understanding, it is no longer, in Gadamer's words, "the resigned ideal of man's experience of life in the dotage of the spirit, as with Dilthey, but it is also not, as with Husserl, an ultimate methodological ideal of philosophy as against the naivety of simply floating along the stream of life, but is on the contrary the original form in which man exists as being-in-the-world." Understanding is no longer a methodological concept or a mode of knowing distinct from scientific explaining and specific to the human sciences alone, but is conceived as the primordial mode of being of human life itself. In this deeper sense, understanding is not just passive awareness but man's potentiality to be, in this way or that; it is man himself in his essence as possibility. Further, all understanding is intrinsically of the nature of project, not in the sense of thinking out plans for the future but as the very mode of being of man as possibility and as essentially ahead-of-himself. By virtue of its character as project--which for Heidegger is always a thrown project determined by the temporal modality of the past and in conformity with the facticity attaching to all existence--understanding is itself that basic movement of transcendence which lifts us above bare entities to their being, i.e., that dimension of ultimate meaning from which they derive their character as such and so. From this perspective, it also becomes evident that understanding is not the detached contemplation of a meaning factually out there but is always self-understanding: whatever and whenever we understand, we always do this in terms of projecting ourselves on our own possibilities. The thrownness and projectivity intrinsic to understanding reflect the temporality of man's very being as care and render it obvious how belongingness to tradition is just

as originally and essentially part of the historical
finitude of man as the projective and creative movement
towards his own future possibilities. In all understanding and interpretation, thus, the totality of this
existential structure of thrownness and projection, of
facticity and existentiality, is at work.

Heidegger's discussion of the relation between
understanding and interpretation or explication in *Being
and Time* is also of considerable importance in clarifying
a disputed question in hermeneutic theory: are these two
different and independent activities and can one take
place without the other? Interpretation, according to
Heidegger, is grounded on understanding and is only the
explicit cultivation and carrying through of the latter.
It is not a subsequent and additional act of taking notice
of what has already been understood but is an explication
of the possibilities projected in understanding and a
constitutive moment in the unfoldment of the latter as the
awareness of something as something. We shall notice
below how explication involves language and how all understanding necessarily occurs within the medium of language.
Of capital importance for the theory of understanding is
Heidegger's analysis of the circularity of understanding.
According to the principle of "the hermeneutic circle,"
recognized as basic in the methodology of interpretation
and exegesis by the predecessors of Schleiermacher, the
parts of a text must be understood in the context of the
whole and the whole in the light of the parts. Schleiermacher applied this principle in the psychological sense
already mentioned above, but he also saw it as a universal
feature of the phenomenon of understanding as such. To
understand is always to execute an unending movement from
the whole to the parts and back again in an ever widening
circle until the relatively total meaning is in our grasp.
But neither the subjective nor the objective interpretation of this circle, the one in terms of comprehending the

author's mind and the other in the sense of a detached,
uninvolved grasping of the text as an objective whole of
meaning within its historical context, really touches the
core of the matter. Beyond having this purely formal
character, understanding is circular also in respect of
the content or subject matter we seek to comprehend.

The marvel of understanding, which is no mysterious
communion of souls, consists in the sharing of a common
meaning and its aim is the achievement of agreement
between oneself and another, or coming to an agreement
with another, in respect of a content, through the
unending circular inter-play between the implicit presuppositions with which we read a text and the meaning
which it conveys to us. This is what Heidegger means when
he says,

> Interpretation is never a presuppositionless
> grasping of something which is already given.
> When in the particular and concrete case of
> explication as attempted in "exact" text-
> interpretation, one appeals to the authority of
> "what is really there," this apparent what-is-
> really-given-there is nothing but the
> presupposition, unexamined and taken for granted,
> with which the interpreter approaches a text and
> which is necessarily the starting point in all
> interpretation.

All understanding has this "pre-structure," as Heidegger
has called it, in consequence of which the interpretation
of something as something is basically and *a priori*
grounded in the pre-possession or prior intention, the
pre-view, the sight which we bring with us, and the
pre-conception or anticipation with which we inescapably
confront a text. And the meaning of the text is "not
something that mysteriously clings to it, lies hidden
behind it, or hovers somewhere in a parenthetical realm"
but is rather that which emerges through the interaction
between the text and the reader's fore-structured project
of understanding. The circle of understanding is thus
not, in Gadamer's words, of a formal character, is neither

subjective nor objective, but is descriptive of the fact
that understanding consists in the inter-play between the
movement of tradition and the movement of the interpreter,
a to-and-fro movement between text and interpreter,
between understanding its meaning and self-understanding.
According to Heidegger's interpretation of the circle, as
he says, "the understanding of a text is necessarily
governed by the anticipatory movement of pre-structured
understanding. The circle of whole and part is not
dissolved in a completed act of understanding but is on
the contrary truly and authentically executed." The
circle of understanding is thus not at all a "methodological" circle but refers to an ontological property of
the structure of understanding itself, such that to
understand is always to be involved in the unending inter-
play of the whole which is tradition, and the part, which
consists of the unconscious presuppositions with which the
interpreter approaches it. There is no understanding which
is presuppositionless and the anticipation of sense which
governs our understanding of a text is not, as Gadamer
says, an act executed by us as subjects, is not the act of
our subjectivity, but is rather an ingression into the
process of tradition in which the past and the present are
continuously mediated. It is itself determined by the
community and mutuality which binds us with tradition, a
community which is not just a pre-given fact but is in
constant formation in consequence of our participation in
the process of tradition through understanding.

   Presuppositions, pre-judgments and prejudices do not
merely restrict our understanding, or necessarily falsify
it, as is generally supposed, but also enable it and are
constitutive elements in it. The prejudice against prejudices in general is, as Gadamer has pointed out, the basic
presupposition of the Enlightenment, manifesting itself in
the rejection and criticism of all authority, especially
that of the religious tradition of Christianity, as a

source of prejudices and is expressed in Kant's formulation at the commencement of his article, "Answering the
question, what is Enlightenment?" Have the courage to use
your *own* understanding; according to this principle, not
tradition but reason is the ultimate source of authority
and final arbiter; what is written down in books need not
be true, for we are capable of knowing better. The
Romantic glorification of tradition and myth, of the past
and the remote, was itself based on the presuppositions of
the Enlightenment, with only the values reversed, and
ultimately led to the emergence of historicism, for which
the last step in the liberation of the human spirit from
enslavement by dogma lay in gaining objective knowledge of
the historical world, thus relegating everything in tradition which cannot stand up to the scrutiny of reason to
the world of the past and interpreting it "historically,"
i.e., in terms of bygone, pre-rational modes of thought
and living. The objectively historical way of understanding tradition is thus the consummation of the spirit
of the Enlightenment, robbing tradition of all potency and
authority and holding up before us the image of a disenchanted, de-mystified and rationalized world which is only
a reflection of the historically generated, subjectivistic
prejudice against our own rootedness in the past and the
naivety of our presumption to have elevated ourselves
above the concrete, historical flow of life and thought.
For, as Gadamer remarks, "The idea of an absolute reason
is in no sense a live possibility for historical mankind.
Reason is for us conditioned and bound up with historical
realities, not master over itself but ever dependent upon
the data to which it applies itself." In reality it is
not to us that history belongs but we who are owned by
history and hence, he adds, the pre-judgments of an
individual, far more than his judgments, constitute the
historical reality of his being. There is no absolute
antithesis between tradition and reason, for the former

depends upon its continuity, not upon the sheer inertia of physical persistence but upon our rational affirmation and critical appropriation, as much as all revolution and innovation.

The hermeneutic act of understanding, we remarked earlier, comes into operation with a sense of alienation from tradition, with a sense of its otherness from our present and remoteness from it. The task of understanding, which does not begin so long as we just live it out unreflectively and without question, is to overcome this alienation by making us explicitly aware of those unconscious presuppositions through which the past is ever operative in our present experience and ways of thinking and speaking. And it does this when we open ourselves to the voice of tradition, let it speak to us and confront us with its claim to communicate a truth. "We can never bring a presupposition in front of us as it were," Gadamer remarks, "so long as a presupposition is in unbroken and unnoticed play, but only when it is so to speak provoked and irritated. What has the power to act as such an irritant is precisely the encounter with tradition." Through such encounter we are enabled to draw out our presuppositions into the open, suspend their blind operation and bring them into play, explicitly as questions, against the truth-claim of what is said in a text handed down from the past. We can then see our relationship to tradition as a game in which we are partners with it, or as a dialogue into which we enter with it, not only putting questions to tradition but allowing ourselves to be questioned in turn by it. The authentic character of a game lies in the fact that here the partners are caught up in a movement which transcends the subjectivity of each of them and which is governed by its own inner law. Phenomenologically, play and the kind of understanding that happens in a conversation or when we occupy ourselves with a traditional text, have a common structure, as Gadamer

has well brought out. As in conversation, when we argue a
point, the give and take of understanding a text occurs in
the medium of language, we may in fact say, as the give
and take of language itself. In a dialogue, each speaker
plays a language-game of his own to begin with and the
authenticity of the dialogue depends upon the extent to
which they gradually surrender themselves to the sway of a
language-game that encompasses them both and which is not
identical with either of their separate games--and thus in
the end let a new common language emerge, and with it a
new horizon of meaning and a new truth that was not in the
possession of either before. It is in this sense that
when we allow ourselves to be addressed by tradition and
play the game of understanding, we participate in a creative process in which new horizons of meaning, resulting
from a fusion of our present horizon and that of a past
world, new ways of speaking and a new truth emerge, not as
something made *by* us but as that which moulds and shapes
us and enables us to live by. The refusal to play this
game is a surrender to philosophical naivety and, beyond
this, it is to let tradition operate blindly and as a
natural force in the form of our own presuppositions and
so to allow our past to creep up towards us as our own
future and take us by surprise.

Just as explication or interpretation is inseparable
from understanding and is an integral moment in it, so
also is application; comprehension, explication and
application together constitute in their unity the fully
executed activity of understanding. We do not really
understand and explicate a text, whether philosophical or
literary, legal or scriptural, so long as we take it only
as an historical document and do not translate it so that
it speaks to us in our present concrete situation, so
long, in other words, as it is not applied to the
historical point where we stand, here and now. Every
encounter with tradition, unfolded explicitly and with

historical self-consciousness in understanding, involves
an experience of the tension in the polar relation between
the text and the present moment, a tension which arises
from the application of what is said in the text to the
present and which understanding then seeks to overcome.
In this manner, tradition, of which our understanding is
itself a moment, is continuously mediated with the present
and is ever renovated, corrected and transformed through
projects of understanding that drive it forward into a
future which holds no more terrors, and understanding
itself is seen as that creative moment of heightened
awareness in which the past transforms itself into a
future truly its own.

Gadamer's explication of the phenomenon of understanding, and his application of this to the philosophical
present of the West as it has attained self-awareness in
the thinking of Heidegger, is determined by an attitude
towards the Western tradition which he shares with Husserl
rather than with Heidegger in its disregard of the existence, claim and world-historical viability of other
traditions. Perhaps it is for the Oriental thinker
himself to seek to achieve clarity about the obscurity and
ambiguity of the situation in which he finds himself today
in respect of his own tradition, however feeble its
breath. We in India can begin to do this only by squarely
facing the issues posed for us by the fact that for us our
own tradition is no embalmed mummy, or not yet, and that
it is still alive in us, for good or ill, as shaping our
attitudes and ways of thinking and speaking; and that, on
the other hand, we live and think in a world which is
under the sway of what we still experience as an alien
destiny. Do we also experience the tension between these
two, and have we attempted to examine the structure of
this field of tension? Have we realized the full otherness of that destiny and investigated, on our part, the
nature and logic of the tradition that has engendered it?

In regard to our own tradition, we have two hundred years
of apologetic, reform and re-interpretation behind us,
since our entry into modernity. But how far have we been
able to achieve that distance from our past which can
enable us to bring before our view and comprehend the
inner, dynamic structure of this tradition from the perspective of the present? The present self-understanding
of the West has been mediated by the dialectic of Athens
and Jerusalem, of the Enlightenment and the Romantic
movement, of this whole past with the scientific, technological present. Can we simply turn our backs on our
own past, just discard it, and appropriate the final
fruits of Western self-understanding as *the* inner telos of
man universally and as such, or shall we reject the
spiritual-philosophical endeavour of the West altogether
as of no consequence and seek to entrench ourselves into a
specifically Indian philosophizing, in the language of the
past and supposedly undistorted by the alien world of
meanings embodied in the English language we employ for
the purpose? Or shall we begin to *understand* both in
their mutual otherness, to learn the language of each and
so to evolve ways of thinking and talking which will be
truly appropriate to our membership of both worlds,
striving in such fashion to transform it into one? I for
one have no doubt that we can gain some help in this
direction if we pay more attention to that moving image of
the West's self-understanding which constitutes its
tradition as also to the ways in which Western scholars
have been seeking to understand our own.

THE PROBLEM OF PHILOSOPHICAL RECONCEPTION
IN THE THOUGHT OF K.C. BHATTACHARYYA

Classical Indian philosophy is rich in examples of the
attention given by Indian thinkers to conceptual problems
arising from their concern with a truth that saves and
liberates. In the Vedānta tradition specifically we have
the two-pronged enterprise of developing a mode of
thinking which is both a hermeneutic and an analytic, both
an explication of what found utterance in the "beginning"
and an analytic of the concepts required for such
explication, the two held together by the unity of a
historically unfolding system. Picking out examples at
random, one may mention the exegesis of *tat tvam asi* in
the *Upadeśasāhasrī* of Śaṁkara and Sureśvara's attempt, in
the *Naiṣkarmyasiddhi*, to inquire into the logical structure of this type of scriptural utterance. What kind of a
sentence is this, in respect of its logical form? Is it
descriptive of a reality standing over against us, to
which it can correspond, or is it more like a call that
awakens a sleeper, thus negating an existent state or
belief, rather than affirming a state of affairs, unless
the way we can be brought to see our true selves be itself
spoken of as a possible state of affairs? Examples of the
more analytical kind of thinking are the conceptual
investigations of "self-luminosity" by Citsukha and of
"falsity" by Madhusūdana, not to speak of the sustained
probing into the nature of the self and of illusion in the
school of Śaṁkara and into what Brahman means by Maṇḍana
and in all schools of Vedānta.

Originally published in *Philosophy East and West*, 24
(1974): 59-70. Reprinted from *Philosophy East and West* by
permission of the University of Hawaii Press.

It would certainly be a task worth undertaking to
determine how, in terms of our present "modern" ways of
thinking and speaking, a philosophical vision has been
developed through conceptualization of religious
experience in the tradition of classical Advaita; what
epistemological, metaphysical, and logical problems have
had to be tackled in the process and why--and to investigate, finally, what light these results, achieved in
this particular religio-philosophical tradition, may throw
on the general problem of the process of symbolization
involved in the conceptualization of truth as disclosed in
religious experience. Implicit in such an enterprise,
however, is the naive belief that the terms in which this
"general problem" is posed provide the standard frame of
reference, the failure to see that categories like
"religion," "philosophy," "religious experience" and
"conceptualization" themselves derive from one particular
tradition, and that they have become questionable even
within that tradition itself. How adequately do the
expressions "religious experience" and "philosophical
vision" represent the self-understanding of the Indian
tradition? Did Indian thinkers understand their task as
one of bringing to the concept specific modes of
experience, and were they concerned with experience and
its conceptual mastery in the way Western thinkers have
always been?

I should like to focus attention here, instead, upon
this last set of questions, upon the hermeneutical task of
understanding the past in terms of the present, of
translating from one to another, and of the impingement of
one tradition upon another. This is not a matter of
merely peripheral relevance to the problem of gaining
access to alien modes of religiousness and of their self-
understanding, but is an intrinsic dimension of the self-
understanding, and thus the very existence and continuity
of every tradition as such. The continuity of a tradition

is one of changing interpretations, of reconception, and
of translation; and in the religious sphere is made
possible by our openness to the past utterance or event,
by letting it claim us in the present and by the faith
that it can become meaningful to us, speak to us, here and
now. But to such faith there always corresponds a predicament. For *homo religiosus*, it is not merely the
existential predicament of finding himself caught in the
necessity of taking account of time and of gathering
together the past and the future in the living present.
It is also, more concretely, the predicament of being torn
between languages and modes of thought, between worlds,
some dead, some alive yet different, others not yet born.
In the Indian religio-philosophical tradition, as in
others, there have been a number of historical nodal
points where such faith and such a predicament has
exhibited itself in dramatic fashion from early Vedic to
late classical Brahmanism and medieval "Hinduism." One
may investigate each of these transition points to determine the quality and the power of faith exhibited, to
analyze the precise character of the predicament and
challenge--linguistic, conceptual-philosophical and
cultural--and of the creative response by which a new
pattern of meanings and a new self-understanding was
generated and handed down to posterity. One fascinating
inquiry of this type would be to study the fateful deci-
sions made from time to time in the long conflict between
classical Sanskrit and the vernaculars and dialects, the
religious significance of the emergence of Sanskrit as a
medium of both religious symbolization and philosophical
understanding and of its eventual abandonment, in the
latter role, in favor of regional languages and dialects.

Much more significant and relevant to our present
concern, however, is the predicament into which a Hindu
seeking to formulate a philosophical vision has been
thrown by India's entry into modernity since the days of

Rammohun Roy. The coming of modernity to India signified not merely the impingement of an alien world of knowledge, ideas, and ideals upon the Indian consciousness but of a world which was itself rapidly reaching out toward a newly conceived future, as well as spreading out its tentacles to encompass the whole world. Under the colonial origins of his modernization, the Indian encountered "philosophy" and "religion" and began forthwith the long journey of reinterpreting his tradition in terms of these Western categories. More importantly, he began thinking about it and reconceiving it in the English language, not just to expound it to English scholars but as the principal medium of his own self-understanding. Such self-understanding was reflected back in new meanings being given to ancient words in the Indian languages, and it also expressed itself in the way traditional meanings were themselves reflected in his use of concepts embedded in English words. In this interplay between the one and the other, between the traditional and the modern, between one's own and the alien, between the present and the past, what was happening to the truth of that tradition itself and to its manner of speaking to us? Was it being gradually covered up and hidden from our view, or was it being brought now to shine forth, at least in promise, in its real purity? How far were the thinkers engaged in the task of reinterpreting their tradition aware of the two players in this game, in their specific distinctness as well as in their mutuality? Did they, in the strength and lucidity of their faith, see that in understanding their tradition in this new fashion, symbolizing its thought in a novel way and for a new age, they were letting a new truth emerge out of this meeting of the past and the present? How clearly did they see that the voice of tradition speaks historically, in varying tongues, and what it says to us depends largely upon our relationship, not merely to our present but to the future as it rushes on toward us?

In one of his brilliant and penetrating studies of
Hinduism, the Indologist Paul Hacker has pointed out how
in the work of men like Bankim, Vivekananda, and
Radhakrishnan modern Hindu thinking has remained a hastily
improvised mixture of traditional heritage on the one hand
and, on the other, of Western and Christian ideas
impinging upon it with inescapable urgency, without any
real fusion of the two and often at the expense of the
heritage of the past, preventing the authentic Hindu
heritage as such from emerging in its real significance
and thus becoming truly effective. More pointedly, he
says there, "Excepting perhaps for Aurobindo Ghose and a
few other, less known thinkers, [Indians] have in general
not succeeded till today in thinking the Indian tradition,
Western and Christian influences, as well as the
requirements of the contemporary situation in their
togetherness and in a unified manner."[1] He admonishes
Indian thinkers, therefore, to overcome now the memory of
the colonial epoch which has so deeply wounded the Indian
spirit and gain back the greater tranquility and inner
self-collectedness requisite for undertaking the task of
seeing, in sober clarity, the multiple and manifold
forces, and sources of insight, still alive and operative
in the spiritual and intellectual space of India and of
orienting itself anew.

Not the least distinguished of these lesser known
thinkers was Krishna Chandra Bhattacharyya, who lived and
thought, like Gandhi, Aurobindo, Tagore, Nehru, and
Radhakrishnan, during the terminal phase of the colonial
epoch. For him, as for these others, the wounds inflicted
by this epoch were not just a memory that darkened their
thinking, as Hacker would seem to imply. As the purest,
most philosophically disciplined and "critical" *thinker* of
them all, he took upon himself this wound at its sharpest
and most intense moment and turned it into an instrument
of lucid vision. By his deep, unbroken faith in the voice

of his spiritual and philosophical tradition, he trans-
muted this wound into the sovereign tranquility and
collectedness of spirit of a true thinker and gained that
rare intellectual honesty that drives a thinker on to
raise new questions and find new answers.[2] He was thus
enabled to search with profound penetration into the truth
of his own tradition and at the same time be genuinely
open, as few Indian thinkers have been, to the call of the
modern, as gathered together in the thought of the
greatest masters of modern Western thought--Kant and
Hegel. What is uniquely characteristic of Bhattacharyya
is the fact that in his massive venture of reappropriating
and critically reinterpreting the Indian philosophical
past in the language of "modern" Western thought, he did
not falsify his understanding of either by an uncritical
superimposition of the one upon the other or by a naive
identification of concepts belonging to these different
traditions. His thought thus embodies and exemplifies the
entire problematic of the hermeneutic enterprise, the
coming together of two intellectual worlds in the act of
understanding, in all its creative significance and power.

Bhattacharyya sought neither to construct a system of
speculative thought nor to create a comprehensive philosophical world-view encompassing all of man's religious
and philosophic experience. His was an enterprise of
genuine spiritual humility, for he only sought to wrench
meaning from an antique philosophical tradition for
himself, to render it meaningful to himself as a thinker
and thereby perhaps also to others. But he thought in the
English language, and wrote in a language which bears a
heavy imprint of the work of Kant and, to a lesser degree,
of Hegel, both of them German thinkers who were available
to him, moreover, in hardly adequate or elegant English
translations. Beyond this, his language strains to
express concepts embedded in the Sanskrit of his own
scholarly tradition, giving to his style and idiom a power

of generating, for the sensitive and educated philosophical ear, echoes emanating from the most diverse
regions of the spirit. The difficulty and occasional
obscurity of his writing is a reflection of the intensity
of effort he spent in bringing about a fusion of intellectual horizons (*Horizontverschmelzung*, as Hans Georg
Gadamer has described it in his *Wahrheit und Methode*), the
horizons of past and present, of the West and India, the
distinct horizons within the Indian philosophico-religious
tradition itself. It is in such fusion, made possible by
creative effort toward a novel understanding, that the
essence of the hermeneutic experience consists, according
to Gadamer. K.C. Bhattacharyya's work exemplifies and
expresses, as hardly any other philosopher's, this kind of
experience in which a tradition achieves new self-
understanding and in which new truth is born.

Although Bhattacharyya wrote extensive studies seeking
to reinterpret the Sāṁkhya and Yoga systems of philosophy
also, he considered Advaita Vedānta as the supreme
expression of the religious quest of freedom in the Indian
tradition. As he remarked, "This philosophy is the most
satisfying formulation of the distinctive spirit of
Hinduism, and in this sense it may claim to be a synthesis
of other systems of Indian philosophy, which all seek to
formulate this spirit; and it has also explicitly
influenced the historical evolution of Hinduism."[3]
Bhattacharyya points out that "Vedānta is primarily a
religion, and it is a philosophy only as the formulation
of this religion. All religion makes for the realization
of the self as sacred, but the religion of Advaita is the
specific cult of such realization understood explicitly as
self-knowledge, as sacred knowledge, and as nothing but
knowledge."[4] The self, which is to be known, is accepted
in the first instance in faith; this faith is "confirmed,
clarified, and formulated by reason" and is in this manner
"inwardized into a vision." This work of reason,

essential to the completion of the process of self-
knowledge in Advaita, may be called philosophy. And
philosophy, as thus understood, is hence "not only an
auxiliary discipline, but an integral part of the religion
and its characteristic self-expression."[5] For Bhattacharyya, Advaitism is thus religion and philosophy in one.

Advaita is religion in the sense that its central
content is given to thought "by something other than
thought and other than sense."[6] The content, in other
words, is here revealed or presented to thought by the
Upaniṣadic Word and is accepted in faith as a demand to be
fulfilled or realized through thought. Such thought,
however, is for Vedānta "itself an emanation of faith,
being spiritual thought that is utterly distinct from
secular thought...."[7] In this respect, Vedānta differs
from the approach of the Sāṁkhya, for which "metaphysical
thought is nothing other than secular thought,"[8] in which
the natural or secular unfolds into the spiritual.
Bhattacharyya describes the Sāṁkhya, therefore, as "a
religion of reflective spontaneity or spiritual natural-
ness,"[9] in which secular thinking, initiated by the
experience of pain, is directed to the service of freedom
from sense and thus itself functions as spiritual
thinking. The metaphysics of Sāṁkhya springs from this
religion and its organon is reflection as the spiritual
process of freeing from sense. The religion of Yoga, as
Bhattacharyya calls it, differs from both of the above and
centers around the discipline of the will as the means of
freedom. "The free realising of freedom is regarded in
Sāṁkhya and Vedānta as a knowing process and in Bhakti-
systems as a feeling process. In Yoga it is taken as
literal willing,"[10] but as willing in its essential or
spiritual form, that is, as will not to will, will to
retract willing.

The category of the "spiritual" plays a pervasive role
in Bhattacharyya's thought, though a precise definition of

what he means by this term is hard to find in his
writings. It may be pointed out, however, that this term
is used by him to express the traditional Indian notion of
adhyatma as integrating the various aspects of existence;
this usage being another example of his practice of
clothing and expressing traditional Indian thought-
schemata in English, "modern," terms, thereby giving them
new meanings not readily intelligible to the reader
unfamiliar with the Indian tradition. The concepts of
adhyātma, *adhibūta*, *adhideva*, and *adhiloka* are traditional
Indian ways of marking "the distinctions among the several
aspects of existence" and Bhattacharyya's first published
work, *Studies in Vedāntism*, gives ample evidence of the
effort he spent in making intelligible this ancient,
Upaniṣadic thought-schema in "modern" terms. In the
second place, his use of the term "spiritual," we may
conjecture, also indicates his dissatisfaction and
uneasiness with the concept of "religion," which he found
hardly adequate to explicate what Vedānta, Sāṃkhya, Yoga,
and the Bhakti systems are about. They are all
"religions" and yet in a sense "transcend the sacred" and
"supersede religion." The category of the "spiritual" is,
for Bhattacharyya, the ultimate, comprehensive category,
of which the "religious" is one mode and manifestation,
and which expresses itself in its highest form in a
consciousness which can only be described as "super-
religious." For example, the consciousness of the
overpersonal Self as identical with I is described by
Bhattacharyya as "the religious form of the spiritual
consciousness,"[11] so that the investigation of the
religious consciousness becomes merely a part of the more
comprehensive discipline, the philosophy of the spirit,
which is a "study of all contents enjoyed in explicit
reference to the subject I."[12] Super-religious spiritual
activity, in which willing is absolutely disinterested,
transcends all activity conceived as religious, for its

final objective is the absolute transcendence that is
freedom or *mokṣa*. As Bhattacharyya says, "All activity
for *mokṣa* (as distinct from *svarga*)--activity as opposed
to self-surrender--where the good is conceived as absolute
and not as coordinate with evil, not, in other words, as
satisfying an interest, is super-religious. Self-
knowledge, for example, is a super-religious good in
Vedānta; so is bhakti in Vaiṣṇava systems."[13] In its
final stage, Yoga also culminates in such super-religious
activity. According to Bhattacharyya, further, the
"spiritual" is itself a concept that points beyond itself.
The philosophy of the spirit (including that of its
expression in the religious form), in which there is a
necessary reference to the subject or "I", culminates in
the philosophy of truth. Here, we reach the region of the
absolute, of "transcendental consciousness," in which even
the "I", as the symbol of reality, is negated. In the
religious consciousness there is experience of self-
abnegation but no theoretic denial of the subject *I*. From
the perspective of the absolute, of which there is no
"enjoying" experience as there is of the overpersonal
reality in religion, and of which the positive character
"is expressible only by the negation of *I* (or more
accurately, by 'what I am not'),"[14] the subject or the
individual self is unreal, for the absolute alone *is*. But
when "we say that the absolute *is*, we mean by 'is' not
reality but truth. Reality is enjoyed but truth is not.
The consciousness of truth as what is believed in but not
understood either in the objective or in the subjective
attitude, as not literally speakable at all but speakable
only in the purely symbolistic way, is extra-religious or
transcendental consciousness."[15]

In Bhattacharyya's description of the Vedānta as
"primarily" a religion, there is implicit thus a critique
of religion as a central concept handed down to us by the
Western tradition. In what sense, we may now go on to

ask, is Advaita a "philosophy"? It is obviously not philosophy in the pure Greek sense of autonomous, open questioning pursued with a view to the attainment of contemplative vision, of truth as *theoria*. The primordial gesture of thinking here is not one of questioning, as with the Greeks, but of hearing, to use Heidegger's language, and the piety of thought, for Vedānta thinking emanates from faith in a revealed content presented to thought and demanding intellectual clarification, but eventually calling for a "spiritual knowing" in which the activity of thought terminates. Bhattacharyya antici- pated, in large measure, the critique to which the central metaphysical tradition of the West has been subjected in the philosophy of the recent past, in particular by Martin Heidegger. He pointed out that "The attitude of meta- physics like that of the sciences including psychology is objective. It seeks to know reality as distinct from the knowing of it, as objective, at least, in the sense of being meant."[16] Metaphysics, and with it logic and epistemology, belongs to what he called the "philosophy of the object," object being defined as what is meant, which is comprehended within and by no means exhausts the realm of the significantly speakable. The concern of Vedānta, however, is with the subject or subjectivity conceived as conscious freedom or felt detachment from the object. This cannot come within the purview of "metaphysics" for, as he says, "There is properly no metaphysic of the subject and the apparent problems about the existence of the subject and its relation to the object are really illegitimate."[17] And yet, the subject and its positive freedom to refer to the object are both speakable, "and it is from the speakable that we must start in philosophy."[18] In the *Critique of Pure Reason*, Kant opened up a whole realm of what is speakable and is not yet objectively meant, namely, the realm of the "transcendental." It is not surprising that, of all Western philosophers,

Bhattacharyya felt himself closest to Kant, took his own point of departure on crucial issues from Kant and developed his thinking in constant debate with Kant.

As mentioned above, Bhattacharyya agreed with Kant in rejecting "the so-called metaphysic of the soul." According to him, the subject is a believed content, is problematically spoken as "I" and is not meanable or is not a meant something. But, he points out

> The understanding here is not a mystic intuition though it may point to its possibility, nor the intuition of a meaning that can be a term of a judgment, nor yet the thought of a meaning that is not known because not intuited or that is known without being intuited. It is somewhere midway between a mystic intuition and the consciousness of a meaning, being the believing awareness of a speakable content, the negation of which is unmeaning and which, therefore, is not a meaning. What is claimed to be mystically intuited is speakable only in metaphor which presents a contradiction in meaning and what is affirmed or denied in metaphysic is a meanable. The subject as I is neither contradictory nor meanable and the exposition of it accordingly is intermediate between mysticism and metaphysic. As, however, the subject is communicable by speech without metaphor, it cannot be taken as falling outside philosophical inquiry. [19]

The philosophical inquiry into the modes or functions of subjectivity or into the ways in which the "I" relates itself freely to the object, and thus may also freely detach itself from it, cannot, however, be content with, far from identifying itself with, the form which transcendental reflection takes in Kant. Bhattacharyya chides Kant for his "persisting objective attitude." The interest of Kantian epistemology, he says, "is still in the object, in the knownness or objectivity of the object which it seeks to understand theoretically as knowing. It does not abandon the objective procedure of metaphysics and the sciences, even though it sets itself to correct the conceit of independent objectivity."[20] It is this that leads Kant to deny self-knowledge and also to

disbelieve in "the possibility of a spiritual discipline of the theoretic reason through which self-knowledge may be attainable."[21] The Kantian analysis misleads insofar as it presents the knowing function "as an objective meaning and does not recognise that it is believed without being meant."[22] Kant's epistemology, further, is reduced to nothing more than a philological study, an enquiry into the significance of the mere phrase "knowing *of* object," "unless it is consciously viewed as rooted in the faith in the facthood of the knowing function and unless the so-called deduction that it presents is definitely known to be not inferential and not literally meant but to be the symbolisation by logical form of what is immediately believed as spiritual fact."[23] According to Bhattacharyya's formulation of the Vedantic view, "the subject is known though neither thought (meant) nor intuited. It is known as what the speaker of *I* is understood to intend by it. The understanding is a direct believing in something that is not meant but revealed as revealing itself....The subject is thus known by itself, as not meant but speakable, and not as either related or relating to the object."[24] The knowing function represents a positive mode of the freedom of the subject to relate to the object without getting related to it and is itself not "known" but only believed, though more indubitably than the knowledge of a meant object.

The task of philosophy, in this view, is the symbolic elaboration of these believed or felt subjective functions "the speaking creation of a system of subjective functions or the symbolising elaboration of the positive freedom of the subject."[25] This is "a special study," "a new philosophical study," not envisaged by Kant, which is "intermediate between the recognition of the subject purely through the intention of the word *I* and the inferential inquiry into the reality behind the meant object which is called metaphysics."[26] To this discipline

Bhattacharyya gives the name of spiritual or transcendental psychology because it seeks to elaborate, into a
system of symbolisms, the believed but not known facthood
of the knowing function and of subjective function in
general. It is a discipline of the theoretic reason, of a
sort inadmissible to Kant, because it investigates the
ways in which the subject freely relates itself to the
object. But it is a spiritual discipline in the sense
that the inquiry into the subject's positive freedom of
relating, into the objective attitude, is in the service
of a cultivation of the subjective attitude, or that of
realizing or inwardizing the subject's negative freedom
from all objectivity. Spiritual psychology is thus conceived of by Bhattacharyya as a philosophical study based
on the method of spiritual introspection, in which one
becomes aware of the subjective functions of relating and
detaching, that is, of the modes of freedom, as distinct
from psychological introspection, which is only concerned
with the consciousness of psychological abstractions like
the knownness and feltness of an object considered in
isolation from the object itself. In this discipline the
subjective attitude is symbolized by the objective attitude from which it seeks to be freed, for the modes of
subjectivity are nothing other than the modes of freeing
oneself from the modes of objectivity. The business of
spiritual psychology, Bhattacharyya says, is not to
explain or to solve a problem but "to interpret empirical
psychology in terms of the positively felt and believed
freedom of the subject from objectivity"[27] and, secondly,
"to elaborate modes of freedom that have no reference to
object at all."[28] As he explains, "In the objective
attitude, the knownness or feltness of the object appears
positive and knowing or feeling appears as its problematic
negation. In the subjective attitude, the case is
reversed: freedom is positively believed and the related-
ness of the object to the subject--its objectivity--

appears as constructed, as not belonging to the object...
and is thus understood as the self-negation or alienated
shadow of the subject."[29]   In his Amalner lectures of 1929
entitled, *The Subject as Freedom*, Bhattacharyya has provided "a rough sketch of transcendental psychology, conceived of as the legitimate substitute for the so-called
metaphysic of the soul,"[30] elaborating the stages of
freedom from objectivity and suggesting "the possibility
of a consecutive method of realising the subject as
absolute freedom, of retracting the felt positive freedom
towards the object into pure intuition of the self."[31]

In consequence of Bhattacharyya's attempt to rethink
the Advaita as "philosophy," the concept of philosophy
itself undergoes a far-reaching transformation at his
hands. The call to thinking comes no longer from a sense
of wonder, as with the Greeks, nor from the need for a
rational justification of established doctrine, as in the
European Middle Ages, nor from the sense of doubt and the
self-assertion of the human will, as in modern philosophy,
but as a demand for making true in one's personal experience a truth heard once as eternally valid and accepted
in faith, as the call to "know" and to be one's self as
absolute freedom through the activity of a faith-full
thinking. In a modern Indian thinker like Bhattacharyya,
open to the highest reaches of the Western philosophical
tradition, the demand springs from the awareness that
ancient texts communicate truth to us only insofar as we
are able to translate them and rethink what they say in
the language and idiom of the present, that a truth, to be
eternal, must be ceaselessly reinterpreted and reformu-
lated and thus made to withstand the exigency of time. It
springs, above all, from the need for a creative response
to the encounter of two traditions, each speaking a
different language, each constituting a world-horizon in
its own right, and of which a certain degree of fusion can
be brought about only by the faith that the utterance of

one's own tradition can sustain itself and even find a
more satisfying articulation in an alien medium, in an
alienated age.

For thinking the "demand" is, as Bhattacharyya puts
it, "that the subjective function being essentially the
knowing of the object as distinct from it, this knowing
which is only believed and not known as fact *has* to be
known as fact, as the self-evidencing reality of the
subject itself."[32]   *Was heisst Denken?*" asked Heidegger,
for the first time explicitly in the history of Western
thought and sought to give an answer adequate to the
unasked question behind the entire philosophico-religious
tradition of the West. Bhattacharyya's thinking, as also
his concept of thinking, gave explicit and appropriate
place to the notion of a "demand," which presupposes faith
in the source of the demand, the recognition of it as in
some sense sacred, and one's response in the act of
thinking as itself religious, as an act of truth and of
truing. As in the thinking of Heidegger, a concept of
thinking is developed here that sheds the traditional
Western dichotomy of theory and practice and of faith and
philosophy, for which thinking itself becomes the highest
form of practice, a process of self-knowledge that is at
the same time a transformation and fulfillment of self,
generated and sustained by faith in the Vedic word. For
Bhattacharyya as for Heidegger there is nothing more
questionable and question-worthy in philosophy than the
nature of philosophy itself. As the former remarks at the
beginning of one of his most seminal essays, "The Concept
of Philosophy," "an explication of the concept of philosophy appears to me more important than the discussion of
any specific problem of philosophy."[33] Coming, however,
as he does from another tradition and inspired by a
different concern than Heidegger's, Bhattacharyya
preferred to retain for his thought the terms "philosophy"
and "subjectivity" rather than rejecting them, along with

some others, as inappropriate on the basis of a historical critique such as Heidegger's.

It may appear incredible that so keen a student of Hegel as Bhattacharyya should have remained unappreciative of the dimension of historicity intrinsic to philosophical understanding, and not so mindful as he might have been of the historicity of his own understanding, both of his own tradition and that of the West, and so of his whole enterprise of interpretation. This failure was due, it may be surmised, in part to the ahistorical climate of philosophical thought at the time in the English-speaking world in general and of its reception of Hegel in particular and in part to the ahistorical bias of the Indian tradition itself. Beyond this, however, it was a legitimate reaction on Bhattacharyya's part to an unbridled historicism that claimed to "explain," and thus to bury, the past historically without concerning itself with the possibility that in them truths may have found utterance that still speak to us and challenge us to renewed thinking. Bhattacharyya was fully aware of the dangers of such historicism, and he reacted sharply on finding how "history thus sits in judgment on philosophy." As he remarked:

> There is the danger, no doubt, of too easily reading one's philosophic creed into the history, but the opposite danger is more serious still. It is the danger of taking the philosophic type studied as a historic curiosity rather than a recipe for the human soul, and of seeking to explain the curiosity by natural *causes* instead of seriously examining its merits as philosophy. This unfortunately is sometimes the defect of Western expositions of Eastern philosophy and religion.[34]

To the present-day reader, Bhattacharyya's work would also appear to be insufficiently sensitive to the role of language in thought, to the particularity of languages and the way they embody, not just express, concepts. He sought in his thinking to provide "problematic construc-

tions on Vedantic lines intended to bring out the relations of the system to modern philosophical systems."[35]
Had he experienced the full impact of Husserl's
phenomenology, or written after the later Wittgenstein and
Heidegger, would Bhattacharyya not have concerned himself
more centrally with the historical and cross-cultural
determinants of his own understanding of the Indian and
Western philosophical traditions?

NOTES

1. "Schopenhauer und die Ethik des Hinduismus," *Saeculum*
12, no. 4 (1961):398-399. My translation.
2. It is interesting to note that, like Tagore,
K.C. Bhattacharyya was linked, through his grandfather,
with some of the pioneers of the "Bengal Renaissance."
Umakant Tarkalankar, as the grandfather was called after
his academic title, was a teacher of Joshua Marshman and
William Ward of the Serampore Mission College and was held
by them, along with William Carey, in the highest respect
as their guru. Cf. Pravas Jivan Chaudhury, "Krishna
Chandra Bhattacharyya: A Biographical Sketch," in *Krishna
Chandra Bhattacharyya Memorial Volume*, ed. S.K. Maitra, et
al. (Amalner, 1958), i.
3. Gopinath Bhattacharyya, ed., *Studies in Philosophy*, 2
vols (Calcutta, 1956), 1:122.
4. Ibid., 1:118-119.
5. Ibid., 1:119.
6. Ibid., 1:150.
7. Ibid.
8. Ibid.
9. Ibid., 1:147.
10. Ibid., 1:285.
11. Ibid., 2:114.
12. Ibid.
13. Ibid., 1:289.

14. Ibid., 2:116.

15. Ibid.

16. Ibid., 2:25.

17. Ibid., 2:27.

18. Ibid., 2:26.

19. Ibid., 2:24-25.

20. Ibid., 2:30.

21. Ibid., 2:31.

22. Ibid.

23. Ibid.

24. Ibid.

25. Ibid., 2:27.

26. Ibid.

27. Ibid., 2:29.

28. Ibid.

29. Ibid., 2:29-30.

30. Ibid., 2:3.

31. Ibid., 2:33. The phenomenological mode of thinking and "doing" philosophy, apparently so close to Bhattacharyya's concerns, had at this time not yet assumed the status of a "modern philosophical system." Even those of Husserl's writings that were published during his lifetime remained inaccessible to the English-speaking student until the appearance of *Ideas* in 1931, one year after the publication of *The Subject as Freedom*. Bhattacharyya read this work in the same year "and recognised a similarity in the general attitude and method between himself and the German thinker." Cf. Pravas Jivan Chaudhury, op. cit., v.

32. Ibid., 2:32.

33. Ibid., 2:100.

34. Ibid., 1:1.

35. Ibid.

THE WILL TO INTERPRET AND INDIA'S DREAMING SPIRIT

An important development in contemporary philosophy is
the emergence of what may be called philosophical hermeneutics or, alternatively, hermeneutic philosophy. This
is concerned not so much with the art or methodology of
interpreting texts as with understanding and interpreting
as themselves basic moments in man's very way of being
human, as forms of be-ing and happening rather than as
operations directed at an objectively given entity or
happening. Wilhelm Dilthey is here the pioneer, but it is
to Martin Heidegger that we owe the basic insights, to
Hans Georg Gadamer the explication and working out in
elaborate detail the implications of these insights and to
Paul Ricoeur the continuation, in the Franco-American
milieu, of this novel mode and dimension of philosophical
thinking. The future alone can show how far and in what
manner Heidegger's call to a planetary thinking, as
against or rather beyond Western "philosophizing", is
heard and turns out to be capable of realization. But in
one respect at least this hermeneutical mode of thinking,
based on Heidegger's critique of the traditional Western
notions of Time, Being, Truth and Man, seems to be immediately helpful. It promises a new sort of freedom and
renewed hope to the Indian thinker reflecting on, and out
of, his own tradition, to the Indian willingly partici-
pating in the larger movement of world civilization and in
the international community of modern scholarship and yet
unwilling to be totally swept off his feet by them. It
enables him to turn a fresh look at the beginnings of his

Unpublished lecture given in the Franklin J. Matchette
Series, Boston University, April 10, 1974.

own tradition, in some measure estranged from it and yet
owned by it, to rethink its cumulative transmission
through successive transformations down to the present and
revaluate it in respect of its truth claims. An awareness
of that whole dimension or form of experience which
Gadamer has called *hermeneutische Erfahrung*, he finds,
strengthens him against what he has long experienced as a
relentless pressure, carrying myriad threats, from the
West, and it also brings to him the assurance of an
unending possibility of creative endeavour in relation to
his tradition in the future.

To a certain extent and in its more popular expressions, this new trend of thought is perhaps a Western
response to a new awareness of the "eternal East" in the
Western soul, of this Western dream, and to the historical
termination of the colonial epoch in the age of Western
dominance; to an awareness of the dreaming East awake and
no longer willing to exist only as a dream within the
Western dream-world. Henri Baudet has described how the
European imagination has reacted to what he calls "the
West's great retreat from Asia and Africa within the space
of less than a generation", and Mircea Eliade has repeatedly spoken of the need of a "creative hermeneutics" as
the only adequate response to the cultural and religious
pluralism of the present. To quote:

> After the Second War, an encounter with the
> "others," with the Unknown, became for Westerners
> a historical inevitability. Now, for some years
> Westerners have not only felt with increasing
> sharpness what a confrontation with "outsiders"
> means; but have also realised that it is they who
> are being dominated. This does not necessarily
> imply that they will be enslaved or oppressed,
> but only that they will feel the pressure of
> "foreign," non-Western spirituality. For the
> encounter--or shock--between civilizations is
> always, in the last resort, an encounter between
> spiritualities--between religions. A true
> encounter implies a dialogue. In order to begin a
> valid dialogue with non-European cultures, it is
> indispensable to know and understand these

cultures. Hermeneutics, the science of interpretation, is the Western man's reply--the only
intelligent reply--to the demands of contemporary
history, to the fact that the West is committed
(one might be tempted to say "condemned") to a
confrontation with the cultural values of the
"others"....The will properly to understand the
"other" is rewarded by an enrichment of the
Western consciousness....might even lead to a
renewal in the philosophical field.

The "other" here, it is worth noticing, is still part of
the Western dream, for which hermeneutics is also a
science of interpretation, an effective instrument for
decoding, unmasking and mastering an unconscious, anxiety-
generating content, in the manner of psychoanalysis, and a
means of achieving cultural totality, if not wholeness, by
assimilating the other as an element in a total dream
image. Strange hermeneutics, in which a valid dialogue
can begin only after understanding has first been
achieved, rather than being itself the locus or the play-
ground in which understanding has its very being. It is
true, as Eliade says, that "Today history is becoming
universal for the first time." But, we ask, must it bring
in its wake the spectral corollary of a "planetary"
culture, as envisaged by him--or by Teilhard de Chardin or
W.I. Thompson--and are Oriental spiritualities destined to
survive only as elements within a planetized culture, to
assist in the birth of which he invites historians of
religion to contribute?

   At the level of religious thought, this quest for
universality, completeness and self-sufficiency in the
West goes far back to, and would seem to be rooted in, the
thinking of the Church Fathers and in the explicitly
formulated principle of "utilization" or *chrêsis*, as
another Catholic scholar, the Indologist Paul Hacker, has
not only described but energetically commended as the
central motivating principle in a religious hermeneutics
of the "other". Hacker has drawn attention to the
phenomenon of what he calls "reorienting assimilation of

foreign materials" in the Old and New Testaments and shown
how in the writings of the Church Fathers the Christian
attitude to the religions of the Gentiles found explicit
formulation in the principle of *chrêsis*. The principle is
implied in the ideas of Justin and Clement and in Origen's
symbolical interpretation of the *spolia Aegyptorum*. In
Gregory's meditation on the Life of Moses three symbols
exhibiting the role of pagan culture in theology are
presented: Pharaoh's daughter, Moses' wife and the
Egyptian treasures, each pointing to the legitimacy of
assimilating the contents of pagan culture. Finally,
Augustine (*De doctrina Christiana*, book II, chapters
40-41) expounds the doctrine of the Egyptian treasures and
of their utilization by Christians, explaining how the
liberal arts and moral concepts to be found among the
Nations constitute their gold and silver which the
Christian is to appropriate to himself, for the gentiles
are unlawful possessors of those treasures and misuse them
perversely and illegitimately. In his discussion of the
views of Karl Rahner and Raimundo Panikkar and of the
implications of the Second Vatican Council, Hacker has
offered his own explication of this principle:

> The practical attitude toward non-Christian
> religions consists mainly in what the Fathers
> called *utilization* (*chrêsis, usus justus*).
> Utilization connotes, (1) that the assimilated
> elements are made subservient to an end different
> from the context from which they were taken, (2)
> that they can be taken over because some truth is
> contained or hidden in them, (3) that they must
> be reoriented in order that the truth might shine
> forth unimpeded.

Hacker addresses himself to the community of believers,
just as Eliade spoke in the name of Western culture, to be
enriched by assimilating "the spiritual universes that
Africa, Oceania, Southeast Asia open to us." He is
therefore not interested in the question whether this same
threefold hermeneutical process may not be at work,
"illegitimately" perhaps, from his point of view, in the

development of these other traditions too, and be adopted
as the creative task of men of faith everywhere, in
relation to *their own* traditions. If it were not for the
fact that the former is professionally a historian of
religion and the latter a distinguished Indologist, I
might have little justification for eavesdropping on what
is said *entre nous*. But both are engaged in scholarly
work in the *Geisteswissenschaften*, work which in its
claim, authority and appeal encompasses East and West,
Christian and non-Christian alike. Or, does the claim to
objective knowledge in such humanistic scholarship, with
its methodologies validating its claim, have something
illusory, dreamlike about it, no more than the pursuit of
a phantom, as Gadamer has put it? Is the "other" present
there only as an object of such scientific knowledge? For
Hacker, the impeccable scholar of Advaita Vedānta,
Indology is a *Fach*, a field of specialized research, a
Wissenschaft with a simple but severely austere methodology for investigating alien texts for the sake of what
is objectively present in them, with all "interpretation"
ruled out of court and its place taken by theological
"utilization". "A text," Hacker says, "does not answer us
like the partner in a conversation. It says, irrespective
of what question the interpreter approaches it with,
always the same, and the interpreter must, *nolens volens*,
let that text speak out with its fixed and established
words." This "*zu Wort kommen*" of the fixed words of the
text, a text belonging to an alien tradition, presumably
occurs by way of translating from the Sanskrit into a
Western language, and is for Hacker a strictly "static"
procedure. Dynamism is introduced into it, he tells
Panikkar, only when the interpreter takes up a stand *vis a
vis* the text, outside its heathen context, exposes its
"daemonic ambiguity and barrenness in that soil and then,
by an act of *chrêsis*, transplants any grains of logos-seed
he picks up there into the soil where alone they can

blossom and bear fruit--in the garden of the Church. The
Hindu Indian can only say amen to this noble enterprise,
for this kind of taking away enriches the other without
leaving the donor any poorer. He too is enriched by the
knowledge that somewhere there is a garden in bloom and is
strengthened in his hope that he too may some day learn to
tend his own garden better. Only, he feels a little left
out in the cold, somewhat bewildered and helpless, to
overhear that in order to grasp the truth in a text that
speaks to him directly, without translation, he must first
secure an Archimidean point outside the entire context of
his tradition. Or is this a hermeneutic only of the
"other," and confined to the foreign, with another, less
urgent hermeneutic for one's own tradition on the shelves?
What is it to understand, oneself or the other, and what
is it to understand a text generally? Is there not a
dynamic moment inherent in all understanding, so that to
understand is not just an independent preliminary act but
is inclusive of interpretation and application as necessary and constitutive moments in the total act, as Gadamer
has shown? Is there such a thing as an objective, unchanging meaning "contained" within a text? Was Heidegger
wrong in holding that all understanding is, as such,
interpretative, or when he said, "Whenever something is
interpreted as something, the interpretation is founded
essentially upon fore-having, fore-sight, and fore-
conception"? As he pointed out,

> An interpretation is never a presuppositionless
> apprehending of something presented to us. If,
> when one is engaged in a particular, concrete
> kind of interpretation, in the sense of exact
> textual interpretation, one likes to appeal to
> what "stands there," then one finds that what
> "stands there" in the first instance is nothing
> other than the obvious undiscussed assumptions of
> the person who does the interpreting.

Must we all think of our relationship to our traditions in
terms of reified entities called "religions," and is there

nothing to be learned here from the liberating insights of
Wilfred Cantwell Smith?

Philosophically more significant, and for our present
purpose closer to the heart of the matter, is the
following classic formulation of the Western concern with
understanding, and its approach toward, the Orient by
Maurice Merleau-Ponty:

> Like everything built or instituted by man, India
> and China are immensely interesting. But like
> all institutions, they leave it to us to discern
> their true meaning; they do not give it to us
> completely. China and India are not entirely
> aware of what they are saying. What they need to
> do to have philosophies is to try to *understand*
> themselves and everything else. Although these
> remarks are commonplace today, they do not settle
> the question. They come to us from Hegel. He
> was the one who invented the idea of "going
> beyond" the Orient by "understanding" it. It was
> Hegel who contrasted the Western idea of truth as
> the total conceptual recovery of the world in all
> its variety to the Orient, and defined the Orient
> as a failure in the same understanding....Hegel
> and those who follow him grant philosophical
> dignity to Oriental thought only by treating it
> as a distant approximation of conceptual under-
> standing. Our idea of knowledge is so demanding
> that it forces every other type of thought to the
> alternative of resigning itself to being a first
> sketch of the concept or disqualifying itself as
> irrational. Now the question is whether we can
> claim as Hegel did to have this absolute know-
> ledge, this concrete universal that the Orient
> has shut itself off from. If we do not in fact
> have it, our entire evaluation of other cultures
> must be re-examined.

Speaking of Husserl's more open attitude in this regard,
Merleau-Ponty adds, however, "Yet the fact remains that
the West has invented an idea of truth which requires and
authorizes it to understand other cultures, and thus to
recover them as aspects of a total truth." As a "historical entelechy" and as itself a historical creation,
the West is "committed to the onerous task of understanding other cultures," though it can learn from Indian
and Chinese philosophers "to rediscover the relationship

to being and the initial option which gave it birth, and
to estimate the possibilities we have shut ourselves off
from in becoming 'Westerners' and perhaps reopen them....
This is why we should let the Orient appear in the museum
of famous philosophers." Merleau-Ponty, too, does not
"settle the question," and still shares, along with
Husserl, the basic presuppositions of Hegel as to the
reality and significance of the East for Western man.

It was Hegel who described India as "the land of
imaginative aspiration," as "a Fairy region, an enchanted
World," "the region of phantasy and sensibility," as
exhibiting the unearthly beauty of a woman in the days
which immediately succeed childbirth, or of women during
the magical somnambulistic sleep, connecting them with a
world of super-terrestrial beauty. "Such a beauty," he
says, "we find also in its loveliest form in the Indian
world; a beauty of enervation in which all that is rough,
rigid, and contradictory is dissolved, and we have only
the soul in a state of emotion;" "the charm of this
Flowerlife...in which its whole environment and all its
relations are permeated by the rose-breath of the soul,
and the world is transformed into a Garden of Love." This
India of the German Romantic imagination, projected by
Hegel on to a distant geographical region, represents for
him "the character of Spirit in a state of Dream," a
character which constitutes "the generic principle of the
Hindu Nature." Hegel goes on to explain, "In a dream, the
individual ceases to be conscious of self *as such*, in
contradistinction from objective existences. When awake,
I exist for myself, and the rest of creation is an
external, fixed objectivity, as I myself am for it." "The
dreaming Indian" has not only never awakened into the
sphere of Understanding, where the self, existing for
itself, stands over against the objective world; he is
lost in his dreams. The Hindu Spirit revels in the most
extravagant maze through all natural and spiritual forms,

and leading "this inebriate dream-life, in which like a desolate spirit, it finds no rest, no settled composure, though it can content itself in no other way; as a man who is quite reduced in body and spirit finds his existence altogether stupid and intolerable, and is driven to the creation of a dream-world and a delirious bliss in opium." Further, "As the Hindoo Spirit is a state of dreaming and mental transiency--a self-oblivious dissolution--objects also dissolve for it into unreal images and indefinitude." This is why Indians have no History, "for history requires Understanding--the power of looking at an object in an independent objective light, and comprehending it in its rational connection with other objects....(And) it is because Hindus have no history in the form of annals (*historia*) that they have no History in the form of transactions (*res gestae*) no growth expanding into a veritable political condition." It is as an embodiment of such spirit in a state of dream that India "forms an essential element in Universal History, as a land of Desire," and as which it has finally consummated her role by surrendering herself and her treasures to her English lords. Is it not indeed the privilege of the spirit in the waking state, as represented by the modern Hegel-speaking Western consciousness, to be master of its dreams, even if they be only his dreams?

More than seventy-five years were to elapse after Hegel's lectures on the philosophy of history, where these views are expressed, before Freud would publish his *Traumdeutung* (1900), and another fifty years or so before Heidegger's critique of the Western waking *Geist* and his exhibition of it as the grandiloquent dream that it is, a critique that was itself rendered possible by the explicit self-exhibition of this as the Will to Power in the thinking of Nietzsche. It was not until 1927 that, with the publication of *Being and Time*, the notion of history and the "power of seeing an object in an objective light,"

the very concepts of Time and of Being, were put into
question by Heidegger. For, it is he who first distinguished between history and *Geschichte*, who said that
unhistorical ages are not as such necessarily *unge-
schichtlich* and that "history" is in a sense the standing
destruction of the future and of the happening character
of our relationship to the arrival of what still remains
hidden, unthought and unsaid, in the beginning that
launched us into our voyage through history. Is history a
continuous movement toward absolute self-consciousness, as
Hegel thought, or is it the *Irrtum* (the empire of confusion and error) that as Heidegger said, constitutes the
Wesensraum of *Geschichte* itself. Not until James Joyce's
Finnegan's Wake was this Western waking dream experienced
as truly a dream and translated back into language appropriate to the dreaming state. Here, it may be added, the
meeting with India is presented as the moment of awaking,
not as the descent into a dream-world, as with Hegel. "It
was a long, dark, all but unending night: now day, slow
day. The lotus bells. It is our hour of risings. In
that European end meets Ind."

Hegel, however, said something profoundly true, unbeknownst to himself, when he prognosticated, continuing his
sentence on the English lordship over India, "for it is
the necessary fate of Asiatic Empires to be subjected to
Europeans; and China will, someday or other, be obliged to
submit to this fate." For the spirit which woke up, or
dreamt that it did, after Socrates in the history of Western thought, *has* conquered the world and incorporated it
into its own big dream. This is world conquest, not in
the political sense, nor even in the cultural sense
(aren't we all today very cheerful and generous plural-
ists?) but in the sense of what Husserl called the
Europaisierung der Erde and, following him, Heidegger.
Nietzsche described this invisible spirit as "that
uncanniest, *unheimlichste*, of all guests, Nihilism,

standing at the door of man's dwelling-place"; Husserl
thought of it, with unrelenting optimism, as the entelechy
inherent in the Greek origins of the Western philosophical
tradition and destined to eventual triumph. Some have
called it secularization, and others have spoken of it, in
more picturesque language, as the virus from the West, as
the whole world being sucked into the current of Christian
history. One manifestation of the modern age, Heidegger
said, is the flight of the gods, the withdrawal of
Divinity as such, adding that the greatest share in
bringing this about falls to Christianity. Arend Theodoor
van Leeuwen seems to agree, even to welcome this modern
phenomenon, not merely of the absence of Deity but of his
passing, so vividly depicted in Nietzsche's story of the
mad man. Heidegger has described this shadow creeping
over the world as the spread of technological thinking, as
the process of the complete Europeanization of the earth
and of man, attacking at the source everything that is of
an essential nature, threatening to bring about a drying
up of these sources. He has also called it, simply,
"world-civilization", which means today "the dominance of
the natural sciences, the dominance and primacy of
economics, politics, technology. Everything else is not
even superstructure any longer, but only an utterly
fragile side-structure. We stand in the midst of this
world-civilization," which is only a form of the world-
destiny of homelessness, not something which modern man
has himself made but a destiny into which he has rather
been sent forth, fated. In this sense at least the
non-Western world has become subject to, and a participant
in, what Heidegger has also called "the destiny, or
history, of Being," originating in the West but now
enveloping the entire earth. In so far as we in the East
are aware of this common destiny, not merely in terms of
the urgency to modernize but also as sharing in a common
"time of need," we cannot but listen to the Western voice

which speaks of the possibility of a "turn," a *Wende*, in
this destiny, if only we are willing to face up to the
task of learning to think Truth and Time, Being, World and
Man in ways other than those laid out by the Greek
founders of this destiny, and wake up at last from this
long Western dream of which we too have become a part,
wake up without forgetting to learn so much that this
dream has yet to teach us.

To return to Hegel and to his view, out-moded in its
formulation but not to be dismissed as just arrant
Hegelian non-sense even today, that the direction of
world-history moves from East to West, for Europe was to
Hegel the culmination of this history, as Asia was its
beginning. As for the future, he said, America is the
land to which it belongs, "where, in the ages that lie
before us, the burden of the World's history shall reveal
itself. The Light of Spirit arises in Asia, but it is in
the West, where the physical Sun sinks down, that there
arises the Sun of self-consciousness which diffuses a
nobler brilliance." In this daylight the Spirit is wide-
awake, having left behind, geographically, historically
and spiritually, the "immediate, unreflected consciousness
which characterises the East," the characteristically
Indian "Idealism of imagination, without distinct conceptions," where Absolute Being is presented "as in the
ecstatic state of a dreaming condition," where "the Spirit
wanders into the Dream-World, and the highest state is
annihilation," "a dreaming unity of Spirit and Nature,
which involves a monstrous bewilderment in regard to all
phenomena and relations." In philosophy as well as
religion thus, Asia represents a form of the Spirit which
has already played its role in history and therefore
belongs to a bygone age. It lives only as a vestige of
the past, for history according to Hegel is "the development of Spirit in *Time*, as Nature is the development of
the Idea in *Space*." Hegel arranges all the philosophies

and religions of the world in a progressive series
culminating in his own philosophy as the final stage in
the self-awareness of the Absolute Religion, Christianity,
and of all philosophies, as history comprehended, forming
together, to quote the great concluding sentence of the
Phenomenology, "at once the recollection and the Golgotha
of Absolute Spirit, the reality, the truth, the certainty
of its throne, without which it were lifeless, solitary,
and alone." In this progression, the religion of India is
one form of the determinate religions, which he calls the
religion of substance, and Indian philosophy likewise
represents the stage of intellectual substantiality and
inner abstraction.

William Ernest Hocking, otherwise so appreciative of
Hegel's "multitudes of penetrating observations" about the
East, saw the crucial weakness in this position, saw that
the East itself cannot be dismissed as a merely consumed
residue in the development of its own traditions of
thought. He recognized that the hermeneutic process of
self-understanding and self-interpretation through which a
religious and philosophical tradition like that of India
has developed continuously does not at a certain point in
time come to a sudden stop, becoming only a dead and
transcended moment in Western thinking. Pointing out "the
ineffectiveness of any attempt to deal with the Oriental
religions by placing them in *an evolutionary or dialectical order*, thus subjecting each in turn to the gentle
fate of being superceded by the next higher member of the
series," Hocking remarks,

> In this respect, I surmise that most Western
> students of Oriental religions are Hegelians at
> heart, tending to conceive the religions as
> members in a rational series whose terminus is
> necessarily one's own view....However genial
> Hegel's insight into the several religions, it
> remains true that the very notion of a serial
> order among the great religions is mistaken; that
> it is, in fact, *inconsistent with the dialectical
> principle itself*. For no people and no religion

ceases to think. If Chinese religion, for example, is defective, it will be Chinese experience
which will discover it, and the cure should come
in China, not in India. Why must the movement of
fundamental racial thought pass from region to
region, as if thought were no longer productive
in its old haunts? If Indian religion is defective, why must the more perfect stage emerge in
Tibet?....There is no advance without new energy
and new insight. But given these conditions, the
dialectical principle must assert itself, and
better *in situ* than in a new sphere where
continuity is lost.

Giving a more adequate formulation of the principle of
development, Hocking continues, "*From any position partially false there is a nisus toward a truer position*....
Living thought and living religion never stand still. The
'dialectic' is incessant and everywhere. And this being
true, the next stage in any dialectical movement is the
natural property of the possessors of the previous
stage....no imperfect position can be fastened upon any
religion as its true definition." Hocking is still too
much of a Hegelian, however, to see here any problem in
the conceptions of "dialectic" and "development," and in
his views on the "logic" and the "structure" of world
history. Perhaps his ideas of the religious traditions of
mankind are too much dominated by the notion of "essence,"
of religions as entities each with its own specific
essence. But he was the first to see religious pluralism
in a new, more adequate perspective and prepared the way
for the bolder, more original and in many ways revolutionary approach of Wilfred Cantwell Smith in our own day.
Preceded only by Royce's account of the role and process
of interpretation in religious thinking, Hocking called
for "the way of Reconception" in the service of a world
faith--not a world religion--in which "the process of
uniting the religious mind of mankind" will be fulfilled
in the comprehension of an identical essence," thus
placing the hermeneutical problem at the very center of
the task of religious self-understanding. This is not the

place to examine in detail the contributions of Royce and
Hocking to philosophical hermeneutics from the perspective
of Heidegger's and Gadamer's thinking, which alone it
seems to me has succeeded in becoming aware of the metaphysical presuppositions or prejudgments implicitly
determining all Western thought and its culmination in
Hegel, including the conceptual concern with the "other,"
i.e., non-Christian traditions. As belonging to one of
these "other" faiths, however, I may be allowed to draw
attention to the following remarks of Hocking regarding
reconception and to question whether they do not exemplify
the continued operation of these same presuppositions.
Hocking says,

> In proportion as any religion gains in self-
> understanding through grasping its own essence,
> it grasps the essence of all religion, and gains
> in *power to interpret* its various forms. To in-
> terpret is the power to say more truly or in more
> understandable language what an idea or a usage
> "means"; to interpret is to give voice to what is
> relatively inarticulate and defenceless....
> Reconception conserves as much as possible of
> what is worth conserving in other faiths.

More explicitly, Hocking goes on to speak of "a certain
noblesse oblige in the relations among religions, of the
obligation to those less skilled in self-explication on
the part of those who have travelled far in the path of
self-understanding, of the chivalrous need to express for
them their meanings better than they themselves could
express them, of the joy of lifting a struggling thought
to a new level of self-understanding, of how much
"fairer--not to say more honourable--would it be to
attempt to anticipate for them what they mean." Without
pausing for the lengthy comment this calls for, let me add
that Hocking does indeed concede reconception to the other
religious traditions and admit the present "unreadiness of
Christianity" to claim triumph in the "competition to
understand and include, a rivalry as to which religion can
best express the meaning of the rest," despite its rela-

tive maturity and its superior "power of self-expression."
But this concession is only provisional, for the time
being only. As he says, "It is right, and indeed
necessary, for the good of men, that the non-Christian
religions should hold to their own, at least until they
find themselves in fact understood, translated, and
included in the growing power of a religion which in
achieving its own full potentiality achieves theirs also."
Are we not here back to Hegel, to his notion of a
potentiality that actualizes itself only by totally
comprehending and swallowing up the other, and to his
vision of hermeneutics as mastery of the other through the
concept, not a hermeneutic of self-understanding but, in
Hocking's words, of going through "the labour of understanding those (other) faiths," hermeneutic as a weapon
directed against the other, rather than as the very heart
of the happening of self-understanding. There is charity
here, it is true, but it is a charity of which the voice
is stifled by the metaphysics of *Geist*.

Except for Karl-Otto Apel in Germany, no one seems to
have attempted to bring Royce's very original and suggestive views on interpretation as a basic cognitive function
and on the concept of a community of interpretation into
relation with contemporary philosophical hermeneutics,
though he might well be described as the pioneer in this
novel mode of thought and the first to say, at least first
after Nietzsche, "Interpretation is, once for all, the
main business of philosophy," and to talk about a "metaphysics of interpretation." Without going into the
fascinating wealth of detail Royce offers us, I shall
mention here just two features of his thought which throw
us back again to Hegel. In the first place, Royce also
operates with the Hegelian notion of dialectic and
mediation, defined in terms of a triadic relation among
three minds, though he was enabled, by what he learned
from Pierce, to conceive it in an extremely generalized

sense. Secondly, Royce's metaphysics of interpretation is explicitly grounded in what he calls Absolute Voluntarism, specifically in that "attitude of the Will" in terms of which Royce interpreted loyalty, the teaching of St. Paul and the concept of charity. On both points Hegel's thought provides the basis, for spirit, according to him, is inherently Will, and Being in its fullness is Absolute Spirit, as the dialectical *Aufhebung* of the past and of the other its relentless instrument. To the will to interpret, or to charity understood in terms of will as the being of what is, the being of the other, far from being acknowledged in its otherness and as a voice trying to reach me with its truth, or in its identity with me in that which escapes the conceptual grasping of either of us, the being of the other can only be seen as "spirit in a state of dream" and as assimilable in that vast megalomanic dream into which reality itself is transformed when conceived as *Geist*.

As I understand it, Heidegger's thinking, with its putting into question of the "metaphysical" concepts of Being, Time, Reason and World, and with its critique of the modern metaphysics of the Will, represents the emergence of the *Western* consciousness in a state of dream into the waking awareness of itself for the first time since the rise in the West, to quote Nietzsche, of "a sublime metaphysical illusion" with Socrates, "the one turning point and vortex of so-called world-history," whose influence "down to the present moment and even into all future time, has spread over posterity like a shadow that keeps growing in the evening sun." The legacy that this dream has brought with it is our waking world of what is common to all, of mankind in the homelessness of "world-civilization" and in that constellation of the relationship between man and being which Heidegger has called the *Gestell*, the framework, which is the mode in which Truth as unhiddenness occurs in this age of

technology. Far from being the handiwork of the human
will, and therefore remediable by it, this mode of the
relationship between what is as such and man is part of
the same destiny by which Being discloses itself as Will,
while concealing its own truth in the hidden aspect of all
unhiddenness. What we need, in this time of planetary
need, is not "philosophy" as an expression of the conceptual mastery over things, but thinking as meditative
recollection and as a gesture of *Gelassenheit*, releasement, of being let into the letting-be in relation to
Being, as releasement toward things and openness to
mystery. These are cryptic utterances, I realize,
impenetrably gnomic and suggestive of a lapse into woolly
mysticism, and I shall not try here to explain them.
Instead, I shall just record my conviction that, in
respect of the ultimate concerns of thinking, a breakthrough has been achieved in Western speculative thought
during the last one hundred years of which the full impact
has yet to be experienced, and which promises not only new
hope for the ongoing process of philosophical and religious self-understanding in the non-Western world but
seems to me to be the only safeguard against the "invasion
from the East," against the abdication of thinking in
favour of the religious sensationalism of the present and
the apparent attenuation of trust in *philosophia* as the
pursuit of wisdom, in the West. Nietzsche's *Birth of
Tragedy*, Husserl's later work, Heidegger's *Being and Time*:
these are the landmarks here, pointing to the current work
of H. G. Gadamer and Eugen Fink, admonishing us to see how
much Hegel persists still in our thinking. For only when
we have seen this can we join together, in this time of
common need, to look for a hermeneutic that lets-be, a
hermeneutics that does not turn the past, or the other,
into a dream-image, an unreality, by the adoption of the
Aufhebung-principle of Hegel, but lets them be, real and
speaking in their own right.

Hegel has been the only Western philosopher of rank to devote serious attention to Indian philosophical and religious ideas and, despite the meager, often biased, scholarly information at his disposal, to analyze and examine them critically. Even though he did not share Wilhelm von Humboldt's ardent admiration for the Bhagavadgītā (Humboldt was thankful to God for letting him live long enough to have a chance of reading it), anyone who reads Hegel's very extensive review of Humboldt's essay on it, cannot but be struck by the intensity of purpose with which Hegel grappled with the difficulties of understanding Indian ideas in terms of Western philosophical conceptuality and by the unsurpassed profundity of his many insights. Apart from the foreignness of the Indian world of ideas, Hegel's reproach against it was not too different from his criticism of early Greek thought, namely, that it represented the stage of abstraction and of beauty rather than truth, a stage *not yet* determined and *not yet* mediated by and in the dialectical movement of absolute subjectivity. The Hegelian principle of *Aufhebung*, in the three-fold sense of *tollere, conservare,* and *elevare,* dismisses the primordial and the pristine as the abstract and the primitive, of value only as taken up and absorbed into a higher stage of thought, needing mediation and through that exhibiting its truth. The first emergence of thought is for Hegel necessarily the most abstract, the simplest and the emptiest, and the happening of history consists in a movement from the less developed to the more. Whether we begin with pure Being, as in the Great *Logic,* or examine experience as the dialectical movement which consciousness exercises on itself, as in the *Phenomenology,* or survey the march of history, it is always the principle of *Aufhebung* which provides the key to interpretation. Having defined history as the development of Spirit in Time, Hegel goes on to admit that the notion of the rise of a new life from the ashes of the

old is "a grand conception; one which the Oriental thinkers attained." But this image of the Phoenix eternally preparing for itself its funeral pile, consuming itself upon it, but so that from its ashes is produced the new, renovated, fresh life, this image, Hegel says, is symbolic only of the life of *Nature* and is "only Asiatic; oriental not occidental." *Spirit*, on the other hand, while consuming the envelope of its existence, does not merely pass into another envelope, nor rise rejuvenescent from the ashes of its previous form; it comes forth exalted, glorified, a purer spirit, elevating itself into a higher grade by working on the debris of the earlier. What is Time, that the primordial must lose itself in the subsequent, and what is Truth, that it must ride on Time's fictitious arrow and can shine forth only on the ruins of a transcended past? What is thinking, that it does not permit the past to retain some treasure in reserve, making possible the arrival of the authentic future, and to Truth the mystery of concealment in the very moment of articulated disclosure?

Heidegger has taught us that interpretative thinking conceived as an act of will, however adequate it may be to acquiring mastery over entities or over facts and events in the non-human realm, totally falsifies our awareness of the human world and of the Being of all entities generally. To that the only appropriate mode of relationship is that of letting-be (*Lassen*). For, the happening of understanding, and of a tradition as its cumulative result, is itself an ontological process, a continuous language event and an event of truth, rather than a series of operations performed by a subject upon something objectively given; remembrance of what has been and upon an anticipative reaching out to the future and openness to it. This is what Heidegger means when he says that the unsaid and the unthought of the earliest past, ever inexhaustible, comes towards us as our future and as a

task for the future, rather than being annulled into the present. This is what Gadamer means by his theory of the *wirkungsgeschichtliche Bewusstein*, of the fusion of horizons and of the productivity of time, and this is the sense of his insistence that understanding is not so much a method as a standing within or entering into a happening of tradition (*Uberlieferungsgeschehen*) in which the past and present are constantly mediated, an experience which we undergo rather than control. And here also lies the extraordinarily illuminating power of his notion of the self-propelled game, as a model for understanding, in which he who understands is taken up, not as master of himself, but as given over to the *Sache*, the matter which seeks utterance in the inter-play between him and the other. As participants in the game we are left without a secure *Stellungnahme* outside of it, for we are already incorporated into a happening of truth and come as it were too late, as Gadamer puts it, when we want to know what we should believe.

We live in a world in which the hitherto relatively closed horizons of the different traditions of mankind are opening out to each other and our divided histories are being joined together, or are being rejoined, in strange, unheard of ways (one recalls in Max Müller's glad astonishment at discovering in the Ṛgveda a documentation of the fact that Indians and Europeans are long-parted brethren, belonging to the same Indo-Aryan family and are meeting now after a divided history of four thousand years). As yet, we have only had a hermeneutic of the "other," i.e., of non-Western cultures and religions, and we have philosophical hermeneutics, of which the concern is self-understanding and in which the "will to interpret" suffers its shipwreck. But so far we have no hermeneutic of a global "we," appropriate to a world factually in process of unification under the common destiny of the *Ge-Stell* mentioned earlier, and aspiring to learn to speak

a common language and share in a heritage which is no
longer sharply partitioned. In the work of Wilfred Smith
we have the beginnings of a global hermeneutic awareness
of diverse religious traditions, an awareness made
possible by a rare renunciation of the voluntaristic
metaphysics of the will to interpret the other, a willingness to let the other be, only inviting him to engage in
the exciting and creative task of reappropriation that
lies ahead, for him and in respect of his own tradition,
endlessly open to the future and its promise. The non-
Western intellectual is brought to see that by joining in
this enterprise he may yet let his tradition deliver him
into a truth, new and fresh, and freer from the contin-
gencies of its historical context, by delivering to him
its treasures of the unsaid and unthought, the treasure of
the *zukünftige* that lies hidden, conserved, held in
reserve, in all living past. And beyond this, Smith
brings home to us, to Western and non-Western scholars
alike, that such reappropriation, guided by scholarly
discipline and close awareness of other traditions than
our own, is also the way in which we can contribute to the
emergence of common ways of speaking, as we move into the
future, and let a community of discourse come about as the
true realization of world-community, without all "other"
religious ways "being understood, translated, and
included," to use Hocking's words, in one's own.

The study of religion and philosophical thought stand
at the opposite ends of the spectrum of academic concern
with things human: the first, intensely personal, revol-
ving around the faith in the hearts of men and rooted in
man's love for man, as Smith has insisted; the other,
passionately impersonal, no less a form of love, and, as
Gadamer has observed, "in a profound and definitive sense
selfless." Neither of these by itself can bring into
being a community of discourse among men, but both
together, of necessity working separately but aware of

their function as creative, as *poiesis*, may yet initiate
the birth of a "we," no longer one in merely sharing a
common nightmare. Every religious tradition constitutes a
historically evolving body of interpretation, disclosing a
reality which it seeks to embody in language, and operating with concepts which it sometimes inquires into. The
Western philosophical tradition, devoted to inquiry into
these concepts of our ultimate concern, was until recently
confined within the horizons of its Greek origins, its
Christian unfoldment during the medieval and modern periods, and its pre-occupation with the sciences in recent
times. There are indications, however, that the spirit of
radical questioning that this tradition represents is not
only reasserting its vitality at the present time but is
also moving out beyond its traditional confines into a
more global awareness, no longer Greek in a restrictive
sense and beyond Orient and Occident, as Heidegger puts
it. I am convinced that such questioning, originating in
a listening to the voice of tradition, and the new ways of
thinking about man and about that from which he derives
his humanity, have an important part to play in enabling
us to realize, in Hölderlin's words, the dialogue that we
are, and the song that we may hope to become.

BEYOND BELIEVING AND KNOWING

> *Über den alten Gegensatz der Vernunft und des*
> *Glaubens, von Philosophie und positiver Religion*
> *hat die Cultur die letzte Zeit so erhoben, dass*
> *diese Entgegensetzung von Glauben und Wissen*
> *einen ganz andern Sinn gewonnen hat und nun* 1
> *innerhalb Philosophie selbst verlegt worden ist.*
>
> ---G. W. F. Hegel

As a Western Indological scholar has remarked,
"Ancient India had no term exactly equivalent to our word
'law', in the same way that it had no word for 'religion'
or 'philosophy'."[2] Even at the present time, though we in
India do study philosophy and speak of religion, the
latter is not a subject of academic study. And, since we
have neither Book nor Church, there are no schools or
departments in universities devoted to the promotion of
studies corresponding to theology in the Christian world.
As one representing in some measure the continuing Indian
religious tradition, and therefore an outsider to the
problematic of the relation of philosophy and theology, I
can hardly contribute significantly to the principal
concern of this conference, of which, moreover, I have a
somewhat nebulous idea. I am grateful, nevertheless, for
this chance of speaking to you, even if it be only to
plead for a loosening of accustomed frameworks and taking
notice of other ways of seeing.

Translation of "*Jenseits von Glauben und Wissen,*" a paper
read at the Fourth International Symposium organized by
Alexander von Humbolt-Stiftung at Ludwigsburg, West Germany, October 12-17, 1976, originally published in *Trans-
zendenz und Immanenz*, edited by Dietrich Papenfuss and
Jürgen Sörig (Stuttgart: Kohlammer Verlag, 1977), 119-130.

Going beyond, the movement of self-surpassing, is as much constitutive of the human state as defining and setting up boundaries. It is this self-transcending movement, this reaching out and reaching down within, inherent in man, which defines him as *homo religiosus*, a bridge thrown across, from the realm of the visible to another shore. It is part of this movement to give itself a symbol or concept of that toward which it strains, its mode of being, its nature, its nearness or remoteness from us. At the same time, this movement seeks to form a conception of its own nature and mode. Is this appropriately describable as an act of believing or as a kind of knowing? Philosophical thought, itself a manifestation of this movement, has ceaselessly wrestled with this problem, aware of the inadequacy of each formulation, constantly moving beyond each, ever since the classic treatments of this question by Kant and Hegel. It is not my intention to examine here these views, or to ask how the problem itself came to be formulated subsequently in terms of believing and understanding (rather than knowing) and why it is theologians rather than philosophers who are at present concerned with this problem, despite the profound and far-reaching insights of a Scheler, a Jaspers and a Heidegger. I only draw attention to the challenge which contemporary theological reflection presents to philosophers to reconsider the problem, to rethink the concepts of believing and knowing and move beyond the charmed circle of traditional formulations of their relationship. A more significant challenge, presented by the relatively new discipline of comparative religion to both philosophers and theologians, will be considered here at some length later.

The term "beyond" in the title of this paper is also intended as a reminder of the fact that the terms belief and knowledge, and indeed this whole manner of posing the question, are proper to one particular group of religious

traditions and it is by no means certain that they are
adequate to the self-understanding of others. The theologian is concerned primarily with an explication of
Christian faith, but as required by his commitment to this
faith, he also has an interest in "other" religions, the
specific character of that interest being determined by
his particular theology of missions. In seeking to understand these other religious traditions he tends to interpret them in terms which have become normative in his own
and thus fails to see them for what they are in themselves. Even when theology is defined in a wider sense as
"a spiritual or religious attempt of 'believers' to explicate their faith,"[3] in Helmut Thielicke's words, the
theologian still projects upon non-Christian religions his
own way of understanding his tradition, still overlooks
the possibility that in other traditions the individual
may have other ways of being related to his tradition, and
to the truth it makes available to him, than that denoted
by the terms "believer" and "religion," other ways of
understanding the task of self-explication. A Hindu finds
it hard to identify himself by this name, given by others
to identify him, following necessities imposed by their
own conception of religion. Like the term "Hinduism", it
is not found in the vocabulary of his classic tradition
and has now been appropriated by him only under the pressure of historical circumstance, in imitation of Islamic
and Christian ways of regarding religious traditions and
one's belongingness to them, to use a favourite word of
Herder's. And what will a Buddhist, who knows neither a
theion nor a *logos*, do with the term "theology"? He seeks
refuge in the Buddha, the *Dhamma* and the *Sangha*, is a man
of faith in so far as he truly does so, but in what sense
is he a believer?

The two major traditions of Indian spirituality,
Vedanta and Buddhism, are as much philosophical as
religious traditions and are therefore neither purely

philosophical systems nor religions, as these terms are understood in the West. They are both theologies in the wider sense, for they are both rooted in the revealing word, the one in the Veda, the other in the teaching of the Buddha, and both are explications and interpretations of a transcendent message. And neither of them is a theology because each understands itself as a quest for a truth which can satisfy and set to rest the disquiet of reason, and because neither is based upon a dogmatically laid down system of beliefs. Further, the truth, however revealed, is not itself something to be believed merely, or even known. It is not enough to acknowledge it as such, pay worshipful homage to it, pledge loyalty to its sway. It is a truth that is at the same time a call, a demand placed on us, to realize it in our own personal experience, within which alone it fulfills its character of being the truth. The Buddhist may worship the Supreme Wisdom and the Advaitin may bow down in prayer to the Highest Truth, but in both cases this is only the beginning of a process, to which a discipline of the intellect is integral, and which culminates ideally in the personal appropriation of that truth, in realizing or actualizing it as one's own truth. So long as we insist on interpreting religious traditions such as these in terms of the believing-knowing dualism, they cannot be understood in their own essence.

In the Indian tradition of Advaita Vedanta and Buddhist philosophy, knowledge in the highest sense is immediate, an experienced reality in which the duality of knowing subject and known object lapses. The lower, empirical, knowledge of entities in the world is mediated by language, concepts and categories, though even here, according to some schools, the conceptual activity of the mind is more a hindrance than an indispensable means of knowing. Empirical knowledge, though of a lower order, is nevertheless knowledge, and what it provides is truth,

though of a lower order. In relation to the highest
truth, the lower may function as a ladder, a path and a
means of gaining access to it, and that is its potentially
religious value. But from the perspective of that truth
itself all else is untruth, all that passes for knowledge
in our ordinary life and all that goes under the name of
religion; it belongs to the realm of ignorance. *Homo
religiosus*, regarded individually or in terms of collective history, is "*ein Pfeil der Sehnsucht nach dem anderen
Ufer*,"[4] on his way to the truth, and all his ways of
symbolizing this truth, all his belief, all the concepts
by means of which he seeks to give to himself an account
of his relationship to reality, even the sense of the
sacred that accompanies him on this journey, his worship
and prayer, all these must fall by the wayside, as being
of this world, mental constructs, though of inestimable
value as leading on to a goal beyond themselves. Taken by
themselves, without relation to the goal, they are false
and empty of meaning; regarded in relation to that end and
its truth, they indeed have an essential pragmatic value
for religious, wayfaring man, but are untrue in the last
resort. Human religiousness, from this point of view, is
a pilgrimage, not the holding true of certain propositions
about the world and what transcends it, and not the
holding fast to certain ways of symbolizing man's longing
for the Infinite. As an *Unterwegssein*, it is necessarily
an *Irregang*, for on this journey idols must be set up and
idols must be broken, these same idols, our own, not those
of others. Without the faith that there is a goal to be
reached, without saying yes to the possibility that the
truth can be actualized, without the sense of something--
word, image, or person--sacred and without conceptual
constructs, we cannot take even the first steps on this
journey. Without the long travail of looking through and
beyond these symbolic, mythical and conceptual representations as constructs and seeing them as pointers on the

way, pointing, and inviting us, to move on, leaving them
behind, without this there cannot be that awareness of
moving closer to port which makes of a mere gazing at the
far horizon into a voyage. And without the final perception of these symbols, including those called concepts,
and of our very belongingness to a tradition, as idols to
be discarded, down to the very last, there can be no
arrival, no homecoming, no recognition that the goal was
not somewhere else but where we always were, beyond all
departure and arrival. Human religiousness culminates and
finds its fulfillment in something that is beyond
"religion," beyond belief and knowledge in the usual
sense. Religion is indeed *aufgehoben* here and the "old
opposition" of believing and knowing is overcome, but not
in favour of mysticism, a concept which belongs properly
to the prophetic religious traditions. A rethinking of
these concepts, a moving beyond their restricted applica-
bility is thus suggested, if violence is not to be done to
other religious traditions.

As the noted American religious thinker Robert Bellah
contends, "the confusion between belief and religion,
which is found only in the religious traditions deeply
influenced by Greek thought--Christianity and Islam--and
is almost completely missing in China and India, involves
a fundamental misapprehension of the nature of religion."[5]
The concept of knowing too is rooted, like that of philosophy itself, in the Greek strand of Western thought and it
is even harder for the Western scholar to realize that it
may not correspond to the self-understanding of non-
Western intellectual traditions. Hegel's extensive and
repeated treatment of Asiatic religions, and of the Indian
in particular, is the classic example of Western attempts
to interpret these traditions as halfway houses in the
march of the Spirit, as needing subordination to and
incorporation within the Greek mode of knowing which is
taken as paradigmatic, as Karl Löwith and Maurice Merleau-

Ponty have pointed out. Husserl also spoke of the *telos*
towards universal acceptability inherent in the Greek gift
of *theoria* to humanity and of the purely theoretical
attitude from which philosophy has arisen in the West. He
asked, rhetorically,

> whether the *telos* which was inborn in European
> humanity at the birth of Greek philosophy...is
> merely a factual, historical delusion, the
> accidental acquisition of merely one among many
> other civilizations and histories, or whether
> Greek humanity was not, rather the first
> breakthrough to what is essential to humanity as
> such, its *entelechy*...whether the spectacle of
> the Europeanization of all other civilizations
> bears witness to the rule of an absolute meaning,
> one which is proper to the sense, rather than to
> a historical non-sense, of the world.[6]

Nietzsche too saw in Socrates "the one turning point and
vortex of so-called world-history,"[7] more than a half
century before Husserl wrote the above words, but he spoke
about "how the influence of Socrates, down to the present
moment and even into all future time, has spread over
posterity like a shadow in the evening sun." When he
speaks here of "the profound *illusion*,...the sublime
metaphysical illusion," and of "the disaster slumbering in
the womb of theoretical culture," Nietzsche puts this
Greek *entelechy* into question and makes the phenomenon of
the Europeanization of the world appear in quite a
different light. It is only when we experience the full
impact of the opposition between these two viewpoints and
grasp the wide-ranging implications of this opposition
that we can appreciate the significance of Martin
Heidegger's life-work. This is not the place to show in
detail how this constitutes a massive, radical critique of
pure reason, a bringing to light of the unexamined presuppositions of the Western heritage, how it requires us to
think anew not only the concept of knowing but also to
consider in what a different light the old contrast
between knowing and believing is bound to appear now, for

in terms of that contrast a critique of knowing is at the same time a critique of believing. The theoretical mode of knowing is happily with us, like that other gift of the West to the rest of the world, Christianity incognito, at work in a secularized form, as the theologian Arend Theodoor van Leeuwen has described it.[8] Both these gifts have jointly contributed to the phenomenon of the Europeanization of the earth, "homelessness in the form of world-civilization," as Heidegger called it.[9] I mention here only in passing that the relevance of Heidegger's thought, not to Christian theology, not to the enterprise of philosophy as such, but to reflection in the context of the study of world religions, is still to be realized adequately, as also the relevance of Hans Georg Gadamer's philosophical hermeneutics to our attitude and approach to the study of other religious traditions. The work of both has exhibited the possibility of a mode of experiencing, of a relationship to what is, which is non-objectifying, in which truth is disclosed and which is not yet a knowing. These insights call for a rethinking of the concept of believing, the other member of that pair of opposites.

It is when we come to this new discipline, variously called *Religionswissenschaft*, comparative religion, history of religion or simply study of religion, that the concepts of believing and knowing and their alleged relationship are seen to be inappropriate to religious traditions other than the prophetic group, as does indeed the concept of religion itself. Even in this field, as one reads some of the older literature, one has the unnerving feeling that this whole academic enterprise constitutes a massive attempt to reinterpret other religious traditions in terms of the Christian tradition, make them available and assimilable to the West, theologically or culturally, and incorporate them within the only history there is, within Western history as world-history,

a continuation by other means, of the Hegelian imperialism of the Spirit. Max Müller, with whom the Science of Religion, as he called it, may be said to begin, a century after the birth of Hegel, said, "The Science of Religion may be the last of the sciences which man is destined to elaborate; but when it is elaborated, it will change the aspect of the world, and give new life to Christianity itself."[10] Max Müller was a humanist scholar of towering stature, with a passionate concern for man's commerce with the Divine, and for whose pioneering work on the Veda Indians will never cease to be grateful. He wrote to his wife on December 9, 1867, "...I feel convinced,...that this edition of mine and the translation of the *Veda* will hereafter tell to a great extent on the fate of India.... It is the root of their religion, and to show them what that root is is, I feel sure, the only way of uprooting, all that has sprung from it during the last 3000 years."[11] Another Oxford humanist Professor and author of the great *Sanskrit English Dictionary*, Monier-Williams occupied the Boden Chair for Sanskrit, a Chair which was established for the special purpose of promoting the translation of the Scriptures into Sanskrit, so as "to enable his countrymen to proceed in the conversion of the natives of India to the Christian religion."[12] The very first public lecture he gave was on "The Study of Sanskrit in Relation to Missionary Work in India."

The distinguished contemporary Indologist, historian and uncompromising critic of Hinduism, Paul Hacker of Münster, has in recent years worked out, in his additional role as theologian of missions, an explicitly stated theology of assimilation, appropriation and utilization (*chrêsis* or *usus justus*, as the Church Fathers called it) by the Christian of whatever elements of value there may lie in non-Christian religions. As he explains,

> Utilization connotes, 1. that the assimilated
> elements are made subservient to an end different
> from the context from which they were taken,

2. that they can be taken over because some truth is contained or hidden in them, 3. that they must be reoriented in order that the truth might shine forth unimpeded.[13]

Elsewhere he elucidates, quoting Gregor von Nyssa,

Das gleiche besagt das bekannte Bild vom Aigyptios ploutos oder von den spolia Aegyptorum: die Schätze der Kirche, verwendet werden, erfüllen sie ihren Sinn. Auf den Umgang mit Texten angewandt, bedeutet das: Solange diese in ihrem Kontext interpretiert werden, bleiben sie, was sie sind: heidnisch, und eine christlich-sachgemässe Interpretation muss gerade ihre dämonische Zweideutigkeit und Unfruchtbarkeit ans Licht bringen.[14]

These words, like others addressed by Hacker to "softer" theologians like Karl Rahner and Raymond Panikkar, are addressed to fellow Catholics and I must apologize for having overheard them. But I have heard them with great admiration for the clarity with which a religious issue has been stated and with amazement at the fact that phenomenologists of religion have hardly taken notice of *this* particular religious phenomenon--this age-old phenomenon of transplantation and borrowing of elements from one culture to another in the religious life of mankind. A Hindu can only be grateful for such criticism and even more so for this *Benutzung* for this double mercy--far from depriving me of my treasure or making it seem worthless so long as it remains mine, it enables me to notice its preciousness all the better, as it stands out from its context, to see it in a new light, when transplanted in another context, and to realize with greater vividness the value of the principle of *chrêsis* for the ongoing and future destiny of "Hinduism" itself. It is not for me to take a position regarding this theological principle or any particular manner of formulating it. But as a phenomenon it appears to me one of the most striking things happening in the religious life of the West, specially the United States, today. The

phenomenon may be given a theological interpretation (as in the extensive literature on the problem of "other religions"), or a humanistic, cultural interpretation (as in the work of Mircea Eliade and others), or a philosophical one, as in the work of W. D. Hocking, Edwin Burtt and other students of comparative philosophy. It may exhibit itself at any of these levels; to a certain extent even the rise of comparative religion is part of this wider phenomenon. Is there something in the modern Western concept of knowing, as Heidegger suggested, that prevents it from letting the other be, which transforms it into an object and thus takes possession of it, which permits no inappropriable mystery in things, in persons, in other cultural and religious traditions, no otherness which is not at the knowing subject's disposal? Is there something in the concept of belief, which is sustained by the existence of an unbelieving other, out in the cold, without the possibility of finding himself, lost?

There are other voices, however, speaking in other tones, voices of scholars who are leading the discipline of comparative religion to maturity. Here is Brede Kristensen, phenomenologist of religion at Leiden until 1937:

> Let us never forget that there exists no other religious reality than the faith of the believer. If we really want to understand religion, we must refer exclusively to the believer's testimony. What we believe, from our point of view, about the nature or value of other religions, is a reliable testimony to our own faith, or to our own understanding of religious faith; but if our opinion about another religion differs from the opinion and evaluation of the believers, then we are no longer talking about their religion. We have turned aside from historical reality and are concerned only with ourselves.[15]

Here, though the language of belief is still naively used, we have moved beyond belief as a proper name for Christian faith, the other is acknowledged as a "believer" in his own right and "knowing" has given place to "understanding."

The Dutch school of phenomenology of religion evolved to
some extent under the influence of Dilthey and Husserl,
but it cannot be said that it has taken seriously into
account the critical ferment generated with the publication of Heidegger's *Sein und Zeit* nor the dynamism of
self-criticism inherent in the naivety of the phenomenological starting point itself. Today, this phenomenological approach to the study of religion is still
confronted with the task of appropriating the criticism
and self-transformation to which phenomenology as a
concept and as a method has been subject during the last
quarter of a century.

The same may be said about the work of Joachim Wach,
who emigrated to the United States in 1935. As a historian of the concept of understanding, he brought to bear
upon *Religionswissenschaft*, of which the central concern
according to him was the understanding of other religions,
the discipline of hermeneutics as a *Geisteswissenschaft*.
Wach himself had little appreciation of the new direction
in which philosophical hermeneutics was moving in his own
lifetime and it is regrettable that the very promising
trend he initiated in the study of religion was allowed to
lapse without bearing fruit. There are signs that with
the recent translation of Gadamer's *Wahrheit und Methode*
into English, sixteen years after its publication, coupled
with the work of Paul Ricoeur, the relevance of the
hermeneutical mode of thinking will become more apparent
in America. Incidentally, Wach's basically theological
concern was evident in his scholarly work in comparative
religion. It exemplifies the not uncommon tendency of
treating comparative religion as second, new ancilla to
theology, as the Jewish scholar Zwi Werblowsky of Jerusalem has perceived and strongly criticized. Theological
concerns must not obtrude here, as he pointed out; but, on
the other hand, is the study of religion a matter solely
of objective, scientific knowledge? Can there be such a

thing as *Religionswissenschaft*, with an objectively given
field of data and equipped with a method guaranteed to
ensure valid knowledge?[16] Scholarly historical information must of course be gathered and organized, but does
not the crucial and central task lie in understanding and
interpretation, beyond that? It seems to me strange that
this humanistic discipline, though free ideally from
theological presuppositions and not confined to antiquarian scholarship, should still remain largely cut off
from liberating contemporaneous developments in philosophical thought, as also from important trends, critical
and visionary, in literature and literary theory. May it
be that the very starting point, the conception of the
study of religion as the study of "other religions" has
resulted in an exaggerated concern with methodology, in an
admirable openness to social science and anthropology, but
in too little regard for the task of religious *thinking*,
of finding an appropriate way of talking about *all*
religious traditions and about the history of religion (in
the singular) in their global togetherness? It is time
that we realize that, as thinkers like W. C. Smith insist,
the rise of this new discipline betokens the emergence of
a novel approach to religion and promises to inaugurate a
new era in the religious history of mankind; in other
words, that it is governed by a religious interest no
longer tied to specific theologies, and yet religious,
pushing towards an integral, universal way of thinking
about *homo religiosus* and about human history as in
essence religious history.[17] Its aim is not to replace
the plurality of the historical traditions by some kind of
universal religion, but to acknowledge them and study them
precisely in their plurality, in their interaction with
one another, in their continued self-renewal, to play a
helpful role in the response of each in the present crisis
in its history.

One example of this new approach is the work of Mircea
Eliade, which is concerned largely with the cultural
appropriation by the West of elements of alien religiosity
by the study of myths and symbols, Yoga and Shamanism and
benefitting from the researches of cultural anthropology
and structuralism. This concern with the development of a
"planetary culture,"[18] as it has been called, seems to
answer to a real spiritual need in this age and is
generating a new form of religiousness, beyond belief and
beyond knowing in the scientific sense. There is a wide-
spread sense today that we stand at the edge of history,
"*an der Zeitmauer*," that we are entering a new phase in
the evolution of human consciousness, a post-modern, post-
traditional age, in which a simultaneity of all places and
times and the availability of all traditions to each has
become possible, where alternative realities have become
accessible. New ways of religiousness are being explored
and the need has arisen to find new ways of conceptualizing these manifestations, of moving beyond the knowing-
believing dichotomy. In so far, however, as this school
claims to arrive by the study of myth, ritual and symbols
at universal, objective, synchronic knowledge about human
religiousness, it seems to be pursuing a chimera. Even if
we take into account the phenomenon of transference from
one culture to another, it remains true that what a
symbol, myth or text means is the meaning it has for
people within a particular tradition, what role it has
played in their lives, what these men have done to or with
it, how it has shaped their history and governed their
perception of truth. For, even in the midst of *Welt-
zivilisation*, planetization, and a sense of the end of
history, the ancient religious traditions, in a world that
has changed, continue to flourish and interact, and others
step into history for the first time. This is a time of a
new kind of crisis for all of them, to be sure, but it by
no means denies to any of them a future, a future which

will be shaped, in some measure at least, by *their* past
and by the way they perceive their present in the light of
that past. Each of them has unexhausted resources within
it to enable it to move forward, and each is now, more
self-consciously than ever before, in a position to
strengthen itself by having a share in the resources of
all the others.

The cumulative religious tradition of India, comparable at the present time to a temple in ruins, has been in
the past an open temple. It was once touched by Greek
power and beauty, and by the traditions of neighbouring
China; Islam and Christianity have massively contributed
to it and Buddhist religious thought has been at the very
heart of its self-awareness. His present crisis can also
be the moment of renewal for the Hindu, thanks to his
wounded history itself, for now as never before, he can
free himself from the dead hand of the past. Now he can
joyfully let his religious imagination be enlarged and
vivified by the heritage of the Greeks, by the vision of
Christianity, and the message of Islam, and he can freely
seek to appropriate through creative reinterpretation the
tradition of which he is both a product and a trustee. He
can accomplish this, but only to the extent that he can
see himself and his tradition in the wider inter-religious
context of world-history. Does he have the fortitude, the
courage and the faith to live creatively, not just reac-
tively, in this new world, not of his own making, and join
in the common quest for a home here, and in the human
pursuit of that which is beyond time?

No one in our time has seen the implications of this
more clearly, is wrestling with them as problems for
creative religious thinking, more energetically, than
Wilfred Cantwell Smith, until recently at Harvard and now
at Dalhousie University in Canada. As a historian of
Islam, he is keenly aware of the historical dimension of
religion and of the fact that the religious history of

mankind, divided so long into several histories, is today
joined in a novel kind of self-awareness. Disciplined
historical information about the diverse religious
traditions is becoming more available and such knowledge
is altering the self-awareness of each tradition. In the
second place, there is a growing appreciation that to
people belonging to these different traditions, their
tradition has been the light by which they have symbolized
the transcendent, glimpsed the truth and experienced the
touch of the Holy. To understand the faith of other men
is to discern what their tradition has meant to them. To
see this means to be able, like them, to use their
religious tradition to enable us to see life through their
eyes. Like learning a foreign language, this can be done
and, as with language, it gives us access to a new world.
This in turn alters our understanding of our own faith,
puts it in a global perspective and thus enables us really
to understand it for the first time, though never finally.
As Smith has said, "An attempt to study Islam (for
example) in itself is inadequate: what in fact one is
studying is the Islamic strand in the history of man's
religiousness,"[19] including that of the student's own
tradition. Every religious tradition can now be seen as
developing within the context of an encompassing, evolving
totality. And in this emergent global awareness, which is
also a novel awareness of one's own faith as Christian or
Hindu, it becomes possible and imperative to re-examine
systematically the central concepts in terms of which each
of us has understood his own faith so far, including the
concept of religion as a reified entity. Smith himself
has been devoting his energies to an analysis and reconception of "religion" and "belief", somewhat as Heidegger
has done in the case of "philosophy" and "knowledge". In
his critical stance towards the notion of method and of
the goal of objective knowledge in this particular
Geisteswissenschaft, he joins hands with Gadamer, as

indeed in his entire hermeneutical concern, without
borrowing from outside. In his widened conception of
faith, as different from belief (again somewhat like
Heidegger's broadened conception of thinking as different
from philosophizing), the intellectual pursuit of truth is
also seen as an expression of faith, rather than being
excluded from it. What we have here is not theology and
not philosophy, but a new kind of thinking demanded by the
present and coming religious consciousness of humanity, so
that one day we may learn to speak as participants in the
shared history of a religiously pluralistic world rather
than opponents in a divided one. Some scholars have been
critical of Smith for giving up too much for a committed
Christian; others for being too hesitant as a thinker.
They forget that such renunciation, far from meaning a
loss, is always a multifold gain, and that in thinking it
is the breakthrough that counts, the sighting of a path,
the opening up of a vista. His sensitivity for the *Sache*
of his thinking and his sense of responsibility for his
calling as a thinker is too strong to ever let him forget
that, as he has said, one must tread softly here, for one
is treading on men's dreams. That these dreams sometimes
turn into nightmares, often into grotesque life-formations,
in which piety becomes paranoia and everything changes
into its unholy opposite, that is only the negative side
of this very human pursuit of transcendence. What other
safeguard is there against this than the single individual's unrelenting watchfulness over the ways of his own
mind and heart?

NOTES

1. *"Glauben und Wissen"* in *Gesammelte Werke* (Hamburg:
Meiner, 1968), 4:315.
2. Daniel H.H. Ingalls, "Authority and Law in Ancient
India," *Journal of the American Oriental Society*,
supplementary volume 17 (1954): 34.

3. "Theology" in *Encyclopedia Britannica* (Chicago, 1975), Macropaedia 18, p. 274.

4. Nietzsche, *Also Sprach Zarathustra*, *"Zarathustras Vorrede,"* 4.

5. *Beyond Belief* (New York: Harper & Row, 1970), p. 220.

6. *Die Krisis der europäischen Wissenschaften* (The Haque: Nijhoff, 1954), Part 1, 6.

7. *Die Geburt der Tragödie*, 15.

8. *Christianity in World History* (New York: Scribners, 1964), 18.

9. *"Dankansprache,"* in *Ansprachen zum 80. Geburtstag-- Martin Heidegger, 26 September 1969* (Messkirch, 1969), 35.

10. *Chips from a German Workshop I* (London, 1867), xix.

11. *The Life and Letters of the Rt. Hon. Friedrich Max Müller* (2 vols.), edited by his wife (London, 1902), 1:346.

12. M. Monier-Williams, *A Sanskrit-English Dictionary* (Oxford, 1889), ixf.

13. "The Christian Attitude Toward Non-Christian Religions" *Zeitschrift für Missionswissenschaft und Religionswissenschaft* 55, 2 (1971): 95f.

14. *"Interpretation und 'Benutzung,'"* *Zeitschrift für Missionswissenschaft und Religionswissenschaft* 51, 3 (1957): 262.

15. *Religionshistorik studium* (Oslo, 1954), 27, cited in Eric J. Sharpe, *Comparative Religion: A History* (London: Duckworth, 1975), 228. See also Brede Kristensen, *The Meaning of Religion* (The Haque: Nijhoff, 1960), Chapter 1. See also Brede Kristensen, *The Meaning of Religion* (The Haque: Nijhoff, 1960), ch. 1.

16. Cp. Eric J. Sharpe, ibid., 275f.

17. See especially Wilfred Cantwell Smith, *The Meaning and End of Religion: A New Approach to the Religious Tradi- tions of Mankind* (New York: Macmillan, 1963) and *Religious Diversity: Essays by Wilfred Cantwell Smith*, edited by Willard C. Oxtoby (New York: Harper & Row, 1976).

18. Cp. Mircea Eliade, *The Quest: History and Meaning in Religion* (Chicago, 1969), 69.

19. "Mankind's Religiously Divided History Approaches Self-Consciousness," Harvard Divinity Bulletin 29, 1 (1964): 11; *Religious Diversity* (New York: Harper & Row, 1975), 108.

HEIDEGGER AND VEDANTA: REFLECTIONS
ON A QUESTIONABLE THEME

What is questionable can sometimes be worthy of
thought, and what is unthinkable can sometimes be glimpsed
as that which thinking is about. Both Heidegger and
Vedanta thought amply illustrate this. No other justification can be offered for the following very questionable
enterprise of bringing together two disparate ways of
thinking, so wide apart in time and in their entire context. The attempt can have unquestioned validity only for
those who believe, like Nicolai Hartmann and many contemporary comparativists, that there are "eternal problems"
in philosophy, everywhere and at all times the same, or,
with Paul Deussen, that it is the same voice of the Eternal Truth that is heard by thinking spirits everywhere.[1]

Perhaps, however, the task of thinking, in the comparative sphere, is not limited to the search for what is
common to the thought-content (the thoughts, the *Gedanke*,
the answers given) of two different philosophical traditions, or the construction of new concepts overarching
them, nor to the quest of motifs in another tradition that
may supplement a deficiency in one's own and so "enrich"
it. Perhaps there is, beyond this, the more exciting, in
the end even more rewarding, task of trying to see and lay
open the hidden truth of the paths taken by thinking (the
Denken, the movement of thinking, the questions asked) in
each, and letting questions arise in the process and stay
with us, without seeking to come up with precipitate
answers. This involves a movement of thought that is less
like an arrow in flight toward its target than a roving

Originally published in *International Philosophical
Quarterly*, 18 (1978): 121-149. Sanskrit words appear as
printed in the original publication.

and a rambling, a movement to and fro, between two different realms of discourse and vision, an exploration of
two different topologies. There are no predetermined
rules for a game of this kind, only the playing of the
game can generate the rules, if at all. So much by way of
apology for the following fragmentary, somewhat
Heideggerian, remarks on this questionable theme.

I

Deussen quotes the following passage from Samkara's
Commentary on the *Brahmasutra* (I, iii, 33) as "characteristic for Samkara's period as well as for his
theological conception":

> For also, what is for us imperceptible was for
> the ancients perceptible; thus it is recorded,
> that Vyasa (the author of the *Mahabharatam*) and
> others used to meet the Gods and (*Rishis*) face to
> face. But if some would assert that, as for
> those now living so for the ancients also it was
> impossible to meet with gods and the like, they
> would deny the variety of the world; they might
> also maintain that, as at present, so also in
> other times, there was no world-swaying prince
> (*sarvabhaumah kshatriyah*) and thus they would not
> acknowledge the injunctions referring to the
> consecration of kings; they might further assume
> that, as at present, so also in other times, the
> duties of castes and *Asramas* had no stable rules,
> and thus treat as vain the canon of law which
> provides rules for them. We must therefore
> believe that the ancients, in consequence of
> pre-eminent merits, held visible converse with
> Gods and (*Rishis*). The *Smriti* also says
> (*Yogasutra* 2, 44): "through study (is gained)
> union with the beloved godhead." And when it
> further teaches, that Yoga bestows as reward the
> mastery of nature, consisting (in the freedom
> from embodied being and its laws, and thereby) in
> the ability to become as small as an atom and the
> like, this is not to be rejected out of hand by a
> mere dictatorial sentence.[2]

Samkara goes on to quote the *Sruti* (*Svetasvatara Upanisad*
II, 12) proclaiming the greatness of Yoga, and adds that

we do not have "the right to measure by our capabilities
the capability of the *Rishis* who see the mantras and
Brahmana (i.e, the Veda)." Samkara remarks in conclusion,

> From all this it appears that the *itihasas* and
> *puranas* have an adequate basis. And the
> conceptions of ordinary life also must not be
> declared to be unfounded, if it is at all
> possible to accept them. The general result is
> that we have the right to conceive the gods as
> possessing personal existence, on the ground of
> *mantras, arthavadas, itihasas, puranas,* and
> ordinary prevailing ideas.[3]

Here, the gods are absent but they are not denied;
they have withdrawn from man's sight but still form a
presence on the horizon. A world has passed, but its
links with the present are not broken. The present,
though impoverished, is still seen, understood and interpreted in the light of a nobler past and as continuous
with it. Samkara would not perhaps have said, with
Heraclitus, that "Here too there are gods," but would have
found little to quarrel with Catullus when he said of the
golden age: then indeed did the gods come down and visit
with men. Life, in this Upanisadic tradition, was still
experienced as touched by the Divine, and the dimension of
the holy provided the context for all inquiry into reality
and into the nature and destiny of man, and for the pursuit of freedom and immortality. The quest for truth was
still a quest for the truth of life, for the living truth,
and its articulation into a coherent body of argued and
examined statements; it was not just a matter of detached
theoretical contemplation. It was a profoundly religious
quest, and yet a passionately intellectual one.

The eighth century in India, when Samkara probably
lived and wrote, was the century that experienced the
impact of the Buddhist thinker Dharmakirti, of Kumarila
and Prabhakara, thinkers of the Purva Mimamsa school, of
Mandana Misra, the lone-wolf in the history of Advaita
Vedanta, as he has been aptly described, and a century

which was heir to the imposing and strikingly original
work of the Speculative Grammarians. But the India of
this century, and of many more centuries to come, was not
yet under the shadow of what Nietzsche called "the spirit
of Socratism," and its thinking was not primarily an
operation with concepts about a reality understood solely
in terms of being, but had something of the quality of
meditation, reflection, and remembrance, even in the midst
of the lively give and take of argument and debate so
characteristic of the Indian philosophical scene. What is
to be heard, thought about, and meditated upon is not a
bare ontological principle or a metaphysical ultimate,
ground, or *arche*, but a reality experienceable and
experienced as sacred. And the hearing, the reflecting
and arguing, the meditating, the learning and teaching,
the composition of commentaries and independent critical
or creative works, all these activities are carried on
within the dimension of the holy and the ambience of
the Divine.[4]

The medium is not irrelevant to the message and is
often part of it. But concern for the "philosophy" of the
Upanisads and of the Vedanta, for their content, has stood
in the way of sufficient attention being paid to the
medium: the literary structure and style; the poetry and
not just the prose of these writings; the rhetoric and
what appear to be minor embellishments; the magico-mythic
elements still clinging to an endeavor where they do not
seem rightfully to belong (for example, the role of the
sacred syllable *Om*); above all, the verses of obeisance
and praise to be found at the beginning and conclusion of
most Vedanta works.[5] It is not just a matter of conven-
tion and good form when Gaudapada concludes his *Karika*
with a salutation to "the state of non-multiplicity" or
when Samkara begins and concludes his commentary on the
same work with an obeisance to "that Brahman which
destroys all fear in those who take shelter in It," and

when, at the commencement of *Upadesasahasri* XVIII, he bows
down "to that Eternal Consciousness, the Self of the
modifications of the intellect, in which they merge and
from which they arise"; or when Suresvara, in the opening
verse of the *Naiskarmyasiddhi*, offers obeisance to "that
Hari, the witness of the intellect, dispeller of darkness." And when, towards the end of this work, he speaks
of the Vedanta as a "science flowing out from the holy
foot of Visnu," this is no figure of speech only.

Nor is the idea, and historically the fact, of a
world-renouncer (*sannyasin*) and a wandering monk as the
only one competent to pursue the inquiry--not just any
"secular" scholar--into this sacred reality, a mere
sociological curiosity. For Vedanta, thinking is not
simply an expression of that universal urge so crisply
stated by Aristotle: all men by nature desire to know
(*eidenai*); the urge which becomes, when joined with the
pathos of wonderment (*thaumazein*), the *arche* of all
philosophy, as Plato said. Nor is it identifiable with
that *episteme theoretike* which, in Aristotle's words,
inquires after the first principles and causes of being or
with that pursuit which he described as "that which is
sought both of old and now and forever and forever missed
is, what is being (*ti to on*)?"[6] In the Upanisadic tradition, too, there is a seeking, to which the intellectual
quest is integral, but there is also a finding, which does
not consist in merely putting at rest the *pathos* of
thaumazein or in the discovery of its inexhaustible power
to nourish unceasing inquiry, but concerns the whole man
and the transformation and fulfillment of his human state.
And both, the seeking and the finding, presuppose the
experienced dimension of the holy and the darkly seen
presence of truth as sacred and saving.

II

Turning now to Heidegger, we find ourselves in a completely different life-world; it is the world of our present-day experience, life as we all experience it, irrespective of how we individually choose to respond to it. The world in which and for which Heidegger writes is a world that has blossomed under the shadow of the Greek theoretical spirit; the world which Nietzsche meant when he spoke of "how the influence of Socrates, down to the present moment and even unto all future time, has spread over posterity like a shadow that keeps growing in the evening sun"; a world under the domination of that "profound illusion," again in Nietzsche's words, which lies in "the unshakable faith that thought, using the thread of logic, can penetrate the deepest abysses of being, and that thought is capable not only of knowing being but even of *correcting* it."[7] It is, further, a world which has been determined by the spread of Christianity and its subsequent secularization, so that, in the words of Arend Theodoor van Leeuwen, "in the spread of modern Western civilization throughout the world something of the spirit of 'Christianity incognito' is at work."[8] It is a world shaped by the Enlightenment and by the spirit of technology, a world disenchanted and desacralized, as Max Weber saw. As Heidegger has also described it, a characteristic feature of the modern world is the flight of the gods (*Entgötterung*):

> This expression does not mean the mere setting
> aside of the gods, a crude atheism. The disap-
> pearance of the gods is a two-sided process.
> First, the world image is Christianized, in so
> far as the ground of the world is set up as the
> infinite, the unconditioned, the absolute; on the
> other hand, Christendom gives a new interpreta-
> tion to its Christian character by transforming
> it into a world-view, thus adapting itself to
> modernity. Desacralization (*Entgötterung*) is the
> state of indecision regarding God and the gods.
> Christendom has the largest share in the

emergence of this state. But desacralization does not exclude religiosity; indeed, it is through it primarily that the relationship with the gods is transformed into religious experience (*Erlebnis*) as a subjective process. Once it comes to this, then the gods have indeed fled. The consequent emptiness is filled up by the historical and psychological investigation of myth, as a substitute.[9]

The question of Being, as Heidegger poses it, is marked by a radical putting into question of all that has led up to this present state, of the entire Greek-Christian tradition of thought which he sums up under the word "metaphysics." Equally radical is his attempt to so transform "the question of Being" itself, from its original formulation by the Greek thinkers, through the thinkers of medieval Europe, down to his own initial manner of posing it that this questioning itself becomes a path of preparing for a possible future in which the dimension of the holy may once again give meaning to our world, no longer forsaken by the gods, and man heal himself through a thinking which has freed itself at last from its tutelage to the Greek paradigm.

The world-historical context in which Heidegger raises the question of Being is one which he has described as "the darkening of the world, the flight of the gods, the devastation of the earth, the transformation of men into a mass, the hatred and suspicion of everything creative."[10] The essence of this darkening of the world is the absence of God, as Holderlin experienced it, in this destitute time, to which we ourselves still belong. Heidegger's explanation of the neediness of this time is worth quoting in full:

For Holderlin's historical experience, the appearance and sacrificial death of Christ mark the beginning of the end of the day of the gods. Night is falling. Ever since the "united three"--Herakles, Dionysos, and Christ--have left the world, the evening of the world's age has been declining towards its night. The world's night is spreading its darkness. The era is

defined by the god's failure to arrive, by the "default of God." But the default of God which Holderlin experienced does not deny that the Christian relationship with God lives on in individuals and in the churches; still less does it assess this relationship negatively. The default of God means that no god any longer gathers men and things unto himself, visibly and unequivocally, and by such gathering disposes the world's history and man's sojourn in it. The default of God forebodes something even grimmer, however. Not only have the gods and the god fled, but the divine radiance has become extinguished in the world's history. The time of the world's night is the destitute time, because it becomes ever more destitute. It has already grown so destitute, it can no longer discern the default of God as a default.[11]

The question of Being, as it unfolds in Heidegger's thinking, is directly relevant to this destitution of the present age, "for which the ground fails to come, hangs in the abyss"; it is a reaching down into the abyss, experiencing and enduring it, so that a "turning of the age" and the return of the gods may be prepared for through a rethinking of Being.

With all his originality and brilliance, Samkara writes as at one with his tradition, a tradition mediated, it is true, by the passing of the Vedic age and by a long period of Buddhist intellectual and religious dominance, but yet unbroken. Heidegger, on the contrary, starts off, with Nietzsche as precursor, as a radical thinker in whom the crises of thought and sensibility in the sciences and philosophy, in theology and in literature, are gathered to a focus. Samkara too was not just a traditionalist intent on restoring the Vedic tradition but was a thinker moved by the experience of his age as destitute, pervaded by an absence and hanging in the abyss. The rise and development of the Buddhist schools (as of some others) in the preceding centuries was only a symptom of this, bringing to the surface a corrosion in the very substance of things, the abyss that was opening up in the very core of

what is and summed up in the formula, "Everything is
without a self," and in the elevation of the subjective
sphere as the ultimate frame of reference. It is from
within this awareness that Samkara understood his work and
started on his way of thought, seeking to exhibit how it
was still possible and supremely needful to think of life
as grounded in Being (*atman*), to show how experience is
unmeaning and an unmitigated pain unless thought of as
grounded in a "self," revelatory of it and therefore alive
with "the radiance of the divine" (in Heidegger's sense).
Samkara said,

> This tree of *samsara*, the round of worldly exis-
> tence, which sprouts from action and constitutes
> the field of confusion and error, must be torn
> out from its very roots. Alone in pulling it out
> lies the fulfillment of life's purpose.[12]

A statement like this can easily be misunderstood as a
classic example of a life-denying philosophy. In reality,
what it denies is not life but the death-in-life that
consists in taking things as empty of a self, without a
ground in Being and yet holding us in their grip through
the illusion of being all that there is, exercising this
magic spell over us. The purpose of life is fulfilled in
exorcising this spell and realizing that the spell arises
from our disregard of the truth, the self, veiled under
things, and is itself a reflection of our identity with
this self or Being.

All great thinkers respond creatively to "the time of
need," and so did Samkara, massively, passionately and
effectively, to the nihilism of his time, seeking to avoid
the extremes of conceiving Being objectivistically, as an
object of representation, and total subjectivism. But he
did so in an age of divided history--of cultures, peoples,
whole civilizations--and he thought from within the confines of a specific culture, and spoke to men sharing a
common tradition, still felt as binding, with common ways
of experiencing life and of speaking and inquiring about

it. Heidegger's thinking, on the contrary, is a response, in full historical self-awareness, to the phenomenon of what he calls "world-civilization," to its correlate, the process of "the Europeanization of the Earth," and to its consequence, homelessness. As Heidegger puts it, "Homelessness has become a world destiny in the form of world-civilization."[13]

This homelessness has come about--has long been coming about, enveloping the future in this inexorable process, as Nietzsche perceived--as a consequence ultimately of the originally Greek comprehension of Being, of the way Being disclosed itself to the Greeks. More accurately perhaps, it is a consequence of the thinking generated by this disclosure (thinking as "philosophy," as metaphysics) and what remained unthought in the Greek understanding of Being. This comprehension, never made explicit, remained dominant in Western thought until Nietzsche's awareness of it as a prejudice, though he never succeeded in adequately formulating this awareness. It also determined the character and nature of this thinking itself, until Nietzsche subjected it to radical questioning, again without clearly seeing the way to a satisfactory formulation of his insight. It is precisely this that Heidegger seeks to accomplish, bringing Nietzsche's insight "to a full unfolding,"[14] inquiring about the predetermined perspective on which the Greek understanding of Being depended and trying to see how the dreary homelessness of our mode of being in the world today has come to pass. It is thus that Heidegger is able to bring Western thought, for the first time in history, to an awareness of its specific limits, as something historically conditioned and "factitious," as based on specific presuppositions which have constituted its unthought, unverbalized foundation. He has thus brought it to a realization of its own parochial character as Western thought, that is, as "philosophy" as distinct from other possibilities and modes of thinking, adumbrated or realized elsewhere, elsewhen.

III

But how has this homelessness, this transformation of
home into wilderness, how has this harvest of what seems
like death, become a world destiny in the form of world-
civilization? Why must the seeds sown once in Greece
generate a desert bound to envelope the whole world of
man? Much of Heidegger's thinking since the late thirties
has been devoted to showing how Nihilism is not just an
isolated phenomenon in the history of the West, nor even
the central feature, but that it is the very law of this
history, its "logic."[15] How this Western history has
assumed in modern times more and more a world-historical
character is a question that has been variously answered
by Hegel, Marx, Nietzsche, and Christian theologians. Is
it because of an inherent entelechy in the Greek idea of
reason (the fountainhead of all philosophy and science)
towards universal and glad appropriation, as Husserl
thought, that a geographically localized history has
become planetary? According to Heidegger, science and
technology, themselves rooted in "philosophy" and in
"metaphysics" as characteristically and uniquely Greek
forms of thought, are universally triumphant because they
are unrivalled instruments of power over that which is,
over every being or entity (*to on, das Seiende*), as
presented in the light of the conception of Being implicit
in the Western metaphysical tradition. It is when beings
are seen in this light that they acquire their character
as sheer entities to be measured and manoeuvred. The
"Europeanization of the Earth" is in reality the
irresistible triumph of this light, through which things
become entities and then (in the modern era of
subjectivism) objects.

But a prerequisite for the irresistible power of this
light is that it should itself remain invisible, that what
has remained unthought in the Greek version of Being, its

presupposition, should remain unthought. It is to the
task of penetrating to this "unthought," of thinking it,
that Heidegger addresses himself, and exhibits in his
thinking how this power of "being" can be broken and
abated, how a turn in the world destiny of universal
homelessness can be brought about. The world has become
one only today, in the sense of being universally under
the sway of the Greek mode of thinking as the thinking of
Being, in terms of Being and as exhibiting everything
under the aspect of Being. In seeking to think the
unthought in all thinking of Being, Heidegger is the first
world-historical, planetary thinker, a thinker who has
attempted at the same time to rethink the nature of
thinking itself as called for by his discovery of the
truth, of that primordial dimension or region from which
Being itself derives its nature, a region no longer Greek
or parochial.[16]

Nietzsche saw the spectral presence of Nihilism, that
uncanniest of guests, standing at mankind's door.
Heidegger has succeeded in clearly seeing his visage,
identifying and touching in thought this threatening
shadow, tracking him down as to his provenance and pin-
pointing the exact character of the threat he poses for
the world. A danger hangs over the world and over man in
it; its presence stalks the world. It is not the loss of
religion in general or the brokenness of a particular
faith which could be healed by taking the road East; it is
not the Atom Bomb and the vividly present possibility of
total annihilation for mankind; it is not even modern
technology and its effects on human personality and
culture. The danger comes from what Heidegger has called
the "framework (*Ge-stell*)," the peculiar constellation of
man and Being that lies hidden, unthought, in technology
as its characteristic mode of concealment.

But, "where there is danger, there grows also what
saves," Heidegger points out, quoting Holderlin. Within

that itself which has generated this danger, and is its
unrecalled foundation, there lies the saving resource,
forgotten, unthought and therefore preserved and held in
reserve. That same Western metaphysical tradition which
has, inevitably, grown into a world-wide destiny contains,
when we reach down into its ground, the remedy which alone
can bring about a turn in this destiny. The cure must
come from the source of the disease, if it is to be effective, because the disease itself is a destiny flowing from
what has not been brought within the reach of thinking
contained in this source itself, lying in it as a guarded
treasure. It is this unthought of the Western tradition,
lying beyond the Greek, out of which alone a planetary
thinking adequate to the phenomenon of "world-
civilization" can emerge. As Heidegger has said,

> The present day planetary-interstellar world
> situation is, in its essential origin that can
> never be lost, through and through European-
> Western-Greek....What alters, is capable of doing
> so only out of that which still remains saved of
> its great origins. Accordingly the present-day
> world situation can receive an essential
> alteration, or at least a preparation for it,
> only from that origin which has become fatefully
> determinative of our age.[17]

The thinking of the unthought of this imperishable
Western beginning, however, is also the liberation of
thought from its parochial mould and its meeting with the
unthought of the other few, really great beginnings in
human history. In no case can it be just a return to
those beginnings, but only the gathering of resources for
a novel beginning in the realm of thinking, for which
perhaps, as Heidegger hopes, the initiative and the
preparation can come from Europe, "this land of evening
out of which the dawn of a new morning, of another world
destiny can come."[18] Heidegger's thinking, as he himself
conceives it, is a waiting and a preparation for the
arrival of what was glimpsed once as promise, but which
came bearing a harsh visage, concealing itself behind it

completely, and which can come again: the holy, the
divine, God, without the "metaphysical" mask. Without
living commerce with the Immortals, man has become incapable of truly experiencing himself as mortal, and the
quest for immortality has become unmeaning. For "mortality," as conceived in terms of the metaphysical conceptions of Being and time, is only a sham and an evasion of
the possibility of that awesome experience.

Heidegger's thinking has little to do with "cultural
synthesis" or with the notion of a "planetary culture," or
with the idea of a "universal philosophy" for the man of
today, gathering together the complementary insights of
the philosophies of the West and the East. His thinking
is post-philosophical, in the sense of being no longer
"metaphysical" and no longer operating on the presuppositions implicitly at work in all "philosophy." Yet it
is finite, in the sense that it does not claim to make an
absolute beginning but can emerge only as mediated by the
course of the Western metaphysical tradition and its
thinking of Being, as still linked to that which it seeks
to overcome. It is, in a sense, the carrying forward
through revolutionary transformation of the tradition of
Western thought, beginning all over again, so to speak, an
enterprise that remains imperishably, essentially Greek
and Western; no longer "philosophy," yet, as thinking and
asking, still concerned with questions that could be
formulated only as mediated by the Greek-Christian course
of Western philosophy, with unconcealment (*aletheia*),
opening (*Lichtung*) and presence (*Anwesenheit*).

Heidegger mentions Indian Philosophy (and Chinese) a
couple of times in his writings, but only to point out
that it is not "philosophy," a term which ought to be
reserved for the uniquely Greek form, mode, and concern of
thought. As compared with several pointed references to
"East Asian thinking," he refers in a positive sense only
once, and that, too, almost casually, to anything in

Indian thought. This happens in the course of a discussion between him and Eugen Fink on Fragment 26 of
Heraclitus, regarding the nature of sleep, where Heidegger
remarks, "For Indians the state of sleep is the highest
life," a remark dismissed by Fink with the words, "That
may well have been the Indian experience."[19]

This unconcern is somewhat surprising in view of the
attention given by Herder, the German Romantics,
Schelling, Hegel, Schopenhauer, and Nietzsche to Indian
philosophy, surprising in view of the fact that Deussen,
who was a friend of Nietzsche, had brought, through his
consummate scholarly work and enthusiastic appreciation,
the philosophy of the Upanisads and the system of the
Vedanta to the notice of the German academic world,
assigning as he also did a position of importance to
Indian philosophy in his *Allgemeine Geschichte der
Philosophie*. It is not likely that Heidegger had no
knowledge of these developments, or of the interest of his
colleagues and contemporaries Rudolf Otto, Max Scheler,
Georg Misch (Dilthey's pupil), and Karl Jaspers in Indian
thought. It is clear that he deliberately steers clear of
the tradition of Indian thought. His interest in "East
Asiatic" ways of thinking (not so much in its content) is
understandable, for here as in Meister Eckhart he finds
the possibility of a nonconceptual, non-metaphysical way
of thinking and speaking in some sense realized, and so of
value to his own quest and to the matter (*Sache*) of his
own thinking. But Heidegger is critical of the Neo-
Kantian presuppositions with which his older contemporaries approached Indian thought; nor does he share
Hegel's diametrically opposite concern for appropriating,
subsuming, and cancelling all non-Western modes of
thought, like all earlier stages of Western thought
itself, into the total self-possession of the Spirit in
the form of the Absolute Spirit. Therefore, in spite of
being as mindful of the historicity of thinking as Hegel

was, Heidegger is under no compulsion to incorporate
non-Western achievements of thought in his thinking and
exhibit them as consummated and superseded in it. Concerning himself with the opaque foundations of the Western
thinking of Being in a ceaselessly backward movement of
thought, rather than with the ever-progressive movement of
the spirit toward complete self-transparency like Hegel,
Heidegger leaves these traditions aside, lets them be, as
repositories of a treasure which may be relevant, at some
future time, to that planetary thinking for which he
claims to do no more than prepare at this critical time of
the in-break of world-civilization in our midst.

Deussen said in his *Allgemeine Geschichte der
Philosophie*,

> One purpose will surely be served when the Indian
> world-view becomes known. It will make us aware
> that we, with our entire religious and philo-
> sophical thought, are caught in a colossal one-
> sidedness, and that there can be found yet a
> quite different way of grasping things than the
> one which Hegel has construed as the only
> possible and rational way.[20]

No less than Deussen and many others who have been
saying this since, and far more acutely, Heidegger is
aware of this "one-sidedness." But Heidegger is extremely
suspicious of the concept of "world-view" and his way,
therefore, has been that of becoming aware, through
radical, persistent questioning and tracking down, of the
origin and nature of this one-sidedness rather than of
hastening to a premature answer like that of Deussen, an
answer that is still rooted in his unexamined Schopenhauerian and Kantian presuppositions. Here, the Indian
Weltanschauung remains an alternative image for mere
aesthetic contemplation and it is an image which is in
itself largely a projection of these presuppositions. As
against Deussen's, the Heideggerian question is: Must not
there be a different way of grasping things than the one
which was launched by the Greeks, a way that needs to be

fashioned yet by becoming aware of the implicit and unquestioned foundations on which they built? And must it not be, not an *alternate* way which can be substituted for the Greek, but rather a *foundational* way which can provide the Greek and the Western enterprise with the foundation of a more primordial awareness and thus break its appearance of absoluteness and independence? For there is no choice between two alternatives today. The Greek way *has* become world destiny. This is our world, and the only choice left is whether through another manner of thinking than the "metaphysical" we can enter into the region, yet to be recognized and articulated in language but not beyond reach, as the invisible basis of that world--the region of what Heidegger has called the event of appropriation (*Ereignis*). The quest of thought here is not personal, the achievement by the single individual of his ultimate human purpose through insight into reality, but world-historical, as "philosophy" is world-historical--the quest of a common world of shared meaning and ways of speaking. It is thus not evident how the Indian tradition can help in this enterprise, as it is becoming evident, partly in consequence of Heidegger's thinking, that the Indian enterprise of self-understanding in respect of its tradition is by no means always helped by being translated in terms of Western conceptuality. This, too, may be a reason for Heidegger's lack of Schopenhauerian warmth for Indian philosophy.

And there is another, more crucial, point worth mentioning perhaps in this regard. Heidegger's quest for the "sense of Being" is at the same time a quest for the right or appropriate language in which to talk about it, in which the region from which Being itself gets its sense can find utterance. This region, as it finally comes into view in Heidegger's thinking is "that realm of the event of appropriation, vibrating within itself, through which man and Being reach each other in their nature, achieve

their real nature by losing those qualities with which metaphysics has endowed them."[21] Thinking this "self-vibrating realm" is building with language "a self-suspended structure" expressive of this realm, inaccessible in the language of metaphysics. Here, "language is the most delicate and thus the most vulnerable vibration holding everything within the suspended structure of the appropriation."[22]

Heidegger's search for the appropriate language with which to build in this realm, that is to think it, leads him progressively away from metaphysical, conceptualizing ways of speaking and makes him even wonder whether Western languages, just because they are superbly suited for metaphysical thinking, can ever lend themselves to non-representational utterance. For the thinking of Being the Greek language is paradigmatic, for it alone, Heidegger says, is *logos*; "what is said in it *is* at the same time in an excellent way what it is called....What it presents (through its *legein*) is what lies immediately before us. Through the audible Greek word we are directly in the presence of the thing itself."[23] Because to the Greeks the nature of language is revealed as the *logos*, Greek is the language uniquely fitted for that "expressly adopted and unfolding correspondence which corresponds to the address of the Being of what is" which is philosophy, as Heidegger describes it, and for that very reason inadequate to the attempt at a thinking responsiveness to that other domain beyond the Being of what is, the domain of the truth of Being, from which Being itself derives. Since we can neither ever again return to this nature of language, nor simply take it over, Heidegger says, we must enter into a dialogue with the Greek experience of language as *logos*.

As Indo-European, Sanskrit also is in some measure "metaphysical," as distinct from the languages of the Far East, with the notions of Being embedded in it, gramma-

tically and conceptually. It is metaphysical in being
representational, concept-generating and in being productive of ontological speculation about Being as the
ground of all that is, and so giving the appearance of
setting up a reality other and higher than this world, in
the sense attacked by Nietzsche. Since *this* possibility
of thinking has been fulfilled in its amplest and purest
form in the Greek tradition, Heidegger is not interested
in how Sanskrit speaks (in the sense in which, according
to Heidegger, it is language that speaks, not man), nor in
the tradition that has evolved out of it.[24] The extreme
opposite of both Greek and Sanskrit, in their characteristic mode of disclosure, the Far Eastern languages hold
greater promise for the thinking that reaches out to a
non-representational mode of utterance. Thus, the very
reasons for the delighted surprise and excitement with
which the discovery of Sanskrit was hailed by European
linguists, along with the thought forms in Indian
philosophy by scholars such as Garbe and Deussen, are
reasons for Heidegger's relative indifference to the
Indian tradition.

IV

In this tradition, *Brahman* plays the same role as
Logos in the Greek and *Tao* in the Chinese, corresponding
to the notions of *verbum*, *oratio*, and *ratio* respectively,
as Johannes Lohmann has pointed out.[25] But whereas with
the Greeks, by virtue of the very *logos* character of the
language, attention was directed away from the light of
the *logos* to what it illumined, that is, the world of
entities, of what is, in the Indian case language itself
entered, so to speak, into the reality it disclosed,
shining forth itself also, while illumining and opening up
the domain of meanings. The original Vedic sense of

Brahman as poetic, creative and sacred utterance (as Paul
Thieme has shown), sliding subsequently into the sense of
the reality finding such utterance, the source of all
utterance and itself beyond human speaking, manifested
itself in the conception of *Vak* or speech as the
primordial reality, in the extraordinary attention given
to grammar (the invention of this discipline itself),
finally in the emergence of the school of speculative
grammar which culminated in the great *Vakyapadiya* of
Bhartrhari and the philosophy of Word-monism.

In the Upanisads themselves and in the schools of
Advaita Vedanta which arose after Bhartrhari this
awareness of language, either as Word principle or as
Sruti, is never absent. Samkara's insistence on the
inseparability of the liberating Brahman-knowledge and the
Vedic word about this knowledge and on the immediacy of
the relationship between the two is as good an example of
this as any. That the word of the *Sruti* itself falls away
and is left behind in the experience of what it has disclosed is no argument against the above, for all saying,
as such, is a showing, a mode of disclosure, and the
former is not just a tool for the latter but itself a
reality inseparable from it, as Heidegger has insisted.
The designation of the Veda, of even all primordial
utterance sometimes, as the Sabda Brahman--an aspect of
Brahman or as the "lower" Brahman--and of the Word-
principle as Brahman itself is not uncommon in Vedanta
literature and expresses this whole way of thinking. When
this is forgotten and language is understood as having a
solely instrumental reality, Vedanta thought is easily
treated as a kind of "theology".

It is not surprising that Professor Lohmann should
take recourse to the concept of "magic" whenever he
touches upon the beginnings of Indian thought. For "magic"
is only the name of a category employed to indicate what a
blind spot prevents one from seeing, what Lohmann's

idealization of the Greek prevents him from thinking.
Greek culture *is* paradigmatic, and perhaps we in India can
do with even more emphatic reminders of this fact. But in
the perspective of Heidegger's quest for what is "never
Greek any more" and for "planetary thinking," in this age
of world-civilization and man's homelessness, there is
little meaning in such idealization. The presence of the
Greek as world destiny is a hard reality to be faced and
interrogated, now and for a long time to come, by thinking
men everywhere. It requires a rethinking of the meaning,
and the negative value, assigned by metaphysical thinking
to the notions of the irrational, the magical, the mythic,
the symbolic, the merely poetic and fanciful and so forth.
It is a demand to rethink the relation between the contrasting spheres of "religion" and "philosophy," and the
contrast itself, generated in Western thought by the
coming together of the Greek and the Christian as major
components in this metaphysical tradition, to rethink the
concept of "mysticism" as a type of religious or
philosophical view or position.

The value of a thinker such as Nietzsche, even more so
Heidegger, lies in this that they invite us to such
"revaluation" and rethinking of concepts, categories and
thought-forms, not in the solutions they supposedly offer
to certain perennial philosophical "problems," nor in the
philosophical doctrine or system they may be thought to
teach or propound. Comparative philosophy so far has
proceeded largely on the basis of an uncritical employment
of these "metaphysical" concepts, assumed as obviously and
eternally valid, in the understanding of "philosophies"
such as those of India.[26] But something remarkable will
be seen to happen when we take seriously Heidegger's talk
of "the end of philosophy" and his "overcoming of
metaphysics" (understanding these phrases in *his* sense,
not just projecting an imaginary meaning into them, out of
context): freedom from this metaphysical bias, the

loosening of the hold of the "concept" on thinking, the liberation from prejudices functioning as norms and as standards of comparison, the openness to "the matter of thinking," wherever going on, East or West. For example, if "philosophy" is a synonym for the mode of thinking arising from the Greek venture and if there is no such thing as Indian or Chinese philosophy, as Heidegger insists, what happens to the concept of "comparative philosophy" itself? If the term philosophy is taken in this strict sense, as a proper noun, there is nothing to compare; if we still insist on comparing, it can only be for the sake of judging the non-Western, in the manner of Hegel, with the Greek-Western as the norm. But if we bring ourselves to share Heidegger's insight in this matter, we may also see the nullity of the contrast between "religion" and "philosophy" in the Western tradition (for, with the end of "philosophy," the opposite number of the pair also meets its "end"), and thus becomes open to the *Sache des Denkens* in those other ventures at thinking.

Comparative philosophy, if we still retain the name, would then be a name for the task, infinitely open, of setting free, bringing into view and articulating in contemporary ways of speaking, in new ways of speaking, the matter of thinking which, in what has actually been realized in thought, still remains unsaid and so unthought, in the traditions of the East. Otherwise, comparative philosophy will amount to no more than an unthinking attempt at perpetuating Western "philosophy" by translating Eastern thinking into the language of Western metaphysics, taken as the universally valid paradigm. And this is bad, not because it is Western but because it hides an unthought opacity that stands in the way of adequately reaching out to the other, for it either prompts to an assimilation of the other or leads to a perpetuation of its otherness.

As Heidegger speaks of it, the end of philosophy as metaphysical thinking does not mean its termination but rather its consummation, the fact that it has reached "the place in which the whole of philosophy's history is gathered in its most extreme possibility."[27] It exhibits itself as "the triumph of the manipulable arrangement of a scientific-technological world and of the social order proper to this world. The end of philosophy means: the beginning of the world civilization based upon Western European thinking."[28] Are we to think of comparative philosophy as a continuation of this consummation or completion, a contribution to it required by the emergence of world-civilization and in its service? Or should we rather not think of it in terms of "the task of thinking" which, according to Heidegger, still remains reserved for thinking at the end of philosophy, a *first* possibility which was contained in its beginning but which it could not acknowledge or realize? Whether we choose the first or the second alternative depends upon whether or not we see this world-civilization as "the world destiny of homelessness," question it (not deny it, or want to substitute something else for it), and are willing to question the thought of Being as Ground which heralded its moment of birth.

For any one in search of "philosophemes" common to Heidegger and Vedanta, or of similar-looking ideas in them, there is a great deal to be found regarding man's nature, the world, and man's relationship to it, the unity of Being, the identity between man and Being. Each of these topics can provide the starting point of an examination in depth of the similarity and the differences between the two, and beyond these, to meditation on these central concerns of thought. There is, above all, the idea of Being (Brahman-Atman) as the ground of all, that appears to offer an interesting point for comparison and contrast, for this is the basic concept of the meta-

physical tradition and in Vedanta thought it is even more emphatically crucial. This is what made the arch-anti-Platonist Nietzsche describe the Vedanta as "the classical expression of the mode of thinking most alien to me," in his letter of 16 March 1883 to Deussen. Following Nietzsche, Heidegger also is engaged in the attempt to root out the very idea of a transcendent ground of things which seems most characteristic of Vedanta thought.

As one looks more closely, however, matters become more intriguing and complicated, calling for a fuller investigation than can be undertaken here. The second sutra of Badarayana's *Sariraka-mimamsa-sutra* both sums up a long tradition and presents a task for centuries to follow when it declares: Brahman is that from which, by and into which, all this arises, is sustained and returns. Is this Anaximander all over again? Is it Aristotle? If Brahman is identified with the Greek notion of Being (not to speak of its scholastic variants), conceived as ground, then Heidegger's whole effort is to demolish this idea, for his entire thinking is a critique of just this single concept. Can Brahman be so identified? If not, then the "all this" of the Upanisads cannot just be identified with the "entity" of Heidegger or with the *to on* of the Greeks, for here the "this" is not thought of solely under the aspect of its being-ness. As for the notion of "ground," here again, despite the seeming similarity, different things were going on in the two traditions, with very different consequences. But into this fascinating problem, perhaps basic to the comparative enterprise, we cannot enter here.[29] Instead, let us discuss in what follows, though again only briefly, two questions of a more general character: Is Heidegger an ontologist, and is Vedanta an ontology? Is Heidegger a mystic and is Vedanta a mystical philosophy, is Samkara a mystic? What makes these questions specially interesting is the fact that none of them can be answered with a simple "yes" or "no," that *as* questions they are themselves questionable.

V

Although taking the question of the "sense" of Being as his starting point, Heidegger is certainly not an ontologist, either in the traditional meaning of the term or in some new sense. The point hardly needs laboring, since he has expressed himself with all clarity on this matter in his later writings. He does not take ontology for granted as the first philosophy or as *metaphysica generalis* and then go on to make some original contribution to it, or provide a novel analysis of the "meaning" of Being but, on the contrary, subjects the very idea of ontology to the most radical questioning. For the first time in the history of Western thought, he exhibits the derivative, contingent, specifically Greek character of this whole notion, this whole manner of conceiving the matter of thought and of thought's response to the matter by which it is addressed. The Being of what-is emerged as the unique matter of thinking at the beginning of Western thought and this, Heidegger points out, is itself the beginning of the West, the hidden source of its destiny.[30] This great beginning of Western philosophy did not arise out of nothing but emerged in the process of overcoming "its extreme opposite, the mythical in general and the Asiatic in particular."[31] Heidegger's quest is for the source from which this thought of Being, indeed from which Being itself, emerged as the first and last for thinking, and a quest for that which remained unthought in this thinking, variously called by him Appropriation (*Ereignis*), Clearing (*Lichtung*) and Truth (*Aletheia*), or unhiddenness. And yet Heidegger is a thinker of Being from beginning to end, gnawing away at this marrow-bone (as Hamann said of his own concern with *Logos*) until he is able to dispel the darkness over this depth (luckier than Hamann perhaps, to have found the key to this abyss).[32]

Throughout his work there is a strange, bewildering
nebulousness or lack of precision in the use of the word
"Being," apparent in the adoption of such expressions as
"the truth of Being," "Being itself," and of variants such
as "*Seyn*" and "Being" struck out with a cross mark, so
that one can always pick out passages from different
periods of his writing to prove that, after all, it is
"Being" Heidegger is really talking about without being
quite clear as to what he is trying to say. This would be
a mistake, for this nebulousness is not confusion but part
of the stringency or rigor (which is something quite
different from "exactness," as Heidegger points out)
necessitated by this path of thinking itself. It must be
remembered, further, that for Heidegger thinking is a
movement and a wayfaring, in which what is thought about
itself undergoes continuous transformation, as thinking
fashions its path and moves forward, that is, away from
the matter as conceived at the starting point, and from
the manner of thinking it, towards a destination of which
it has no foreknowledge. Seeking for what can have no
name until it is seen, Heidegger uses the word "Being" as
a provisional first name for the greater part of his path
of thinking, until the long drawn out act of renunciation
is completed.

The starting point is the Greek thought of Being, but
the path is one of continuous overcoming of this thought,
until thinking is itself set free from its bondage to this
thought and from the determination of its own nature by
it. Heidegger is a thinker of Being, yet not an
ontologist; he is a thinker of Being who has caught a
glimpse of the truth covered over by the thought of Being.
Heidegger said in 1935, "In the seemingly unimportant
distinction between being and thinking we must discern the
fundamental position of the Western spirit, against which
our central attack is directed."[33] From the perspective
of the successful carrying through of this attack in the

following three decades, we can say that thinking is not,
in its true nature, the sort of activity which can be
about Being, with Being confronting it as its *Sache* or
matter, but must be *of* Being; that Being is not the sort
of thing which, eternally there, self-established and
shining in its own light, beckons thought to grasp it in
its three-pronged onto-theo-logical movement; that both
Being and thinking (man) belong together in a deeper unity
(inaccessible to any form of dialectic), from which they
both derive their nature and which exhibits itself, while
yet concealing itself, as the proper matter of thinking
that is no more a grasping, no longer a striving to form a
system of concepts for what is beyond all conceptualizing.

VI

Neither the Upanisads nor Samkara can be said to be
concerned with a theoretical inquiry (*episteme theoretike*)
into being as being (*on he on*) or into the *ontos on* and
their question is not identical with the Greek "What is
Being (*ti to on*)?" nor with Heidegger's questioning of the
ambiguities and the unthought presuppositions of that
question. Brahman, that one being (*sat*) which the wise
speak of in many ways, is not identical with the *to on* of
Aristotle, "spoken of in many ways"; and the Brahman-vidya
is not a *legein* of Brahman (so that it is as inappropriate
to speak, with Paul Hacker, of Atomology as it would be to
describe Vedanta as a Brahmology). It is not the conceptual knowledge of Being, though wisdom about Being
(*sad-vidya*) or about Brahman as Being, is part of it.
Brahman is *sat* (Being), the ground of all that is,
including my own being, which is of the nature of sheer,
pure *chit* (awareness, of which "knowing" is itself a
derivative mode) and potentially capable of rising above
all otherness and, therefore, pure bliss. Thus Brahman is

Being, but not in the sense in which it is other than what it is Being for or to, not in the sense of what knowing, thinking and speaking are about, other than them, as a reality confronting them, but inclusive of these as themselves modes of Being. It is *sat*, *chit* and *ananda* in one and as one, and my being is one with it. We can, if we choose--and as metaphysics does--consider things (including my self) solely and exclusively under the aspect of their being (is-ness), only taking notice of the fact that they *are*. But this would be something like Blake's "Single vision and Newton's sleep," for no being, as simple is-ness, is exclusive of the fact of being lit up, of lighting up, of being gathered into a unity with what it lights up and with where this lighting up occurs-- in me, who am in essence (as *atman*) just this lighting up itself and so identical with that is-ness. So regarded, however, is-ness (Being) becomes an aspect, though integral and essential, of something more "comprehensive" than it, thinkable separately and by itself, even as an aspect, only by an illegitimate abstraction. Brahman, therefore, is beyond Being and Non-being; "it cannot be spoken of either as being or as not being," as the *Bhagavadgita* has it.

It has been rightly pointed out by Paul Hacker that Samkara was wary and hesitant, for this reason, of dwelling too much on Brahman as Being, unlike his followers, but focused instead on Brahman as awareness (*chit*) and preferred hence an Atman-oriented approach to ultimate truth.[34] Being, taken by itself, carries a suggestion of objectivity, as being for another than it, for which reason K.C. Bhattacharyya also relegates metaphysics to the "philosophy of the Object." The self should first be realized as existing, but only as a stepping-stone to the self-revelation of its essence, to which the ideas of being and not-being are not applicable, as Samkara says.[35] In so far as Brahman, in itself devoid

of all distinctions, is the basis (from our human perspective) of all diversification and the seed of all activity, it can be spoken of as existing; or, because only by thinking of it as being can we be prompted to realize it.[36]   But, being beyond the reach of the senses, it cannot be an object of consciousness accompanied with the idea of either existence or non-existence, as we have it in ordinary experience.   Further, Brahman does not belong to any class or genus, and therefore cannot be denoted by the word *sat*, for we cannot speak about anything that exists in the empirical mode without referring it to a class.[37]   And if *sat* were itself regarded as only a class name, it would be no more than the "Being of or in beings" and cannot be the prior ground of all that is.[38]   Brahman has a unitary nature and we cannot define it as merely "that which is (*sat*)," or as merely consciousness or thought (*bodha*) or as being made up of the two together; "for he who would maintain that Brahman is characterized by thought different from existence, and at the same time by existence different from thought, would virtually maintain that there is a plurality in Brahman."[39]

The *locus classicus* of the more ontologically oriented treatment of Brahman as Being (*Sad-Brahman*) is chapter VI of the *Chandogya Upanisad* and later Advaita thinkers have attached relatively greater importance to the notion of Brahman as *ens primum* (*Satta*), as Paul Hacker points out. But it is in the *Brahmasiddhi* of Mandana Misra that we find a view of Brahman as the universal Being that is presented in and animates all experience.   Mandana himself was probably influenced in his ontological interpretation of Brahman by the speculative grammarian Bhartrhari, according to whom Brahman is the Highest Universal (*Mahasamanya*) the Great Being (*Mahasatta*) which expresses itself in all words.   For Samkara, however, such a view would be intolerable because it objectifies Brahman by making it an object of knowing.   As he says,

> The purport of this science is not to represent
> Brahman definitely as this or that object, its
> purpose is rather to show that Brahman as the
> eternal inward self is never an object, and
> thereby to remove the distinction of objects
> known, knowers, acts of knowledge, etc,, which is
> fictitiously created by Nescience.[40]

We thus see that "ontology" hardly provides a basis
for comparison between Samkara and Western thinkers like
Parmenides, Eckhart, or Aquinas. Deussen made use, though
sporadically, of Greek ontological concepts to illumine
Samkara's thought. More systematic attempts have been
made to compare Samkara with Eckhart by Rudolf Otto and
with Thomas Aquinas by Richard De Smet and Paul Hacker.
But in so far as the final point of reference in these
latter comparisons also perforce remains the Greek notion
of Being, they cannot be regarded as shedding light on
what *Brahma-vidya* is about or what *Atman-bodha* stands for.
In this respect, at least, a consideration of Advaita
Vedanta in a Heideggerian perspective perhaps offers a
better chance, for the thinking of Heidegger and Samkara
may be found to have a touching point somewhere in that
"region of all regions," beyond the thought of Being and
Non-being, in which it has its sojourn. About these two
thinkers also it may with some truth be said that they
"dwell near to one another" though standing "on mountains
farthest apart."[41]

VII

Is Heidegger a mystic? It is true that he refers to
Meister Eckhart and Angelus Silesius, mentions Tao, speaks
of Way and Topos and Leap, talks of the identity of man
and Being in a primordial belonging-togetherness, of the
abruptness of an unbridged entry into the region of the
Ereignis. There is enough evidence to show that Heidegger
has been deeply interested, from his early writings, in

medieval mysticism in general and Eckhart in particular
and in his later writings he borrows freely from the
vocabulary of Eckhart. As John D. Caputo has shown,
Eckhartian concepts such as those of *Abgeschiedenheit*
(detachment) and *Gelassenheit* (abandonment, releasement)
have substantially contributed to this thinking.[42] Yet,
it must be kept in mind that all this happens in the
context of *thinking* and in its service. Heidegger appropriates what he finds to be genuine thinking contained in
the works of the mystics, takes them as gestures of
thought, as happenings on the path of thinking, never in
the sense of finding access to a realm and an experience
which lie beyond the reach of thinking, never as the
necessary or even possible abrogation of thought. As he
points out even in his early Duns Scotus book, the notion
of mysticism in the sense of an irrationalistic *Erleben*
(immediate inner experience) rests on an extreme rational-
ization of philosophy, on the conception of philosophy as
a rationalistic structure divorced from life.[43] Almost a
quarter of a century later, Heidegger makes the same point
when he asserts that mysticism is the mere counterpart of
metaphysics, into which people take flight when, still
wholly caught in their slavery to metaphysical thinking,
they are struck by the hiddenness in all revealment and
lapse into unthinking helplessness.[44] When we abandon the
presuppositions of such thinking and the traditional
conception of *Lichtmetaphysik*, however, we can acknowledge
this mystery of concealment as manifest, *as* concealment,
in all disclosure, and can think it as such. "Mysticism"
then loses all meaning and becomes both unnecessary and
impossible. It should also not be forgotten that,
according to Heidegger, pointing to and intimating something are gestures of thinking, not of the resignation of
thought. As he says,

> What makes itself known only in such a way that
> it becomes apparent in its self-concealment, to
> that we can respond also only by alluding to it,

> indicating it....This simple pointing is one of
> the distinctive marks of thinking.

Such pointing in words is not a relegation of the *Sache*
(the matter) to the realm of the ineffable and the unknown
but a way of being related to it in thought, the seeing of
what is pointed out. Thinking is a seeing of what comes
into view and so a form of experiencing, the profoundest
modality of experience in fact. The traditional,
metaphysical contrast between entities known by reason
(thought conceived as *ratio*) and what is experienceable
breaks down.

Thus, Heidegger speaks of the *experience* of thinking,
of thinking as itself an experience, appropriating within
thinking the precious element of immediacy in all mysticism. Little attention has been paid to this extraordinary role of "experience" in Heidegger's writings. He
speaks of the experiencing of Being, of the hiddenmost
history of Being, of the basic experience of nothingness,
of "undergoing an experience with language."[46] According
to Heidegger, thinking is thus in a profound sense
experiencing. "To experience," Heidegger says, "means
eundo assequi to obtain something along the way, to attain
something by going on a way....To experience is to go
along a way."[47] And thinking is the pre-eminent mode of
going along a way for man. Further, what one undergoes on
the path of thinking is not just "intellectual insight"
but experience in the most transforming sense. As
Heidegger describes it,

> To undergo an experience with something--be it a
> thing, a person, or a god--means that this
> something befalls us, strikes us, comes over us,
> overwhelms and transforms us. When we talk of
> "undergoing" an experience, we mean specifically
> that the experience is not of our own making; to
> undergo here means that we endure it, suffer it,
> receive it as it strikes us and submit to it. It
> is this something itself that comes about, comes
> to pass, happens.[48]

> To experience something means to attain it
> alongthe way, by going on a way. To undergo an
> experience with something means that this
> something, which we reach along the way in order
> to attain it, itself pertains to us, meets and
> makes its appeal to us, in that it transforms us
> into itself.[49]

If we ponder these remarks and undergo, with
Heidegger, an experience with thinking, we may come to see
that there is something wrong with the current and
unquestioning characterization of Eastern thought as
"mystical," especially by scholars of religion, and thus
with the perpetuation of *Erleben* as the alternative to
"mere" thought. Such an attempted perpetuation may be
understandable in theologians like Rudolf Otto, with their
quest for the "inner relationship of types of human
experience and spiritual life,"[50] carried on in unexamined
acceptance of "metaphysics" as the normative mode of
thought. We can see what is wrong here if we understand
why Heidegger, "having experienced theology in its own
roots, both the theology of the Christian faith and that
of philosophy, prefers to remain silent about God in the
realm of thinking,"[51] and if we recall his remark in *Being
and Time* about "those residues of Christian theology
within the problematics of philosophy which have not as
yet been radically extruded."[52] It is this extrusion
which has enabled Heidegger to reclaim for thinking its
proper plenitude, to set it free to reach out limitlessly
to its *Sache*, and widen its sphere to an unbounded
horizon. Such liberation of thinking can enable us to
look out for the thinking going on in other religious and
philosophical traditions. "Mysticism," too, is one such
residue that has fused in recent religious thought with
subjectivism, the form which metaphysics has assumed since
Descartes, according to Heidegger, resulting in the
present day pursuit of *Erlebnis* and the quest for types,
patterns, and structures of inner experience or of its
correlate, the world of objectivity as disclosed in such
experience.[53]

VIII

From the perspective opened up by Heidegger's thinking
we may seek in the Upanisads and in the tradition of
Vedanta thought for "the thinking experience" of Uddalaka
and Yajnavalkya, of Samkara and his successors. For what
is central, at least in the Advaita tradition of Vedanta
philosophy, is the "way of knowledge," the way of insight
through meditative thought, the way of "the experience of
thought." Here, as in Heidegger, such realization of
truth in and through thinking comprises a two-fold
movement, the movement of "hearing" and the movement of
questioning, with the former as basic and first, as in
Heidegger. It culminates in a "seeing," which is not the
act of a subject directed toward objective being, either
in the Greek sense of *theoria* or in the modern subjectivistic sense, but as the shining forth of the *Sache*
itself, in the sense of being appropriated by it and owned
into an identity with it, prior and primordial, as in
Heidegger. Finally, this whole process in which truth is
realized in thinking experience occurs within the dimension of the holy, as Heidegger thinks it, as a sacred
happening, within an experience of Being "which is still
capable of a god," which is not yet "too late for the gods
and too early for Being."

This comparison is not intended to establish any
thesis about the similarity of two entities, the structure
of Heidegger's thought (thus transforming it into a
"philosophy") and Advaita Vedanta as a thought-form (thus
devaluing its essentially religious character), but to
imply that it is thinking that is happening in the latter,
not just the rational justification of a set of assertions
in the *Sruti*, in acknowledgement of it as an "authority,"
nor just the construction of an intellectually satisfying
system of speculative philosophy, but a thinking which is
experienced *as* thinking of ultimate concern. But this

thinking is neither "no-more-metaphysical" nor "not-yet-metaphysical" (in the sense Heidegger speaks of these in *Heraklit*); it has not been mediated by medieval Christianity, nor by the new awareness introduced into modern Western thought by the rise of historicism. It is not haunted by the reflective sense of the finitude of thinking as such, as Heidegger naturally is, in reaction against Plato and Hegel and the entire metaphysical tradition. As thinking, it moves straight ahead toward its *Sache* not thematically mindful of its own character as a "thrown project," but seeking the impossible, fullness of light, all light, without shadows and dark corners, seeking the total elimination of pain and fear, of the ensnarement by things and all forms of objectivity and otherness in life, seeking the annulment of mortality.

But this naivety, if it must be called such, is minimal in the Vedanta tradition. For we have indeed here a vivid and energetic awareness of the possibility, ever present for thinking, of grasping, in Hegel's words, only "clouds of error instead of the Heaven of truth."[54] This is exhibited in the very extensive treatment of the problem of knowledge--its nature, sources and criteria of validity--and the nature of error in Vedanta, as in all schools of Indian thought. Guarded by the equally primal awareness of the voice of the Upanisadic word, undistracted from listening to it, Vedanta thinking could move on, however, without that fear of erring which, in Hegel's words again, is already the error itself. Is it not precisely in this straining towards the impossible, the Absolute, that the very passion, the ecstasy, and the moving power of all great thinking lie, in this incessant, relentless pushing beyond its ever incomplete accomplishment, in this unceasing self-transcendence, in this movement of unending self-overcoming which Nietzsche has so penetratingly seen and described, and which attains a straining and a stretching to the utmost in the thinking

of Heidegger, just because he is aware as no other thinker
of the West of thought's finitude and in spite of his
disclaimer that his thinking has no wisdom to deliver and
is not put forward as a *Heilsweg*, a promise of salvation?
What greater healing can there be than the thinking
experience by man of being at one with that from which, in
his all too human state, he experiences division and of
being freed from the tyranny of that thing out there, and
this, here inside his mind, confronting him as an other
to himself?

It is true that we find in the founders of systematic
Advaita thought, Gaudapada and Samkara, a great deal of
insistence on setting aside, suspending and even nihilating the activity of the mind, so that we may have a
vision of the true self and of what truly is, without
being obstructed and tricked by this seed-bed of all
seeming. A number of considerations, impossible to enter
into here, account for this: the starting point with the
self (rather than with the Being of beings, in the Greek
sense), the prevailing conceptions about the mental
faculty and the concern for distinguishing it from the
self (which is the self or "being" of the mind itself),
the discovery of the constructive, projective and representational functions of the mind as sources of error in
our understanding of the world and ourselves by the Buddhist thinkers, and, above all the uncompromising resistance to the two "nihilistic" and "semi-nihilistic" ways
of thinking dominant at the time (though as possibilities
ever present threats to the Advaita mode of thinking),
namely, the Madhyamika and the Vaisesika philosophies.

According to the first, thinking is the positing of an
"it is" where there is in reality no entitative Being;
according to the latter, thinking moves within and knows
only the realm of entities and is intrinsically categorial
in its procedure. In its concern to preserve the primal
reality undiminished by the least vestige of opacity

(somewhat in the Sartrian sense), the former replaces Being by Nothingness, giving to thinking the preliminary and solely negative role of a dialectical cancellation of its own thetic, positing activity. The latter takes cognizance only of beings, of Being only as a class concept and of Non-being as the absence of a being. Each denies Being as the ultimate "that from which"; each conceives thinking in accordance with its view of the *Sache* of thinking.

Advaita thinking lives in the tension between these two stances, refusing to go the way of systematic denial but acknowledging the illusions to which thought is ever exposed, and refusing also to accept the position that there is nothing for thinking to be addressed by except entities and that there is no other mode of thinking than the ontic-categorial. This is the Upanisadic way of "yea-saying," of saying yes to the realm of entities (for they are "beings in Being," upheld in and by Being, are grounded in a self; the "is" in any entity cannot be denied, for it is none other than the "is" that I myself am); of saying yes to the negativity infecting all mortal experience (for I, ever in the midst of entities, am "always already forfeited to them," am duped by them-- *"genarrt durch das Seiende, dem Sein so entfremdet,"* as Heidegger puts it--am caught in the play of seeming, in this mirror-game of reflecting and being reflected in beings, confused between the realm of beings and the self of which and for which they are beings); of saying yes to that other dimension, beyond beings and yet in them, the dimension from which all is-ness derives, which is the primordial openness and truth and which is also the dimension of the holy, that *"Wesensraum"* of Divinity from which the real shines forth as the god, as God; of affirming that gesture of thinking which lies in saying, "It is." Does not the *Katha Upanisad* (VI, 12 and 13) say, "Not by speech, not by mind, not by sight can he be

apprehended. How can he be apprehended except by him who says, 'He is'?" Intellection "dissolves" in such thinking of the self, Samkara points out in his comment on this verse, but only as pregnant with a notion of existence (*satpratyayagarbhaiva viliyate*).

The thinkers of the Upanisadic-Buddhist-Advaita tradition were acutely, intensely, and vividly alive to the havoc wrought by representational thinking because they lived in awareness of a dimension other than the workaday world in which such thinking is valid, perhaps inevitable as well as necessary. This sensitivity was all the more heightened by the fact that this "other" dimension was not thought of as wholly transcendent but as the truth of this workaday existence itself. However, the doctrine of two truths, or two levels of reality, as developed by Nagarjuna and Samkara in different ways and to different ends, is not quite the same as the distinction between the grasping, conceptual, and representational thinking generated in the metaphysical-philosophical tradition of the West and the notion of non-representational, meditative, reminiscent, topological, and preparatory thinking as we have it in Heidegger. Also, Heidegger's distinction should not itself be understood in a "metphysical" sense, or as a philosophical thesis about the nature of thinking, for it is itself part of a movement of thought that seeks to overcome and get behind, so to speak, the Greek metaphysical thought of Being, so that someday "the farewell from all 'It is'" may come to pass,[55] so that there may be a turn in the world destiny of homelessness.

The Brahman-Atman of the Upanisads is not the same as the Being of Western thought; they are different starting points, each uniquely itself, for thinking in the two traditions, and they are untranslatable one by the other, for we do not yet have a name for what may be identical in them (though perhaps "Brahman" has the advantage of

including in itself, but not being exhausted by, the
notion of Being!). The history of Being, its mittence
(*Geschick*) is the hidden history of the West, now over-
spreading the world and culminating in the all-consuming
"Europeanization of the earth," in world-civilization and
the loss of world as home for man. Brahman-Atman, too is
Geschick and yet, not in the sense of historical destiny;
perhaps a *Geschick* still, indeed in a more real sense so,
when we have once achieved the "releasement toward things
and openness to the mystery" of which Heidegger speaks in
his address on *Gelassenheit*?[56]

Vedantic thought or Vedantism, in so far as it is a
way of thinking and is not simply a name for what has at
any time been actually thought in it (in respect of content, structure, and style), has been and will remain,
like all genuine, original thinking, a thinking of the
unthought in what has been thought, to speak in
Heidegger's language, and a perpetually novel start.
Historically, the challenge to this thinking has come from
the existence of opposing systems and paths of thought and
spirituality. It has therefore itself a history. The
Upanisads do not say, could not have said, what Gaudapada
found it possible and necessary in his time to say. Did
he falsify the intent of the Vedic utterance, importing
into its thought elements borrowed from alien sources, or
was he able in some measure to set free the unsaid,
implicit truth of those ancient thinkers, while appropriating a new language and speaking in a new age? Did
Samkara do this in respect of his predecessors, and in
which regard and with what success? And so with his
followers and with the other schools of Vedanta.

Much of Heidegger's work has been devoted to attempts
at saying, by means of a series of "phenomenological
interpretations" (as he described many of his early
seminars on the great Western philosophers), what remains
unsaid and unthought in their works. Should it not be

possible to attempt the same with these Indian thinkers,
"looking beyond the language which these philosophers
employ to what they intended to say," in the words of
Kant, or "wresting from the actual words that which these
words 'intended to say,'" as Heidegger puts it?[57] To be
able to do so, however, requires, as he goes on to point
out, that

> ...the interpretation must be animated and guided
> by an illuminative idea. Only through the power
> of this idea can an interpretation risk that
> which is always audacious, namely, entrusting
> itself to the secret elan of a work, in order by
> this elan to get through to the unsaid and to
> attempt to find an expression for it.

With which "illuminative idea" have subsequent thinkers in
the Vedanta tradition approached the earlier thinkers? Is
there such a directive idea, capable of confirming itself
by its own power of illumination, available to us today
for the task of interpreting the thinkers of this tradition?

These thinkers themselves did not conceive their task
in these terms but thought of themselves as continuators
and defenders of a tradition--ahistorically, reaching the
limits of impersonality and anonymity in their creative
work. How could they ever come upon the idea that
Samkara's thinking, for example, drew its sustenance from
its own unthought depths, that there was something he
himself could not think, but which Suresvara or Padmapada,
his immediate disciples, could bring out into the open,
but without their own thinking being totally transparent
to themselves? Every great thinker has his own explicitly
seen task, which he seeks to accomplish with the tools,
the energy and the gifts at his command. But in the midst
of what he actually manages to accomplish and sees himself
as achieving, something else also goes on within his work,
all unbeknownst to himself, to his contemporaries and
immediate successors almost always, often to the entire
tradition that springs out of his work. The continuity of
the mostly hidden operation of this unknown and unsaid is

the mittence (*Geschick*) which carries all history, giving it an inexhaustible potentiality of meaningfulness in the oncoming, endless future. Thus Vedantic thinking has a history, that continuity of hidden unrest that pushes it forward. Can we say about it, as Heidegger does about the "end" of the Western tradition of metaphysical thinking with Hegel and Nietzsche, that it reached its completion with Madhusudan Saraswati, or even with K.C. Bhatta-charyya? Perhaps not, perhaps the beginning (in the Upanisads) still hides a secret for future thinking and saying; perhaps Samkara's thinking still contains a meaning, still awaiting the work of thought to be clearly seen, from which his school itself was side-tracked, even while bringing it to *one* consummation, carrying it to dizzy heights of intellectual effort in a white heat of luminous creativity rarely paralleled anywhere. If so, Vedanta thinking, far from being a closed and completed whole, remains a task for the open future.

CONCLUSION

In the world of today, in this one world of "world-civilization," our relationship to tradition is an irreparably broken one and our thinking is determined by an unheard-of simultaneity of times and places, all equally remote, all equally close. If the bringing together of "Heidegger" and "Vedanta" is to have any sense it can only lie in enabling us to see that there is more to Vedanta--something that is its very own and yet unfulfilled--than providing those who are in revolt against the establishment (the religious, the Western metaphysical), and in flight from thinking, with a "mystical" alternative; that as a way or path of thinking, not so much as a doctrine, Vedanta may also have some relevance to that other task to which Heidegger points,

the task of planetary thinking, in an age of homelessness
and of the coming together of East and West in the
extremity of fate, in the task of overcoming this
universal misery of lost home by "staying on the path,
in genuine need, and learning, without straying from the
path, even though faltering, the craft (*Handwerk*)
of thinking."[58]

NOTES

1. *Vedanta und Platonismus im Lichte der Kantischen
Philosophie* (Berlin, 1922), 40-41. The penultimate
paragraph of this interesting study may be quoted here in
full since it states most concisely and lucidly the
approach to comparative philosophy most widely favoured
and which appears so questionable when we look at it from
the perspective of Heidegger's thinking. Deussen says,

> *In allen Landern und zu allen Zeiten, in all
> Nähen und Fernen ist es eine und dieselbe Natur
> der Dinge, welcher einer und derselbe Geist
> betrachtend gegenubersteht. Wie sollte es da
> anders sein konnen, als dass der denkende Geist,
> sofern ihn nicht Traditionen und Vorurteile
> blenden, sofern er der Natur rein und unbefangen
> gegenubersteht, in seiner Erforschung derselben
> überall, in Indien wie in Griechenland, in alter
> wie in neuer Zeit zu den gleichen Ergebnissen
> gelangen musste! Wir haben die drei glänzendsten
> Erscheinungen der Philosophie, den Vedanta,
> Platon und Kant miteinander verglichen. Wir
> haben nicht an ihnen gedreht und gedeutelt,
> gebogen und gerenkt, sondern wir haben jede
> Erscheinung in ihrer vollen individuellen Eigen-
> tumlichkeit bestehen lassen. Aber indem wir bei
> jeder von ihnen in die letzte Tiefe drangen, ge-
> langten wir zu dem inneren Einheitspunkte, aus
> dem die Anschauungen der indischen, griechischen
> und deutschen Denker entsprungen sind, und diese
> ihre innere übereinstimmung bei aller Verschie-
> denheit der Aussenseite ist eine nicht geringe
> Gewähr dafur, dass wir in allen dreien die Stimme
> der einen und mit sich einstimmigen Natur, dass
> in ihnen die Stimme der ewigen Wahrheit vernehmen.*

2. Paul Deussen, *The System of the Vedanta* (Delhi: Motilal Banarsidass, 1972), 38-39.

3. *The Vedanta Sutras of Badarayana with the Commentary by Sankara,* translated by George Thibaut (New York: Dover, 1962), Part 1, 223.

4. Keeping in mind Heidegger's conception of world as the "Fourfold (*Geviert*)" of earth and sky, divinities and mortals, a systematic examination of the meaning of *devata* (divinity), of God and the gods, in the Upanisads (particularly in the *Brhadaranyaka*) and Samkara's interpretation of it may prove rewarding. The comparative task here would be to differentiate this Vedic and post-Vedic conception from the Greek. In his early work, *Studies in Vedantism*, K.C. Bhattacharyya gave an original interpretation of the notions of *devata* and *loka* (region) as part of his treatment of "Vedantic metaphysics," but these suggestions have never since been examined or followed up. See Krishnachandra Bhattacharyya, *Studies in Philosophy* (Calcutta: Progressive Publishers, 1956), 1:31-68.

5. A major exception is Paul Hacker. See his remarks on Suresvara's style as compared with Samkara's in *Untersuchungen uber Texte des fruhen Advaitavada, I. Die Schüler Sankaras* (Wiesbaden, 1951), 16-21, and on verses of praise in Samkara and the early Advaita writers in "Relations of Early Advaitins to Vaisnavism", *Wiener Zeitschrift fur die Kunde Sud- und Ostasiens,* 9 (1965), and "Sankara der Yogin und Sankara der Advaitin," ibid. 12-13 (1968-1969) (Frauwallner *Festschrift*).

6. For references to these quotations from Plato and Aristotle, see Heidegger, *What is Philosophy?* (New Haven: Yale University Press, n.d.).

7. See *The Birth of Tragedy,* Section 15 (*Basic Writings of Nietzsche,* edited by Walter Kaufmann, New York: Random House, 1968, 93-95). These quotations by no means represent adequately Nietzsche's complex attitude to Socrates.

8. *Christianity in World History* (New York: Scribners, 1964), 18.

9. *"Die zeit des Weltbildes"* in *Holzwege* (Frankfurt: Klostermann, 1950), 70.

10. *An Introduction to Metaphysics* (New York: Doubleday, 1961), 31.

11. *Poetry, Language, Thought* (New York: Harper and Row, 1971), 91-92.

12. Samkara's Commentary on the *Brhadaranyaka Upanisad*, I, iv. 7, beginning.

13. *"Dankansprache von Professor Martin Heidegger"* in *Ansprache zum 80. Geburtstage* (Messkirch: Stadt Messkirch, 1969), 35. This is a recurrent motif in Heidegger's post-*Being and Time* writings, in which he keeps coming back to the ideas of "home," "world destiny," and "world-civilization" from the perspective of the question of Being.

14. *An Introduction to Metaphysics*, 30.

15. *Nietzsche* (Pfullingen: Neske, 1961), 2:278.

16. On the notion of "planetary" thinking, see *The Question of Being* (New Haven: Yale Univ. Press, n.d.), 107 and Kostas Axelos, *Einfuhrung in ein kunftiges Denken--uber Marx und Heidegger* (Tubingen: Niemeyer, 1966), passim. See also this author's *The Philosophy of Martin Heidegger* (New York: Harper and Row, 1971), 244-254, for this as well as the whole general topic of this paper.

17. *"Holderlins Erde und Himmel"* in *Erlauterungen zu Holderlins Dichtung* (Frankfurt: Klostermann, vierte, erweiterte Auflage, 1971), 177.

18. "Der Spruch des Anaximander," in *Holzwege* (Frankfurt: Klostermann, 1950), 300.

19. Martin Heidegger--Eugen Fink, *Heraklit* (Frankfurt: Klostermann, 1970), 212.

20. *Allgemeine Geschichte der Philosophie* (Leipzig, 1894-1917), 1:36.

21. *Identity and Difference* (New York: Harper and Row, 1969), 37.

22. Ibid., 38.

23. *What is Philosophy?* 45.

24. Granting the metaphysical component in Sanskrit, however, it may be instructuve to investigate the correctives it has developed against this representational or objectifying element, thus exhibiting its own unique genius: a mode of utterance in which representation and the cancellation of the representative force are held in tension and balance. Perhaps the uniqueness of Indian philosophy and religion lies in the simultaneous de-objectification of the objectified, in the iconoclastic moment which is never for long absent from its iconism. If, as Heidegger admits (*Discourse on Thinking*, New York: Harper and Row, 1966, 46), thinking is of two kinds, calculative and meditative or representational and non-representational, it may yet be of significance to his concern to see how Indian thought took notice of the problem which it so explicitly recognized as crucial, the forms in which the problem presented itself as a haunting, ever-present task for thinking, and the solutions offered. Looked at from this point of view, the history of Indian philosophy may prove to be not just an antiquarian, humanistic pursuit but a treasure house of direct promise to the Heideggerian quest.

25. See the preface in Latin to the first issue of *Lexis*, a periodical on comparative linguistics edited by Lohmann; also "*Uber den paradigmatischen Charakter der grieschischen Kultur*," in *Die Gegenwart der Griechen im neueren Denken* (Gadamer Festschrift. Tübingen: Mohr, 1960).

26. See this author's "Heidegger and the Comparison of Indian and Western Philosophy," *Philosophy East and West* 20 (1970), for a methodologically oriented consideration of the problem of comparative philosophy, as well as Eliot Deutsch's "Commentary" on the article in the same number. The entire issue is devoted to the subject of "Heidegger and Eastern Thought."

27. *On Time and Being* (New York: Harper and Row, 1972), 57.

28. Ibid., 59.

29. Another, if possible even more basic and ultimate problem, concerns the meaning and nature of truth. The crucial, and culminating, point in Heidegger's thinking is how truth (*Wahrheit*) itself can be understood in terms of the profounder notion of *aletheia* or unhiddennness. In the Upanisadic tradition truth (*satya*) and Being (*sat*) are even more intimately connected than in the Greek. But, beyond this, we have also the conception of the truth of what is commonly called true. See *Brhadaranyaka Upanisad* II.i.20 for "the truth of truth (*satyasya satyam*)" as the secret name of the Self and Samkara's commentary on this. How far the Advaita conception of *avidya-maya* (nescience-illusion) as the "seed" of all presentedness of entities is comparable to Heidegger's conception of *aletheia* as necessarily involving the element of hiddenness is also a question worth pursuing in this connection.

For a systematic and lucid exposition of Hedegger's life-long concern with truth as *aletheia*, see Walter Biemel, *Heidegger* (Hamburg: Rowohlt, 1973).

30. *Vortrage und Aufsatze* (Pfullingen: Neske, 1954), 227.

31. *Schellings Abhandlung über das Wesen der Menschlichen Freiheit (1809)* (Tübingen: Niemeyer, 1971), 175.

32. See the entire quotation from Hamann in Martin Heidegger, *Poetry, Language, Thought* (New York: Harper and Row, 1971), 191.

33. *An Introduction to Metaphysics*, 99.

34. Hacker has pointed this out repeatedly in a number of articles. See "Notes on the *Mandukyopanisad* and Sankara's *Agamasastravivarana*" (in *India Maior*, edited by J. Ensink and P. Gaeffke, Leiden: Brill, 1972), 125, 129-30, though he seems to be arguing from a position extraneous to the Vedanta (from the point of view of what we have called "the Greek thought of Being," as mediated in Hacker's interpretation through the Christian Thomist tradition) when he finds that "the inadequacy of his argumentation landed Sankara in that very nihilism which he made such

valiant efforts to combat," and when he concludes that
"Sankara never succeeded in facing the overwhelming fact
of existence." A statement like this, coming from the
most competent scholar of Advaita Vedanta in the West
since Deussen, brings to a focus the basic issues in the
comparative enterprise, whether in religion or in
philosophy. See also Hacker's (*"Sankara der Yogin und
Sankara der Advaitin"* in *Beitrage zur Geistesgeschichte
Indiens--Festschrift für Erich Frauwallner* (Wien: Gerold,
1968), 131 and *"Essere e Spirito nel Vedanta,"* in
Filosofia e Vita, 4 (1969), passim, where the problem of
Being in Samkara is dealt with extensively in the context
of a comparison of Samkara and Advaita generally with
Thomas Aquinas.

35. Commentary on *Katha Upanisad* II.iii.13.

36. Commentary on *Taittiriva Upanisad* II.vi.

37. Commentary on the *Bhagavadgita* XIII.12.

38. Commentary on *Chandogya Upanisad* VI.ii.1.

39. Commentary on *Brahma Sutra* III.ii.21.

40. Commentary on *Brahma Sutra* I.i.4.

41. Heidegger says this about the hidden relationship
between the thinker and the poet, quoting from Holderlin's
Patmos. See "What is Metaphysics?" in Werner Brock,
Existence and Being (London: Vision Press, 1949), 392.

42. See his articles "Phenomenology, Mysticism and the
'Grammatica Speculativa': A Study of Heidegger's
'Habilitationsschrift,'" *Journal of the British Society
for Phenomenology*, 5 (1974), and "Meister Eckhart and the
Later Heidegger: The Mystical Element in Heidegger's
Thought," forthcoming in *The Journal of the History
of Philosophy*.

43. See *Fruhe Schriften* (Frankfurt: Klostermann, 1972), 352.

44. *Nietzsche*, 2:28.

45. *Vortrage und Aufsatze, 134.*

46. *On the Way to Language* (New York: Harper and Row,
1971), 57.

47. Ibid., 66-67.

48. Ibid., 57.

49. Ibid., 73-74.

50. Rudolph Otto, *Mysticism East and West* (New York: Meridian, 1959), xvi.

51. *Identity and Difference*, 54-55.

52. *Being and Time* (New York: Harper and Row, 1962), 272.

53. Recognizing "*das Kreisen der Gedanken*" in Suresvara and in Advaita thinkers generally and also the fact that they are all concerned with what is "*ein einziger Gedanke*" (both features so readily intelligible from a Heideggerian perspective), Paul Hacker does not find any special virtue here but, operating with the category of "mysticism" judges Suresvara's *Naiskarmyasiddhi* in the following words, "*Die Naisk, is für uns eine geistesgeschichtlich hochbedeutsame Mischung von Logik und Mystik, wobei die Mystik der Logik, auf die das Zeitalter doch nicht verzichten kann, immer wieder Gewalt antut.*" (*Untersuchungen über Texte des frühen Advaitavada, I. Die Schüler Sankaras*, Wiesbaden, 1951). Would it not enable a reader of Suresvara's work to come closer to the thinking in it if he were to set aside, following Heidegger's critique, the concepts of "Logic" (which is not quite the same as the Indian *tarka*) and "Mysticism" as both suspect "in the realm of thinking?"

54. *Phänomenologie des Geistes* (Hamburg: Meiner, 1952), 65; 2nd paragraph of the "Introduction," *Phenomology of Mind*.

55. *On the Way to Language*, 54.

56. *Discourse on Thinking* (New York: Harper and Row, 1966), 55.

57. *Kant and the Problem of Metaphysics* (Bloomington: Indiana University Press, 1968), 207.

58. *Vortrage und Aufsatze*, 185.

DATE DUE

NOV 29 1993	

The Editor

David O'Connell is professor of French at Georgia State University. He received his Ph.D. in 1966 from Princeton University, where he was a National Woodrow Wilson Fellow, the Bergen Fellow in Romance Languages, and a National Woodrow Wilson Dissertation Fellow. He is the author of *The Teachings of Saint Louis: A Critical Text* (1972), *Les Propos de Saint Louis* (1974), *Louis-Ferdinand Céline* (1976), *The Instructions of Saint Louis: A Critical Text* (1979), and *Michel de Saint Pierre: A Catholic Novelist at the Crossroads* (1990). He has edited more than sixty books in the Twayne World Authors Series.

The Author

David A. Fein (B.A., Brown University, 1971; Ph.D. Cornell University, 1976) is Professor of French at the University of North Carolina at Greensboro. He is the author of *Charles d'Orléans* (Twayne, 1983), *A Reading of Villon's "Testament"* (Summa Publications, 1984), and *François Villon and His Reader* (Wayne State University Press, 1984), as well as numerous articles on medieval French literature. He has also published articles on the teaching of literature, and recently coauthored a literary reader designated for first-year French courses, *Architextes* (Harcourt Brace, 1996). In 1995 he was named "Teacher of the Year" by the North Carolina chapter of the American Association of French Teachers.